## NOVELL OBJECTIVE

MW01103774

# NetWare 5 CNE: Core Technologies Study Guide Test Objectives

## Course 580 *Service and Support* (Test 51-635)

| NOVELL OBJECTIVE | COVERED IN |
|---|---|
| 1. List and describe tasks related to providing service and support on a NetWare network. | Chapter 13 |
| 2. Describe the six-step troubleshooting model used in this course. | Chapter 13 |
| 3. Describe good service and support techniques, such as static protection and record keeping, and describe how to use diagnostic tools. | Chapter 13 |
| 4. Describe static protection measures. | Chapter 13 |
| 5. Describe record keeping practices. | Chapter 13 |
| 6. Use the Novell Support Connection website to find solutions to service and support problems. | Chapter 13 |
| 7. Install and use SupportSource to find information about system boards, hard disks, and network interface boards. | Chapter 13 |
| 8. Choose which tool is most likely to provide a solution to a specific type of problem. | Chapter 13 |
| 9. Describe network cabling types. | Chapter 14 |
| 10. Demonstrate skills prerequisite to installing network boards, such as identifying the appropriate board type; setting the IRQs, memory addresses, and port addresses; setting jumpers and DIP switches; and ensuring network board and slot compatibility. | Chapter 14 |
| 11. Configure, install, and troubleshoot Token Ring network. | Chapter 14 |
| 12. Configure, install, and troubleshoot an Ethernet network. | Chapter 14 |
| 13. Describe FDDI. | Chapter 14 |
| 14. Describe ATM. | Chapter 14 |
| 15. Describe basic hard disk principles, including the purpose of hard disks and the various interface types used by these devices. | Chapter 15 |
| 16. Configure, install, prepare, and troubleshoot SCSI and IDE disks on a workstation and a NetWare Server. | Chapter 15 |
| 17. Establish NetWare file storage by creating NetWare partitions and volumes, spanning hard disks, and mirroring hard disks. | Chapter 15 |

The exam objectives listed here were current as of this book's publication date. However, exam objectives are subject to change at any time without prior notice and at Novell's sole discretion. Please visit Novell's website (www.novell.com) for the most current listing of exam objectives.

# NetWare® 5 CNE®: Core Technologies Study Guide

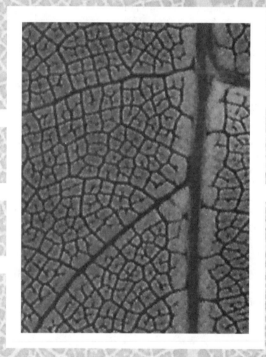

Michael G. Moncur
David Groth
with James Chellis

San Francisco • Paris • Düsseldorf • Soest • London

Associate Publisher: Guy Hart-Davis
Contracts and Licensing Manager: Kristine O'Callaghan
Acquisitions & Developmental Editor: Bonnie Bills
Editor: Lawrence Frey
Project Editors: Gemma O'Sullivan, Bronwyn Shone Erickson
Technical Editor: Mark Kovach
Book Designer: Bill Gibson
Graphic Illustrator: Tony Jonick
Electronic Publishing Specialist: Bill Gibson
Production Coordinator: Catherine Morris
Indexer: Ted Laux
Cover Designer: Archer Design
Cover Illustrator/Photographer: The Image Bank

SYBEX, Network Press, and the Network Press logo are registered trademarks of SYBEX Inc.

Screen reproductions produced with Collage Complete.
Collage Complete is a trademark of Inner Media Inc.

Novell, NetWare, and LANalyzer are registered trademarks of Novell, Inc. in the United States and other countries.

Novell Test Objectives from Novell, Inc.'s Web site, www.novell.com, ©1998, Novell, Inc. All Rights Reserved. Reprinted and used with permission.

TRADEMARKS: SYBEX has attempted throughout this book to distinguish proprietary trademarks from descriptive terms by following the capitalization style used by the manufacturer.

The author and publisher have made their best efforts to prepare this book, and the content is based upon final release software whenever possible. Portions of the manuscript may be based upon pre-release versions supplied by software manufacturer(s). The author and the publisher make no representation or warranties of any kind with regard to the completeness or accuracy of the contents herein and accept no liability of any kind including but not limited to performance, merchantability, fitness for any particular purpose, or any losses or damages of any kind caused or alleged to be caused directly or indirectly from this book.

Copyright ©1999 SYBEX Inc., 1151 Marina Village Parkway, Alameda, CA 94501. World rights reserved. No part of this publication may be stored in a retrieval system, transmitted, or reproduced in any way, including but not limited to photocopy, photograph, magnetic or other record, without the prior agreement and written permission of the publisher.

Library of Congress Card Number: 99-60004
ISBN: 0-7821-2389-9

Manufactured in the United States of America

10 9 8 7 6 5 4 3 2

# Acknowledgments

I would like to especially thank my wife, Linda, who tirelessly edited my work, brought me coffee, and gave me the support (or kick in the butt) when I needed it. Additionally, I would like to thank my Brainshare friend Jutta VanStean and brother-in-law Matthew Perkins, who each made their Sybex writing debut in this book. They can be proud of their work done here.
—D.G.

I would like to thank my family and friends, particularly my wife, Laura, and my parents, Gary and Susan Moncur. Thanks also go to the rest of my family and my friends, particularly Chuck Perkins, Cory Storm, Robert Parsons, and Dylan Winslow. Everyone at Cummins Intermountain and CallWare Technologies, and Karl Davis of Reliant Data Systems.
—M.M.

Thanks to my family—Kiki, Mary Jo, Gayle, David, Paul, Aaron, Ray, and Bill—as well as Sibylla, Matt, John, Lisa, Salman, Jairo, Bo, Oşcar, Arica, Kewei, Gin, Donese, Mike and Laura, Howarth, Jenny, Travis, Heidi, Stefene, Rick, Esmerelda La Cat, Guy, Kristine, and Neil.
—J.C.

# Contents at a Glance

# Appendices                                                    **599**

# Table of Contents

# Introduction

**W**ith over 81 million users and 4 million servers worldwide, NetWare is by far the most popular server operating system in the world. According to a report released by International Data Corporation (IDC) in June of 1998, NetWare servers comprise 38 percent of all servers out there, while the various Unix operating systems together rank second at 21 percent, Windows NT Server is third at 16 percent, OS/2 is fourth at 11 percent, and several others make up the last 14 percent. Clearly, there is a demand for professionals capable of managing NetWare. With the release of NetWare 5, the opportunity for professional NetWare administrators trained in Novell's latest product has risen again.

## Why You Should Buy This Book

So you're standing in the bookstore with this book in your hand. Should you buy it?

YES—if you just want to learn to work with Novell's latest and greatest operating system. Building on your basic understanding of previous versions of NetWare, this book will quickly and directly update your knowledge and skills.

or

YES—if you are a CNE and want to upgrade your certification to the most current level. This book gives you an affordable, efficient means of learning NetWare 5 and preparing for the CNE certification upgrade exam.

or

YES—if you are with a training company, because this book offers the best alternative to the very expensive Novell Education training manuals.

## What Subjects Are Covered in This Book?

The short answer to this question is the information you need for the CNE update test and much more. To be more specific, the information presented in this book can help you in two distinct areas:

- The realm of Novell Education, with its unique perspective on how things are and what you should know about networking.

- The real world, where tough demands on your time and energy require you to focus on only the most important information.

This book contains not only the information you need to achieve success on the CNE update test, but also the information that will enable you to implement actual networks under real-world conditions. We know that you don't want materials that will be of little use to you once you've taken the tests, so we've packed this book with information that will continue to help you in your work with NetWare networks.

Specifically, the following topics are covered in this book:

- Networking technologies: concepts and services

- The various network components found on a network

- A detailed discussion of the OSI model

- TCP/IP protocol theory and concepts (including addressing, supernetting, and subnetting)

- IPX protocol theory and concepts

- Bridging, switching, and routing concepts

- Network troubleshooting basics

- Installing and troubleshooting disk systems

- NetWare workstation client information and configuration

- Troubleshooting NDPS and queue-based printing

- Disaster recovery and network optimization

## How Do I Update My CNE to NetWare 5?

If you are a CNE and considering updating your certification, there are two options:

**Option 1:** If you are a NetWare 4 or intraNetWare CNE, pass the following exam:

**50-638:** NetWare 4.11 to NetWare 5 Update

**Option 2:** If you are a NetWare 3, GroupWise, or Classic CNE, pass the following exam:

**50-640:** NetWare 5 Advanced Administration

If you don't already have a CNE-4 and would like to study for the NetWare 5 CNE program from scratch, we recommend these Sybex titles: *NetWare 5 CNA/CNE: Administration and Design Study Guide* and *NetWare 5 CNE: Integrating Windows NT Study Guide.*

Novell's tests are administered by Sylvan Prometric and VUE, both independent-testing companies. At the time of writing, the tests are $95 each. For more information on testing, you can reach Sylvan at 1-800-RED-EXAM and VUE at 1-800-511-8123. You can also register for tests online at the Sylvan Prometric or VUE Web site:

`http://www.prometric.com/`

`http://www.vue.com/novell/`

## How to Use This Book

The best way to prepare for the test is:

- Study a chapter carefully, making sure that you fully understand the information.

- Consider setting up a practice network to help you work through the procedures and to review as you study for the tests.

- Answer the Practice Questions related to that chapter. (The answers to the Practice Questions are located in Appendix A.)

- Notice which questions you did not understand, and study those sections of the book again.

- Review the Practice Questions until you have mastered the appropriate material.

- Study the next section, and repeat the previous process.

- After you have read all of the chapters, go to Sybex's web page at http://www.sybex.com. Once there, click Catalog. Under Browse by Category, and the subsection Certification, select CNE/CNA. Find the title to this book, and select that link, which will take you to a page where you can access the most recent updates to the book, as well as take an online test, the Sybex CNA EdgeTest for NetWare 5.

- If you prefer to learn in a classroom setting, you have many options. Both Novell-authorized and independent training are widely available.

- Having access to a NetWare 5 network on which you may practice is definitely an advantage in the process of studying. If you are practicing on a network used by others, be sure you do not try anything that may influence their data in any way.

- The following pages contain a lot of information. To learn all of it, you will need to study regularly and with discipline. Try to set aside the same time every day to study, and select a comfortable and quiet place in which to do it. If you work hard, you will be surprised at how quickly you learn this material. Good luck.

## Obtaining a Free Copy of NetWare 5

At the time of publication of this book, Novell is offering a three-user demo of NetWare 5, with no expiration date, for only $15 dollars plus shipping. (This is a full version of the NetWare 5 operating system, but it includes licenses for only three clients.) The demo can be an excellent support tool in your efforts to become skilled with NetWare 5.

 The worldwide price is $15 (U.S. dollars) plus shipping. Orders take approximately two weeks to arrive.

To order:

- In the United States, call 1-800-395-7135 Monday–Friday 7 A.M.–5 P.M. U.S. PST.

- In Latin America and Asia Pacific regions, call 925-463-7391 Monday–Friday 6 A.M.–5 P.M. U.S. PST.

- In Europe, the Middle East, and Africa, call 353-1-8037035.

## Conventions Used in This Book

Where possible, we have tried to make things clearer and more accessible by including Notes, Tips, and Warnings based on our personal experiences in the field of networking. Each has a special margin icon and is set off in special type.

Notes provide you with helpful asides, reminders, and bits of information that deserve special attention.

Tips provide you with information that will make the current task easier. Tips include shortcuts and alternative ways to perform a task.

Read any Warnings to help you avert a possible disaster. Warnings will help you avoid making mistakes that could require a tremendous effort to correct.

## How to Contact the Authors

If you have questions or comments about the content of this book, you can contact the authors at nw5update@starlingtech.com. This e-mail address will reach Michael G. Moncur and James Chellis.

David Groth's e-mail address is not reached through this address; it is dgroth@corpcomm.net.

# PART

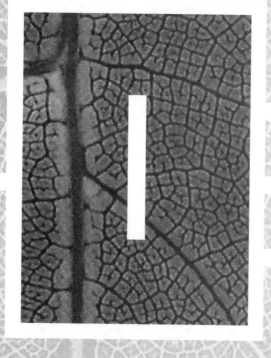

# I

## Networking
## Technologies

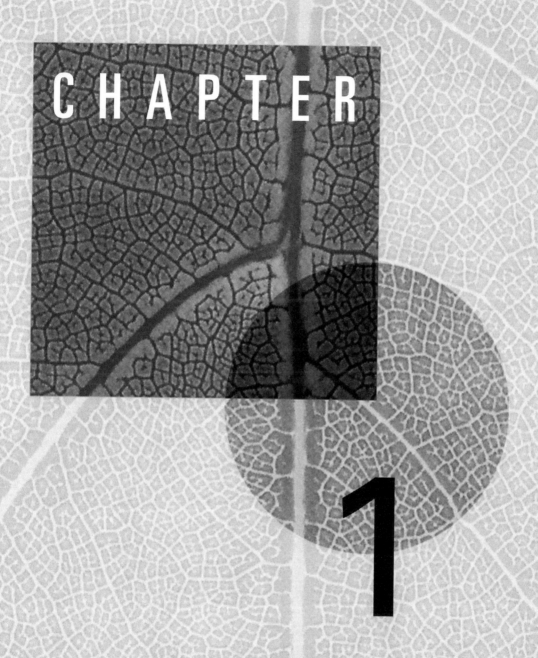

# CHAPTER

# 1

Networking Technologies:
Concepts and Services

# Roadmap

This chapter covers the basic elements of a network.

### Topics Covered

- Definition of a network
- Models of computer networking
- Sizes of networks
- Components of a network
- Popular network services

### Skills You'll Learn

- Define computer networking
- Compare the features of the different computing models
- Differentiate between LAN, MAN, and WAN
- Identify the basic networking elements
- Describe the interaction of servers, clients, and other network components delivering basic network services
- Describe the use and function of the five basic network services
- Describe when the various network services should be implemented
- Describe how network services are affected by the different network architectures

While society is experiencing an explosion in the types of information available across computer networks, the people who maintain these networks are experiencing a dramatic increase in the amount of information they need to know. It isn't surprising that many network administrators are experiencing another type of explosion, the type that occurs from mental overload!

Novell's Networking Technologies course is a tour through the complex field of networking, including network hardware and the various conceptual models used to understand what happens on that hardware. It covers the basics of networking technologies, as well as numerous abstract theoretical models used to give some order to network events.

This chapter begins the tour of networking technologies by covering some fundamental information about networks: what they are made of and what they have to offer us.

Keep in mind that you don't need to memorize all this information to be a good network administrator. Much of this information is required for Novell's Networking Technologies exam, but it isn't often needed in the real world. In extraordinary cases when you need to know about these particular details, you can use this book as a quick reference. For the real world, you will benefit most by focusing on the general concepts and simply "cramming" the details for the exam.

# The Basics of Networking Technologies

Y ou are probably familiar with the basics of computer networks. But, to establish working definitions of some fundamental aspects of networking, this chapter reviews the following:

- Computer networking models

- Network size categories

- Components of networks

## Models of Computer Networking

A computer network is fundamentally an arrangement of computers and peripheral electronic equipment, such as printers and modems. These computers and peripherals are connected in a computer network so that they can communicate with each other and share data and resources.

There are several markedly different models of how computers work together in a network. Three general models are called centralized, distributed, and collaborative, which will be discussed in detail in the next sections.

## Centralized Computing

*Centralized* computing centers around large *host* computers. These monster computers, which are generally referred to as *mainframes,* handle all the data storage and processing. The *dumb terminals* connected to the mainframes normally serve as mere input/output devices because they have little or no processing power.

The mainframes may be connected together in some kind of a network, but usually one mainframe is connected to disciple computers, which can't think on their own. Some would argue that this is not a true network because no information is being shared. The disciple computers do not process or store any data, they just serve as input/output devices. Figure 1.1 illustrates the centralized computing model.

---

**FIGURE 1.1**

In the centralized computing model, a host computer handles all the data storage and processing.

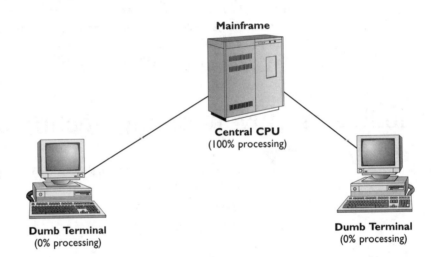

True network or not, mainframe computers offered the first type of computer connectivity. They are expensive and hard to work with, but they have the advantage of facilitating central management. (They also provided Hollywood with some fantastic imagery for sci-fi flicks: people wearing white suits in hermetically sealed rooms filled with blinking lights.)

When personal computers began to take over the world of organizations in the mid-1980s, the decline of centralized computing began. This marked the rise of distributed computing.

## Distributed Computing

The *distributed* model of computing involves a network of *intelligent* computers, called *clients,* which are able to share the processing load. The advent of PCs, which offered low-cost processing power for individual users, made this type of computing possible.

In the distributed computing model, each client can process its own tasks. In a NetWare network, for example, a client (workstation) can execute an application entirely on its own. When the client requests an application from a file server, the application can be loaded into the client's memory and run from there without further resources from the network.

In the distributed model, some data is actually stored and processed on the clients, while services are requested from and provided by the server. The computers in the network are actually sharing capabilities and information. Figure 1.2 illustrates the distributed computing model.

**FIGURE 1.2**

The distributed computing model has clients that can share the processing tasks.

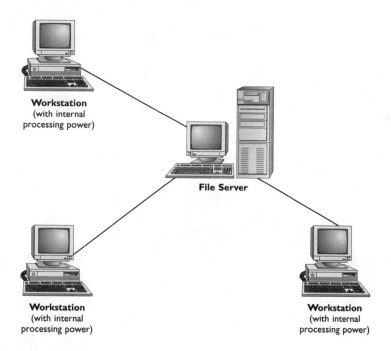

**Workstation**
(with internal processing power)

**File Server**

**Workstation**
(with internal processing power)

**Workstation**
(with internal processing power)

In a nutshell, there are two main features that distinguish distributed computing from centralized computing:

- Clients with internal processing power
- True exchange of data and services

## Collaborative Computing

The distinguishing feature of the *collaborative* computing model is the notion of computers working together to process the same task. In collaborative computing, also called *cooperative* computing, a computer might run part of a program on another computer in order to maximize processing power.

Collaborative computing is essentially an extension of the distributed computing model. Like distributed computing, it involves clients with internal processing power that can share data and services. But the collaborative model adds another vital factor, cooperation among multiple computers to perform a task.

Collaborative computing is becoming more and more important in the networking world, as administrators strive to maximize network processing power with today's powerful workstations. Figure 1.3 illustrates the collaborative computing model.

**FIGURE 1.3**

In the collaborative computing model, computers cooperate to perform a task.

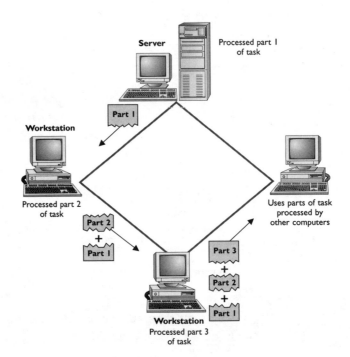

## Sizes of Networks

Another way of categorizing networks is by size. The exact definitions of these categories generally depend on the person who is doing the explaining, but the size categories most often employed are local area network (LAN), wide area network (WAN), and metropolitan area network (MAN). The following sections describe these categories of network sizes.

## Local Area Networks

LANs are the smallest of the networks in these three categories. They tend to cover just a single building or college campus. If you have two PCs in your bedroom linked together with parallel-port cables, that's a LAN. The network a small business runs in the offices on the second floor is also a LAN. And what the local university has might well be a LAN too, depending on how spread out it is. Typically, LANs use only one type of transmission medium (such as coaxial cable).

The most common types of LANs are:

- ARCnet

- Ethernet

- FDDI

- Token Ring

Figure 1.4 illustrates a typical LAN.

**FIGURE 1.4**

A local area network (LAN) consists of computers located in a single location.

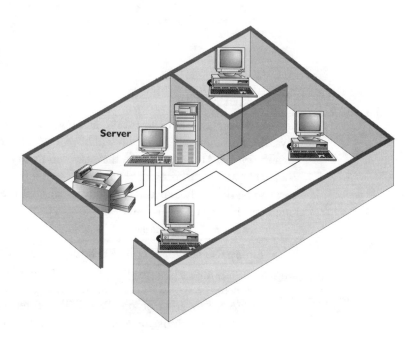

## Metropolitan Area Networks

The name metropolitan area network produces a snappier acronym than either local area network or wide area network, but most people don't bother with this term. For a working definition, MANs are a bit bigger than LANs (up to the size of a metropolitan area) and usually require different hardware and transmission media (which are covered in detail in the next chapter). Figure 1.5 shows an example of a MAN.

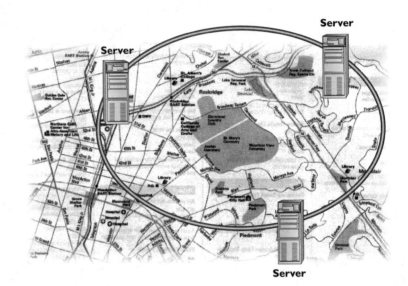

**FIGURE 1.5**

A metropolitan area network (MAN) is similar to a LAN but covers a wider area— up to a good-sized metropolis.

## Wide Area Networks

Any small business can have a LAN, and few people use the term MAN these days. But no mom-and-pop shop will have a WAN. At their largest, WANs span the globe. At the very least, they cover multicity areas. Typically, WANs use telephone lines to provide the link between different network sites; and they can be relatively expensive, mainly because of the cost of leasing those long lines. Figure 1.6 shows an example of a heavy-duty WAN.

There are two subcategories of WANs:

- *Enterprise* networks connect the computers of a single organization. For example, MegaMoney Corporation may have sites on every continent in the world (with the possible exception of Antarctica), all connected together on one WAN. This enterprise WAN would be a private network used exclusively by a single organization, a single enterprise.

**FIGURE 1.6**

A large wide area network (WAN) can span the globe. At its smallest, a WAN consists of a couple of LANs connected together.

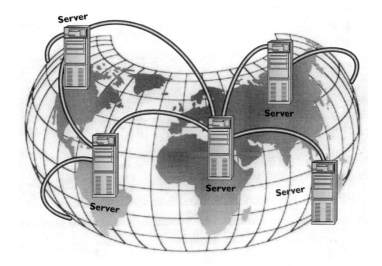

- *Global* networks serve multiple organizations and cover multiple continents. The Internet, the network of networks serving thousands of different organizations and millions of individuals, is considered a global network because it is transcontinental and serves many separate organizations.

## The Nuts and Bolts of a Network

Every network needs to have certain components in order to work properly. The required elements are:

- Network services, such as printing, e-mail, and file sharing, exchanged between service requesters and service providers

- Transmission media, such as coaxial cable and fiber optics

- Protocols, such as TCP/IP, IPX/SPX, and AppleTalk

Figure 1.7 shows how these elements form a network.

### Network Services

The reason for connecting computers is to share *services*. Services are simply what computers have to offer on a network. For example, network services include print services, file services, e-mail, and database services. Some of these services are covered in more detail later in this chapter.

**F I G U R E   1.7**

The components of a
network

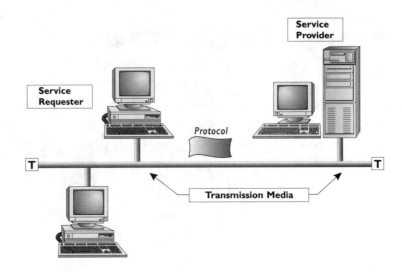

When a computer is offering a service on a network, it is what Novell calls a *service provider*. A server is an example of a service provider. The list of resources that a service provider puts onto the network is what makes it possible for other computers to request services. When a computer requests services on the network, it is called a *service requester.*

NetWare, starting with version 3.1*x*, focuses on the server as the logical center of network services, and is defined as using a *server-centric* approach. In the traditional server-centric model of networking, servers usually function only as service providers, and clients only play the role of service requesters. This is in contrast to the *peer-to-peer* approach, which does not center around a network server, and the *network-centric* approach presented by NetWare 4 and versions since then (including NetWare 5), which focus on a logical rather than physical network.

In the world of peer-to-peer networking, the line between those who give and those who receive is not so clear. A computer on a peer-to-peer network will often both request and provide services.

## Transmission Media

The physical cables and wireless technology across which computers are able to communicate are the *transmission media*. Words like *coaxial*, *twisted-pair*, *radio*, *microwave*, and *fiber-optic* are part of the transmission media jargon.

Transmission media provide a network with physical connections. This physical equipment between one computer and another on a network ensures that, if everything else goes right, there will be communication.

Until recently, the type of transmission media you used depended on the type of topology design you employed. Now, however, there is much more interchangeability, and any topology can use most transmission media. Transmission media and topology design are discussed in more detail in Chapter 2.

### Network Protocols

In order for humans to communicate, they must speak the same language. In much the same way, for computers to communicate, the guidelines for communication must be clearly defined. Computers use *protocols* for this purpose. Protocols are rules that specify how devices on a network communicate (Chapters 7 through 11).

# Popular Network Services

From the point of view of a network user, the whole purpose of a network is to provide services. Users want to log in to a network and have access to as many useful services as they could possibly need. The easier the services are to access, the better.

The five most common network services that users like to use are:

- File services

- Print services

- Message services

- Application services

- Database services

The following sections cover the various services that a network can perform.

## File Services

File services allow network users to share files. File services are the network applications that store, retrieve, or move data. This type of service is probably the single most important reason companies invest in a network. With a network, users can exchange, read, write, and manage shared files and the data contained in them.

Although NetWare is the primary concern in this book, there are other popular types of file servers, such as AppleShare, Windows NT Server, and Banyan VINES.

File services include several more specific components:

- File transfer

- File storage and data migration

- File archiving

- File update synchronization

## File Transfer

Before networking computers became a popular way of sharing files, *sneakernet* was the dominant method. To transfer a file from one computer to another, you would save the file to a floppy disk, put on your sneakers, and walk it over to the other computer. Even in a small office, this was inconvenient, especially when files were too large for a single floppy. For longer distances, it was impossible. The more sophisticated option was to dial the other computer and transfer your files with a modem or across a direct serial connection, a bit of an improvement but still an impractical method of sharing files regularly.

Fortunately, networks became more sophisticated and began to offer file transfer services. Under NetWare, users can transfer files between clients and servers, and between servers. Figure 1.8 illustrates how file transfer works.

**FIGURE 1.8**

Files can be transferred between clients and servers, as well as between servers.

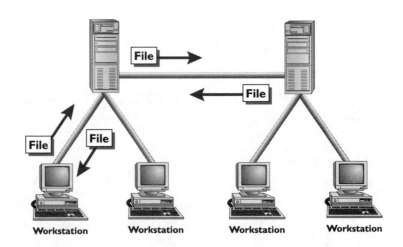

Workstation          Workstation          Workstation          Workstation

NetWare 3.1x, 4.x, and 5.x do not support file transfers from client to client, only between servers and between clients and servers. You can transfer a file between clients by temporarily saving it in a server directory.

With all this file transferring taking place, the need for file security arises. Every network operating system has its own level of file security. Higher levels use passwords to control system access, file attributes to limit file usage, and encryption schemes to prevent data from being obtained by unauthorized individuals.

For more on NetWare 5 File System Security, see *NetWare 5 CNA/CNE: Administration and Design Study Guide*, by Michael G. Moncur et al., and *Mastering NetWare 5*, by James Gaskin, both published by Sybex.

## File Storage and Data Migration

One by-product of the information explosion era is a huge amount of data that must be stored somewhere. Nowhere is this more evident than on the networks of the world.

Twenty years ago, the idea of gigabytes of data would make your average computer enthusiast's eyes roll. Now, there are teenage Internet surfers whose 5.7GB hard drives are completely full. On networks, terabyte storage systems may become fairly common before too long. As a network administrator, you must find the most affordable and efficient means of storing all this data.

A megabyte equals 1,048,576 bytes. A gigabyte equals 1,073,741,824 bytes. A terabyte equals 1,099,511,627,776 bytes!

Not long ago, most storage took place on hard drives. Hard drives can be accessed quickly, but there are still more affordable network storage devices, despite the falling cost of gigabytes on hard drives.

There are three main categories of file storage:

- Online storage
- Offline storage
- Nearline storage

*Online* storage consists, most notably, of hard drive storage. Information stored on a hard drive can be called up quickly. For this reason, hard drives are used to store files that are accessed regularly. But hard drive space is relatively expensive. There is also another limitation specific to internal hard drives (but not external hard drives): because they are a fairly permanent part of a computer, they cannot be conveniently removed, placed in storage, and replaced when needed.

Much of the heavy data load most file servers take on is not urgent data. For example, financial records from previous years may be stored on a company's network, waiting only for the day when an audit is necessary. This type of data can be stored just as well on less accessible, less expensive devices.

*Offline* storage devices include media such as data tapes and removable optical disks. This type of storage offers high-capacity, low-price options to online storage. One disadvantage of this type of storage, however, is that it requires a person to retrieve the disk or tape and mount it on the server. In this age of convenience, that is enough to make a network administrator almost want to cry. This type of storage is best for data that is rarely used and for data backup.

Fortunately, there is a happy medium. *Nearline* storage devices offer fairly low costs and high storage capacities, without requiring the network administrator to wake up, go to the archive shelf, and mount the tape or disk on the server. Instead, a machine, such as a tape carrousel or jukebox, automatically retrieves and mounts the tape or disk. These systems tend to offer faster, more efficient data access than offline systems, but they are still only fast enough for infrequently used data and applications.

The process by which data is moved from online to offline or nearline storage is called *data migration*. Network operating systems usually have some type of facility that automatically migrates files from hard drives to nearline or offline storage. Files are selected for migration based on factors such as the last time the file was accessed, the file owner, or the file size. Novell publishes the following standards for file storage and migration:

- *Real Time Data Migration* (RTDM) automatically migrates data from online hard drives to a nearline system.

- *High-Capacity Storage System* (HCSS) supports optical jukeboxes.

- *Mass Storage Services* (MSS) coordinates distributed hierarchical storage.

## File Update Synchronization

*File update synchronization* has the lofty goal of ensuring that each user of a file has the latest version. By using time and date stamping and user tracking, file synchronization works to ensure that changes made to a file are organized in the chronological order in which they actually took place and that files are properly updated.

Imagine that you download some files from a network server onto a laptop. You then take the laptop on a trip to Africa. Meanwhile, back on the network, people are changing those same files left and right. You also make some changes to your copies of the files. When you log on to the network and begin to copy those files back to the network, all the changes will need to be synchronized in some way to make sure that the server keeps them in order and your files are updated with the latest changes. Both your files and the server files need updates to put everything in order. This is where file update synchronization comes into play.

Ideally, update utilities would be able to resolve any conflicts. However, at present, there are many cases in which update utilities cannot solve problems. These utilities will merely alert you by flagging files when there are conflicting updates.

## File Archiving

File archiving is the process of backing up files on offline storage devices, such as tapes or optical disks. Because networks occasionally destroy files arbitrarily, without any concern for anyone's feelings, it is best to use a file-archiving system, such as Novell's Storage Management Service (SMS), as insurance.

Because you can back up all the servers on a network onto a single backup device, file archiving is really not very difficult. Some backup systems even allow central backup for client workstations, which means you can back up files that reside on multiple client workstations without leaving your chair. This way, it may be possible to store every file on a network on a single central storage device.

It's best not to procrastinate when it comes to backing up data. Do it now, or wish you had later.

## Print Services

Another important factor in the genesis of computer networking was the demand for the ability to share printers. Before networks made this possible, there were few alternatives. You could employ sneakernet. You could use a manual switching device that hooked a few computers up to a single printer. Or you could keep your printer on a cart, and wheel it from computer to computer.

The advent of networking represented a whole new level of computer printing, because a network can:

- Allow users to share printers

- Allow you to place printers where convenient, not just near individual computers

- Achieve better workstation performance by using high-speed network data transfer, print queues, and spooling

- Allow users to share network fax services

Print services manage and control printing on a network, allowing multiple and simultaneous access to printing facilities. The network operating system achieves this by using *print queues*, which are special storage areas where print jobs are stored and then sent to the printer in an organized fashion. When a computer prints to a queue, it actually functions as if it were printing to the printer. The print job is simply stored in the queue, and then forwarded to the printer when the printer has finished the jobs scheduled ahead of it. Figure 1.9 illustrates how a print queue works.

Under NetWare, jobs in print queues may be forwarded in the order received, or they may be prioritized in accordance with other criteria (such as by the size of the users' egos whose jobs are in the queue).

To keep everyone happy, you might consider setting up a separate printer for the important users. Then the other users won't get frustrated when they need to wait for their lower-priority print jobs.

Printers can be placed anywhere on a network, and anyone on the network can use any one of those printers. For example, if you want to print on a special 11×17-inch network printer that resides five miles away, you can do that, no problem. (Well, at least in theory—in actuality, it seems that the words *print* and *no problem* can rarely be used in the same sentence.) Figure 1.10 shows how printing to a remote network printer works.

**FIGURE 1.9**
Print jobs wait in a
print queue until the
printer is ready
for them.

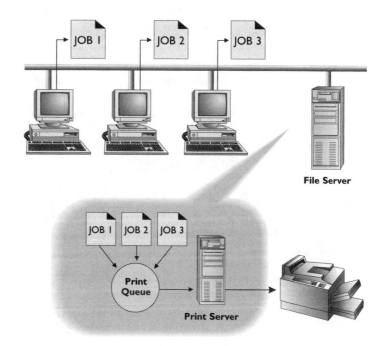

**FIGURE 1.10**
Print jobs can be sent
to distant printers.

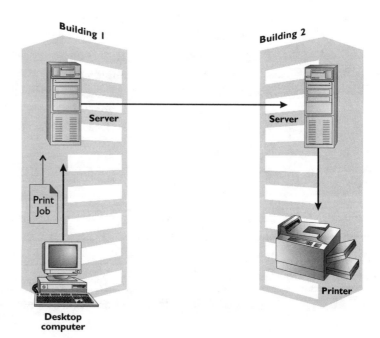

Printing on a network with queues can be a more efficient way for users to work. The print data is transferred to the queue at network speed. With this done, the user can then continue working in an application, while the network takes care of the printing.

Network printing also cuts costs by allowing shared access to printing devices, which is especially important when it comes to the more expensive varieties of printers. High-quality color printers, high-speed printers, and large-format printers and plotters tend to cost big bucks. It is seldom feasible for an organization to purchase one of these for every individual computer that should have access to one.

---

### Distributed Print Services. . .A Better Way

A new technology that is taking hold in the networking community is *distributed print services*. This new type of printing technology is an improvement over traditional queue-based printing because it allows the printer and server to talk directly and exchange information. It also allows the network administrator to centrally manage all the aspects of network printing. Additionally, by leveraging a directory service, the printers can tell the network what drivers to use and automatically download them to the workstations. Anyone who has ever set up and managed traditional queue-based printing can appreciate these features.

Novell, together with Hewlett Packard and Xerox, has developed its own implementation of this technology. Called *Novell Distributed Print Services* (or NDPS), it is the preferred method of setting up network printing services in NetWare 5. Additionally, it is backward-compatible with older versions of queue-based printing. NDPS is covered in more detail in Chapter 17.

---

Another print service is fax services. Fax machines are now a fundamental communication device around the world. With network print services, you can fax straight from your workstation to a receiving fax machine. This way, you can eliminate the step of printing a hard copy and scanning it into a fax machine. From an application, you can send a document to a fax queue, which then takes care of the faxing. Furthermore, with a fax server, you can receive faxes directly onto your workstation. Optical character recognition (OCR) software can even convert these faxes into editable text, thereby saving a lot of time and effort.

# Message Services

Message services include a wide variety of communication methods that go far beyond simple file services. With file services, data can pass between users only in file form. With message services, data can take the form of graphics, digitized video, and audio, as well as text and binary data. As hypertext links (electronic connections with other text, images, sounds, and so on) become more common in messages, message services are becoming an extremely flexible and popular means of transmitting data across a network.

Message services must coordinate the complex interactions between users, documents, and applications. For example, with message services, you can send an electronic note, attached to a voice-mail message, to a fellow user on a network.

There are four main types of message services:

- Electronic mail
- Workgroup applications
- Object-oriented applications
- Directory services

## Electronic Mail

Electronic mail, or e-mail, is an increasingly popular reason for installing a network. With e-mail, you can easily send a message to another user on the network or on other networks, including the Internet (once your network is connected to other networks, of course).

Originally, e-mail was text-based—it contained only text characters. Now e-mail systems can transfer video, audio, and graphics as well. E-mail is much faster than traditional snail mail (regular postal mail delivery), much cheaper than courier services, and much simpler than dialing the recipient's computer and transferring the files to it.

E-mail systems are quickly becoming more complex. Integrated voice mail is one of the most popular recent developments, rapidly fusing computers and telephones into a single communication system.

Users can now call into the network from a distant telephone and, using a text-to-speech program, have their computer read their e-mail messages in a synthesized voice. In the not-too-distant future, speech-to-text systems that allow you to talk to your computer, and convert your speech to an e-mail message, may be perfected.

## Workgroup Applications

Workgroup applications are used to produce more efficient processing of tasks among multiple users on a network. The two main workgroup applications are:

- Workflow management applications
- Linked-object documents

*Workflow management* applications route documents, forms, and notices among network clients. Tasks that require the input of multiple network users are often much easier using this type of application. Scheduling programs are one application of this sort. More complex applications can take care of otherwise difficult paperwork processes. For example, for a supply clerk to complete a requisition at a military base, approval from several higher-ups may be needed. This process could be automated so each person whose approval is routinely needed would receive the requisition form on the network. The application would send the form around from one person to the next, in the correct order, until all approvals had been granted (or refused).

*Linked-object* documents are documents containing multiple data objects. A variety of types of data objects can be linked to construct a document. For example, a single linked-object document could contain voice, video, text, and graphics linked together. Network message services can then act as an agent for each of these objects, passing messages between the objects and their originating applications or files.

## Object-Oriented Applications

*Object-oriented* applications are programs that can accomplish complex tasks by combining smaller applications, called *objects*. By using a combination of objects, object-oriented applications gain the ability to handle large tasks.

Message services facilitate communication between these objects by acting as a go-between agent. This way, objects do not need to communicate with other objects on the network. Instead, an object can simply pass data to the agent, which then passes the data on to the destination object.

## Directory Services

Directory services provide a comprehensive database, or directory, of all the services available on a network. The directory services under NetWare 5 are called Novell Directory Services (NDS).

Because directory services consolidate information about all network objects, including their current network addresses, in one centralized database, messaging services become greatly simplified. Under NDS, user addresses and configuration information are maintained in a database that is replicated and distributed across a network and that updates itself using message services.

# Application Services

Application services allow client PCs to access and use extra computing power and expensive software applications that reside on a shared computer. You can add specialized servers to provide specific applications on a network. For example, if your organization needs a powerful database, you could add a server to provide this application.

Application servers can be dedicated computers set up specifically for the purpose of providing application services, or they can serve multiple functions. A single NetWare server, for example, can provide file, print, communication, and database services.

An application server dedicated solely to the task of providing application services can be useful. An organization can use an application server to accommodate growth, because you can increase network computing power as necessary simply by upgrading the application server. This server can use NetWare or another operating system. Windows NT Server, for example, makes an excellent application server.

Although in the earlier days of networking, application services were not often found on networks, they have recently become more popular. In terms of network models, they reflect more directly the centralized processing model of the mainframe world. When they do appear on a network, application servers are usually dedicated machines, minimizing the drain on file servers' resources. For example, an accounting department of a large corporation might have an AS/400 machine running OS/400 to handle its accounting database software.

NetWare provides server applications via NetWare Loadable Modules (NLMs) and by providing support for third-party applications.

# Database Services

Database services can provide a network with powerful database capabilities that are available for use on relatively weak PCs. Most database systems are client/server based. That is, the database applications run in two separate components:

- The *client end* portion of the application runs on the client, providing an interface and handling less-intensive functions such as the data requests.

- The *server end* portion of the application handles the intensive performance of database operations. It runs on the database server, managing the database, processing queries, and replying to clients.

For example, imagine a network with a 100GB database. This database could be managed by a centralized database application based on the client/ server model. Clients could request information from the server, which would then perform a query and report the results to the client. The client could then access the data, process it on the client end, then return it to the server.

Database servers are becoming increasingly powerful, providing complex services including security, database optimization, and data distribution. Distributed databases, utilizing database management systems such as NDS, are becoming increasingly popular.

Distributed databases maximize network efficiency by storing data where it is needed. From the user end, the database appears as a single entity, even though the data might be stored across the network, close to the users who need those parts. This can boost performance by helping to ensure that users are using local resources to access data, rather than, for example, using WAN lines to access it.

When a database is distributed, it can be either divided into portions, which are stored on various computers across the network, or *replicated*. Replication can be used to reproduce and distribute an entire database. Replication can be based on either of the following models:

- In the *master database* model, a single server receives all changes and additions. Database management software then distributes updated replicas of the database to other servers. This type of model is illustrated in Figure 1.11.

- In the *distributed database* model, local servers distribute changes and receive updates in synchronized coordination with other servers, which also distribute changes and receive updates. This type of model is shown in Figure 1.12.

F I G U R E  1.11

A master database
receives all changes
and distributes
updates to replicas.

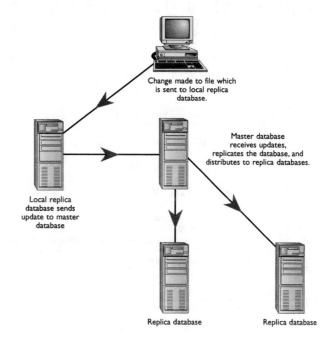

Change made to file which
is sent to local replica
database.

Master database
receives updates,
replicates the database, and
distributes to replica databases.

Local replica
database sends
update to master
database

Replica database

Replica database

F I G U R E  1.12

In a distributed
database, multiple
servers coordinate
changes and updates.

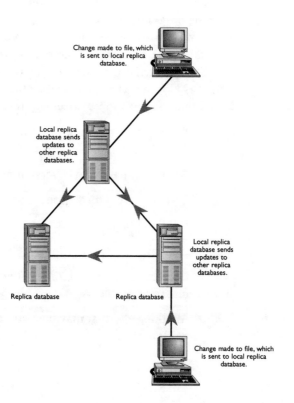

Change made to file, which
is sent to local replica
database.

Local replica
database sends
updates to
other replica
databases.

Local replica
database sends
updates to
other replica
databases.

Replica database

Replica database

Change made to file, which
is sent to local replica
database.

# The Basics of Network Management

The job of a network administrator is multifaceted and ever changing. However, it can generally be viewed in terms of the following five functional management categories:

- Configuration management
- Fault management
- Security management
- Accounting management
- Performance management

The following sections describe the tasks that each of these types of network management involves.

## Configuration Management

It is important to document network components and their configuration so this information is available for future reference. When something goes wrong or you need to make changes (such as upgrading your operating system), you will benefit greatly from detailed descriptions of the components of your network and how they are configured.

These descriptions can be organized in network management software, such as Novell's ManageWise, or other third-party products. In these descriptions, you should document the following:

- Workstation configuration files, including CONFIG.SYS and AUTOEXEC.BAT as well as the Registry (if present)
- Application and driver version numbers
- User security information
- Database tables
- Network software, including NetWare shell and Requester versions
- Network history, including network idiosyncrasies, peculiarities, and recurrent problems
- Anything else that may help you or someone else work with the network in the future

Keep in mind that this documentation will not only serve to provide you with a map of your network, but could also prove invaluable to the person who inherits your network when you move onward and upward.

## Fault Management

One of the most important functions of a network administrator is to ensure the reliability of a network. Another is to be able to quickly resolve problems when they do arise. Fault management employs hardware, software, and well-established procedures to alert you to potential and actual problems with network reliability, and it also offers you resources to deal with these problems.

When you analyze your network in terms of its reliability, consider using or implementing the following:

- Disk mirroring or disk duplexing. These techniques (described in detail in Chapter 15) use redundant network hardware to provide added fault tolerance. The secondary system can take over when the first one fails. This allows you to identify and correct a problem without interrupting normal network activity.

- A network management system, such as Novell's ManageWise. This type of system uses protocols such as SNMP (Simple Network Management Protocol) and CMIP (Common Management Information Protocol) to alert you to network problems and to provide network performance information. For example, ManageWise includes a console with an audio alarm and a visual notification of failed network devices.

- Protocol analyzers, such as LANalyzer for Windows (described in Chapter 18). These software-based tools interpret packets captured from the network to detect any errors.

- A cable tester, to help you pinpoint failures in specific areas of network cables.

- Data archiving and backup. Although these won't help you analyze your network for problems, they will give you a safety net when things go wrong. As explained earlier in this chapter, there are a number of ways to provide backup and archiving, including online, offline, and nearline storage.

## Security Management

NetWare provides numerous security features to help you prevent unauthorized access, destruction, or theft of information on your network. Along with using these features to secure your network, you must also work to make sure network hardware is carefully guarded. By restricting access to both network information and hardware, you can minimize the risks of theft and destruction.

## Accounting Management

Novell Education uses this category to refer to the practice of monitoring network usage and interpreting it in terms of costs.

Some organizations do actually ascribe certain costs to network usage, such as numbers of packets sent across the network, and bill departments for that usage. Others use accounting information simply to determine when it is affordable and appropriate to improve the system.

## Performance Management

The goal of performance management is optimal network performance. It can be seen as proactive rather than merely reactive. Some of the performance parameters you may wish to consider when optimizing your network include the following:

- Throughput
- Error level
- Response time
- Cost of improvements
- Capacity of network currently being used

This information can help you determine when you need to improve your system to perform at a higher level. See Chapter 18 for more information about techniques for optimizing your network.

# Review

This chapter presented the basics of computer networking. The different types and sizes of networks were covered, as were the services networks offer and the basic tasks of network administrators.

# Network Models

Computer networks have developed from their origins in the centralized computing model of mainframe computers to the distributed processing model reflected in most current networks. In the distributed model of computing, clients are able to share the processing load. As they become more sophisticated, networks are beginning to integrate distributed computing capabilities.

Like distributed computing, the collaborative model involves clients that can do their own processing. The additional factor is that multiple computers can cooperate to perform a task.

# Network Sizes

Networks are classified according to size:

- Local area networks (LANs) usually reside in a single location and use only one type of transmission medium. Common types of LANs are ARCnet, Ethernet, FDDI, and Token Ring.

- Metropolitan area networks (MANs) are somewhat bigger than LANs (up to the size of a metropolitan area) and usually require different hardware and transmission media.

- Wide area networks (WANs) are the largest type. They can span the globe. WANs usually use telephone lines to provide the link between different network sites. The two subcategories of WANs are enterprise networks, which connect the computers of a single organization, and global networks, which serve multiple organizations and cover more than one continent.

# Network Components

Networks have the following elements:

- Network services are what computers have to offer on a network. For example, network services include print services, file services, e-mail, and communication services.

- Transmission media provide a network with physical connections (such as coaxial or fiber-optic cable).

- Protocols are the rules of communication that allow devices on a network to communicate.

## Types of Network Services

The following are commonly used types of network services:

- File services include file transfer, file storage and data migration, file update synchronization, and file archiving.

- Print services allow users to share printers and fax services.

- Message services include e-mail, workgroup applications, object-oriented applications, and directory services.

- Application services allow clients to access and use extra computing power and software applications that reside on a shared computer.

- Database services provide a network with powerful database capabilities. Distributed databases maximize network efficiency by storing data near where it is needed.

## Network Management Basics

Network management can be analyzed in terms of the following:

- Configuration management centers around documenting network components and their configuration.

- Fault management involves maintaining a fault-tolerant system. Fault management uses tools such as network management systems, redundant network systems, data archiving and backup, protocol analyzers, and cable testers to achieve its goals.

- Security management is concerned with the privacy and protection of the information on a network.

- Accounting management provides data that helps the accounting department bill for network usage and determine when improvements make financial sense.

- Performance management involves proactive steps to maximize network speed and efficiency.

# CNE Practice Test Questions

**1.** Centralized computing is best described as

   **A.** Computing taking place on the motherboard, rather than the peripherals

   **B.** When data processing is completed at corporate headquarters

   **C.** Computing that centers around a mainframe computer

   **D.** Server-centric networking

**2.** Which of the following is NOT characteristic of the distributed computing model?

   **A.** Clients with internal processing power

   **B.** Exchange of data and services

   **C.** Clients with data storage capacity

   **D.** Clients serving mainly as input/output devices

**3.** What is a WAN?

   **A.** A wide-apple network

   **B.** A work-associate nexus

   **C.** A wide area network

   **D.** A work-area network

**4.** Which one of the following is currently NOT a common network service?

   **A.** Print services

   **B.** File services

   **C.** Communication services

   **D.** Photocopying services

**5.** What is a protocol?

   **A.** A set of rules of communication that allow network devices to communicate

   **B.** A device used by proctologists

   **C.** A hardware device used by TCP/IP

   **D.** The most important part of the CPU

**6.** What are the three main types of file storage?

   **A.** Online storage

   **B.** Offline storage

   **C.** Nearline storage

   **D.** Downline storage

**7.** What is the primary function of a print queue?

   **A.** Ensure that fonts maintain precise integrity

   **B.** Store print jobs before they are printed

   **C.** Provide important information about printer specifications

   **D.** Store backup paper for the printer

**8.** Which one of the following is NOT a type of message service?

   **A.** E-mail

   **B.** Workgroup applications

   **C.** Directory Services

   **D.** Secretarial databases

# CHAPTER

# 2

## Network Hardware:
## Transmission Media and Connections

# Roadmap

This chapter covers the basic connectivity components of a network, including transmission media and connectivity devices.

## Topics Covered

- Choosing a media type
- Types of cable media
- Types of wireless media
- Types of public and private network services
- Types of network connectivity devices
- Types of internetwork connectivity devices

## Skills You'll Learn

- Define transmission media as it applies to networks
- Choose which transmission media to use in a given situation
- Describe the function of connectivity devices in networks and internetworks
- Choose which network or internetwork connectivity devices to use in a given situation

The physical basis of a computer network is composed of two fundamental components, the devices that communicate on a network and the hardware that connects them.

The hardware that connects network devices can be grouped in two main categories:

- Transmission media, which include cabling (such as twisted-pair, fiber-optic, and coaxial cable), wireless connections (such as radio wave, microwave, and infrared), and public and private networks (such as the Internet and Public Switched Telephone Network).

- Transmission media connections, which include communication devices (such as modems, multiplexers, and repeaters) and internetwork connectivity devices (such as routers and CSUs/DSUs).

This chapter covers the different types of transmission media and connectivity devices. This information will give you a solid background in these fundamental components of network hardware.

# Choosing a Media Type

In order to share network resources (such as applications, printers, and servers), computers must be able to communicate with each other. Computers send electronic signals to each other using electric currents, radio waves, microwaves, or light. These signals represent network data as binary impulses (zeros and ones). The physical path that computers send and receive these signals through is called *transmission media*.

Scientifically, light and radio waves are part of the *electromagnetic spectrum*. This spectrum provides a wide variety of ways in which signals may be passed through transmission media from one computer to another. The electromagnetic spectrum ranges from electric currents to infrared light and gamma rays. Figure 2.1 shows the electromagnetic spectrum divided into waveforms and their frequencies.

Transmission media are divided into two categories:

- *Cable* media have a central conductor enclosed in a plastic jacket. They are typically used for small LANs. Cable media normally transmit signals using the lower end of the electromagnetic spectrum, such as simple electricity and, sometimes, radio waves.

- *Wireless* media typically employ the higher electromagnetic frequencies, such as radio waves, microwaves, and infrared. Wireless media are necessary for networks with mobile computers or those that transmit signals over large distances, and are especially prevalent in enterprise and global networks.

Cellular phone networks use microwaves to broadcast signals.

**FIGURE 2.1**

The electromagnetic spectrum

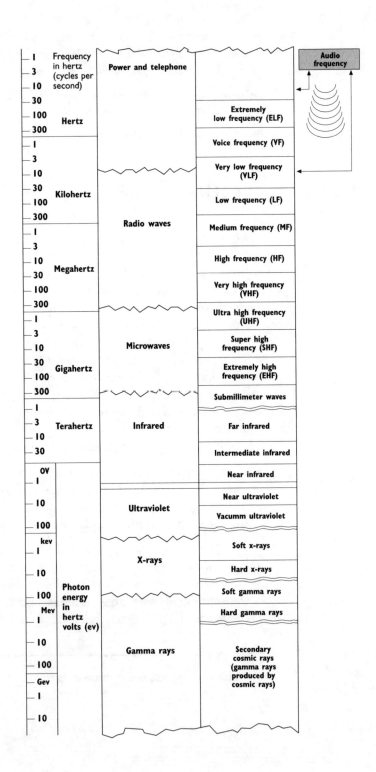

Networks that cover multiple sites frequently use combinations of cable and wireless media to link computers and devices.

Each media type has certain characteristics that make it suitable for particular networks. To choose the best type of media for your network, you should know how each medium's characteristics relate to the following factors:

- Cost

- Installation

- Capacity

- Attenuation

- Electromagnetic interference (EMI)

The following sections describe how these factors affect a network. The specifics of how each medium performs in these areas are covered later in this chapter.

## Cost

The cost of each media type should be weighed against the performance that it provides and the resources that are available. For example, it is a common practice among network integrators to attempt to run a network across unused, leftover telephone cabling. Although this could reduce costs, in many cases it's not a viable solution, for example, when cable drops of greater than 100 meters are required.

Each network installation is different, and you must look for the most affordable, but viable, solution. Take into consideration the real needs of the network. For example, fiber-optic cable is fast, but you may not need that much speed. It's easy to spend too much if you're not writing the checks.

## Installation

How difficult installation will be depends on the individual situation, but some general comparisons between the media are possible. Some types of media can be installed with simple tools and little training; others require more training and knowledge, and may be better left to professionals. For example, unshielded twisted-pair cable is easy to install, but fiber-optic cable requires professional training. To connect two lengths of fiber together, you may need to use electric fusion or a chemical epoxy process. These are jobs that you probably don't want to undertake unless you know how to do them. Installation will be covered later in this chapter.

## Capacity

The capacity of a medium is usually measured in *bandwidth*. In the world of networking, bandwidth is measured in terms of megabits per second (Mbps). Ethernet, for example, has a bandwidth of 10Mbps. A transmission medium with a high capacity has a high bandwidth; a medium with a low capacity has low bandwidth.

In the field of communications, the term *bandwidth* refers to the range of frequencies a medium can accommodate. In networking, bandwidth is measured in terms of the number of bits that can be transmitted across a given medium per second.

A high bandwidth normally increases throughput and performance, but the cable length and signaling techniques affect the bandwidth a cable can accommodate.

## Attenuation

Electromagnetic signals tend to weaken during transmission. This is referred to as *attenuation*. As the signals pass through the transmission medium, part of their strength is absorbed or misdirected. This phenomenon imposes limits on the distance that a signal can travel through a medium without unacceptable degradation. The farther you are from a person, the harder it is to hear what that person is saying. Part of this is attenuation, and part is interference.

## Electromagnetic Interference and Eavesdropping

Electromagnetic interference (EMI) affects the signal that is sent through the transmission media. EMI is caused by outside electromagnetic waves affecting the desired signal, making it more difficult for the receiving computer to decode the signal. Some media are more influenced by EMI than others. EMI is often referred to as *noise*. If you are in a quiet room, it is easier to hear a person than if you are at a rock concert.

Another concern is eavesdropping, especially if your network data requires a high level of security. The properties of each media affect how vulnerable it is to eavesdropping.

# Cable Media

**C**ables have a central conductor, a wire or fiber, surrounded by a plastic jacket. Three types of cable media are twisted-pair, coaxial, and fiber-optic cable. Two types of twisted-pair cable are used in networks, unshielded (UTP) and shielded (STP). Table 2.1 summarizes the characteristics of these different types of cable media.

**T A B L E   2.1:**   Characteristics of Cable Media

| Factor | UTP | STP | Coaxial | Fiber-Optic |
|---|---|---|---|---|
| Cost | Lowest | Moderate | Moderate | Highest |
| Installation | Easy | Fairly easy | Fairly easy | Difficult |
| Capacity | 1 to 100 Mbps (typically 10Mbps) | 1 to 155 Mbps (typically 16Mbps) | Typically 10Mbps | 2Gbps (typically 100Mbps) |
| Attenuation | High (range of hundreds of meters) | High (range of hundreds of meters) | Lower (range of a few kilometers) | Lowest (range of tens of kilometers) |
| EMI | Most sensitive to EMI and eaves-dropping | Less sensitive than UTP but still sensitive to EMI and eavesdropping | Less sensitive than UTP but still sensitive to EMI and eavesdropping | Not affected by EMI or eavesdropping |

## Twisted-Pair Cable

*Twisted-pair* cable uses two twisted copper wires to transmit signals. It is commonly used as telecommunications cable.

When copper wires that are close together conduct electric signals, there is a tendency for each wire to produce interference in the other. One wire interfering with another in this way is called *crosstalk*. To decrease the amount of crosstalk and outside interference, the wires are twisted. Twisting the wires allows the emitted signals from one wire to cancel out the emitted signals from the other, and protects them from outside noise.

Twisted pairs are two color-coded, insulated copper wires that are twisted around each other. A twisted-pair cable consists of one or more twisted pairs in a common jacket. Figure 2.2 shows a twisted-pair cable.

**FIGURE 2.2**

Twisted-pair cable has two twisted copper wires.

**Insulation**                                **Copper wire conductor**

There are two types of twisted-pair cable, unshielded and shielded.

## Unshielded Twisted-Pair Cable

*Unshielded twisted-pair* (UTP) cable consists of a number of twisted pairs with a simple plastic casing. UTP is commonly used in telephone systems. Figure 2.3 shows a UTP cable.

**FIGURE 2.3**

Unshielded twisted-pair (UTP) cable

The Electrical Industries Association (EIA) divides UTP into different categories by quality grade. The rating for each category refers to conductor size, electrical characteristics, and twists per foot. The following categories are defined:

- Categories 1 and 2 were originally meant for voice communication and can support only low data rates, less than 4 megabits per second (Mbps). These cannot be used for high-speed data communications. Older telephone networks used Category 1 cable.

- Category 3 is suitable for most computer networks. Some innovations can allow data rates much higher, but generally Category 3 offers data rates up to 16Mbps. This category of cable is the kind currently used in most telephone installations.

- Category 4 offers data rates up to 20Mbps.

- Category 5 offers enhancements over Category 3, such as support for Fast Ethernet, more insulation, and more twists per foot, but Category 5 requires compatible equipment and more stringent installation. In a Category 5 installation, all media, connectors, and connecting equipment must support Category 5, or performance will be affected.

Data-grade UTP cable (Categories 3, 4, and 5) consists of either four or eight wires. A UTP cable with four wires is called a *two-pair*. Network topologies that use UTP require at least two-pair wire. You may want to include an extra pair for future expansion. Figure 2.4 shows a four-pair cable.

**FIGURE 2.4**

A four-pair UTP cable

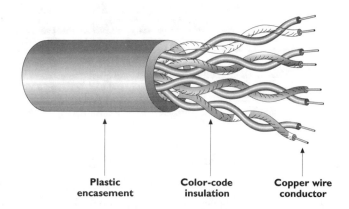

Plastic  Color-code  Copper wire
encasement  insulation  conductor

Because UTP cable was originally used in telephone systems, UTP installations are often similar to telephone installations. For a four-pair cable, you need a modular RJ-45 telephone connector. For a two-pair cable, you need a modular RJ-11 telephone connector. These connectors are attached to both ends of a patch cable. One end of the patch cable is then inserted into a computer or other device, and the other end is inserted into a wall jack. The wall jack connects a UTP drop cable (another length of cable) to a punch-down block.

Most UTP network installations done today use all four pairs and RJ-45 connectors.

The other side of the punch-down block is wired to a patch panel. The patch panel provides connectivity through patch cables to other user devices and connectivity devices. Figure 2.5 shows how UTP might be installed.

**FIGURE 2.5**

A common UTP
installation

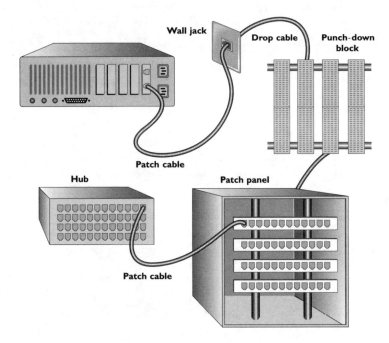

UTP cable has the following characteristics:

- Cost: Except for professionally installed Category 5, the cost of UTP is very low when compared with other transmission media. It continues to be mass-produced for telecommunications applications, such as computer and telephone networks.

- Installation: UTP cable is easy to install, so it can be done with very little training. Because UTP uses equipment similar to telephone equipment, maintenance and network reconfiguration should be relatively simple.

- Capacity: With current technologies, UTP may support data rates from 1 to 100 Mbps at distances of up to 100 meters (328 feet). The most common rate is 10Mbps.

- Attenuation: Transmissions across copper wire tend to attenuate rapidly. Because of this, UTP is normally restricted to distances of 100 meters.

- EMI: UTP is very susceptible to EMI. Twisting reduces crosstalk, but some interference still exists. Also, external devices that emit electromagnetic waves, such as electric motors and fluorescent lights, can cause problems. In addition, because copper wire emits signals, UTP is very susceptible to eavesdropping.

## Shielded Twisted-Pair Cable

The only difference between *shielded twisted-pair* (STP) and UTP is that STP cable has a shield—usually aluminum/polyester—between the outer jacket or casing and the wires. Figure 2.6 shows STP cable.

**F I G U R E   2.6**

Shielded twisted-pair (STP) cable

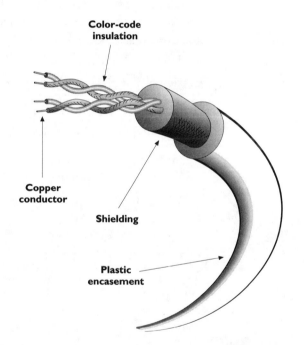

The shield makes STP less vulnerable to EMI because the shield is electrically grounded. If a shield is grounded correctly, it tends to prevent signals from getting into or out of the cable. It is a more reliable cable for LAN environments. STP was the first twisted-pair cable to be used in LANs. Although many LANs now use UTP, STP is still used.

Transmission media specifications from IBM and Apple Computer use STP cable. IBM's Token Ring network uses STP, and IBM has its own specifications for different qualities and configurations of STP. A completely different type of STP is the standard for Apple's AppleTalk networks. Networks that conform to each vendor's specifications have their own special requirements, including connector types and limits on cable length.

STP has the following characteristics:

- Cost: Bulk STP is fairly expensive. STP costs more than UTP and thin coaxial cable but less than thick coaxial or fiber-optic cabling.

- Installation: The requirement for special connectors can make STP more difficult to install than UTP. An electrical ground must be created with the connectors. To simplify installation, use standardized and prewired cables. Because STP is rigid and thick (up to 1.5 inches in diameter), it can be difficult to handle.

- Capacity: With the outside interference reduced by the shielding, STP can theoretically run at 500Mbps for a 100-meter cable length. Few installations run at data rates higher than 155Mbps. Currently, most STP installations have data rates of 16Mbps.

- Attenuation: STP does not outperform UTP by much in terms of attenuation. The most common limit is 100 meters.

- EMI: The biggest difference between STP and UTP is the reduction of EMI. The shielding blocks a considerable amount of the interference. However, because it is copper wire, STP still suffers from EMI and is vulnerable to eavesdropping.

See Table 2.1 (shown earlier) for a comparison of the characteristics of STP and UTP cable.

## Coaxial Cable

*Coaxial* cable, commonly called *coax,* has two conductors that share the same axis. A solid copper wire or stranded wire runs down the center of the cable, and this wire is surrounded by plastic foam insulation. The foam is surrounded by a second conductor, a wire mesh tube, metallic foil, or both. The wire mesh protects the wire from EMI. It is often called the *shield*. A tough plastic jacket forms the cover of the cable, providing protection and insulation. Figure 2.7 shows a coaxial cable.

Coaxial cable

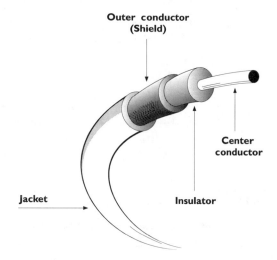

Coaxial cable comes in different sizes. It is classified by size (RG) and by the cable's resistance to direct or alternating electric currents (measured in ohms), also called *impedance*.

The following are some coaxial cables commonly used in networking:

- 50 ohm, RG-8 and RG-11, used for Thick Ethernet

- 50 ohm, RG-58, used for Thin Ethernet

- 75 ohm, RG-59, used for cable TV

- 93 ohm, RG-62, used for ARCnet

Coaxial cable has the following characteristics:

- Cost: Coax is relatively inexpensive. The cost for thin coaxial cable is less than STP or Category 5 UTP. Thick coaxial is more expensive than STP or Category 5 UTP, but less than fiber-optic cable.

- Installation: Installation is relatively simple. With a little practice, installing the connectors becomes easy, and the cable is resistant to damage. Coaxial cable is most often installed either in a device-to-device daisy-chain (Ethernet) or a star (ARCnet). The interface may involve T-connectors or vampire clamps (or taps). Coaxial cable must be grounded and terminated. Grounding completes the electrical circuit. Terminating keeps the signals that reach the end of the cable from reflecting and causing interference.

- Capacity: A typical data rate for today's coaxial networks is 10Mbps, although the potential is higher. Coaxial cable's bandwidth potential increases as the diameter of the inner conductor increases.

- Attenuation: Because it uses copper wire, coaxial cable suffers from attenuation, but it is much less than attenuation for twisted-pair cables. Coaxial cable runs are limited to a couple thousand meters.

- EMI: Coaxial cabling is still copper wire and vulnerable to EMI and eavesdropping. However, the shielding provides a much better resistance to EMI's effects.

## Fiber-Optic Cable

*Fiber-optic* cable transmits light signals rather than electrical signals. It is enormously more efficient than the other network transmission media. As soon as it comes down in price (both in terms of the cable and installation costs), fiber-optic will be the best choice for network cabling.

Each fiber has an inner core of glass or plastic that conducts light. The inner core is surrounded by *cladding*, a layer of glass that reflects the light back into the core. Each fiber is surrounded by a plastic sheath. The sheath can be either tight or loose. Figure 2.8 shows examples of these two types of fiber-optic cables.

**F I G U R E   2.8**

Fiber-optic cables with tight and loose sheaths

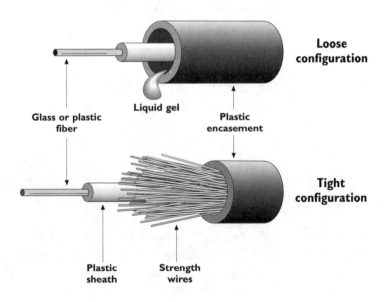

Tight configurations completely surround the fibers with a plastic sheath, and sometimes include wires to strengthen the cable (although these wires are not required).

Loose configurations leave a space between the sheath and the outer jacket, which is filled with a gel or other material. The sheath provides the strength necessary to protect against breaking or extreme heat or cold. The gel strengthens wires, and the outer jacket provides extra protection.

A cable may contain a single fiber, but often fibers are bundled together in the center of the cable. Optical fibers are smaller and lighter than copper wire. One optical fiber is approximately the same diameter as a human hair.

Optical fibers may be multimode or single-mode. *Single-mode* fibers allow a single light path and are typically used with laser signaling. *Multimode* fibers use multiple light paths. The physical characteristics of the multimode fiber make all parts of the signal (those from the various paths) arrive at the same time, appearing to the receiver as if they were one pulse. Single-mode fiber can allow greater bandwidth and cable runs than multimode, but is more expensive. If you want to save money, look into multimode, because it can be used with LEDs (light-emitting diodes), which are a more affordable light source than lasers. Figure 2.9 shows single-mode and multimode fibers.

**FIGURE 2.9**

Single-mode and multimode optical fibers

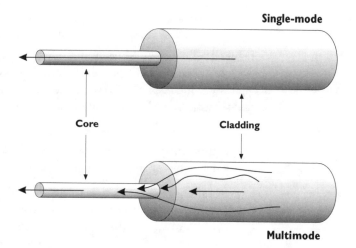

Optical fibers are differentiated by core/cladding size and mode. The size and purity of the core determine the amount of light that can be transmitted.

The following are the common types of fiber-optic cable:

- 8.3 micron core/125 micron cladding, single-mode

- 62.5 micron core/125 micron cladding, multimode

- 50 micron core/125 micron cladding, multimode

- 100 micron core/140 micron cladding, multimode

A typical LAN installation starts at a computer or network device that has a fiber-optic NIC. This NIC has an incoming interface and an outgoing interface. The interfaces are directly connected to fiber-optic cables with special fiber-optic connectors. The opposite ends of the cables are attached to a connectivity device or splice center.

Splicing fiber-optic cable can involve electric fusion, chemical epoxy, or mechanical connectors. Fiber-optic cables, with cores as thin as 8.3 microns, can be very difficult to line up precisely.

Optical interface devices convert computer signals into light for transmission through the fiber. Conversely, when light pulses come through the fiber the optical interface converts them into computer signals. For single-mode fiber, light pulses are created by injection laser diodes (ILDs), which create a higher quality of light. For multimode fiber, Light Emitting Diodes (LEDs) are used. When the light pulse is received, it is converted back into electric signals by P-intrinsic N diodes or photodiodes.

Fiber-optic cable has the following characteristics:

- Cost: Fiber-optic cable is expensive, but costs are falling. Associated equipment costs can be much higher than for copper cable. Fiber-optic cable is by far the most expensive to install.

- Installation: Fiber-optic cable is more difficult to install than copper cable. Every fiber connection and splice must be carefully made to avoid obstructing the light path. Also, the cables have a maximum bend radius, which makes cabling more difficult.

- Capacity: Because it uses light, which has a much higher frequency than electricity, fiber-optic cabling can provide extremely high bandwidths. Current technologies allow data rates from 100Mbps to 2 gigabits per second (Gbps). The data rate depends on the fiber composition, the mode, and the wavelength (the frequency) of the transmitted light. A common multimode installation can support 100Mbps over several kilometers.

- Attenuation: Fiber-optic cable has much lower attenuation rates than copper wires, mainly because the light is not radiated out in the way that electricity is radiated from copper cables. Fiber-optic cables can carry signals over distances measured in kilometers.

- EMI: Fiber-optic cable is not subject to electrical interference. In addition, it does not leak signals, so it is immune to eavesdropping. Because it does not require a ground, fiber-optic cable is not affected by potential shifts in the electrical ground, nor does it produce sparks. This type of cable is ideal for high-voltage areas or in installations where eavesdropping could be a problem.

# Wireless Media

**W**ireless media do not use an electrical or optical conductor. In most cases, the earth's atmosphere is the physical path for the data. Wireless media is, therefore, useful when distance or obstructions make bounded (cable) media difficult. There are three main types of wireless media: radio wave, microwave, and infrared.

## Radio Wave Transmission Systems

Radio waves have frequencies between 10 kilohertz (KHz) and 1 gigahertz (GHz). The range of the electromagnetic spectrum between 10KHz and 1GHz is called *radio frequency* (RF).

Radio waves include the following:

- Short-wave

- Very-high frequency (VHF) television and FM radio

- Ultra-high frequency (UHF) radio and television

Most radio frequencies are regulated; some are not. To use a regulated frequency, you must receive a license from the regulatory body over that area (the FCC in the United States). Getting a license can take a long time, costs more, and makes it more difficult to move equipment. However, licensing guarantees that, within a set area, you will have clear radio transmission.

The advantage of unregulated frequencies is that there are few restrictions placed on them. One regulation, however, does limit the usefulness of unregulated frequencies: unregulated frequency equipment must operate at less than 1 watt. The point of this regulation is to limit the range of influence a device can have, thereby limiting interference with other signals. In terms of networks, this makes unregulated radio communication bandwidths of limited use.

Because unregulated frequencies are available for use by others in your area, you cannot be guaranteed a clear communication channel.

In the United States, the following frequencies are available for unregulated use:

- 902 to 928 megahertz (MHz)
- 2.4GHz (also internationally)
- 5.72 to 5.85 GHz

Radio waves can be broadcast omnidirectionally, or directionally. Various kinds of antennas can be used to broadcast radio signals. Typical antennas include the following:

- Omnidirectional towers
- Half-wave dipole
- Random-length wire
- Beam (such as the Yagi)

Figure 2.10 shows these common types of radio frequency antennas.

**FIGURE 2.10**

Typical radio frequency antennas

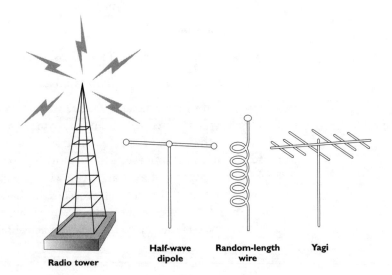

Radio tower        Half-wave dipole        Random-length wire        Yagi

The power of the RF signal is determined by the antenna and transceiver. Each range has characteristics that affect its use in computer networks. For computer network applications, radio waves are classified in three categories:

- Low-power, single-frequency
- High-power, single-frequency
- Spread-spectrum

Table 2.2 summarizes the characteristics of the three types of radio wave media that are described in the following sections.

**T A B L E  2.2:**  Radio Wave Media

| Factor | Low-Power, Single-Frequency | High-Power, Single-Frequency | Spread-Spectrum |
|---|---|---|---|
| Frequency Range | All radio frequencies (typically low GHz range) | All radio frequencies (typically low GHz range) | All radio frequencies (typically 902 to 928 MHz in U.S; 2.4 also used) |
| Cost | Moderate for wireless | Higher than low-power, single-frequency | Moderate |
| Installation | Simple | High | Moderate |
| Capacity | From below 1 to 10 Mbps | From below 1 to 10 Mbps | 2 to 6 Mbps |
| Attenuation | High (25 meters) | Low | High |
| EMI | Poor | Poor | Fair |

## Low-Power, Single-Frequency

As the name implies, single-frequency transceivers operate at only one frequency. Typical low-power devices are limited in range to around 20 to 30 meters. Although low-frequency radio waves can penetrate some materials, the low power limits them to the shorter, open environments.

Low-power, single-frequency transceivers have the following characteristics:

- Frequency range: Low-power, single-frequency products can use any radio frequency, but higher gigahertz ranges provide better throughput (data rates).

- Cost: Most systems are moderately priced compared with other wireless systems.

- Installation: Most systems are easy to install, if the antenna and equipment are preconfigured. Some systems may require expert advice or installation. Some troubleshooting may be involved to avoid other signals.

- Capacity: Data rates range from 1 to 10 Mbps.

- Attenuation: Attenuation is determined by the radio frequency and power of the signal. Low-power, single-frequency transmissions use low power and consequently suffer from attenuation.

- EMI: Resistance to EMI is low, especially in the lower bandwidths where electric motors and numerous devices produce noise. Susceptibility to eavesdropping is high, but with the limited transmission range, eavesdropping would generally be limited to within the building where the LAN is located.

## High-Power, Single-Frequency

High-power, single-frequency transmissions are similar to low-power, single-frequency transmissions but can cover larger distances. They can be used in long-distance outdoor environments. Transmissions can be line-of-sight or can extend beyond the horizon as a result of being bounced off the earth's atmosphere. High-power, single-frequency can be ideal for mobile networking, providing transmission for land-based or marine-based vehicles as well as aircraft. Transmission rates are similar to low-power rates, but at much longer distances.

High-power, single-frequency transceivers have the following characteristics:

- Frequency range: As with low-power transmissions, high-power can use any radio frequency, but networks favor higher gigahertz ranges for better throughput (data rates).

- Cost: Radio transceivers are relatively inexpensive, but other equipment (antennas, repeaters, and so on) can make high-power, single-frequency radio moderately to very expensive.

- Installation: Installations are complex. Skilled technicians must be used to install and maintain high-power equipment. The radio operators must be licensed by the FCC, and their equipment must be maintained in accordance with FCC regulations. Equipment that is improperly installed or tuned can cause low data-transmission rates, signal loss, and even interference with local radio.

- Capacity: Bandwidth is typically between 1 and 10 Mbps.

- Attenuation: High-power rates improve the signal's resistance to attenuation, and repeaters can be used to extend signal range. Attenuation rates are fairly low.

- EMI: Much like low-power, single-frequency transmission, vulnerability to EMI is high. Vulnerability to eavesdropping is also high. Because the signal is broadcast over a large area, it is more likely that signals can be intercepted.

## Spread-Spectrum

Spread-spectrum transmissions use the same frequencies as other radio frequency transmissions, but instead of using one frequency, they use several frequencies simultaneously. Two modulation schemes can be used to accomplish this, direct frequency modulation and frequency hopping.

*Direct frequency modulation* is the most common modulation scheme. It works by breaking the original data into parts (called *chips*), which are then transmitted on separate frequencies. To confuse eavesdroppers, spurious signals can also be transmitted. The transmission is coordinated with the intended receiver, who is aware of which frequencies are valid. The receiver can then isolate the chips and reassemble the data while ignoring the decoy information. Figure 2.11 illustrates how direct frequency modulation works.

The signal can be intercepted, but it is difficult to watch the right frequencies, gather the chips, know which chips are valid data, and find the right message. This makes eavesdropping difficult.

Current 900MHz direct-sequence systems support data rates of 2 to 6 Mbps. Higher frequencies offer the possibility of higher data rates.

*Frequency hopping* rapidly switches among several predetermined frequencies. In order for this system to work, the transmitter and receiver must be in nearly perfect synchronization. Bandwidth can be increased by simultaneously transmitting on several frequencies. Figure 2.12 shows how frequency hopping works.

**FIGURE 2.11**

Direct frequency
modulation

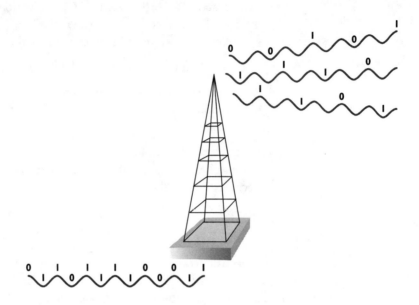

**FIGURE 2.12**

Frequency hopping

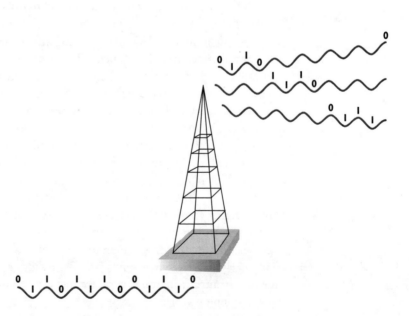

Spread-spectrum transceivers have the following characteristics:

- Frequency range: Spread-spectrum generally operates in the unlicensed frequency ranges. In the United States, devices using the 902 to 928 MHz range are most common, but 2.4GHz devices are becoming available.

- Cost: Although costs depend on what kind of equipment you choose, they are typically fairly inexpensive when compared with other wireless media.

- Installation: Depending on the type of equipment you have in your system, installation can range from simple to fairly complex.

- Capacity: The most common systems, the 900MHz systems, support data rates of 2 to 6 Mbps, but newer systems operating in gigahertz produce higher data rates.

- Attenuation: Attenuation depends on the frequency and power of the signal. Because spread-spectrum transmission systems operate at low power, which produces a weaker signal, they usually have high attenuation.

- EMI: Immunity to EMI is low, but because spread-spectrum uses different frequencies, interference would need to be across multiple frequencies to destroy the signal. Vulnerability to eavesdropping is low.

## Microwave Transmission Systems

Microwave communication makes use of the lower gigahertz frequencies of the electromagnetic spectrum. These frequencies, which are higher than radio frequencies, produce better throughput and performance. There are two types of microwave data communication systems, terrestrial and satellite.

Table 2.3 shows a comparison of the terrestrial microwave and satellite microwave transmission systems.

### Terrestrial

Terrestrial microwave systems typically use directional parabolic antennas to send and receive signals in the lower gigahertz range. The signals are highly focused, and the physical path must be line-of-sight. Relay towers are used to extend signals. Terrestrial microwave systems are typically used when the cost of cabling is cost-prohibitive.

Because they do not use cable, microwave links are often used to connect separate buildings where cabling would be too expensive, difficult to install, or prohibited. For example, if two buildings are separated by a public road, you may not be able to get permission to install cable over or under the road. Microwave links would be a good choice in this type of situation.

Because terrestrial microwave equipment often uses licensed frequencies, additional costs and time constraints may be imposed by licensing commissions or government agencies (the FCC in the United States).

**T A B L E  2.3:**  Terrestrial Microwave and Satellite Microwave

| Factor | Terrestrial Microwave | Satellite Microwave |
|---|---|---|
| Frequency range | Low gigahertz (typically between 4 to 6 or 21 to 23 GHz) | Low gigahertz (typically 11 to 14) |
| Cost | Moderate to high | High |
| Installation | Moderately difficult | Difficult |
| Capacity | 1 to 10 Mbps | 1 to 10 Mbps |
| Attenuation | Depends on conditions (affected by atmospheric conditions) | Depends on conditions (affected by atmospheric conditions) |
| EMI | Poor | Poor |

Figure 2.13 shows a microwave system connecting separate buildings. Smaller terrestrial microwave systems can be used within a building as well. Microwave LANs operate at low power, using small transmitters that communicate with omnidirectional hubs. Hubs can then be connected to form an entire network.

Terrestrial microwave systems have the following characteristics:

- Frequency range: Most terrestrial microwave systems produce signals in the low gigahertz range, usually at 4 to 6 GHz and 21 to 23 GHz.

**F I G U R E  2.13**

Terrestrial microwave
connecting two
buildings

- Cost: Short-distance systems can be relatively inexpensive, and they are effective in the range of hundreds of meters. Long-distance systems can be very expensive. Terrestrial systems may be leased from providers to reduce startup costs, although the cost of the lease over a long term may prove more expensive than purchasing a system.

- Installation: Line-of-sight requirements for microwave systems can make installation difficult. Antennas must be carefully aligned. A licensed technician may be required. Also, because the transmission must be line-of-sight, suitable transceiver sites could be a problem. If your organization does not have a clear line-of-sight between two antennas, you must either purchase or lease a site.

- Capacity: Capacity varies depending on the frequency used, but typical data rates are from 1 to 10 Mbps.

- Attenuation: Attenuation is affected by frequency, signal strength, antenna size, and atmospheric conditions. Normally, over short distances, attenuation is not significant. But rain and fog can negatively affect higher frequency microwaves.

- EMI: Microwave signals are vulnerable to EMI, jamming, and eavesdropping (although microwave transmissions are often encrypted to reduce eavesdropping). Microwave systems are also affected by atmospheric conditions.

## Satellite

Satellite microwave systems transmit signals between directional parabolic antennas. Like terrestrial microwave systems, they use low gigahertz frequencies and must be in line-of-sight. The main difference with satellite systems is that one antenna is on a satellite in geosynchronous orbit about 50,000 kilometers (22,300 miles) above the earth. Because of this, satellite microwave systems can reach the most remote places on earth and communicate with mobile devices.

Here's how it usually works. A LAN sends a signal through cable media to an antenna (commonly known as a *satellite dish*), which beams the signal to the satellite in orbit above the earth. The orbiting antenna then transmits the signal to another location on the earth or, if the destination is on the opposite side of the earth, to another satellite, which then transmits to a location on earth.

Figure 2.14 shows a transmission being beamed from a satellite dish on earth to an orbiting satellite and then back to earth.

**F I G U R E   2.14**

Satellite microwave transmission

Because the signal must be transmitted 50,000 kilometers to the satellite and 50,000 kilometers back to earth, satellite microwave transmissions take about as long to cover a few kilometers as they do to span continents. Because the transmission must travel long distances, satellite microwave systems experience delays between the transmission of a signal and its reception. These delays are called *propagation delays*. Propagation delays range from .5 to 5 seconds.

Satellite microwave systems have the following characteristics:

- Frequency range: Satellite links operate in the low gigahertz range, typically between 11 and 14 GHz.

- Cost: The cost of building and launching a satellite is extremely expensive—as high as several hundred million dollars or more. Companies such as AT&T, Hughes Network Systems, and Scientific-Atlanta lease services, making them affordable for a slightly larger number of organizations. Although satellite communications are expensive, the cost of cable to cover the same distance may be even more expensive.

- Installation: Satellite microwave installation for orbiting satellites is extremely technical and difficult, and certainly should be left to professionals in that field. The earth-based systems may require difficult, exact adjustments. Commercial providers can help with installation.

- Capacity: Capacity depends on the frequency used. Typical data rates are 1 to 10 Mbps.

- Attenuation: Attenuation depends on frequency, power, antenna size, and atmospheric conditions. Higher frequency microwaves are more affected by rain and fog.

- EMI: Microwave systems are vulnerable to EMI, jamming, and eavesdropping. (Microwave transmissions are often encrypted to reduce eavesdropping.) Microwave systems are also affected by atmospheric conditions.

## Infrared Transmission Systems

Infrared media use infrared light to transmit signals. LEDs or ILDs transmit the signals, and photodiodes receive the signals. Infrared media use the terahertz range of the electromagnetic spectrum. The remote controls used for television, VCR, or CD players use infrared technology to send and receive signals.

Because infrared signals are in the terahertz (higher frequency) range, they have good throughput. Infrared signals do have a downside; the signals cannot penetrate walls or other objects, and they are diluted by strong light sources.

Infrared media use pure light, normally containing only electromagnetic waves or photons from a small range of the electromagnetic spectrum.

Infrared light is transmitted either line-of-sight (point-to-point) or broadcast omnidirectionally, allowing it to reflect off walls and ceilings. Point-to-point transmission allows for better data rates, but devices must remain in their locations. Broadcast, on the other hand, allows for more flexibility but with lower data rates (part of the signal strength is lost with each reflection).

## Point-to-Point

Infrared beams can be tightly focused and directed at a specific target. Laser transmitters can transmit line-of-sight across several thousand meters.

One advantage of infrared is that an FCC license is not required to use it. Also, using point-to-point infrared media reduces attenuation and makes eavesdropping difficult. Typical point-to-point infrared computer equipment is similar to that used for consumer products with remote controls. Careful alignment of transmitter and receiver is required. Figure 2.15 shows how a network might use point-to-point infrared transmission.

**FIGURE 2.15**

Point-to-point infrared media in a network

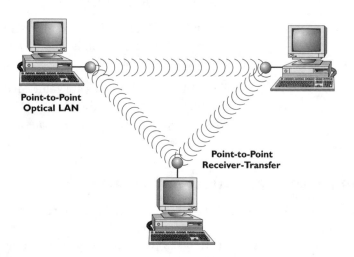

Point-to-point infrared systems have the following characteristics:

- Frequency range: Infrared light usually uses the lowest range of light frequencies, between 100GHz and 1,000 terahertz (THz).

- Cost: The cost depends on the kind of equipment used. Long-distance systems, which typically use high-power lasers, can be very expensive. Equipment that is mass-produced for the consumer market and can be adapted for network use is generally inexpensive.

- Installation: Infrared point-to-point requires precise alignment. If high-powered lasers are used, take extra care because they can damage or burn eyes.

- Capacity: Data rates vary between 100Kbps to 16Mbps (at one kilometer).

- Attenuation: The amount of attenuation depends on the quality of emitted light and its purity, as well as general atmospheric conditions and signal obstructions.

- EMI: Infrared transmission can be affected by intense light. Tightly focused beams are fairly immune to eavesdropping because tampering usually becomes evident by the disruption in the signal. Furthermore, the area in which the signal may be picked up is very limited.

## Broadcast

Broadcast infrared systems spread the signal to cover a wider area and allow reception of the signal by several receivers. One of the major advantages is mobility; the workstations or other devices can be moved more easily than with point-to-point infrared media. Figure 2.16 shows how a broadcast infrared system might be used.

**FIGURE 2.16**

An implementation of broadcast infrared media

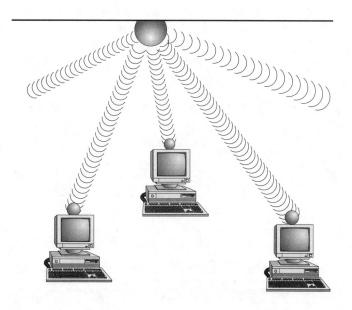

Because broadcast infrared signals are not as focused as point-to-point, this type of system cannot offer the same throughput. Broadcast infrared is typically limited to less than 1Mbps, making it too slow for most network needs. Broadcast infrared systems have the following characteristics:

- Frequency range: Infrared systems usually use the lowest range of light frequencies, between 100 GHz to 1,000 THz.

- Cost: The cost of infrared equipment depends on the quality of light required. Typical equipment used for infrared systems is quite inexpensive. High-power laser equipment is much more expensive.

- Installation: Installation is fairly simple. When devices have clear paths and strong signals, they can be placed anywhere the signal can reach, making reconfiguration easy. One concern should be the control of strong light sources that might affect infrared transmission.

- Capacity: Although data rates are less than 1Mbps, it is theoretically possible to reach much higher throughput.

- Attenuation: Broadcast infrared, like point-to-point, is affected by the quality of the emitted light and its purity, and by atmospheric conditions. Because devices can be moved easily, however, obstructions are generally not of great concern.

- EMI: Intense light can dilute infrared transmissions. Because broadcast infrared transmissions cover a wide area, they are more easily intercepted for eavesdropping.

# Public and Private Network Services

Although this information is not covered on the new NetWare 5 Networking Technologies exam, it is very good information to know in your career as a CNE.

**W**hen faced with the costs of installation, rather than choosing to start your system from scratch, you may want to consider using the services (transmission media) of networks that already exist, which can lower expenses considerably.

Public and private networks can help extend your own transmission media. Quite often, it is much cheaper to use provider services (pay to use their media) than to try to install your own transmission media.

A number of different services exist. Two of the most popular are the Public Switched Telephone Network and the Internet.

## Public Switched Telephone Network

Virtually every country in the world has a Public Switched Telephone Network (PSTN). All these networks together represent the world's largest network. PSTNs were originally designed exclusively for telephones but have evolved to high levels of sophistication, with the ability to handle different kinds of data transmission, including digital data transmission.

PSTNs are not the same in every country. Each country's PSTN may differ slightly, but they all use one of the types of transmission media described in this chapter.

The United States PSTN consists of various categories of components. Subscriber wiring and equipment is the customer's wiring and equipment, such as telephones, modems, and other devices. Typically, subscriber wiring consists of UTP cabling with RJ-11 or RJ-45 connectors. Often, the wiring extends back to a telephone closet, which then connects to a specific point, called the *demarcation point* or *demarc*. The demarc is the point where the telephone company's wiring connects with your wiring. It is a grounded, protected, physical connection point. You are responsible for maintaining wiring and equipment on your side of the demarc.

*Local loops* begin at the demarc and extend back to the *central office* (CO). The local loop normally consists of high-grade UTP cable, fiber-optic cable, or a combination of the two. The CO provides various services, the most important of which is switching incoming signals to outgoing trunk lines. It also provides reliable DC power to establish an electronic circuit on the local loop. A number of COs are connected by trunk lines to other switching offices.

Groups of central offices and switching offices then use long-distance carriers to provide transmission capability to COs almost anywhere in the world. Long-distance carriers often make use of a number of transmission media, such as high bandwidth coaxial cable, fiber-optic cable, and microwave transmitters and receivers.

Where the lines from the long-distance carriers enter the central office is called a *point of presence*. Figure 2.17 shows how the components of a PSTN work together.

**F I G U R E   2.17**

PSTN components

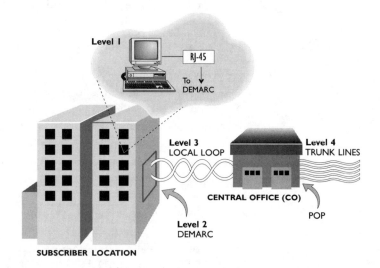

The PSTN provides a number of options for data transmissions, including services that route packets between different sites. Among these services are X.25, frame relay, SONET (Synchronous Optical Network), and ATM. The following are some examples of the available services and possible transmission rates:

- Dedicated 56 (56Kbps)
- Switched 56 (56Kbps)
- X.25 (56Kbps)
- T1 circuits (1.544Mbps)
- Switched T1 (1.544Mbps)
- Frame relay (1.544Mbps)
- SMDS (1.544Mbps)
- ISDN (1.544Mbps)

- E1 and above, available in Europe (2.048Mbps)

- T3 circuits (44.736Mbps)

- ATM (44.736Mbps)

These data transmission rates can be compared with common LAN services such as Ethernet (10Mbps and 100Mbps), Token Ring/4 (4Mbps), and Token Ring/16 (16Mbps). The expense of operating the network is distributed among various subscribers. Figure 2.18 shows an example of a PSTN.

**FIGURE 2.18**

An example of a PSTN

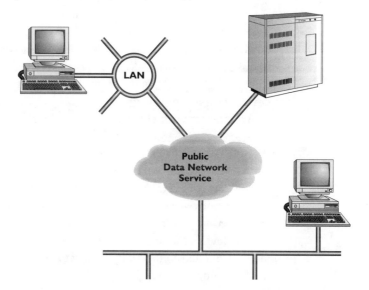

## The Internet

You're probably very familiar with the Internet, which is a shared network of government agencies, educational institutions, and private organizations from more than 100 nations. No one owns the Internet; everyone can have access to the transmission media. In fact, estimates of the number of people who have access to the Internet reach as high as 50 million or greater worldwide.

The United States has begun to put its weight behind the development of the National Information Infrastructure (better known as the "information superhighway"). The stated goals are to connect networks through "superhighways" with data rates of greater than 3Gbps. Research includes strategies for using fiber-optics and other high-bandwidth transmission media.

# An Overview of Transmission Media Connections

**N**ow that you know something about transmission media—the physical path through which the computer signals are transmitted—you can examine how to connect transmission media to devices and how to connect different segments of transmission media to each other. These connections allow you to connect devices and create a network, or connect networks to create an internetwork. Novell distinguishes between the terms *network* and *internetwork*.

A network consists of a single independent network that is not connected to any remote networks. On a network, devices are connected together to form a single unit. A network is alone, not talking to anyone else but the devices in its own little group.

An internetwork consists of multiple independent networks that are connected together and can share resources. Another way of saying this is that internetworks consist of physically connected, but logically separate, networks. Internetworks can consist of different kinds of networks. The device that connects them is said to be "intelligent" because it must decide whether packets should stay on the local network or be sent to another connected network.

The devices and interfaces used to connect computers and transmission media are called *connectivity hardware*. Connectivity hardware is used to do the following:

- Connect devices (such as workstations, printers, and modems) to transmission media

- Connect transmission media to transmission media

- Connect remote networks (internetworking)

# Network Connectivity Devices

**F**irst, let's examine network connectivity devices in terms of how they work on local networks, rather than when they are used to connect remote networks (internetworking). This section describes the following devices:

- Network interface boards

- Transmission media connectors

- Modems

- Hubs

- Repeaters

- Bridges

- Multiplexers

The first three of these components (network interface boards, transmission media connectors, and modems) are responsible for connecting individual computers to media segments. Each of the media segments must then be connected to form a network. The task of connecting all the transmission media segments is aided by hubs, repeaters, bridges, and multiplexers.

# Transmission Media Connectors

Every medium has one or more connectors used to attach the transmission media to network devices and other transmission media. The following sections cover several of these connector types.

## Multiple Wire Cable Connectors

Many Physical layer standards require cable with multiple wires. Several types of connectors are used for these connections. The following are three common types:

- D-type connectors are available in a wide variety. Two common types are DB-9 and DB-25 connectors. The number indicates the number of pins or sockets the connector has. DB-9 connectors are often used with Token Ring network cards. DB-25 connectors are often used with RS-232 connections.

- DIX connectors are similar to DB-15 connectors. DIX connectors connect to a mating connector with a clip that slides (instead of using screws). Thick Ethernet cable uses these connectors.

- DIN connectors have a number of different pin count arrangements. If you've worked on an AppleTalk network, you may have encountered a DIN connector.

Figure 2.19 illustrates the types of connectors for multiple wire cables.

**FIGURE 2.19**

Connectors for
multiple wire cables

**Twisted-Pair Cable Connectors**

The RJ-45 connector is the most common connector used with UTP cable. The biggest advantages of these connectors are that they are easy to install on the cables and easy to connect to and disconnect from each other. RJ-45 connectors are for four-pair UTP, so they have eight pins for the eight wires in the cable. Figure 2.20 shows an RJ-45 connector.

**FIGURE 2.20**

An RJ-45 connector

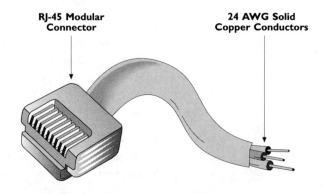

The RJ-11 connector is similar to the RJ-45 except that it is used for two-pair cable (cable with four wires rather than eight). Because RJ-11 connectors are used to plug your telephone into the telephone jack, they are probably familiar to you.

AppleTalk and Token Ring networks now typically use UTP cables with RJ-45 connectors, but both started out using STP cable. The connectors for STP cable are different. AppleTalk networks use a DIN connector with STP (see Figure 2.19). STP Token Ring uses IBM Data Connectors, except that the connection to the workstation is made by a DB-9 connector.

IBM uses the IBM Data Connector, which is distinguished by the fact that it does not come in the usual two-gender configuration. There is only one type of IBM Data Connector. Figure 2.21 shows an IBM Data Connector.

**FIGURE 2.21**

An IBM Data Connector

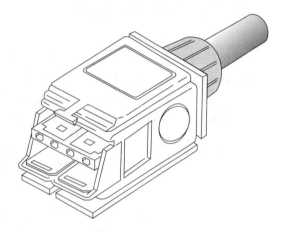

## Coaxial Cable Connectors

The BNC (*Bayonette Connector*) and the N-connector are typically used for coaxial cable. BNC connectors use a twist-lock fitting. N-connectors screw on and may be used to connect Thick Ethernet cable, but the more common approach now is to use vampire clamps (clamp-on transceivers) to penetrate the cable without cutting it.

## Fiber-Optic Cable Connectors

The most common type of fiber-optic connector is the ST-connector (Figure 2.22).

Fiber-optic cable can accommodate a number of fibers, which is usually necessary because two-way communication requires a pair of fibers.

**FIGURE 2.22**

An ST-connector

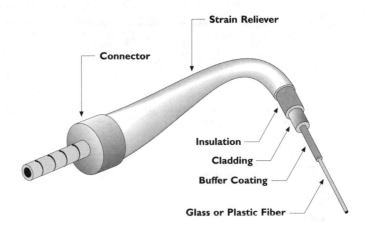

Eventually, each fiber will probably be connected to an individual device. When this becomes necessary, a connection center, called a *splice center*, is often used to connect individual fibers to individual connectors. Figure 2.23 illustrates how fibers are divided and attached to connectors.

**FIGURE 2.23**

Fiber-optic cable in a splice center

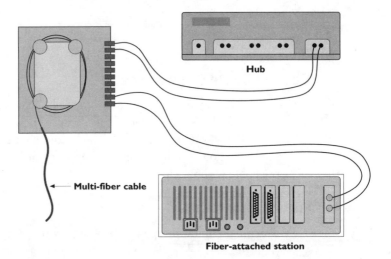

## Network Interface Boards

A *network interface board* provides the necessary hardware and logical connections between a device and the transmission media. In other words, a network interface board allows you to connect your computer (or other device) to the network. Network interface board is a generic term because it could be any of the following devices:

- A network interface card installed in one of the computer's expansion slots
- Network interface circuitry on the computer's main board
- A transmission media adapter

Figure 2.24 shows some sample network interface boards.

**FIGURE 2.24**

Examples of network
interface boards

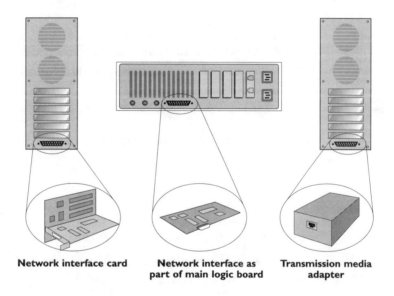

**Network interface card**    **Network interface as**    **Transmission media**
                            **part of main logic board**    **adapter**

You will need to be familiar with the following three terms:

- Transceiver
- Network interface card
- Transmission media adapter

## Transceivers

Whatever kind of network interface board you use, it will include some type of *transceiver*. Transceivers both transmit and receive signals. The fundamental purpose of transceivers of every type is to transmit or receive electricity, light, or electromagnetic waves.

Transceivers change the computer's signal into the form necessary to send the signal through the transmission medium. For example, when a computer sends data through a fiber-optic cable, the transceiver changes the computer's electrical signal into the light pulses to send through the cable. And it does the opposite when the signals come from the transmission media, using devices that can detect light and change them into the signals that the computer can use.

## Network Interface Cards

If a computer does not come with the necessary circuitry included, a network board called a *network interface card* (NIC) can be installed in the computer's expansion slot. NICs are a common way to connect computers to a network. The NICs have circuitry that changes the computer's signals to those needed by the transmission medium (except in the case of Thick Ethernet, which uses an external transceiver in addition to the card). Each NIC incorporates a transceiver and may provide one or more types of connections.

## Transmission Media Adapters

When a network transmission medium comes with a connector that is different from the connector on a network interface board, a *transmission media adapter* is used to connect the two. Novell Education categorizes several types of devices as transmission media adapters. The following are examples of types of transmission media adapters:

- *SCSI port adapters* allow you to connect devices to a network through a SCSI interface.

- *Parallel port adapters* allow you to network laptop computers by their parallel ports for communication.

- *PCMCIA adapters* allow you to connect a laptop computer to a network using credit-card-size interface cards.

- *Transceivers (or MAUs)* connect computers to Thick Ethernet (thick coaxial cable).

- *Media filters* adapt DB-9 connectors to connect with RJ-45 connectors for use with a UTP network.

# Modems

Modems are used to change digital signals (zeros and ones) to analog signals (waveforms). Changing a signal from digital form to analog form is called *modulation*. The process of changing a signal back from analog to digital is called *demodulation*. Modems get their name from this process (MOdulation/DEModulation).

The process begins at one computer where the modem changes (modulates) a digital signal into an analog waveform. The waveform (data) is then sent to the receiving device through the transmission medium. At the receiving device, the waveform is changed back (demodulated) into digital signals by a second modem. Figure 2.25 illustrates the process.

**F I G U R E   2.25**

Modems sending and receiving data

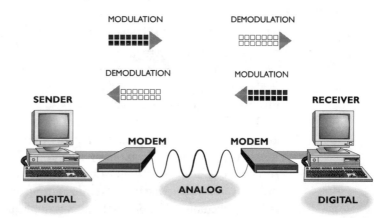

Digital signals must be changed to analog to transmit them through telephone lines or microwave media. Modems can be used to connect different devices over long distances. Modems are also occasionally used when a transceiver's signal is not powerful enough to travel the desired distance, because modems can amplify signals.

Modems generally use telephone lines or microwave transmission. Some modems operate on dedicated telephone lines; others use PSTNs to dial up and connect only when necessary. Typical modem use on LANs includes the following:

- Dial-up users accessing the LAN

- Mail servers exchanging e-mail

- Fax servers transmitting and receiving faxes

- LANs exchanging data on demand

Modem speeds are measured in bits per second (bps). Modems that transmit at 33,600bps are currently the most common. The latest standard supports speeds up to 56,000bps with the V.90 standard.

Modems are not internetworking devices. The amount of data modems can exchange is limited. They do not allow remote networks to connect to each other and truly share network data. Modems, however, can be used with an internetwork device (a router, for example) to connect remote networks.

If you wish to connect two devices but do not wish to use a modem, and the devices are less than 100 meters apart, you can make a connection using a cable called a *null modem cable*. This type of cable provides a connection between the transmit circuit of one device to the receive circuit of another.

# Repeaters

All transmission media attenuate (weaken) the electromagnetic waves that travel through them. Attenuation, therefore, limits the distance any medium can carry data. Adding a device that amplifies the signal can allow it to travel farther, increasing the size of the network. Devices that amplify signals in this way are called *repeaters*.

Repeaters are classified in two categories, amplifiers and signal-regenerating repeaters. *Amplifiers* simply amplify the entire incoming signal. Unfortunately, they amplify both the signal and the noise. *Signal-regenerating repeaters* create an exact duplicate of incoming data by identifying it amidst the noise, reconstructing it, and retransmitting only the desired information, reducing the noise. The original signal is duplicated, boosted to its original strength, and sent. Figure 2.26 shows where a repeater might be used.

**FIGURE 2.26**

An example of repeater use in a network

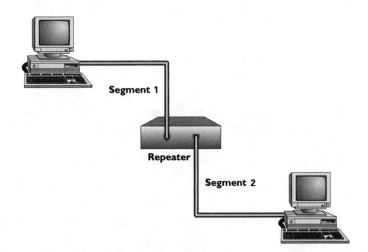

Theoretically, repeaters could be used to combine an unlimited number of transmission media segments. But in reality, network designs limit the number of repeaters.

# Hubs

All networks (except those using coaxial cable) require a central location to bring media segments together. These central locations are called *hubs* (or *multiport repeaters* or *concentrators*). The easiest way to understand this concept is to think of the necessity of connecting multiple cables. If you just connected the media segments together by soldering them, the signals would interfere with each other and create problems. A hub organizes the cables and relays signals to the other media segments. Figure 2.27 shows a hub.

**FIGURE 2.27**

An example of a hub

There are three main types of hubs: passive, active, and intelligent.

## Passive Hubs

All a *passive hub* does is combine the signals of network segments. There is no signal processing or regeneration. Because it does not boost the signal (in fact, it absorbs some of the signal), a passive hub reduces the maximum cabling distances. The maximum distance is reduced to half of what it would normally be for that medium. For example, if a segment normally allows a reliable transmission distance of 200 meters (656 feet), the distance between a passive hub and a device can only be 100 meters (328 feet). Also, with a passive hub, each computer receives the signals sent from all the other computers connected to the hub.

### Active Hubs

*Active hubs* are like passive hubs except that they have electronic components that regenerate or amplify the signals. Because the signals are regenerated or amplified, the distances between devices can be increased. The main drawback to some active hubs is that they amplify noise as well as the signal, depending on whether they function as simple amplifiers or as signal regenerators. They are also much more expensive than passive hubs. Because some active hubs function as repeaters, they are sometimes called *multiport repeaters*.

### Intelligent Hubs

In addition to signal regeneration, *intelligent hubs* perform some network management and intelligent path selection. A switching hub chooses only the port of the device where the signal needs to go, rather than sending the signal along all paths. Many switching hubs can choose which alternative path will be the quickest and send the signal that way. One advantage to using intelligent hubs is that you can permanently connect all transmission media segments because each segment will only be used when a signal is sent to a device using that segment.

## Bridges

*Bridges* connect network segments. The use of a bridge increases the maximum possible size of your network. Unlike a repeater, which simply passes on all the signals it receives, a bridge selectively determines the appropriate segment to which it should pass a signal. It does this by reading the address of all the signals that it receives. The bridge reads the physical location of the source and destination computers from this address. The process works like this:

1. A bridge receives all the signals from both segment A and segment B.

2. The bridge reads the addresses and discards (filters) all signals from segment A that are addressed to segment A because they do not need to cross the bridge.

**3.** Signals from segment A addressed to a computer on segment B are retransmitted to segment B.

**4.** The signals from segment B are treated in the same way.

Figure 2.28 illustrates how signals pass through a bridge.

**F I G U R E  2.28**

A bridge connects
different types of
networks.

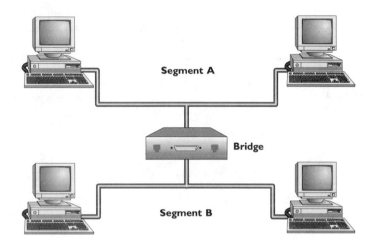

Through address filtering, bridges can divide busy networks into segments and reduce network traffic. To use a bridge effectively, networks will often be divided into groups by physical location and shared resources (such as printers, network servers, and applications). If most signals do not frequently cross the bridge, using bridges can help reduce traffic on your network.

Bridges cannot be used to connect LANs of different types. For example, an Ethernet segment and a Token Ring segment cannot be connected with a bridge, because each network type uses different physical addressing.

# Multiplexing

**I**n some cases, a transmission medium can handle more capacity than a single signal can occupy. *Multiplexing* allows you to use more bandwidth of the medium by combining two or more separate signals and transmitting them together. The original signals can then be extracted at the other end of the medium. This is called *demultiplexing*.

A familiar example of multiplexing is cable TV. Most cable TV networks send numerous signals (30 or more) through a single coaxial cable. The cable box or VCR demultiplexes the signals into what we think of as channels.

Figure 2.29 illustrates multiplexers on a computer network.

**F I G U R E  2.29**

Multiplexers on a computer network

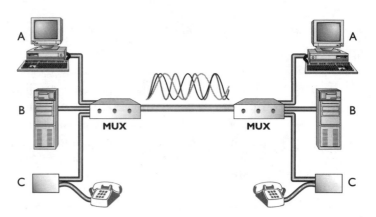

# Internetwork Connectivity Devices

**A**n *internetwork* consists of two or more independent networks that are connected and yet maintain independent identities. An internetwork may include different types of networks (an Ethernet and an ARCnet network, for example). To connect independent networks, you use *internetwork connectivity devices*.

The three internetwork connectivity devices discussed here are routers, brouters, and CSUs/DSUs.

## Routers and Brouters

*Routers* use logical and physical addressing to connect two or more logically separate networks. They accomplish this connection by organizing the large network into logical network segments (sometimes called *subnetworks* or *subnets*). Each of these subnetworks is given a logical address, allowing the networks to be separate but still access each other and exchange data when necessary. Data is grouped into *packets*, or blocks of data. Each packet, in addition to having a physical device address, has a logical network address. Figure 2.30 shows networks connected by routers.

**FIGURE 2.30**

Networks connected
by routers

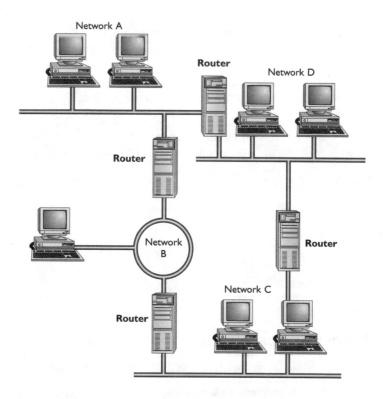

The network address allows the routers to more accurately and efficiently calculate the optimal path to a workstation or computer. Routers perform a function very similar to that of a bridge, but routers keep the networks separate. Because they must check both the device address and the network address, router processing is generally slower than bridge processing. However, routers are more "intelligent" than bridges because they use algorithms to determine the best route for each packet. Even if a router is not directly connected to a network, it will know the best way to get a packet there.

Many routers may be more appropriately called *brouters*. A brouter is a router that can also act as a bridge. A brouter first tries to deliver the packet based on network protocol information. If the brouter does not support the protocol used by the packet or cannot deliver the packet based on protocol information, it bridges the packet using the physical address. A true router will simply discard a packet if it doesn't have a correct logical address.

## CSUs/DSUs

As explained earlier in this chapter, sometimes it is less costly and easier to use existing public networks, such as the PSTN in your area. Connecting to some of these networks requires the use of *CSUs/DSUs (channel service units/digital service units).*

Network service providers may require you to use a CSU/DSU to translate the signals of your LAN into a different signal format and strength for use on their transmission media. CSUs/DSUs are also useful for shielding your network from both noise and dangerous voltage currents that can come through the public network.

# Review

This chapter surveyed the wide array of transmission media and connections available for creating network connectivity.

## Transmission Media

This chapter described the two main types of transmission media:

- Cable media
- Wireless media

There are also public and private network services, including Public Switched Telephone Networks (PSTN) and the Internet. These services are composed of cable and wireless media, and they offer the option of using established services rather than starting from scratch.

Cable media typically use the lower end of the electromagnetic spectrum for signaling and consist of the following varieties:

- Shielded twisted-pair (STP) cable

- Unshielded twisted-pair (UTP) cable

- Coaxial cable

- Fiber-optic cable

Wireless media typically use the higher frequencies of electromagnetic wavelengths. Types of wireless media include:

- Radio wave

- Microwave

- Infrared

Transmission media connect by means of a variety of network connectivity devices, including the following:

- Network interface boards

- Modems

- Repeaters

- Hubs

- Bridges

- Multiplexers

There are also several types of internetwork connectivity devices:

- Routers

- Brouters

- CSUs/DSUs (channel service units/digital service units)

# CNE Practice Test Questions

**1.** Thin Ethernet uses which type of cable?

   **A.** UTP

   **B.** STP

   **C.** Coaxial

   **D.** Fiber-optic

**2.** Which type of cable supports the highest bandwidth?

   **A.** UTP

   **B.** STP

   **C.** Coaxial

   **D.** Fiber-optic

**3.** Which device is used to send data over telephone lines?

   **A.** Repeater

   **B.** Hub

   **C.** Bridge

   **D.** Modem

**4.** What is the most common connector used with UTP cable?

   **A.** RJ-14

   **B.** RJ-45

   **C.** DB-15

   **D.** BNC

**5.** What is the process of converting a signal to analog form?

   **A.** Modulation

   **B.** Demodulation

    **C.** Transmission

    **D.** Attenuation

**6.** Which two categories are used to classify repeaters?

    **A.** Amplifiers and transmitters

    **B.** Amplifiers and regenerating repeaters

    **C.** Modems and codecs

    **D.** Bridges and routers

**7.** What is the device that connects multiple nodes to the network?

    **A.** A modem

    **B.** A repeater

    **C.** A hub

    **D.** An amplifier

**8.** What are the three main types of hubs?

    **A.** Passive, active, and FDDI

    **B.** Passive, active, and amplifying

    **C.** Passive, active, and intelligent

    **D.** Passive, regenerative, and amplifying

**9.** Which is the most complicated type of hub?

    **A.** Intelligent

    **B.** Passive

    **C.** Active

    **D.** Regenerative

**10.** What device passes signals selectively between network segments?

   **A.** A repeater

   **B.** A hub

   **C.** A bridge

   **D.** A modem

**11.** What is sending two signals over the same cable called?

   **A.** Routing

   **B.** Multiplexing

   **C.** Multicoding

   **D.** Combining

**12.** What does attenuation refer to?

   **A.** A signal growing weaker as it travels

   **B.** A signal growing stronger as it travels

   **C.** Sending the same signal again

   **D.** Increasing the strength of a signal

# CHAPTER

# 3

The OSI Model and Its Lower Layers

# Roadmap

This chapter covers the general overview of the OSI model and a detailed discussion of the lower two layers (Physical and Data Link).

**Topics Covered**

- The need for rules in computer networking
- The OSI model
- Relationship of the OSI model to protocols
- Physical layer definition
- Physical layer characteristics
- Data Link layer definition
- Data Link layer characteristics

**Skills You'll Learn**

- Explain why rules are needed in networks
- List the seven layers of the OSI model and how they interact
- Explain the relationship between the OSI model and network protocols
- Explain the purpose of the Physical layer of the OSI model
- Identify the characteristics of the most common Physical layer connection types used in computer networks
- Explain the five most commonly used physical topologies
- Distinguish between analog and digital signals
- Explain the various methods of digital encoding
- Explain the various methods of analog encoding
- Describe the various methods of bit synchronization
- Explain the two most common bandwidth use methods and explain how multiplexing uses each
- Explain the purpose of the Data Link layer of the OSI model
- Explain the details of the two most common logical topologies

- Explain the characteristics of the three media access methods

- Detail the reason behind and uses of the Data Link layer addresses

- Define the three ways transmission synchronization occurs at the Data Link layer

- Detail the way connection services are used at the Data Link layer

---

**T**he International Organization for Standardization (ISO) began developing the *Open Systems Interconnection (OSI)* reference model in 1977. It has since become the most widely accepted model for understanding network communication.

This chapter begins the examination of the OSI reference model, which divides network communication into seven separate processes, called *layers*. It describes how the OSI model operates, and then starts working through the model's layers. This chapter includes details about the bottom two layers, called the Physical and Data Link layers. Chapter 4 will cover the next two layers: the Network and Transport layers. Finally, Chapter 5 will cover the top three layers: Session, Presentation, and Application.

# Understanding the OSI Model

**C**hapter 1 said that in order for computers to communicate, there must be accepted rules of communication, or protocols. For communication to take place on a network composed of a variety of network devices, these rules must be clearly defined. The OSI model (and other networking models developed by other organizations) attempts to define rules that apply to the following issues:

- How network devices contact each other and, if they have different languages, how they communicate with each other.

- Methods by which a device on a network knows when to transmit data and when not to.

- Methods to ensure that network transmissions are received correctly and by the right recipient.

- How the physical transmission media are arranged and connected.

- How to ensure that the network devices maintain a proper rate of data flow.

- How bits of data are represented on the network media.

The OSI model is nothing tangible; it is simply a conceptual framework that you can use to better understand the complex interactions taking place among the various devices on a network. The OSI model does not perform any functions in the communication processes. The actual work is done by the appropriate software and hardware. The OSI model simply defines which tasks need to be done and which protocols will handle those tasks, at each of the seven layers of the model:

1. Physical

2. Data Link

3. Network

4. Transport

5. Session

6. Presentation

7. Application

A good way to remember these seven layers is illustrated in Figure 3.1.

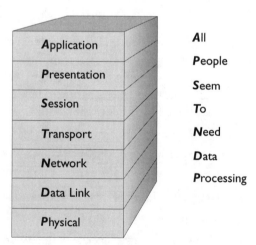

**FIGURE 3.1**

The OSI model and a mnemonic device for remembering it

The OSI model divides communication tasks into smaller pieces called *subtasks*. Protocol implementations are computer processes that relate to these subtasks. Specific protocols fulfill subtasks at specific layers of the OSI model. When these protocols are grouped together to complete a whole task, you have what is called a *protocol stack*. The following sections examine how protocol stacks work and how they communicate with protocol stacks on other computers.

## Protocol Stacks

A protocol stack is a group of protocols that are stacked on top of each other as part of a communication process. Each layer of the OSI model has different protocols associated with it. When more than one protocol is needed to complete a communication process, the protocols are grouped together in a stack. An example of a protocol stack is TCP/IP, which is a widely used protocol for UNIX and the Internet.

Each layer in the protocol stack receives services from the layer below it and provides services to the layer above it. Novell likes to explain the relationship like this: Layer $N$ uses the services of the layer below it (*layer N-1*), and provides services to the layer above it (*layer N+1*).

In order for two computers to communicate, the same protocol stacks must be running on each computer. Each layer of the protocol stack on one computer communicates with its equivalent, or *peer,* on the other computer. The computers can have different operating systems and still be able to communicate if they are running the same protocol stacks. For example, a DOS machine running TCP/IP can communicate with a Macintosh machine running TCP/IP. This is illustrated in Figure 3.2.

**FIGURE  3.2**

Peer communication between two computers

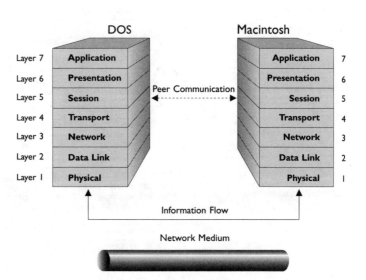

## Peer Layer Communication between Stacks

When a message is sent from one machine to another, it travels down the layers on one machine and then up the layers on the other machine. This route is illustrated in Figure 3.3.

**FIGURE 3.3**

A message sent from one peer layer to another

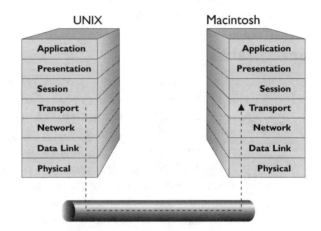

As the message travels down the first stack, each layer it passes through (except the Physical layer) adds a *header*. These headers contain pieces of control information that are read and processed by the corresponding layer on the receiving stack. As the message travels up the stack of the other machine, each layer strips the header added by its peer layer. This process is illustrated in Figure 3.4.

**FIGURE 3.4**

The OSI model and headers

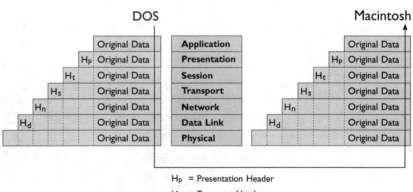

As an example, suppose that you are using two networked applications based on the DOS and Macintosh operating systems. At layer 7, the DOS application requests something from the Macintosh application. This request is sent to the DOS application's layer 6. This layer receives the request as a data packet, adds its own header, and passes the packet down to layer 5, where the process is repeated. As the request travels down the layers, headers are added until the request reaches the Physical layer (which does not add a header), loaded down with headers.

Next, this request packet travels across the network transmission media and begins its journey up the layers on the Macintosh. The header that was put on at the Data Link layer of the DOS application is stripped at the Data Link layer of the Macintosh application. The Macintosh Data Link layer performs the tasks requested in the header, and then passes the request on to the next higher layer. This process is repeated until the Macintosh application's layer 7 receives the packet and interprets the request inside.

At each layer, the data packages, called *service data units*, are comprised of data and headers from the layers above. For this reason, they are commonly referred to with different names when they are at different layers, as shown in Figure 3.5. The term *packet* is applicable to a service data unit at any layer.

**F I G U R E   3.5**

Common data
package names

| Application | | Messages & Packets |
|---|---|---|
| Presentation | H₁ | Packets |
| Session | H₂ | Packets |
| Transport | H₃ | Datagrams, Segments & Packets |
| Network | H₄ | Datagrams & Packets |
| Data Link | H₅ | Frames & Packets |
| Physical | | Bits & Packets |

## The Lower Layers of the OSI Model

The lower layers of the OSI model provide a pathway for data transmission.

At the bottom is the Physical layer, which consists of the physical media, such as cable, and the electrical specifications that determine its functionality. The second layer from the bottom is the Data Link layer, which provides the first layer of logic on top of the Physical layer. From the perspective of the Physical layer, the data that traverses the medium is simply a string of bits without form or structure. The Data Link layer adds structure by grouping the bits into frames.

# The Physical Layer of the OSI Model

The Physical layer's job is to transmit and receive bits over the physical media, the network cable. It also controls the physical layout or structure of the network and defines the rules for bit-transmission encoding and timing.

The following topics are addressed at the Physical layer:

- Network connection types, including multipoint and point-to-point connections.

- Physical topologies, which are physical layouts of networks, such as bus, star, or ring.

- Analog and digital signaling, which include several methods for encoding data in analog and digital signals.

- Bit synchronization, which deals with synchronization between sender and receiver.

- Baseband and broadband transmissions, which are different methods for using media bandwidth.

- Multiplexing, which involves combining several data channels into one.

## Connection Types

There are two basic types of network connections, *multipoint* and *point-to-point* connections. The type of connection defines whether multiple devices are connected to the medium or if there is a one-to-one connection between two devices. A simple rule of thumb is that if two devices are connected, the connection is point-to-point. If three or more devices are connected, the connection is multipoint. Networking systems are almost always multipoint. The following sections discuss these two types of connections in detail.

### Multipoint Connections

If a network is using multipoint connections, multiple devices are connected to the transmission medium. Figure 3.6 shows an example of a network using multipoint connections. In this example, there are four devices connected to the cable. These four devices will, of necessity, share the same cable, and the bandwidth of the cable will be divided among all four of them.

**FIGURE 3.6**

An example of
multipoint
connections

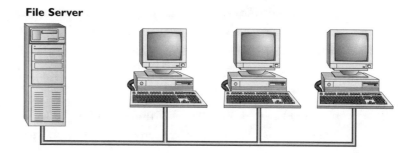

## Point-to-Point Connections

A point-to-point connection is one between two devices. Two computers
connected via modem are an example of a point-to-point link. Figure 3.7
illustrates some examples of point-to-point links.

**FIGURE 3.7**

Point-to-point
connections

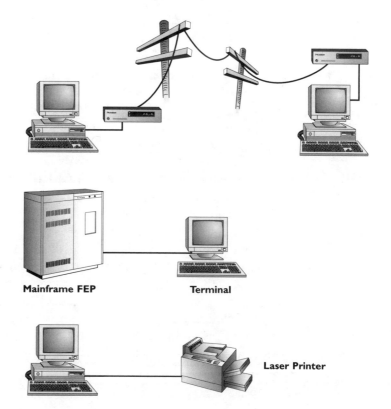

Because only two devices are connected in this type of link, the media bandwidth is divided between those two devices. Obviously, this provides the devices a higher percentage of the media bandwidth than they would receive with a multipoint connection.

## Physical Topology

The physical topology of the network is the network's physical structure or layout. There are several possible ways to connect the devices that make up a network.

To give you some perspective before going into the details of each type, here is a brief history of my personal experiences with some different physical topologies.

The first physical topology I saw when I began to install networks was a star. Each computer was directly cabled to an active (powered, eight-port) or passive (not powered, four-port) hub using coaxial cable. If you guessed that this was ARCnet, you are right. It was a dependable network that did not require much troubleshooting.

Next, I ran into another type of network layout. It consisted of a long piece of coaxial cable with terminators on both ends. Every so often, there was a computer attached to the cable with a connector in the shape of a letter T. I'm quite sure you know that this one was Thin Ethernet. Its physical topology is a bus. The wiring of a bus topology functions like old-fashioned Christmas lights—the failure of one connection brings down the whole bus. Let's just say that I have experienced many stressful moments when bus topology networks have gone down at the wrong time.

Later, I was introduced to another type of Ethernet, called 10BaseT, that uses unshielded twisted-pair (UTP) cable connected to a powered hub in a star topology. The star topology makes every computer independent of the others; if one computer has a bad connection or a bad cable, no other computer is affected. My experience with 10BaseT has been very positive. No wonder it is the most popular type of LAN being installed today.

Along with the popular star and bus topologies, other common physical topologies for a network include ring, mesh, and cellular topologies.

The following sections cover some important points about each topology: its relative ease of installation, troubleshooting, reconfiguration, and its advantages and disadvantages. These are all important factors to consider when choosing a physical topology.

## Physical Bus Topology

A bus topology is a backbone configuration in which all the computers tie into one long cable segment. This topology is considered to be a multipoint connection, as you can see in Figure 3.8.

**FIGURE 3.8**

Physical bus topology

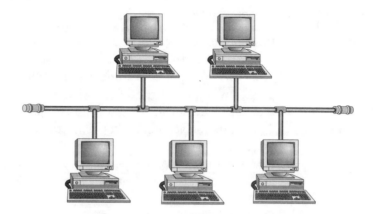

In a bus topology, both ends of the network segment must be terminated to avoid harmful signal reflections, and the machines are attached to the common media via some type of connector, such as T-connectors. In some variations on the bus topology, the machines connect to the bus with drop cable, which are 2- to 4-foot cables that connect the main network cable to each computer.

**Bus Topology Installation** Installing a network with a bus topology is relatively simple, although you must follow certain guidelines, such as maximum backbone cable length and minimum distance between devices. Also, don't forget those terminators!

A network *terminator* is a device you attach to the end of a cable segment. The terminator contains an electrical device called a resistor. Its function is to connect the two conductors together partially. The network can detect when a signal reaches the terminator, and knows it does not need to send it further.

Ethernet networks are the most common type of bus topology network. In a Thick Ethernet bus configuration, the devices must be at least 2.5 meters (8 feet) apart. The cable used for Thick Ethernet will usually have these markings already on the cable. The cable run itself has distance limitations (500 meters or 1,500 feet) and the attenuation (loss) of the signal will increase as the distance increases. A Thin Ethernet segment must be 185 meters (550 feet) or less.

**Bus Topology Troubleshooting and Reconfiguration**   Because of the way that all the devices in a bus topology are connected, troubleshooting can be a challenge. If there is a break in the cable or a bad connection at any point, it will affect all the other devices on that network segment. Because all the devices are down, it is difficult to isolate the problem.

You can troubleshoot bus topology segments one workstation at a time, terminating each one in turn in order to discover the bad cable or connector. However, this can become very time-consuming, not to mention frustrating. It also creates difficulties when the cables have been strung through walls or through the ceiling. In these cases, you'll need a map of the cable layout. Otherwise, how do you know which workstation is the next one on the bus? Reconfiguration can be moderately difficult, depending on the type of bus topology used. For example, Thick Ethernet uses taps that cut into the backbone cable (called *vampire* taps). These are not likely to be moved on a whim. Also, because there are limitations on the length of the backbone, as well as on the number of devices that can be connected to it, once that maximum is reached, reconfiguration becomes a challenge.

On the other hand, with Thin Ethernet, it is relatively easy to insert another device as long as the maximum specifications have not yet been reached. Simply substitute two shorter cable segments for the existing one and attach the PC at this point with a T-connector.

**Bus Topology Advantages and Disadvantages**   Some advantages of the bus topology are that it uses less cable than other topologies, uses established standards, and is easy to install.

The main disadvantage to bus topology networks is that all the devices on the segment are affected by media failure. This means that when something goes wrong you have 30 users calling you, not just one. The second disadvantage is the difficulty of troubleshooting. Finally, a bus topology can be difficult to reconfigure, especially if the maximum specifications have been reached.

## Physical Ring Topology

A ring topology network is set up in circular fashion, as its name implies. Data travels around the ring in one direction, and each device on the ring acts as a repeater to keep the signal strong as it travels. Each device incorporates a receiver for the incoming signal and a transmitter to send the data on to the next device in the ring. Figure 3.9 illustrates a physical ring topology.

**FIGURE 3.9**

Physical ring topology

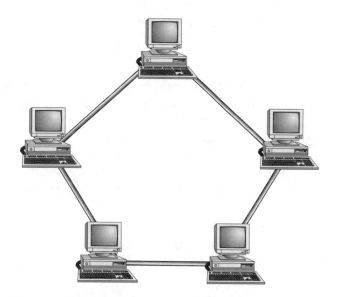

**Ring Topology Installation** A network using the ring topology is not particularly difficult to install. The installer must be careful not to exceed specifications, such as maximum number of devices on the ring, maximum ring diameter, or maximum distance between devices (repeaters).

A ring topology will require more cable than a bus topology because the cable must be brought back around to the starting point.

**Ring Topology Troubleshooting and Reconfiguration** Troubleshooting is easier on a ring topology network than on one with a bus topology. Because each device is expecting to receive a signal from the device upstream to it, it will begin to beacon if it does not receive the signal within a specified amount of time. Unfortunately, all the devices downstream from the break will beacon, making it a challenge to find the station that is located next to the problem area. As in the bus topology, all the devices in a ring are brought down if there is a media failure. The ring topology is dependent upon the ability of the signal to travel around the ring. If the signal is halted from making its rounds, communication comes to a standstill. Some ring topology networks have addressed this problem by connecting stations to dual rings. This built-in fault-tolerance feature allows a break to occur without bringing down all the stations on the rings. Because the signal travels in the opposite direction on the second ring, one station, upon noting a problem in the media, can detour the signal onto the second ring, thus maintaining the circular pathway. Reconfiguring a ring network can be difficult, because ring segments need to be divided. You also need to consider the maximum distances possible between repeaters and the number of devices you can have on the network.

**Ring Topology Advantages and Disadvantages**   Two advantages of the ring topology are that cable faults can be isolated relatively easily, and that the ring topology can be very fault tolerant if configured with dual rings.

Disadvantages include the fact that ring topologies are more difficult to install and reconfigure than bus topologies and use more cable. An important disadvantage when using a single ring configuration is that a failure in the media will bring down all the devices on the ring.

## Physical Star Topology

The star topology is one of the more popular configurations. It requires a central hub, which is usually a concentrator or repeater. Each computer has a dedicated cable to the hub, which gives it a star-like appearance. Some examples of networks that use the star topology are ARCnet and 10BaseT Ethernet. In fact, even IBM Token Ring is cabled in a physical star (however, the data travels around a Token Ring network in a logical ring).

The star topology is popular for two main reasons: media failure does not usually bring down the entire segment (as in the whole star), and star configurations are much easier to troubleshoot. Some enlightened hubs allow you to verify at a glance whether or not there is a good connection between the hub and the workstation's network interface board. Some network interface boards are also blessed with indicator lights that allow you to verify the connection from the workstation side as well.

**Star Topology Installation**   Installing a star configuration network is more difficult than installing a bus in that there must be a cable brought from each node to the hub. Other than that, however, installation is not difficult. As with all topologies, the installer must be careful to follow specifications. With ARCnet, for example, it is important to terminate unused ports on the hubs.

It is also important to consider distance limitations. Each different star topology network has different distance limitations depending on the characteristics of the media and the hubs. A common distance limitation between a node and the hub is 100 meters (328 feet). This is the case with 10BaseT using UTP and with ARCnet between a node and a passive hub. You must make sure that a hub is located within 100 meters of all nodes.

The star topology requires substantially more cable (whether fiber-optic, coaxial, or twisted-pair) than the bus or ring topologies.

**Star Topology Troubleshooting and Reconfiguration**   In a star configuration, it is usually quite easy to locate where the problem is. If any one workstation cannot communicate, the problem probably lies between that workstation and the hub. Something could be wrong with the workstation's network interface board, the connector between the board and the cable, the cable itself, or the port on the hub. If all the workstations are down, the problem probably lies with the hub itself. Fault isolation is more logical and straightforward because of the hierarchical nature of the star topology.

Reconfiguration is not particularly difficult. Adding another node involves extending a cable from that node to an available port on the hub. If the hub's ports are full, another hub can usually be daisy-chained onto the first.

**Star Topology Advantages and Disadvantages**   One of the main advantages of the star topology is that it's easy to troubleshoot. It is also relatively easy to reconfigure, and media failure on a leg of a star affects only the one node attached to it.

A disadvantage of the star topology is that a large amount of cable is required. Also, you might need to do a lot of crawling through ceiling spaces to install that cable.

## Physical Mesh Topology

The mesh topology is distinguished by having redundant links between devices. A true mesh configuration has a link between each and every device in the network. As you can imagine, this gets ridiculous beyond a very small number of devices. Most mesh topology networks are not true mesh networks. Rather, they are hybrid mesh networks that contain some redundant links but not all. Figure 3.10 illustrates both a true mesh and a hybrid mesh topology.

FIGURE 3.10

Physical mesh
topology

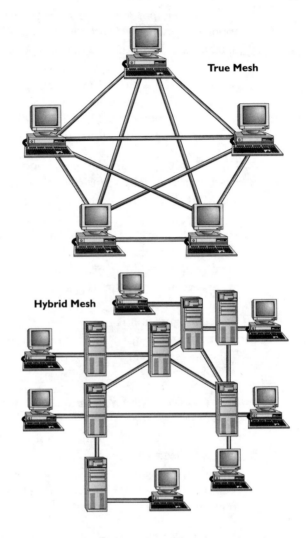

**Mesh Topology Installation**   Mesh topology networks become more difficult to install as the number of devices increases because of the sheer number of connections that must be made. A true mesh of only six devices would require 15 connections (5+4+3+2+1). A true mesh topology of seven devices would require 21 connections (6+5+4+3+2+1), and so on.

**Mesh Topology Troubleshooting and Reconfiguration**   Mesh networks are easy to troubleshoot and are very fault tolerant. Media failure has less impact on a mesh topology than on any other topology. The redundant links enable data to be sent over several different paths.

Reconfiguration, like installation, gets progressively more difficult as the number of devices increases.

**Mesh Topology Advantages and Disadvantages**   The major advantage of the mesh topology is fault tolerance. Other advantages include guaranteed communication channel capacity and the fact that mesh networks are relatively easy to troubleshoot.

Disadvantages include the difficulty of installation and reconfiguration, as well as the cost of maintaining redundant links.

## Physical Cellular Topology

First and foremost, the cellular topology is a wireless topology, making it a completely different animal than the topologies discussed so far.

In a cellular topology, the network is made up of circular areas called *cells*, each of which is serviced by a central station or hub. Communication takes place through radio signals that carry data from nodes within the cell to the central station. The central station can then route data to devices in other cells by way of their central stations. This topology is well-suited for mobile computing environments. The cellular topology is illustrated in Figure 3.11.

**FIGURE 3.11**

Physical cellular topology

It is interesting to note that a device can roam from cell to cell and still remain connected to the network. As it crosses a cell boundary, it will begin to communicate with the central hub of the new cell.

**Cellular Topology Installation**   Installation of a cellular topology network is very different from installation of topologies that use cable. The main consideration is finding suitable hub locations. For example, if the network will cover a wide area, it may be difficult to acquire the property on which to place the central hub. If the network will be local, there should not be any obstructing walls between nodes and the hub.

**Cellular Topology Troubleshooting and Reconfiguration**   The complexity of solving problems on a cellular topology network depends on how the network has been constructed. Troubleshooting node-to-hub links is relatively simple because each device interacts with the hub independently of other devices. If the central hub fails, all devices in the cell are affected. Because user devices are mobile, however, they can be relocated to another cell with a working central station, thus virtually eliminating downtime.

Reconfiguration is not much of an issue with mobile users in a cellular topology.

**Cellular Topology Advantages and Disadvantages**   Advantages of the cellular topology are that installation and troubleshooting are not difficult. Reconfiguration, at least in the case of adding new users or moving existing users, is a not a concern.

A disadvantage is that the failure of a hub will bring down all the devices that depend on it, but that is the case for any topology that uses hubs. Another disadvantage is related to security. It is not difficult to listen in on radio communications. Therefore, secure encryption methods must be used to protect company information. (Encryption is discussed in Chapter 5.)

# Signaling

Signaling is the way that data is transmitted across the medium. It involves using electrical energy to communicate. Somehow the data, or the bits and bytes, must be represented in a way that the sender can create a message and the receiver can understand it. This is done by means of *encoding* (also called *modulation*). The original signal is altered in a certain way to allow it to represent data.

The information to be communicated can exist in either of two forms, analog or digital. A characteristic of analog information is that it changes continuously. An example of this is an analog clock. It is always changing its representation of time because the second hand never stops (as long as it's working).

Digital data, on the other hand, consists of discrete states: On or Off, 1 or 0, and so on. A digital clock does not show the variations of time between minutes. It's either 12:01 or 12:02, not anything in between.

The two signaling methods correspond to the two types of data described above:

- Digital signaling
- Analog signaling

Figure 3.12 shows the difference between an analog signal and a digital signal.

**FIGURE 3.12**

Analog and digital signals

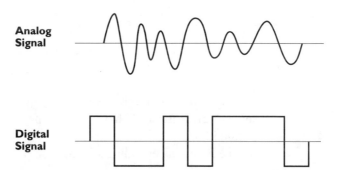

Note that the analog signal is constantly changing and represents all values in a range. It is actually an electromagnetic waveform. In contrast, the digital signal represents discrete states, and the state change is practically instantaneous.

These signaling methods are discussed in detail in the following sections.

## Digital Signaling

Most computer networks use digital signaling because computers are inherently digital. There are many methods of encoding data in a digital signal. These methods are called *encoding* schemes. They can be grouped into two general categories based on whether the recognition of a given state is triggered by a certain voltage level or by the transition from one level to another.

The two categories of signal-encoding techniques are:

- Current-state encoding
- State-transition encoding

**Current-State Encoding**   In current-state encoding strategies, the data is encoded by the presence or absence of a signal characteristic or state. For example, a voltage of +5 might represent a binary 0, while a voltage of −5 could represent a binary 1, as shown in Figure 3.13.

**F I G U R E  3.13**

Current-state encoding

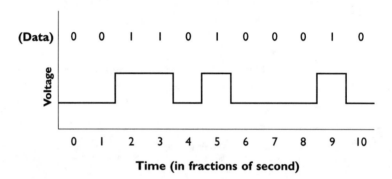

The signal is monitored periodically by network devices in order to determine its present state. That state will then indicate the data value encoded within it.

The following encoding schemes use current-state encoding:

- Unipolar
- Polar
- Return-to-Zero (RZ)
- Biphase

These encoding schemes are described after the discussion of state-transition encoding.

**State-Transition Encoding**   State-transition encoding methods differ from current-state encoding in that they use transitions in the signal to represent data, as opposed to encoding data by means of a particular voltage level or state. For example, a transition occurring from high to low voltage could represent a 1, while a transition from low to high voltage could represent a 0.

Another variation might be that the presence of a transition represents a 1, and the absence of a transition indicates a 0. This type of state-transition encoding is illustrated in Figure 3.14.

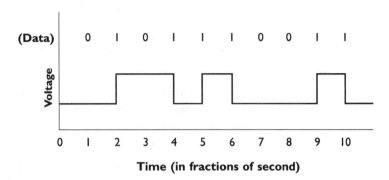

The following encoding schemes use state-transition encoding:

- Bipolar-Alternate Mark Inversion (AMI)

- Non-Return-to-Zero (NRZ)

- Manchester

- Differential Manchester

- Biphase Space (FM-0)

These methods are described in the next section.

**Digital Encoding Schemes**    Here are brief descriptions of some common digital encoding schemes:

- Unipolar: This encoding scheme uses two levels for encoding data. One of the levels is zero, which could represent a binary 1, and the other level can be either positive or negative. If a particular implementation of unipolar is using negative voltages, a –3 V, for example, would represent the other value, a binary 0.

- Polar: This encoding scheme is similar to unipolar, except that it can use both positive and negative voltages for encoding data. For example, a –3 V could represent a 1 and a +3 V could represent a 0.

- Return-to-Zero (RZ): This is an encoding scheme in which the signal transitions to zero in the middle of each bit interval. A positive voltage level transitioning to zero could represent a 0, and a negative voltage transitioning to zero could represent a 1. The mid-bit transition is included to make this strategy self-clocking.

- Biphase: This encoding scheme requires at least one mid-bit transition per bit interval. An example of a biphase encoding scheme is Manchester encoding.

- Manchester: In Manchester encoding, a low-to-high mid-bit transition represents one value, such as a binary 0, and a high-to-low transition represents the other, such as a binary 1. Manchester encoding is used in Ethernet LANs.

- Differential Manchester: This encoding scheme is also considered to be a biphase coding scheme because it uses a mid-bit transition. In this case, however, the mid-bit transition does not represent data; it is used for clocking. The actual data is represented by a transition at the beginning of the bit interval. The presence of a transition indicates one value, such as a 0, for example. The absence of a transition indicates a 1. Differential Manchester is used in Token Ring LANs.

- Non-Return-to-Zero (NRZ): This encoding scheme is similar to Differential Manchester in that the presence or absence of transition at the beginning of the bit interval determines the bit value. For example, if a transition occurs, it could represent a 1, and no transition means a 0. NRZ is unlike Differential Manchester in that there is no mid-bit transition for clocking.

The details of these encoding methods are considered beyond the scope of this portion of the CNE study program. The brief descriptions here are intended to give you a better understanding of digital signaling in general.

## Analog Signaling

Analog signals consist of electromagnetic waves. An analog wave is constantly changing. A wave *cycle* is the change from high to low and back to high (or low to high and back to low). Three characteristics are used to measure or describe electromagnetic waveforms: amplitude, frequency, and phase. Characteristics of an analog signal are illustrated in Figure 3.15.

**FIGURE 3.15**

Characteristics of
analog signals

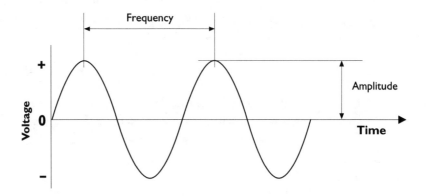

**FIGURE 3.15**

Characteristics of
analog signals

*Amplitude* measures the strength of the signal, or the height of the wave. Amplitude is expressed in volts for electrical potential, amps for electrical current, watts for electrical power, and decibels to indicate the ratio between the power of two signals. Figure 3.16 illustrates a wave that is varying in amplitude.

**FIGURE 3.16**

This wave is varying in
amplitude, or signal
strength.

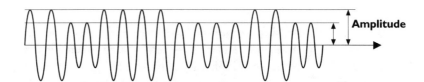

*Frequency* is the amount of time it takes for a wave to complete one cycle. For example, if a signal takes one second to go from high to low and back to high (in other words, to complete one cycle), the frequency of the wave is one. Frequency is measured in hertz (Hz), or cycles per second. Figure 3.17 shows a wave that is varying in frequency.

**FIGURE 3.17**

This wave is varying in
frequency.

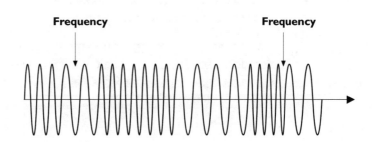

*Phase* is a different type of measurement than amplitude or frequency in that it requires more than one wave. Phase is the relative state of one wave when timing began; that is, relative to another reference wave. An illustration is particularly helpful in this case. Figure 3.18 shows three waves or signals that differ from each other in phase. Phase is measured in degrees. The easiest phase shift to spot visually is that of 180 degrees. In Figure 3.18, signal B and signal C differ from each other by 180 degrees; that is, signal B goes down when signal C goes up and vice versa.

**F I G U R E 3.18**

These signals have different phases.

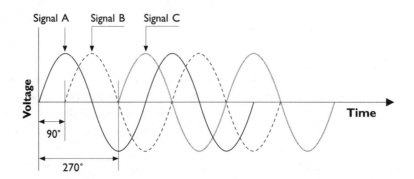

**Analog Signal Modulation**    All three of these characteristics—amplitude, frequency, and phase—can be used to encode data in an analog signal. For example, a higher amplitude could represent a 1, and a lower amplitude could represent a 0. Or a higher frequency could represent a 0, and a lower frequency could represent a 1. Analog signals are periodically measured by network devices to determine the encoded value.

There are three main strategies for encoding data using analog signals. The first two, amplitude shift keying and frequency shift keying, are considered current-state encoding schemes because a measurement is made to detect a particular state or level.

The third strategy, phase shift keying, is a state-transition encoding scheme because it relies on the presence or absence of a transition from one phase to another to indicate the value.

**Amplitude Shift Keying**    Amplitude shift keying, or ASK, can be used to encode binary data by varying the amplitude of the signal. In the example shown in Figure 3.19, a stronger voltage could represent a 1, and a weaker voltage could represent a 0.

**FIGURE 3.19**

Amplitude shift keying represents bits by varying amplitude.

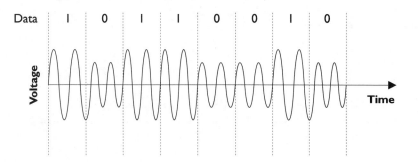

**Frequency Shift Keying**   Frequency shift keying, or FSK, is similar to ASK, except that the frequency of the signal varies instead of the amplitude. In the example shown in Figure 3.20, one frequency could represent a 1, and another could represent a 0.

**FIGURE 3.20**

Frequency shift keying represents bits by varying frequency.

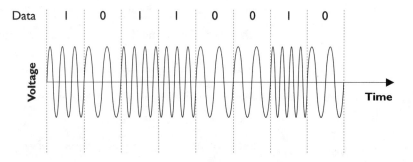

**Phase Shift Keying**   Phase shift keying, or PSK, uses a transition or shift from one phase to another to encode data. As in other state-transition encoding schemes, the presence or absence of a transition can be used to encode data. Figure 3.21 shows an example of PSK in which a 1 is represented by the presence of a transition (in this case, a 180-degree phase shift), and a 0 is represented by the absence of a transition (as in no phase shift).

F I G U R E   3.21

Phase shift keying
represents bits by
varying phase.

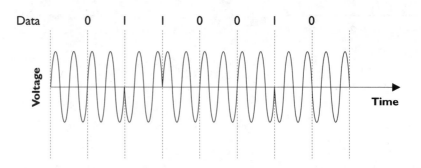

FIGURE 3.21

Phase shift keying represents bits by varying phase.

## Comparing the Signaling Methods

In general, digital signaling provides the following advantages over analog signaling:

- Fewer errors from noise and interference
- Uses less expensive equipment

On the other hand, one disadvantage is that digital signals suffer from greater attenuation than analog signals over the same distance.

In general, analog signaling provides the following advantages:

- Less attenuation than digital signals over the same distance
- Can be multiplexed to increase bandwidth

One disadvantage is that analog signals are more prone to errors from noise and interference.

# Bit Synchronization

The previous sections described ways of encoding data in analog or digital signals. These encoding schemes rely on changes or modulations to a particular characteristic of the signal. The receiving network device must then interpret the signal by measuring that modulated or changed characteristic. Timing is important because the receiver needs to know when to measure the signal in order to extract the correct meaning from it.

The coordination of signal measurement timing is *bit synchronization*. The two major methods of bit synchronization are *asynchronous* and *synchronous*.

## Asynchronous Bit Synchronization

Asynchronous communication requires that messages begin with a start bit so that the receiving device can synchronize its internal clock with the timing of the message. When no data is being transmitted, the media is idle and the sender's and receiver's clocks are not synchronized.

Asynchronous transmissions are normally short, and the end of the message is signaled by a stop bit.

## Synchronous Bit Synchronization

Synchronous communication requires that some kind of clocking mechanism be put into place to keep the clocks of the sender and receiver synchronized. The following three methods are used for synchronous timing coordination:

- Guaranteed state change

- Separate clock signal

- Oversampling

Each of these three methods has implemented a distinct clocking technique.

**Guaranteed State Change**   Guaranteed state change describes a method in which the clocking information is embedded in the data signal. This way, the receiver is guaranteed that transitions will occur in the signal at predefined intervals. These transitions allow the receiver to continually adjust its internal clock.

The guaranteed state change is the most common method, and it is frequently used with digital signals. The digital encoding schemes described earlier as *self-clocking* use this method.

**Separate Clock Signals**   Separate clock signals is a method in which a separate channel is used between the transmitter and receiver to provide the clocking information. Because this method requires twice the channel capacity, it is inefficient. This method is most effective for shorter transmissions, such as those between a computer and a printer.

**Oversampling**   Oversampling is a method in which the receiver samples the signal at a much faster rate than the data rate, which permits the use of an encoding method that does not add clocking transitions. If the receiver samples the signal ten times faster than the data rate, out of any ten measurements, one would provide the data information, and the other nine would determine if the receiver's clock is synchronized.

## Baseband and Broadband Transmissions

Bandwidth use refers to the ways of allocating the capacity of transmission media. The total media capacity or bandwidth can be divided into channels. A *channel* is simply a portion of the bandwidth that can be used for transmitting data.

The two ways of allocating the capacity of bounded (cable) transmission media are the following:

- Baseband: These transmissions use the entire media bandwidth for a single channel. Baseband is commonly used for digital signaling, although it can also be used for analog signals. Most LANs use baseband signaling.

- Broadband: These transmissions provide the ability to divide the entire media bandwidth into multiple channels. Because each channel can carry a different analog signal, broadband networks support multiple, simultaneous conversations over a single transmission medium.

Figure 3.22 shows the difference between baseband and broadband transmission.

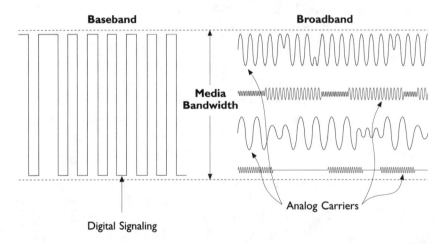

**FIGURE 3.22**

Baseband and broadband transmission

# Multiplexing Methods

Multiplexing is a technique that allows both baseband and broadband media to support multiple data channels. In other words, multiplexing provides a way of sharing a single medium segment by combining several channels for transmission over that segment. There are different ways to combine the channels. The ideal method depends on whether the media in question is baseband or broadband.

The three major methods of multiplexing are:

- Frequency-division multiplexing

- Time-division multiplexing

- Statistical-time-division multiplexing

## Frequency-Division Multiplexing

Frequency-division multiplexing (FDM) uses separate frequencies to combine multiple data channels onto a broadband medium. FDM can be used to separate different direction traffic in a broadband LAN. Figure 3.23 illustrates frequency-division multiplexing.

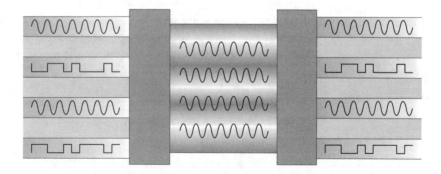

**FIGURE 3.23**

Frequency-division multiplexing (FDM)

## Time-Division Multiplexing

Time-division multiplexing (TDM) is a technique in which a channel is divided into time slots. Each of the devices communicating over this multiplexed line is allocated a time slot in a round-robin fashion, as shown in Figure 3.24. TDM can be used with baseband media or even with an individual channel of a broadband FDM system.

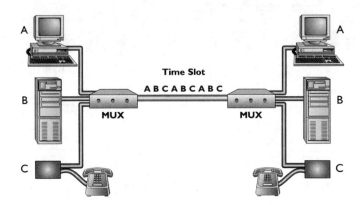

Conventional TDM multiplexers are sometimes called *synchronous TDM* because the time slots do not vary. If a device does not use its time slot, that slot is wasted.

## Statistical-Time-Division Multiplexing

Statistical-time-division multiplexing, or StatTDM, addresses the issue that conventional TDM systems can be inefficient if many slot times are wasted. StatTDM provides an intelligent solution to this problem by dynamically allocating time slots to devices on a first-come, first-served basis. The number of time slots allocated to a particular device depends on how busy it is. Priorities can be used to allow one device greater access to time slots than another. In order for the multiplexer on the receiving end to determine which signal a particular time slot is carrying, there must be a control field attached to the data that identifies the owner. Figure 3.25 shows statistical-time-division multiplexing.

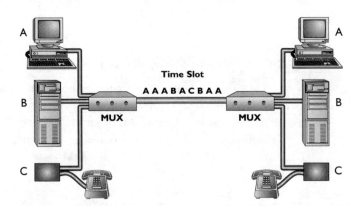

Because terms like *statistical-time-division multiplexer* are a bit tedious to say, network technicians often use jargon to refer to them: a multiplexer is a *mux* or *TDM*, and a statistical multiplexer is commonly called a *StatMux*.

# The Data Link Layer of the OSI Model

**T**he Data Link layer of the OSI model has several primary responsibilities, one of which is to organize bits into groups or packets, also known as *frames*. The Data Link layer can also detect errors, control the flow of data, and identify computers on the network.

Bridges, intelligent hubs, and network interface cards are devices that are typically associated with the Data Link layer.

Two sublayers make up the Data Link layer:

- The Media Access Control (MAC) sublayer, which controls the way that multiple devices share the same media channel.

- The Logical Link Control (LLC) sublayer, which is in charge of establishing and maintaining links between the communicating devices.

Figure 3.26 shows the LLC and MAC sublayers of the Data Link layer.

**FIGURE 3.26**

The LLC and MAC sublayers of the Data Link layer

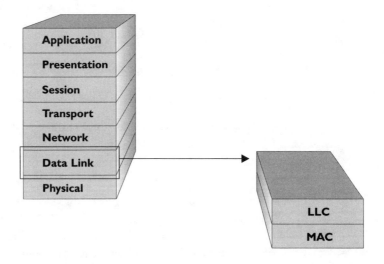

The sections that follow focus on the following topics associated with the Data Link layer:

- Logical topology
- Media access control
- Addressing
- Transmission synchronization
- Connection services

# Logical Topology

The logical topology of a network is the path that the signal takes as it travels around the network. A network has both a physical topology and a logical topology. As explained in the discussion of the OSI model's Physical layer, the physical topology is the physical structure or layout of the network. For example, if the devices are linked into a hub, the network has a physical star topology.

On the other hand, you could not guess the logical topology of a network just by looking at it. You need to know how the network functions at the Data Link layer, or, in other words, how the data flows around the network. In some cases, a network's logical topology is the same as its physical topology, but sometimes these topologies are different.

The two main logical topologies are bus and ring. Here are some rules for distinguishing between the two:

- In a logical bus topology, every signal is seen and received by all devices. Each device checks the address to see if the data frame is meant for it.

- In a logical ring topology, the signal is sent from one device to the next in the ring. A device will receive only those signals that were sent to it.

## Logical Bus Topology

A typical example of logical bus topology is an Ethernet network. Thin Ethernet (Ethernet 10Base2) uses coaxial cable wired in a physical bus topology. The logical topology is also a bus. The signal travels the distance of the cable and is received by all stations on the backbone.

Ethernet 10BaseT differs from other types of Ethernet in that it is set up in a physical star configuration using hubs and UTP wiring. However,

10BaseT is still a logical bus topology because, as in Thin Ethernet, the signal is seen and received by every device.

### Logical Ring Topology

A Token Ring network is a common example of a physical ring topology. As mentioned previously, the physical topology of Token Ring is actually a star. Token Ring is wired by connecting stations to a central hub, called a multi-station access unit (MSAU). However, the logical topology of Token Ring is a ring because of the way the signal travels around the network. The signal travels in a ring from workstation to workstation and is only routed through the MSAU. Figure 3.27 illustrates a logical ring configured as a physical star.

**F I G U R E  3.27**

A logical ring configured as a physical star

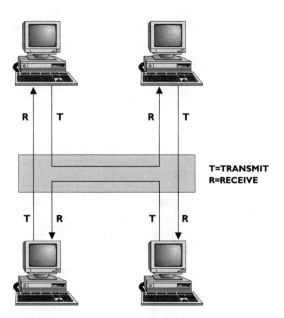

T=TRANSMIT
R=RECEIVE

## Media Access Control

Media access control is the process of controlling which devices can transmit and when they can transmit. In other words, it controls access to the transmission medium. Media access control could be compared to a traffic policeman. His purpose in being there in the busy intersection is the same as the purpose of media access control, to try to prevent collisions and keep traffic running smoothly.

Three types of media access control are discussed in the following sections: contention, token-passing, and polling.

## Contention

Contention is a media access method that basically allows any computer to transmit whenever it has data to transmit. However, it is possible that two (or more) computers will transmit at the same time, and a collision will occur. Because a collision causes the data to be destroyed, it must be resent. The more computers on the network, the greater the chance that collisions will occur, and the worse the performance will be. Fortunately, there are mechanisms that can be used to help reduce the number of collisions.

**Carrier Sensing and Collision Detection**   The first method for reducing collisions is *carrier sensing*. In this method, before a device transmits data, it listens to, or senses, the cable to see if it is busy. If it detects a signal, indicating that another station is transmitting, it will wait until the cable is free. If it doesn't detect any traffic, the computer will place its own data onto the medium for transmission. For example, when you're in your car merging onto the freeway, and you stop to check for oncoming traffic, you're practicing a kind of carrier sensing.

The second method, *collision detection*, comes into play when a station has decided that the media was available and has begun to transmit. During the transmission, the station monitors the cable to ensure that nothing is interfering with the signal being sent. If it detects a collision, it will first transmit a jam pattern so that all stations will be made aware of the collision. Then it will stop transmitting and wait for a random amount of time before attempting to retransmit.

Together, these two methods make up *CSMA/CD*, which stands for carrier sense multiple access with collision detection. All types of Ethernet use the contention with CSMA/CD media access method.

AppleTalk networks use a similar method, called CSMA/CA, which stands for carrier sense multiple access with collision avoidance. Apple Computer's LocalTalk uses a request-to-send/clear-to-send exchange to gain access to the media.

**Contention Method Advantages and Disadvantages**  An advantage of the contention media access method is that the software used for control is relatively simple and involves little overhead. Also, the media is accessed immediately if no other device is transmitting.

Disadvantages include the following:

- Access times are not predictable.
- Priorities cannot be assigned.
- Collisions increase significantly as network traffic increases.

## Token-Passing

In the token-passing media access method, a small frame with a special format, called the *token*, is passed around in an orderly fashion from one device to the next. The station that is in possession of the token has control of the media, which gives it permission to transmit. If a station has data to send, it must wait for control of the token before it can transmit the information. After a station has transmitted its data, it will retransmit the token. The next device can then use it to gain control of the media and transmit its data. Figure 3.28 illustrates a system that is using token-passing access.

**FIGURE 3.28**

Token-passing access

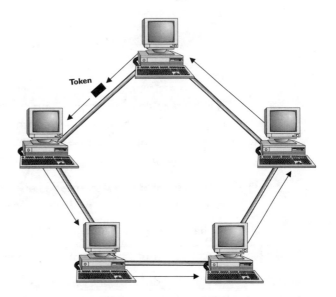

Some network systems that use token-passing are IBM Token Ring and the IEEE standard that was modeled after it, IEEE 802.5. Another is FDDI. These systems are discussed in more detail in Chapter 6.

**Token-Passing versus Contention**   It is interesting to compare the contention and token-passing media access methods. Contention is kind of a free-for-all, whereas token-passing is logical and methodical. Figure 3.29 illustrates the comparative performance of contention and token-passing as the network traffic load increases.

**F I G U R E   3.29**

Comparison of contention and token-passing

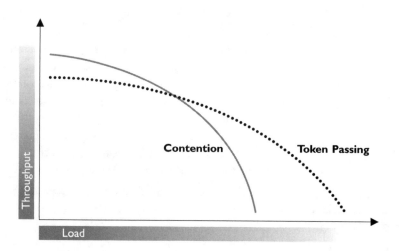

As you can see, contention provides better performance when the traffic load is light, because contention requires less overhead than token-passing. However, as the load increases, the performance of contention falls off more drastically because of the increase in the number of collisions. Token-passing maintains better performance when there is a heavy load on the network.

**Token-Passing Method Advantages and Disadvantages**   The following are some advantages of the token-passing media access method:

- It has a predictable load and delay.

- Some token-passing schemes support the assignment of priorities.

- Collisions do not occur.

- It provides the best throughput under high-load conditions.

Some disadvantages of using this method rather than the contention method include the following:

- It is more complex.
- More overhead is required.
- It is relatively more expensive.

## Polling

Polling uses a central device, called a master or controller, to regulate access to the network. This central device queries secondary devices in a certain order to see if they have information to transmit. If the device being queried has information to transmit, it will do so. Then another device will be polled.

**Polling Method Advantages and Disadvantages**   The advantages of the polling method include:

- Access times and data rates are predictable.
- Control is centralized and collisions do not occur.
- Priorities can be assigned.

Its disadvantages include the following:

- There can be an unacceptable delay while other devices are being polled.
- Secondary devices cannot initiate communication.

# Data Link Layer Addressing

Network addressing is comparable to the addresses used by the postal service. For example, a letter needs a house number, a street name, a city, and a state. If the recipient lives in an apartment building, the address will also include the apartment number. The addresses used on a computer network include a hardware address, a network number, and a software process ID. The hardware address is similar to the house number, the network number is analogous to the street, and the software process ID is like the apartment number.

The Data Link layer is concerned with the hardware address, which it uses to differentiate devices on the network. The network number and software process ID are handled at the Network layer, and they are discussed in Chapter 4.

The hardware address is a unique address usually assigned by vendors and hard-coded into network interface cards. It is also called the *physical* address or the *MAC* (media access control) address because the format depends on the media access method being used.

In the case of Ethernet, the physical address is a six-byte address. The first three bytes are assigned by the IEEE to each vendor to ensure uniqueness. The last three bytes are given a unique value by the vendor and the whole address is hard-coded into the NIC.

It is important to understand the process by which the data arrives at a particular device on a LAN. It is not like the mail carrier delivering letters to the correct house. Instead, the data is broadcast over the wire, and all the devices on the network see it. Each device reads the physical or hardware address of the data frame, and the one with the matching address reads the rest of the frame. The other devices ignore it.

On a busy network, a *bridge* might be used to help direct data to the device that should receive it. The bridge, which works at the Data Link layer, divides a network into separate segments. The bridge is aware of the hardware addresses of the devices on either side of it. When it receives a data frame, it decides whether or not to let it "cross" to the other side, based on which segment the destination device address pertains to. That way, more of the traffic stays local, and the devices don't need to read and reject so many frames.

One type of bridge, a transparent bridge, is capable of learning the location of network devices and building internal tables of device/segment pairs.

## Transmission Synchronization

Transmission synchronization deals with the coordination of transmitted frames. It is related to bit synchronization, which happens at the Physical layer, discussed earlier in this chapter. Bit synchronization, however, is only concerned with coordinating bit transmissions between sender and receiver. At the Data Link layer, transmission synchronization is concerned with meaningful groups of bits, such as characters or frames.

There are three main transmission synchronization methods:

- Asynchronous transmission, in which start and stop bits are used to indicate the beginning and end of the transmission.

- Synchronous transmission, in which communicating devices must provide their own clock or timing.

- Isochronous transmission, in which communicating devices depend on another device to provide the timing.

## Asynchronous Transmission

*Asynchronous transmission* is a method in which the sender and receiver maintain their own internal clocks. They do not synchronize their clocks to each other. Each frame is transmitted separately, using asynchronous bit synchronization. As you may recall from the section on bit synchronization, a start bit indicates the beginning of a frame transmission, and a stop bit denotes the end. The start bit allows the receiver to synchronize its clock so that it can begin to measure the signal to check for data.

A simple error-checking mechanism called *parity* is used with asynchronous transmission. An extra bit, called the *parity bit*, is tacked onto the end of each byte. The devices agree on whether they will use even or odd parity. In even parity, the bits must add up to an even number. The parity bit is assigned the necessary value to make the calculation come out even. On the receiving end, the parity is checked. An odd number in this case would indicate an error. Unfortunately, parity will miss errors when multiple bits are involved.

Figure 3.30 shows the bits in an asynchronous frame transmission.

**F I G U R E   3.30**

Asynchronous transmission

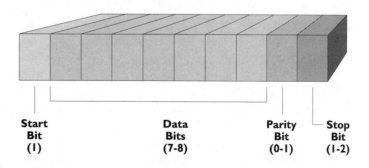

| Start Bit (1) | Data Bits (7-8) | Parity Bit (0-1) | Stop Bit (1-2) |

Some advantages of asynchronous transmission are that it is a simple, mature technology, and it is relatively inexpensive. The disadvantages of asynchronous transmission are that it requires a large amount of overhead (as high as 20 to 30 percent) and that it is relatively slow. Also, parity cannot detect multiple bit errors.

## Synchronous Transmission

In *synchronous transmissions*, the transmitting and receiving devices must provide the clocking signal. One way of doing this is to use special bit strings or control characters for synchronization. Another way is to have a separate channel dedicated to the clock.

With synchronous transmissions systems, the sender and receiver use the same clock, which reduces timing errors. To maintain timing, fill bits are inserted if there is not enough data to fill the block.

Synchronous error control is usually provided by a cyclic redundancy check (CRC), which is a better method than parity. A CRC is computed using a certain algorithm on the block of data to be transmitted. This CRC value is then appended to the block of data. The receiver recalculates the CRC, and if no errors have occurred, it should match the received CRC value.

Figure 3.31 illustrates how synchronous transmission works.

**FIGURE 3.31**

Synchronous
transmission

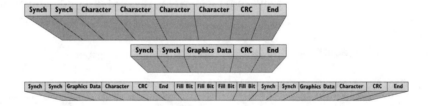

Synchronous transmission is faster and more efficient than asynchronous transmission, and it resists timing errors better. Also, CRC provides better error detection than parity. A disadvantage of synchronous transmission is that it is more expensive because of the more complex logic required.

## Isochronous Transmission

*Isochronous transmission* requires a separate device on the network to provide the timing clock. The designated device generates a clock signal that creates time slots. Devices that wish to communicate fill an available time slot with data. Network devices themselves do not need to be concerned with sending timing information.

Advantages of isochronous transmission are that it provides a guaranteed and deterministic transmission rate while requiring very little overhead. The main disadvantage is that it requires a special device to provide the clock. Because this device becomes a single point of failure for the network, it must be fault-tolerant.

# Connection Services

Network connection services provide the flow, error, and sequence controls for data transmission.

*Flow control* determines the amount of data that can be transmitted in order to prevent a sender from overwhelming a receiver. Flow control can occur at several levels of the OSI model, including the LLC sublayer of the Data Link layer.

*Error control* detects corrupted data in received frames and can request retransmission. Error control can also occur at several OSI model layers, including the LLC sublayer of the Data Link layer.

*Sequence control* allows a receiver to reassemble the pieces of a message into their original order. Sequence control occurs at the Network layer, and will be discussed in Chapter 4.

The three types of connection services provide different combinations of these transmission controls:

- Unacknowledged connectionless service provides no flow, error, or sequence control.

- Connection-oriented service provides flow, error, and sequence control through the use of acknowledgments.

- Acknowledged connectionless service uses acknowledgments to provide flow and error control on point-to-point connections.

The next section covers the different ways that flow and error control can be implemented at the LLC sublayer.

## LLC-Level Flow Control

The purpose of flow control is to control the amount of data that can be transmitted within a given period of time. It is necessary because networks are made up of devices with varying abilities to transmit and receive data. A device that has data to transmit cannot simply assume that the receiver will be able to process that data as fast as the sender can send it. Flow control defines methods that the receiving device can use to tell the sending device to slow down, or at least to agree on a rate before starting.

The two types of flow control used at the Data Link layer are *guaranteed rate flow control* and *window flow control*. Guaranteed rate flow control is a method in which the sender and receiver agree on a mutually acceptable transmission rate before transmission begins. This rate remains in effect, and therefore is guaranteed, for the duration of the conversation.

Window flow control uses buffering to allow the sending device to get a few frames ahead of the receiving device. The sending device transmits several frames before receiving an acknowledgment from the receiving device. The receiving device stores the data frames in its buffers (a *buffer* is an area set aside in memory that is used to hold data) until it can process them and send out the acknowledgment to the transmitting device. The number of frames that the sending device can send before it must receive an acknowledgment is referred to as the window.

The two types of window flow control are *static window* and *dynamic window* flow control. Static window flow control, as the name implies, uses fixed-size windows. The number of frames that fit in the receiving device's buffers usually determines the size of the window. If, for example, the window size is eight, after the transmitting device has sent eight frames that were still outstanding, it will wait until it receives an acknowledgment for one of those frames before sending another.

Dynamic window flow control allows the receiving device to adjust its window size. This technique is also referred to as *floating* or *sliding* window flow control. This technique is useful because it provides greater flexibility to communicating devices. A network device will likely be busy at times and idle at other times. During idle times, it can process data frames it receives much faster than when it is busy. Some network devices, such as a NetWare server, have the ability to dynamically increase the size or number of buffers available for network communications.

One method of dynamic window flow control uses a special acknowledgment packet, called a *choke packet*, that the receiving device can send when its buffer is nearly full. The transmitting device will take the hint and slow down for a while. It then will gradually increase the transmission rate until it receives another choke packet, in effect, adjusting the window size and optimizing the use of the network bandwidth.

### LLC-Level Error Control

LLC-level error control is concerned with the following error conditions:

- CRC or checksum errors

- Expected acknowledgments that have not been received

The first error condition indicates corrupted data. The CRC or checksum is a value that is calculated based on the data and then sent along with the data. The receiving device does the same calculation, and if the two values do not match, the data has been corrupted in transit. This error can be dealt with by transmitting a negative acknowledgment (NAK) that requests that the data be retransmitted.

The second error condition indicates lost data. Connection-oriented and acknowledged connectionless service types specify that the receiver must acknowledge received frames. The transmitter, therefore, expects to receive an acknowledgment within a specified amount of time. If the expected acknowledgment does not arrive, the transmitter will send the frame again.

# Review

This chapter introduced the OSI model as a method for understanding the complex interactions taking place among the various devices on networks. The OSI model has seven layers: Application, Presentation, Session, Transport, Network, Data Link, and Physical.

Protocols, the rules that determine how network devices communicate, are organized into groups, or *stacks*, to make different types of network communication possible. Finally, this chapter began to explore the lower layers of the OSI model.

## Physical Layer

The Physical layer of the OSI model defines the following:

- Network connections, including multipoint and peer-to-peer connections

- Physical topologies, including bus, ring, star, mesh, and cellular topologies

- Signaling, including analog and digital signaling
- Bit synchronization, including synchronous and asynchronous bit synchronization
- Baseband and broadband transmission
- Multiplexing, including frequency, time division, and statistical time-division multiplexing

## Data Link Layer

The next higher layer of the OSI model, the Data Link layer, defines the following:

- Logical topologies, including logical bus and logical ring topologies
- Media access control, including the methods of contention, token-passing, and polling
- Addressing
- Asynchronous, isochronous, and synchronous transmission
- LLC-level error control and LLC-level flow control

# CNE Practice Test Questions

1. Which of the following devices functions at the Data Link layer?

   A. Repeater

   B. Router

   C. Bridge

   D. Gateway

2. Which of the following access methods requires centralized management?

   A. Token-passing

   B. Contention

    **C.** Collision avoidance

    **D.** Polling

**3.** Which flow control method is the most efficient use of network bandwidth?

    **A.** Dynamic window flow control

    **B.** Static window flow control

    **C.** Guaranteed rate flow control

    **D.** Static rate flow control

**4.** Which of the following access control methods is NOT deterministic?

    **A.** Token-passing

    **B.** Contention

    **C.** Polling

    **D.** Primaries and secondaries

**5.** Which of the following physical topologies is most susceptible to a single point of failure?

    **A.** Star

    **B.** Mesh

    **C.** Ring

    **D.** Bus

**6.** Which transmission synchronization method introduces a single point of failure into the network?

    **A.** Asynchronous

    **B.** Isochronous

    **C.** Synchronous

    **D.** Oversampling

**7.** In which logical topology is the data seen and received by every device on the network?

   **A.** Bus

   **B.** Ring

   **C.** Mesh

   **D.** Cellular

**8.** Which analog encoding method uses the presence or absence of a transition to encode data?

   **A.** FSK

   **B.** PSK

   **C.** ASK

   **D.** MUX

**9.** Which multiplexing technique can be used on baseband channels?

   **A.** FDM

   **B.** MUX

   **C.** ASK

   **D.** TDM

**10.** How would a polar digital signal encoding scheme in which a −3 V represents a 1 and a +3 V represents a 0 be categorized?

   **A.** Current-state

   **B.** State-transition

   **C.** Unipolar

   **D.** Guaranteed state change

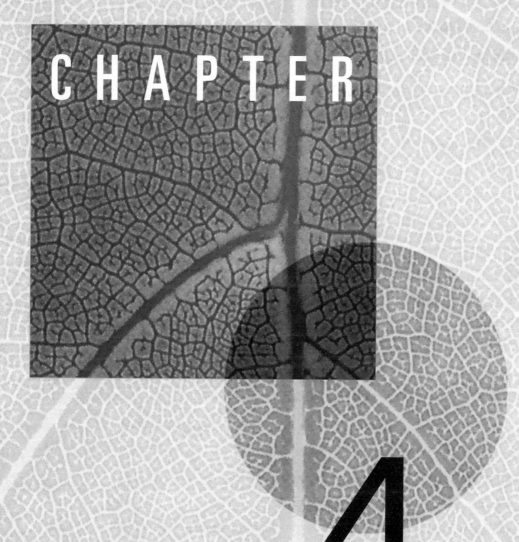

# CHAPTER

# 4

The Middle Layers of the OSI Model

## Roadmap

This chapter covers the middle two layers of the OSI model, the Network and Transport layers.

**Topics Covered**

- Network layer definition
- Network layer characteristics
- Transport layer definition
- Transport layer characteristics

**Skills You'll Learn**

- Define the purpose of the Network layer
- Explain the way addresses are defined and used at the Network layer
- Explain the three Network layer switching methods
- Explain the two route discovery methods
- Explain the two route selection methods
- Explain the ways connection services are implemented at the Network layer
- Explain Network layer gateway services
- Define the purpose of the Transport layer
- Explain the two Transport layer name/address resolution techniques
- Explain various types of addressing used at the Transport layer
- Explain Transport layer segment development techniques
- Explain the way connection services are implemented at the Transport layer

Threlower layers of the OSI model—the Physical and Data Link layers—provide the transmission media and protocols for local network communications. The next two layers, the Network and Transport layers, enable the user to define logical internetworks that surpass physical cabling boundaries.

Routing and the control of errors are two of the key functions provided by the middle layers of the OSI model. Routing provides an internetworking pathway across which WAN traffic can travel. Error checking and acknowledgments add reliability and ensure that the data arrives at the destination, or at least that the sender is notified if the data must be retransmitted. The main function of the Network layer, the first of the middle layers, is to provide a logical pathway for network communications, including internetworking, routing, and network control functions. The Transport layer, the second of the middle layers, adds reliability by providing end-to-end flow control, segmentation, and error checking. This chapter will examine both of these layers and their functions in detail.

# The Network Layer of the OSI Model

The purpose of the Network layer is to move data to its specific destination. On a single network, the Data Link layer can accomplish this alone. The Network layer is required when moving information between multiple independent networks, or *internetworks*. Thus, the basic purpose of the Network layer is to move data across an internetwork (rather than a network).

The Network layer also performs several important functions that enable the data to arrive at its destination. The protocols at this layer may choose a specific route through an internetwork in order to avoid the excess traffic caused by sending data over networks and segments that don't need access to it. This is accomplished through switching, addressing, or routing.

*Addressing* is necessary because logically separate networks depend on unique network addresses. In the Network layer, addressing refers to logical network addresses and service addresses.

To maximize the speed and efficiency of data transfer, *routers* can determine the best data path through the internetwork to minimize costs and improve access time. *Routing* describes how to discover the available pathways through the internetwork, and then how to choose the best path. Routers use various methods to discover the possible routes and then use that information to build routing tables. Based on those routing tables, routers can choose the best route through the internetwork.

*Switching* is an important technique that determines how connections are made and how the movement of data is handled on an internetwork. Many large internetworks include multiple paths from sender to receiver. Switching is a way of sending data along different routes, similar to trains being switched over multiple tracks.

Network layer products or services can implement different levels of *connection services*, depending on the number of errors expected in the internetwork. The previous chapter described some of the connection services related to the LLC sublayer of the Data Link layer. The level of connection services required at the Network layer depends on the way these services have been implemented at other OSI layers. For example, it is common for a Network layer protocol to be more concerned with efficient data delivery and to leave reliability issues, such as error control, to the Transport layer protocol. But in a protocol suite, where the Transport layer does not perform these functions, these connection services must be addressed at the Network layer or at some other layer.

When the networks that must be connected are using completely different protocols from each other, a *gateway* is required. This device can interpret and translate the different rules that are used on two distinct networks. The Network layer handles *gateway services* to allow interfacing between distinctly different networks.

There may be several different ways to achieve any single Network layer objective. The following sections describe the functions handled at this level and the various ways that these functions can be accomplished.

## Network Layer Addressing

As explained in the previous chapter, the addresses that are normally used for designating the source and destination of a packet include the physical address (also called the hardware or MAC address), a logical network address, and a specific service address. The MAC address is a physical address used to transmit frames to and from a specific workstation within a single LAN segment. This addressing is handled at the Data Link layer, and it was explained in the discussion of that layer in Chapter 3.

When messages must cross LAN boundaries and travel over an internetwork, it is necessary to identify the logical network as well as the physical device. The logical network address (created by the network administrator when configuring the servers or routers) is required to identify each individual network.

Network addressing allows routers to choose an optimal path for LAN-to-LAN communications. Using the logical network address, a router forwards the packet to the correct network segment. Once the packet has arrived at the destination network, a router uses the physical address to identify a specific device on the network.

The process is not finished here, however. Once the packet reaches the destination device, the router identifies a specific network service, such as file sharing, printing, application, e-mail, or routing. Each service is identified by a unique service address.

The logical network address and service address are handled at the Network layer of the OSI model, and they are described in more detail in the following sections.

### Logical Network Address

The logical network address uniquely identifies each network within an internetwork. Each data packet includes a logical network address, which enables the router to determine the proper path for sending that packet. (Remember, a router is a device that can connect two or more networks.) The router uses *routing tables* compiled by route discovery protocols (such as RIP) to determine the correct path for sending the data. Without logical network addressing, routing would not be possible.

In many cases, a network administrator will assign the logical network address. Different protocols use different naming and numbering conventions, which must be followed in the assignment of network addresses.

In some cases, such as when the network in question will be connected to the Internet, the assigned network number or name must be unique to that particular network. In the case of the Internet, these are official IP addresses assigned by the InterNIC. See Chapter 8 for details on IP addressing.

## Service Addresses

Any program or process capable of sending or receiving data on the network needs to have a service address for identification. Because networked computers can run a number of different processes at the same time, they need to have several different service addresses—one for each process. The term *entity* is also used to refer to an addressable process or, in even more general terms, to the hardware and software which fulfills each individual role. Service addresses specify entities, upper-layer processes, or protocols.

Some protocol specifications refer to service addresses as ports or sockets.

Some networks or protocols reserve a bank of addresses that identify common network services. This bank of addresses is called *well-known addresses*. When one entity wishes to communicate with another, it appends a service address to the logical network and physical device address. Figure 4.1 shows the relationship of service addresses to physical addresses and network addresses.

**FIGURE 4.1**

Service, physical, and network addresses

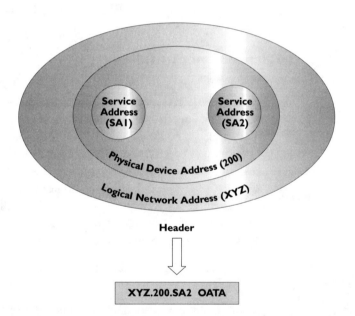

As you can see, the packet header includes the three address types:

- The *logical network address* indicates the source or destination network and corresponds to the external network number on a NetWare server.

- The *physical device address* identifies the source or destination computer and is unique for each node on the network.

- The *service address* refers to the specific application process on the source or destination computer and indicates what will be done with the packet, or which program will handle it.

# Switching

Three major switching techniques can be used to route messages through internetworks:

- Circuit switching connects the sender and receiver by a single physical path for the duration of the conversation.

- Message switching does not establish a dedicated path between two stations; instead, messages are stored and forwarded from one intermediate device to the next.

- Packet switching combines the advantages of both circuit and message switching by breaking longer messages into small parts called *packets*. Packet switching is the most efficient switching technique for data communications.

## Circuit Switching

In circuit switching, a dedicated physical connection is established between the sender and the receiver and maintained for the entire conversation. For example, the public phone system (the PSTN, or Public Switched Telephone Network) uses a circuit-switching system. When you make a call, a physical link between the two phones is dedicated during the entire conversation. When one phone hangs up, the connection is terminated and the circuit is released. A computer network performs circuit switching in a similar way. Figure 4.2 shows the dedicated channel that exists with circuit switching.

Before any two computers can transfer data, a dedicated circuit must be established between the two. The sending machine requests a connection to the destination, after which the destination machine signals that it is ready to accept data. The data is then sent from the source to the destination, and the destination sends acknowledgments back to the source. When the conversation is finished, the source sends a signal to the destination indicating that the connection is no longer needed and then disconnects itself.

**FIGURE 4.2**

Circuit switching uses
a dedicated
connection.

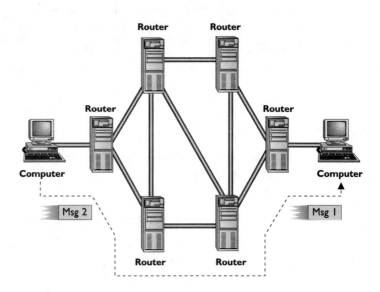

**Advantages and Disadvantages of Circuit Switching**   The major advantage of circuit switching is that the dedicated transmission channel that the machines establish provides a guaranteed data rate, which is important for time-critical applications such as audio and video. Also, once the circuit is established, there is virtually no channel access delay; because the channel is always available, it does not need to be requested again.

Circuit switching does have its disadvantages. One is that circuit switching is often an inefficient use of the transmission media. Because the connection is dedicated even when it is idle, no other devices can use the channel. Dedicated channels require more bandwidth than nondedicated channels, so transmission media can be expensive. Also, this method can be subject to long connection delays; it may take several seconds to establish the connection.

## Message Switching

A message-switching network is sometimes referred to as a *store-and-forward* network. Message switching is unlike circuit switching in that it does not establish a dedicated path between two communicating devices. Instead, each message is treated as an independent unit and includes its own destination and source addresses. Each complete message is then transmitted from device to device through the internetwork. Each intermediate device receives the message, stores it until the next device is ready to receive it, and then forwards it to the next device.

Message switches may be programmed with information about the most efficient routes, as well as with information regarding neighboring switches that can be used to forward messages to their ultimate destination. Because of this information, and because network conditions vary, message-switching systems typically route messages through the network along different paths, as shown in Figure 4.3.

**FIGURE 4.3**

Message switching can route messages along different paths.

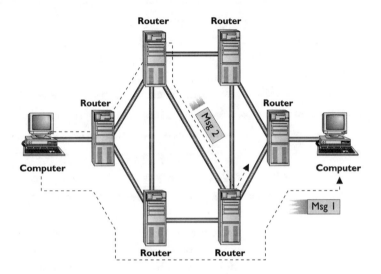

The devices that perform message switching are often PCs using custom software for this purpose. They must be prepared to store potentially long messages until those messages can be forwarded. This information is stored on a hard disk or in RAM. The amount of storage space needed depends on the network traffic through the switch.

One example of a store-and-forward system is e-mail. An e-mail message is forwarded as a complete unit from server to server, until it reaches the correct destination. It may take several seconds to several minutes (or in the case of slow connections to the Internet, several days), but it usually beats the postal service. Clearly, e-mail would be an inefficient use of a dedicated connection. Scheduling and calendaring applications, and group databases such as Lotus Notes, can also send updates as messages in this system.

**Advantages and Disadvantages of Message Switching**  Some of the advantages of message switching are the following:

- It provides efficient traffic management. By assigning priorities to the messages to be switched, you can ensure that higher-priority messages get through in a timely fashion, rather than being delayed by general traffic. Resources are set aside to handle these messages, similar to the extra resources a post office or parcel-delivery service maintains for priority mail.

- It reduces network traffic congestion. The intermediate devices (the message switches) are able to store messages until a communications channel becomes available, rather than choking the network by trying to transmit everything in real time.

- Its use of data channels is more efficient. Unlike circuit switching, with message switching the network devices share the data channels, which increases efficiency, because more of the available bandwidth can be used.

- It provides asynchronous communication across time zones. Messages can be sent even though the receiver may not be present, which can make communication across time zones easier. For example, if you have corporate offices in Sydney, Frankfurt, and Chicago, the last thing you'll want to do is communicate regularly in real time.

On the other hand, the delay introduced by storing and forwarding complete messages makes message switching unsuitable for real-time applications such as voice or video. For these applications (and especially video-conferencing), you need circuit switching. Another disadvantage to message switching is that it can be costly to equip intermediate devices with enough storage capacity to store potentially long messages.

## Packet Switching

Packet switching provides the advantages of circuit switching and message switching, and avoids the main disadvantages of both. In packet switching, messages are broken up into smaller pieces, called *packets*, each of which includes a header with source, destination, and intermediate node address information. Individual packets don't always follow the same route; this is called *independent routing*. There are two advantages to independent routing:

- Bandwidth can be managed by splitting data onto different routes in a busy circuit.

- If a certain link in the network goes down during the transmission, the remaining packets can be sent through another route.

The main difference between packet switching and message switching is that packet switching restricts packets to a maximum length. This length is short enough to allow the switching devices to store the packet data in memory, without writing any of it to disk at all. By cutting the disk out of the process, packet switching works far faster and more efficiently than message switching.

The following sections discuss two methods of packet switching: datagram packet switching, which has many similarities to message switching, and virtual-circuit packet switching, which is quite similar to circuit switching.

**Datagram Packet Switching**   *Datagram packet-switching* services treat each packet as an independent unit—as if each packet were a complete message rather than being a piece of something larger. The switching devices route each packet independently through the internetwork, with each intermediate node determining the next network segment in the packet's route. The switching devices can direct packets around busy network links (rather than blindly sending them into the thickest of the traffic) and make sure they reach their destination without undue delay. As Figure 4.4 illustrates, the packets that make up a message may arrive at their destination after taking very different routes through the internetwork.

**FIGURE 4.4**

Datagram packet switching can send individual packets through different routes.

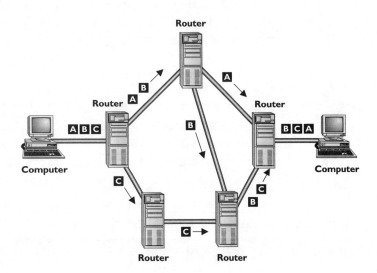

Because the datagram packets can follow different routes through the internetwork, they're likely to arrive at their destination out of order. The packet headers include a sequence number that the receiving device uses to reorder the packets and reconstruct the original message.

Datagram packet switching is frequently used on LANs with multipoint physical topologies. Network layer protocols deliver the datagrams to the network they're destined for, and devices on the local segment use the destination address information to recognize and receive datagrams that are intended for them.

Packet switching enables you to transmit large messages quickly and efficiently by using the smaller frame size. The Network layer on the sending device divides the messages from upper layers into smaller datagrams than the Data Link layer can handle. Then the packets are transmitted through the internetwork. Finally, the Network layer on the receiving machine reconstructs the messages from the Data Link layer frames into messages for the upper-layer protocols.

**Virtual-Circuit Packet Switching**   *Virtual-circuit packet switching* establishes a logical connection between the sending and receiving devices, called a *virtual circuit*. The sending device starts the conversation by communicating with the receiving device and agreeing on communication parameters, such as maximum message size and the network path to be taken. Once this virtual circuit is established, the two devices use it for the rest of the conversation, or for as long as the two devices are operational.

Virtual-circuit packet switching is radically different from datagram packet switching. In virtual-circuit packet switching, all the packets travel through the logical connection established between the sending device and the receiving device. In datagram packet switching, the packets travel different routes through the internetwork.

The logical connection that the sending and receiving machines establish is termed *virtual* because there is no dedicated physical circuit between the machines, even though the machines act as if they had established one. Each node in the logical path can perform switching and error control.

One of the main areas in which you'll see virtual circuits used frequently is connection-oriented services such as audio and video, which will be discussed later in this chapter.

**Advantages and Disadvantages of Packet Switching**   Packet switching has a great advantage over circuit switching in that it improves the use of network bandwidth by enabling many devices to communicate through the same network channel. A switching node may concurrently route packets to several different destination devices, and is able to adjust the routes as required by changing network conditions in order to get the packets through in good order.

Another advantage of packet switching is that it suffers far shorter transmission delays than does message switching because the switching nodes are handling the packets entirely in memory rather than committing them to disk before forwarding them.

When considering packet switching, you need to take the following factors into account:

- RAM versus hard disk space: Switching nodes for packet switching requires large amounts of RAM to handle large quantities of packets successfully. By way of compensation, they won't need such big hard drives (because they won't be writing the messages to disk).

- Processing power: The packet-switching protocols, such as IPX, are more complex than message-based protocols, so the switching nodes will need more processing power.

- Lost packets: Because the data is divided into a larger number of pieces, packets are more easily lost than entire messages. Packet-switching protocols need to be able to recognize which packets have been lost and to request that those packets be retransmitted. The sequence numbers play an important role in helping to identify missing packets.

# Routing

As mentioned earlier in this chapter, *routing* is the process of forwarding messages between dissimilar networks to build an internetwork. It involves determining the possible paths through the internetwork (route discovery) as well as choosing the best of the available paths (route selection). A router uses the logical network address that appears in the header of a packet to determine the possible routes for delivery of that packet.

## Cost Information in Routing Tables

As well as storing information about possible paths, routing tables (also known as *route tables*) also store estimates of the *cost* to send a message through a given route. The cost of a particular route can be defined in several terms: a time estimate, a distance estimate, or an estimate that includes monetary terms, such as if one link were more expensive than another.

The following are terms used to quantify the routing cost:

- Hop count describes the number of routers that a message must pass through to reach its destination.

- Tick count describes the amount of time required for a message to reach its destination. A tick is 1/18 of a second.

- Relative expense is a number you can assign based on the actual monetary cost (if you are charged for the network link) or some other relevant criteria required to use a given link, such as bandwidth on busy links.

Some routers can be preprogrammed with preset routing information by the network administrator. The disadvantage is that preprogrammed routers cannot adjust to changing network conditions and are susceptible to delays when there are network problems. In most cases, it makes more sense to use routers that can identify possible routes through the internetwork and store that information in routing tables that they can quickly access (and indeed, most routers are built this way).

# Route Discovery

Route discovery is the process of finding the possible routes through the internetwork, and then building routing tables to store that information. Because network conditions change over time, routers need to perform route discovery regularly (typically about once per minute) to ensure their routing tables are up-to-date and accurate.

The two methods of route discovery are distance-vector and link-state. The following sections describe these methods in detail.

**Distance-Vector Routing**   In *distance-vector routing*, each router advertises its presence to other routers on the network. Periodically (for example, every 60 seconds), each router on the network broadcasts the information contained in its routing table. The other routers then update their routing tables with the broadcast information they receive.

Distance-vector routing is commonly used in LANs. NetWare's main routing protocol, RIP (Routing Information Protocol), uses distance-vector routing.

As you can imagine, these periodic broadcasts of routing table information by the routers performing distance-vector route discovery add up to a noticeable amount of traffic. This traffic is not a problem in LANs because plenty of bandwidth is available and the number of routers is usually low. However, it can seriously affect performance in a WAN. In a large internetwork, distance-vector routing tends to be quite inefficient. Because route changes must be broadcast through the network from router to router, and because changes are contained within complete routing tables, it can take a long time (as long as several minutes) before all the routers on the network know of a change.

**Link-State Routing**   Because distance-vector routing generates enough network traffic to cause a problem on internetworks that have a lot of routers, *link-state routing* was developed as an improvement. Link-state routers broadcast their complete routing tables only at startup and at certain intervals— much less frequently than distance-vector broadcasts. Thus, this type of routing generates less network traffic than the distance-vector method.

The major difference between the link-state and distance-vector methods is that once the initial routing-table exchange has occurred, a link-state router will generally only broadcast routing updates when it detects a change in its routing table. And when it does broadcast, it sends only information about the change; it doesn't send its complete routing table.

Other routers that receive broadcast messages regarding changes in the state of network links use this information to update their own routing tables. Because only the changes are sent, these updates can be done in less time.

Link-state routing is the method used by an alternate NetWare routing protocol, the Network Link-State Protocol (NLSP), which may be substituted for RIP on a NetWare network.

## Route Selection

Once a router has created its routing table, it can use the cost information contained within that table to calculate the best path through the internetwork. As explained earlier in this chapter, routing protocols can select the best path based on the minimum number of hops, number of ticks, or relative expense. Selection of the optimum route can be dynamic or static. Dynamic route selection permits routers to constantly adjust to changing network conditions. With static route selection, on the other hand, packets must always follow a predetermined path. These two route-selection methods are discussed in the following sections.

**Dynamic Route Selection**    *Dynamic route selection* uses the cost information that is continually being generated by routing algorithms and placed in routing tables to select the best route for each packet. As network conditions change, the router can select different paths to maintain the lowest possible costs. The router can even select new paths on-the-fly as it is transmitting packets. If changes occur during a transmission that make one route suddenly less attractive than another, the router can send the remaining packets of the transmission along a different path (or several different paths) than the packets in the first part of the transmission.

Remember that each router along the path makes routing selections for the next hop.

**Static Route Selection**    With *static route selection*, the data path is not selected on-the-fly by the routers involved. Instead, the data path is designated in advance. Either the network administrator or a computer on the network (the initial router or a controlling device) selects a route for the data from a predefined table. All packets are then forced along that route, and intermediate routers are not allowed to make route-selection decisions. Static route selection tends to be less efficient than dynamic route selection because it cannot adapt to changing network conditions.

# Connection Services

Chapter 3 introduced the concept of connection services. These services are used at several layers of the OSI model. You may recall that the LLC sublayer of the Data Link layer is concerned with connection services that control the amount of data that can be transmitted between two devices and that check for lost or corrupted frames. As you learned in Chapter 3, the three types of connection services are:

- Unacknowledged connectionless service, in which packets are sent and received with no flow, error, or packet sequence control.

- Connection-oriented service, in which flow, error, and packet sequence control are provided by the use of acknowledgments.

- Acknowledged connectionless service, in which acknowledgments are used to furnish flow and error control between point-to-point transmissions.

At the Network layer, the following connection services are commonly provided:

- Network layer flow control, which controls the amount of data following a particular path.

- Network layer error control, in which packet delivery errors are detected and retransmission can be requested.

- Packet sequence control, which allows packets that have been received out of order at the destination to be reordered.

Acknowledgments are used at the Network layer to provide each of the listed services.

## Network Layer Flow Control

Chapter 3 explained how Data Link layer flow control is based on the capabilities of the devices that are in communication, so that one device cannot flood a slower device with more data than it can process. Network layer flow control, on the other hand, is based on the capabilities of the network infrastructure—the wires, cables, routers, and other devices that make up the network.

Network layer flow control is also called *congestion control* because its principal aim is to avoid congestion on the network by controlling the amount of data sent over a given route.

There are several methods of performing flow control at the Network layer:

- A guaranteed transmission rate negotiated by sender and receiver
- Window flow control using static windows
- Window flow control using dynamic windows

These flow-control methods are explained in Chapter 3, in the discussion of LLC-level flow control.

For example, one method of Network layer flow control uses a delay in the acknowledgments used by window flow control as a signal that a network error has occurred. The problem with this method is that there is no way of differentiating between a real error condition and network congestion, either of which could have caused the delayed acknowledgment. For this reason, many protocols implement Network layer flow control by defining special packets that indicate network congestion has been detected between intermediate devices.

## Network Layer Error Control

Lost packets, duplicate packets, and erroneous data are three of the many error conditions that can be detected at the Network layer. At this point, routers use cyclic redundancy check (CRC) algorithms to detect data errors. CRC was described in Chapter 3, in the discussion of the Data Link layer's transmission synchronization functions. As you'll recall, each time a packet crosses a router, the packet header information changes because of the address change, so CRC values must be recalculated at each hop. Alternatively, CRC values can be calculated based on the data only, ignoring the header information.

As mentioned earlier, lost and duplicate packets can be detected at the Network layer, but they're normally handled at the Transport layer. Packet sequence control is also commonly handled at the Transport layer (although it can be addressed at the Network layer).

## Packet Sequence Control

Earlier this chapter discussed how packets routed over varying paths will often arrive at their destination out of order. After they reach their destination, the packets that make up a message must be arranged in the correct order so that they can be handed off to upper layers. Packet sequence control can be required for both datagram and connection-oriented networks. In the latter, an error condition can occur in which one link fails, requiring that a new link be set up, and causing out-of-order or even duplicate packets to arrive at the destination.

## Gateway Services

Routers can successfully connect networks whose protocols function in similar ways. When the networks that must be connected are using completely different protocols from each other, however, a more powerful and intelligent device is required. A *gateway* is a device that can interpret and translate the different rules that are used on two distinct networks.

You'll find many gateways used to connect mainframes and LANs. For example, IBM networks using SNA (Systems Network Architecture) have a totally different protocol architecture from LANs, so gateways are used to connect the two.

Gateways may be implemented at any layer of the OSI model, depending on where protocol translation is required. However, they are usually implemented at the Network or higher OSI layers.

# The Transport Layer of the OSI Model

The next higher layer above the Network layer in the OSI model is the Transport layer. Whereas the lower-layer protocols are concerned with delivering messages between devices, the Transport layer is concerned with delivering messages between processes or services on those devices. Any device capable of running multiple processes requires a method of distinguishing each individual process with an identifier so that messages can be delivered from a particular process on the sending device to the correct process on the receiving device. The identifier that accomplishes this is the service address, port, or socket. The Transport layer is concerned with communicating between ports or sockets.

Another one of the important functions of the Transport layer is to reliably deliver packets or segments to upper-layer protocols. This layer must enable upper-layer protocols to interface with the network, but hide the complexities of network structure and operation from them.

The reliability that can be provided by the Transport layer is often used to compensate for a lack of reliable service in lower layers, such as with connection-oriented protocols. The reliability built into the Transport layer does not guarantee data delivery, but at least it can usually confirm whether data has been delivered or not. If data does not arrive at its destination correctly, the Transport layer can initiate retransmission of that data or it can notify upper-layer protocols of the problem.

These Transport layer subjects are discussed in the following sections:

- Transport layer addressing, which is concerned with identifying conversations between processes.

- Address/name resolution, which is concerned with mapping names to addresses.

- Message segment development, which has to do with the division and combination of messages into segments.

- Connection services, which handle flow control and error control.

## Transport Layer Addressing

As you have learned, the Transport layer is responsible for sending and receiving messages between a process on one computer and the corresponding process on another. The service address, which was discussed in the sections on the Network layer earlier in this chapter, is used to identify individual processes or services on network devices.

Many service providers are capable of maintaining conversations with multiple service requesters at a time. For example, a NetWare server running a print server process is capable of handling multiple print jobs from many clients concurrently. Each client in this case would be considered a service requester.

Service providers must keep track of each conversation that is occurring with different service requesters. The messages that make up each conversation can be identified by means of connection identifiers or transaction identifiers. Both the connection identifier and transaction identifier methods are discussed in the following sections.

## Connection Identifiers

A connection ID is used to identify each conversation. Depending on the specific protocol implementation, this connection identifier could also be termed a *socket* or a *port*. The connection ID enables a service provider process to communicate with client processes running on other devices. Each conversation is assigned a numeric identifier or address that labels it.

The service provider uses the connection ID to refer to each conversation. Given this ID, the Transport layer is then responsible for coordinating the lower-layer addressing required to deliver the message.

## Transaction Identifiers

An alternate method of identifying exchanges of data is the transaction identifier. The transaction identifier is different from a connection ID in that a transaction identifier refers to a single exchange consisting of a request and a response. This request and response "package" is called a *transaction*.

AppleTalk is a protocol stack that uses transaction identifiers. AppleTalk service providers and requesters track individual transactions and not complete conversations.

# Address/Name Resolution

Many networking protocols include the ability to allow users to refer to network devices by logical alphanumeric names that are easier to remember than network addresses. However, if a user refers to his computer as Barney, there must be some way of translating this name into an address that is recognizable to the network. This process is known as *address/name resolution*. Address/name resolution can be performed by each individual network device or by a special service provider called a *name server* or a *directory server*.

The two different methods of performing address/name resolution are distinguished by the process that initiates the resolution. In one method, the service requester initiates the address/name translation process; in the other, the service provider initiates it.

## Service-Requester-Initiated Address/Name Resolution

In service-requester-initiated address/name resolution, a device or requester that needs an address translated into a name or vice versa will notify the other network devices by broadcasting a special type of packet. This packet requests that any device with the particular known name, address, or service type respond with the corresponding unknown name or address.

For example, if a device wanted to send something to the computer, Barney, but didn't know Barney's network address, it would send out a packet that essentially said, "Will Barney please give me his address?" If Barney received this query packet, it would respond with its address.

### Service-Provider-Initiated Address/Name Resolution

In the service-provider-initiated address/name resolution, a network service provider (such as a print server) will periodically broadcast a special type of packet that gives its name, address, and the service it provides, letting other network devices know that it is available. This information can be stored by all network devices, including service requesters, which can then use it to find the service provider when that particular service is required.

The information about service providers and their availability can also be collected in a central location such as a directory server. The directory server's main role is to keep track of network devices and their names and addresses.

Using the Barney example again, suppose that Barney is a service provider. Barney periodically broadcasts its availability, and the directory server has collected its name and address. Then, when a service requester wants to communicate with Barney, it asks the directory server, "Where's Barney?" The directory server responds with Barney's address.

## Message Segment Development

Message segment development is the process of creating *segments* or packets of the proper size so that they can be transported across the network to their destinations. The Transport layer is responsible for dividing messages received from upper-layer protocols that are too large for the lower-layer protocols to handle into segments of an acceptable size. This is called *message division*.

The Transport layer can also combine several small messages intended for the same destination (but from different sources) into a single segment to improve network efficiency. This is called *message combination* or *aggregation*. As shown in Figure 4.5, each of the small messages within the segment is identified by a header consisting of a connection ID, which enables the receiving device to deliver each of the messages within the segment to the proper process or service.

**F I G U R E  4.5**

Message aggregation
combines messages
intended for the same
destination.

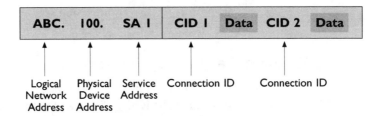

## Connection Services

Connection services can be performed at several levels of the OSI model. Not only can the Data Link and Network layers perform connection services, but the Transport layer can as well. In fact, many protocol stacks, such as Apple-Talk, place most of the responsibility for connection services on the Transport layer, which allows the Network and Data Link layer protocols to concentrate on efficiency and minimizes redundancy. See the discussion of Network layer connection services, earlier in this chapter, for the three types of connection services used by networks.

At the Transport layer, the following connection services are commonly provided:

- Segment sequencing, which has to do with reordering segments at the destination.

- Transport layer error control, in which the Transport layer ensures that segments arrive at correct destinations.

- End-to-end flow control, which employs acknowledgments to manage flow control between two devices.

The following sections describe these services in more detail.

### Segment Sequencing

The Transport layer can perform segment sequencing, which is the reordering of message segments after they arrive at their destination. As you'll recall from the earlier discussion of segment development, the Transport layer divides upper-layer-protocol messages into segments for transport across the network. When these segments arrive at their destination, they must be returned to the correct order to re-create the original message.

Segment sequencing is also known as *segment synchronization*. Segment synchronization typically requires each segment to have a segment number appended to it before it is handed off to the lower layers.

## Transport Layer Error Control

Transport layer error control is concerned with detecting lost, delayed, or corrupted segments. It is also concerned with detecting the error condition that occurs when two completely different segments arrive with duplicate segment sequence numbers. Transport layer protocol implementations use one or more of the following strategies for controlling or eliminating these error conditions:

- Unique segment sequence numbers

- Virtual circuits, allowing only one virtual circuit per session

- A timeout value or a counter to detect and drop packets that have been passed around the network too long

The timeout strategy is used by TCP/IP. It uses a counter called time-to-live, which enables packets that have been passed around the network too long to be dropped.

Corrupted segments can be detected at the Transport layer by appending a checksum to each segment. A checksum, as you may recall from Chapter 3, is a value calculated by submitting the header and data portions of a segment to an algorithm. The result of this calculation is appended to the segment. When the packet is received, the calculation is performed again, and the result should be the same. If not, the receiving device requests that the packet be resent.

## End-to-End Error Control

Transport layer error control is called *end-to-end error control* because the sending and receiving devices are the only ones concerned. The intermediate devices simply pass the message segments along and do not perform any error control.

Transport layer flow control is performed using acknowledgments and negative acknowledgments in a similar way to Data Link layer flow control (described in Chapter 3). Briefly, if a segment reaches its destination success-fully, the receiving device sends an acknowledgment to the sending device. If the segment does not reach its destination or is corrupted, the receiving device sends a negative acknowledgment requesting that the sending device resend the segment.

In addition to acknowledgments and negative acknowledgments, two special types of acknowledgments can be used at the Transport layer:

- Go back *n* acknowledgments, which can request retransmission of a portion of the message consisting of the last n packets.

- Selective repeat acknowledgments, which can request retransmission of only those specific packets that were not received correctly.

These special acknowledgments are useful in situations where the end node buffers have been exceeded; that is, when the buffers on the receiving device are unable to keep pace with the data that the sending device is transmitting.

# Review

This chapter covered the middle layers of the OSI model, which are the Network and Transport layers.

## Network Layer

The Network layer serves to support communication between logically sep-arate networks. This layer is concerned with the following:

- Addressing, including logical network addresses and services addresses

- Circuit, message, and packet switching

- Route discovery and route selection

- Connection services, including Network layer flow control, Network layer error control, and packet sequence control

- Gateway services

## Transport Layer

The Transport layer facilitates reliable message delivery between processes running on network devices. This layer addresses the following topics:

- Addressing and the use of connection identifiers and transaction identifiers

- Service-requester-initiated and service-provider-initiated address/name resolution

- Message segment development

- Connection services, including segment sequencing, Transport layer error control, and end-to-end flow control

# CNE Practice Test Questions

1. Which Transport layer addressing method identifies conversations?

   A. Connection ID

   B. Transaction ID

   C. Transport ID

   D. Conversation ID

2. What is the name of the table that includes information about hops and ticks?

   A. Switching

   B. Routing

   C. Addressing

   D. Hop and tick

3. What type of switching does store-and-forward refer to?

   A. Packet switching

   B. Message switching

   **C.** Circuit switching

   **D.** Bait and switching

**4.** Which type of route selection allows intermediate devices to select a packet's next hop?

   **A.** Dynamic

   **B.** Static

   **C.** Virtual

   **D.** Hop

**5.** Which device is used to connect networks that are running distinctly different protocols?

   **A.** Bridge

   **B.** Repeater

   **C.** Router

   **D.** Gateway

**6.** Which type of route discovery method does Novell's RIP protocol use?

   **A.** Link-state

   **B.** State-link

   **C.** Vector

   **D.** Distance-vector

**7.** Which type of packet switching is the closest to message switching?

   **A.** Datagram

   **B.** Circuit

   **C.** Virtual circuit

   **D.** Repeater

**8.** Which type of address/name resolution uses name servers or directory servers?

   **A.** Service-provider-initiated

   **B.** Service-requester-initiated

   **C.** Name/directory initiated

   **D.** Address/name initiated

**9.** Which connection service is concerned with alleviating network congestion?

   **A.** Transport layer error control

   **B.** Network layer error control

   **C.** Transport layer flow control

   **D.** Network layer flow control

**10.** What does the term *aggregation* refer to?

   **A.** Dividing messages into segments of the proper size

   **B.** Combining segments into messages at the destination device

   **C.** Combining small messages into one segment

   **D.** Combining small segments into one message for transport

# CHAPTER

# 5

The Upper Layers of the OSI Model

# Roadmap

This chapter covers the details of the upper layers of the OSI model.

**Topics Covered**

- Session layer definition
- Session layer characteristics
- Presentation layer definition
- Presentation layer characteristics
- Application layer definition
- Application layer characteristics

**Skills You'll Learn**

- Define the basic function of OSI Session layer
- Explain the details of the three Session layer dialog control methods
- Explain the three ways of session administration
- Define the basic function of the OSI Presentation layer
- Explain the translation methods that can occur at the OSI Presentation layer
- Explain the various encryption methods that can be used at the Presentation layer
- Define the basic function of the OSI Application layer
- Explain the two service advertisement methods most commonly used at the Application layer
- Explain the service use methods that are implemented at the Application layer

Chapter 3 began the coverage of the OSI reference model. At the top of the OSI model are the Session, Presentation, and Application layers.

- The Session layer is responsible for connection establishment, which means setting up the dialog between sender and receiver. It's also responsible for connection release, which is the orderly process of ending the dialog.

- The Presentation layer covers functions such as translation, which enables disparate computer systems to communicate, and encryption, which encodes messages for security reasons.

- The Application layer houses the actual network services, such as file services, print services, message services, and so on.

These upper layers are more closely related to the user and his or her perception of the network. The user is not aware of how the packets are transported across the network (Network layer), but is aware of whether his or her workstation is connected to the network (Session layer).

This chapter will cover how a service provider makes its services known to the other devices on the network.

# The Session Layer of the OSI Model

The Session layer, as its name implies, has to do with setting up and tearing down a *session*. Other names for a session are *dialog* or *connection*. For example, a session might be the whole time a workstation is connected to a NetWare file server. The NetWare server assigns a connection ID that identifies the workstation for that session.

To see the connection ID for each current workstation connection, use the Connections option of NetWare 5's MONITOR utility.

The Session layer is aware of services available on the network and the corresponding service addresses. Upper-layer protocol implementations can request a particular service and depend on the Session layer to initiate a dialog with the desired service provider.

The two major areas of responsibility for the Session layer are dialog control and session administration.

## Dialog Control

Dialog control describes the direction the data can travel through the medium. You can think of it in terms of a street. A street can be one-way, it can be two-way, or, as sometimes happens during construction, traffic may take turns, first going one direction, then the other. (Fortunately, the data doesn't get upset like some motorists.)

Another way of looking at dialog control is that it is the control of whose turn it is to talk when two entities are communicating. Depending on the system used, it may be possible for both the sender and receiver to talk at the same time.

The three possible directions that data can travel through the medium are called *simplex* (one-way), *half-duplex* (taking turns), or *full-duplex* (two-way). Figure 5.1 illustrates these dialog control modes, which are described in more detail in the following sections.

**FIGURE 5.1**

Dialog control modes

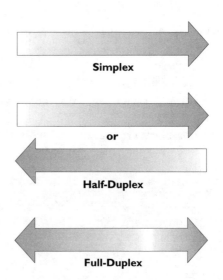

Simplex

or

Half-Duplex

Full-Duplex

## One-Way Communication: Simplex

Simplex communication is one-way communication. An obvious example of simplex communication is broadcast communication, such as radio or television. Another example of a simplex dialog would be a burglar alarm with a one-way connection to the alarm company. When a door or window is opened, and the burglar alarm is activated, an alarm goes off at the alarm company's headquarters to alert a security guard. In this case, the full bandwidth of the channel is available for a one-way dialog.

**Simplex Advantages and Disadvantages**    Advantages of simplex communication include the fact that the hardware is relatively inexpensive and there is no channel contention.

Simplex communication, however, is limited by its one-way nature. Just as it's difficult to tell how many people are watching a certain television channel, there is no way to verify that data was received successfully, or to know which device received it.

## Taking Turns: Half-Duplex

In a half-duplex dialog, the communicating entities take turns talking. An example of a device that requires half-duplex dialog is a walkie-talkie, which can be in either transmit mode or receive mode, but is not capable of transmitting and receiving at the same time.

The use of half-duplex dialog implies that the channel is only capable of one-way transmission at a time.

**Half-Duplex Advantages and Disadvantages**    The advantages of half-duplex over simplex are that two-way communication is possible and that one channel can be used to both transmit and receive. One disadvantage of half-duplex is that there is a delay while the channel direction is changed. Another limitation is that only one entity can transmit at a time.

## Two-Way Communication: Full-Duplex

The third option, full-duplex, allows both entities to communicate at the same time. A telephone conversation is full-duplex, because both parties can, if they wish, talk at the same time. However, if both people decide to take advantage of the full-duplex properties that the telephone system offers, they probably won't get much real communication accomplished. Yet computers can talk at the same time without this problem.

In order for a computer network to offer full-duplex communication, both devices must have a physical or logical channel available for transmitting and another channel available for receiving.

A *physical channel* is represented by an actual wire or cable. A *logical channel* is controlled by software. Techniques such as multiplexing can be used to create multiple logical channels over a single physical channel. Multiplexing is explained in Chapter 3.

**Full-Duplex Advantages and Disadvantages**   The ability to communicate through the medium in both directions concurrently is an advantage of full-duplex mode. There are disadvantages to this scenario, however. The hardware required tends to be more expensive. Also, there is more transmission media required to provide the additional physical channel, or broadband media, or techniques must be used to provide an additional logical channel.

# Session Administration

Session administration is an important component of the Session layer. There are several steps involved in setting up a dialog or connection between communicating entities, maintaining it, and then terminating it gracefully. Session administration also provides some way of identifying the parties involved in the dialog. Many networking systems, including NetWare, use a connection ID to identify each session.

The administration of a session involves three parts:

- Connection establishment
- Data transfer
- Connection release

## Establishing the Connection

Connection establishment is the first step in setting up a session. In order to establish a session, certain tasks need to be performed. First, the entity that wants to initiate the connection must, in most cases, meet certain security requirements, such as using a valid user ID and password. Another important task of connection establishment is assigning the connection ID that will be used throughout the session. In addition, it may be necessary to specify the exact services desired from the service provider and for what duration they will be required.

Other responsibilities that fall under connection establishment are specifying which entity will begin the conversation—who gets to talk first—and managing the exchange of acknowledgments.

An *acknowledgment* is simply a brief message indicating that the data was sent successfully. See Chapter 3 for more information about how acknowledgments are used in data transfer.

## Data Transfer

Data transfer is really the purpose of establishing a session. Having arrived at this phase means that all the initial security requirements have been met, and that both entities have been able to agree on communications parameters.

The major task of data transfer is, obviously, the actual transmission and reception of the desired data. Besides this, however, certain control information must be exchanged, such as acknowledgments and negative acknowledgments that manage the transfer.

A key responsibility of session administration involves the issue of interrupted dialogs. The Session layer is made aware that a dialog has been interrupted when it is informed by lower-layer protocols that expected acknowledgments have not been received. It may be possible to resume the dialog where it left off when lower-level communications are restored. If not, the Session layer implementation must inform upper layers, in order to provide the user with options.

## Releasing the Connection

Connection release consists of formal procedures to close the dialog. The most common kind of connection release happens when you type LOGOUT from a workstation, ending the session in an orderly way and releasing the resources on the service provider so that someone else can log in.

Sometimes the connection is broken without going through the connection release procedure. This occurs when a user reboots a workstation without logging out, when a cable is accidentally pulled out far enough to break the connection, or when power is lost. If the Session layer implementation is capable of rebuilding the session, it can be resumed where it left off. If not, a new session can be requested.

# The Presentation Layer of the OSI Model

The Presentation layer comes into play when it is necessary to change the format of the message, which often occurs when different computer systems need to communicate. Its function is similar to that of a human translator when two people wish to communicate but do not share a common language.

The two main functions of the Presentation layer are data translation, which includes several methods for changing data from one format into another, and encryption, which describes methods for encoding data for security reasons.

## Data Translation

Data translation is concerned with translating data from one format into another so that different types of computer systems can exchange data.

The following sections cover four different approaches to data translation:

- Bit order translation
- Byte order translation
- Character code translation
- File syntax translation

### Bit Order Translation

Bit order translation is somewhat like agreeing on whether a book should be read from left to right or from right to left.

As you learned in math class, for any decimal number, such as 325, the 3 represents (3 * 100), the 2 represents (2 * 10), and the 5 represents (5 * 1). Of all the digits, the 3 is the digit that represents the highest value, and is, therefore, the *most significant digit*. The 5 is the *least significant digit* because it represents the lowest value.

The binary numbering system works in the same way. For a seven-digit binary number such as 1100110, the leftmost bit is the most significant digit because it represents (1 * 64). The rightmost bit is the least significant digit because it represents (0 * 1).

Numbers are transmitted one bit at a time across the Physical layer of a network. The transmitting device could either send the binary number left bit first (most significant) or right bit first (least significant). The receiving device must be aware of the bit order in order to properly interpret the number.

Bit order translation may be required between systems that differ in which bit they transmit first.

## Byte Order Translation

A similar issue exists with byte order as with bit order. Complex numbers can take up more than one byte, and the question becomes whether to transmit the least significant byte first or the most significant byte first. Note how two common, but very different, microprocessors have implemented byte order:

- Intel microprocessors start with the least significant byte, which is called the *little endian* method.

- Motorola microprocessors start with the most significant byte, which is called the *big endian* method.

Byte order translation is commonly required when different types of computer systems attempt to communicate.

## Character Code Translation

Different types of computers use different character sets to represent letters, numbers, and special characters. Some of the more common character code sets include ASCII (American Standard Code for Information Interchange), commonly used on microcomputers and LANs, and EBCDIC (Extended Binary Coded Decimal Interchange Code), used on IBM mainframes. Another character code set called Shift-JIS is used to represent Japanese language characters.

The ASCII and EBCDIC character code sets are shown in Tables 5.1 and 5.2.

**T A B L E   5.1:**   The ASCII Character Set

**First Three Bit Positions**

|        | 000 | 001 | 010 | 011 | 100 | 101 | 110 | 111 |
|--------|-----|-----|-----|-----|-----|-----|-----|-----|
| 0000   | NUL | DLE | SP  | O   | @   | P   | '   | p   |
| 0001   | SOH | DCI | !   | \|  | A   | Q   | a   | q   |
| 0010   | STX | DC2 | "   | 2   | B   | R   | b   | r   |

**T A B L E  5.1:**   The ASCII Character Set *(continued)*

### First Three Bit Positions

| 0011 | ETX | DC3 | # | 3 | C | S | c | s |
|------|-----|-----|---|---|---|---|---|---|
| 0100 | EOT | DC4 | $ | 4 | D | T | d | t |
| 0101 | ENQ | NAK | % | 5 | E | U | e | u |
| 0110 | ACK | SYN | & | 6 | F | V | f | v |
| 0111 | BEL | ETB | ' | 7 | G | W | g | w |
| 1000 | BS  | can | ( | 8 | H | X | h | x |
| 1001 | HT  | EM  | ) | 9 | I | Y | i | y |
| 1010 | LF  | SUB | * | : | J | Z | j | z |
| 1011 | VT  | ESC | • | ; | K | [ | k | { |
| 1100 | FF  | FS  | ,< | L | \ | I | l |   |
| 1101 | CR  | GS  | - | = | M | ] | m | } |
| 1110 | SO  | RS  | + | > | N | ^ | n | ~ |
| 1111 | SI  | US  | / | ? | O | - | o | DEL |

**T A B L E  5.2:**   The EDCDIC Character Set

### First Four Bit Positions

|      | 0000 | 0001 | 0010 | 0011 | 0100 | 0101 | 0110 | 0111 | 1000 | 1001 | 1010 | 1011 | 1100 | 1101 | 1110 | 1111 |
|------|------|------|------|------|------|------|------|------|------|------|------|------|------|------|------|------|
| 0000 | NUL  | DLE  |      |      | SP   | &    | -    |      |      |      |      |      |      |      |      | 0    |
| 0001 | SOH  | SBA  |      |      |      | /    |      |      | a    | j    |      |      | A    | J    |      | 1    |
| 0010 | STX  | EUA  |      | SYN  |      |      |      |      | b    | k    | s    |      | B    | K    | S    | 2    |
| 0011 | ETX  | IC   |      |      |      |      |      |      | c    | l    | t    |      | C    | L    | T    | 3    |

**T A B L E  5.2:**  The EDCDIC Character Set *(continued)*

**First Four Bit Positions**

| 0100 |     |     |     |     |     |     |     | d | m | u |   | D | M | U | 4 |
|------|-----|-----|-----|-----|-----|-----|-----|---|---|---|---|---|---|---|---|
| 0101 | PT  | NL  |     |     |     |     |     | e | n | v |   | E | N | V | 5 |
| 0110 |     |     | ETB |     |     |     |     | f | o | w |   | F | O | W | 6 |
| 0111 |     |     | ESC | EOT |     |     |     | g | p | x |   | G | P | X | 7 |
| 1000 |     |     |     |     |     |     |     | h | q | y |   | H | Q | Y | 8 |
| 1001 |     | EM  |     |     |     |     |     | i | r | z |   | I | R | Z | 9 |
| 1010 |     |     |     |     | ¢   | !   | \|  | : |   |   |   |   |   |   |   |
| 1011 |     |     |     |     | .   | $   | ,#  |   |   |   |   |   |   |   |   |
| 1100 |     | DUP |     | RA  | <   | .   | %   | @ |   |   |   |   |   |   |   |
| 1101 |     | SF  |     | NAK | (   | )   | —   | ' |   |   |   |   |   |   |   |
| 1110 |     | FM  |     |     | +   | ;   | >   | = |   |   |   |   |   |   |   |
| 1111 |     | ITB |     | SUB | \|  | _   | ?   | " |   |   |   |   |   |   |   |

Character code translation may be required at the Presentation layer to translate from one code to another.

NOTE

NetWare 5 supports a new character code set, called Unicode, to improve the portability of NetWare products into different languages. Unicode is a 16-bit character code set defined by the Unicode Consortium. It can represent 65,536 unique characters, which allows it to represent the characters for multiple languages in one code set.

## File Syntax Translation

Some computer systems differ in the way that they store files. For example, IBM-compatible personal computers running DOS store files as one data file. Apple Macintosh computers, on the other hand, store files in two parts, the *data fork* and the *resource fork*.

Other differences that can exist between disparate computer systems include the following:

- Distinct methods of marking the beginning and end of files
- Varying methods of organizing files on storage media
- Unique methods of assigning read and write security

All of these differences must be addressed in order for a Presentation layer implementation to translate from one file syntax to another.

# Encryption

*Encryption* refers to the encoding of messages for security reasons. It is important because certain data, such as passwords, must be kept secure. Because there are ways to listen in on a network and read what is being sent, such as with a device called a *sniffer*, many institutions prefer to encrypt their data instead of sending it as plain ASCII text.

Older NetWare versions (before version 3.*x*) sent passwords across the wire as readable text during the workstation login process. Today's versions send only encrypted passwords.

Two methods of encryption are commonly used, private key and public key. These encryption methods are described in the following sections.

## Private Key Encryption

The private key encryption method uses one key. This key can be hard-coded into firmware or chip sets, or established by network administrators. Only devices with the key can encrypt and decrypt messages.

If the key needs to be changed, all devices must be updated. If the network is used to transmit the new key to all devices, security is compromised.

## Public Key Encryption

The public key method uses two keys, a public key and a private or secret key. A known value is combined with the secret key to create the public key.

An entity that initiates communication will send the public key across the wire to the destination device. That device, in turn, combines the public key with its own secret key and thus derives the encryption value. Both keys are necessary to decode a message; if the public key is discovered, it is of no value without a private key.

NetWare 3.12, 4, and 5 use a variation of the public key encryption method for user authentication.

# The Application Layer of the OSI Model

The Application layer of the OSI model is concerned with network services, the advertisement of those services, and the way in which they are used. Network services, such as file services, print services, and messaging services, are discussed in Chapter 1. The benefits these services provide are the reason for installing a network in the first place.

The Application layer handles service advertisement and service use. Service advertisement involves letting other network devices know of the services provided by service providers. Service use has to do with the different ways that service requesters make use of network services. The user application running on a given client machine may or may not be aware of the network. There are varying degrees of cooperation possible between service requesters and service providers.

## Service Advertising

Service advertising is the process by which service providers make their services known to other devices on the network. A given service is identified by a service address. As explained earlier, the service address is analogous to the apartment number in an apartment building. It identifies a particular service process on a network device.

Service providers can use either active or passive service advertisement, as explained in the following sections.

### Active Service Advertisement

As its name implies, active service advertisement requires that a service provider actively make its services known, by means of periodic network broadcasts that include the service provider's name and service address. Potential service requesters collect this information in tables. A client may also poll or query other devices on the network if it is in need of a particular service. If a service provider responds to the query, the client will add the information to its table.

A client's service table needs to be kept current. An entry in the table that is not refreshed after a certain period of time will be removed.

A NetWare protocol, SAP (Service Advertising Protocol) actively broadcasts service information every 60 seconds. One example where SAP is used is with a single-reference time server. See Chapter 11 for more information about SAP.

### Passive Service Advertisement

Passive service advertisement requires a global directory of network services. Service providers list their services in this directory, and clients can refer to that directory to find a needed service. The directory contains all the necessary information, such as device and service addresses. NetWare 5 provides a global directory called NDS (NetWare Directory Services).

For more information on NDS, see *NetWare 5: CNA/CNE Administration and Design Study Guide* by Michael Moncur et al.

## Service Use Methods

Service use methods are the ways network services can be used once a desired service has been located and a connection has been made between the service requester and service provider.

Varying degrees of cooperation are possible between a service requester and service providers. For example, a client device may be unaware of the network and may require a piece of software to act as an interface and coordinate requests that must be sent to the network. On the other hand, a service provider may be unaware of client devices, and a way must be devised to communicate with them. Another possibility is that a high degree of cooperation exists between service providers and requesters, and they can actually share the processing of an application.

The three service use methods are as follows:

- OS (operating system) call interception

- Remote operation

- Collaborative computing

## OS Call Interception

OS call interception is used when the client devices are unaware of the network. In order to use network services, the devices require a software module to act as an interface between the local operating system and the network. This module coordinates network requests. In the NetWare environment, this task is handled by the NetWare DOS Requester or Client 32. (In earlier versions of NetWare, this interception was handled by the shell or NETX.)

Imagine that a DOS user wants to retrieve a letter to make a few changes to it. This letter happens to be stored in a directory on a file server, which the user considers to be his F drive. The user selects the proper commands in his word processor to retrieve the file. At this point, the DOS Requester steps in. It intercepts the call that normally would have gone to the local DOS operating system and packages it as a network request to the file server. The file server retrieves the file and sends it back to the client. The letter appears on the user's screen, and as far as that user is concerned, the file works no differently than if it had been on the local hard drive.

## Remote Operation

Remote operation addresses the situation where servers are unaware of clients on the network. The clients are network-aware and have the ability to request services from service providers. As far as the service provider is concerned, however, the request appears as if it were generated by its own operating system.

Remote procedure calls (RPCs) and operating systems that allow terminal emulation are examples of remote operation.

## Collaborative Computing

Collaborative computing is a more advanced method of sharing processing power between devices on the network. Both service provider operating systems and service requester operating systems must be aware of the network and of each other in order to accomplish this type of resource sharing. Peer-to-peer network operating systems use collaborative computing methods.

# Review

This chapter covered the three upper layers of the OSI model: the Session, Presentation, and Application layers.

## Session Layer

The Session layer establishes, manages, and terminates communications between computers. It does this through the following:

- Control over simplex, half-duplex, and full-duplex dialogs
- Administration of the establishment of connections, data transfer, and connection release

## Presentation Layer

The Presentation layer deals with the format, or syntax, of messages. It does this in the following ways:

- Bit order, byte order, character code, and file syntax translation
- Public key and private key encryption

## Application Layer

The Application layer is involved with the advertisement and use of network services in the following ways:

- Active and passive advertisement of services
- Service use methods, including OS call interruption, remote operation, and collaborative computing

# CNE Practice Test Questions

1. Which layer is responsible for encryption?

   A. Application

   B. Presentation

   C. Session

   D. Transport

**2.** A walkie-talkie would be an example of which kind of dialog?

   **A.** Simplex

   **B.** Half-duplex

   **C.** Full-duplex

   **D.** Broadcast

**3.** Which type of communication requires the most cooperation between operating systems?

   **A.** Remote operation

   **B.** OS call interception

   **C.** Full-duplex

   **D.** Collaborative computing

**4.** Which encryption method does NetWare 5 use?

   **A.** Public key

   **B.** Private key

   **C.** Algebraic

   **D.** Transposition

**5.** Which character code set is the one most commonly used on microcomputers and LANs?

   **A.** ASCII

   **B.** EBCDIC

   **C.** Shift-JIS

   **D.** Unicode

**6.** Which translation method does "little endian" have to do with?

   **A.** Bit order

   **B.** Byte order

    **C.** File syntax

    **D.** Character code

**7.** Which layer is responsible for establishing and maintaining dialogs?

    **A.** Application

    **B.** Presentation

    **C.** Session

    **D.** Network

**8.** Which one of the following does not belong in connection establishment?

    **A.** Verify valid user ID and password

    **B.** Assign the connection ID

    **C.** Release the resources on the service provider

    **D.** Specify the services required

**9.** Which one of the following is not an Application layer service?

    **A.** File syntax

    **B.** Database

    **C.** Message

    **D.** Print

**10.** What does NetWare use SAP for?

    **A.** Passive service advertising

    **B.** Collaborative computing

    **C.** Active service advertising

    **D.** Character code translation

# CHAPTER

# 6

Lower Layer Protocols

## Roadmap

This chapter describes the basic details of the lower layer protocols used in LANs and WANs.

**Topics Covered**

- Overview of the IEEE 802.*x* Standards & Protocols
- IEEE 802.3 and Ethernet
- IEEE 802.3u and Fast Ethernet
- IEEE 802.5 and Token Ring
- Fiber Distributed Data Interface (FDDI)
- Wan Protocols

**Skills You'll Learn**

- Explain the function of IEEE 802.*x* standards implemented in today's computer networks
- Explain the details of the IEEE 802.3 standard and its relation to Ethernet
- Explain the details of IEEE 802.3u standard and its relation to Fast Ethernet
- Explain the details of the IEEE 802.5 standard and its relation to Token Ring
- Explain the details of Fiber Distributed Data Interface (FDDI)
- Explain the various WAN protocols in use today

T he past few chapters covered the OSI model. This chapter will discuss a few networking standards that apply to the lower layers of the OSI model. A standard differs from a model in that you can't implement a model. *Networking models* like the OSI model are used to provide a framework with which to describe network protocols. On the other hand, *networking standards* describe the way network protocols actually are supposed to function.

# The Institute of Electrical and Electronic Engineers (IEEE) Standards

The Institute of Electrical and Electronic Engineers (IEEE) is a group that develops standards for the use of electric and electronic components. It consists of various committees and subcommittees who come up with these standards. One of these subcommittees is the 802 subcommittee. It is responsible for coming up with standards for the Physical and Data Link layers of the OSI model.

## IEEE Protocols

The IEEE defines several standards for protocols at the lower layers of the OSI model. Each of them is unique with its own lower layer details.

You can find more information about all the IEEE 802.x protocols on the Internet at http://www.ieee.org.

### 802.1

The IEEE 802.1 standard defines standards for the Physical and Data Link layers that allow any two IEEE 802 LAN stations to communicate over a LAN or WAN. This is usually referred to as the *internetworking standard*.

### 802.2

This standard defines the Logical Link Control (LLC) sublayer of the entire 802.x series of protocols. The standard specifies the adding of special header fields that tell the receiving protocol stack which upper layer sent the information. It is most commonly used with the IEEE 802.3, 802.4, 802.5 and 802.6 implementations.

### 802.3

IEEE 802.3 is probably the most commonly used standard. It specifies many Physical layer attributes, like signaling types, data rates, and topologies. It also specifies the media access method. The media access method used by all the different variants is carrier sense multiple access with collision detection (CSMA/CD).

The different variants are differentiated from one another through the use of a special naming scheme. The naming scheme looks like the following:

*nnxxxxxyyy*

where *nn* is the speed in Megabits per Second (Mbps), *xxxxx* is the signaling method (Baseband or Broadband), and *yyy* is a unique identifier (either the maximum distance, in meters, or something else that makes the implementation unique). Some common examples of this naming scheme are 10BaseT (10 Mbps, Baseband signaling, Twisted pair cable), 10Base2 (10Mbps, Baseband signaling, approximately 200 Meters maximum segment length) and 10Base5 (10 Mbps, Baseband signaling, and 500 Meters maximum segment length).

More of the 802.3 standard, as well as the different variants, are covered later in this chapter.

## 802.4

This standard does not see much use in the corporate LANs. It is more often seen in factories as a standard protocol for connecting production machines together. Before the 802.4 standard, there were many different methods of connecting machines together.

IEEE 802.4 defines a common LAN protocol designed for use in factory automation. It specifies a physical bus topology, token passing media access, either 75-ohm copper or fiber-optic media, and either broadband or baseband signaling.

## 802.5

IEEE 802.5 is primarily based on IBM's Token Ring technology. The main difference between Token Ring and 802.5 is that 802.5 doesn't specify either a particular physical topology or a transmission medium. 802.5 uses a data rate of 1, 4, or 16 Mbps and a token-passing media access method.

## 802.6

This is the standard that uses the Distributed Queue Dual Bus (DQDB) technology for high-speed data transfer between nodes. It provides for both asynchronous and synchronous transmission modes.

## 802.7

Defines several standards for broadband communications including design, installation, and testing.

## 802.8

This standard defines a group (the Fiber Optic Technical Advisory Group) to work with the other 802 groups to advise them on the various fiber optic technologies and standards.

## 802.9

Defines a standard for Isochronous Ethernet (or IsoEnet). This standard focuses on the integration of voice and data transmissions.

## 802.10

The IEEE 802.10 standard defines a standard way for protocols and services to exchange data securely using encryption mechanisms. This standard is not dependant on any particular transmission media or encryption method.

## 802.11

IEEE 802.11 defines standards for implementations of wireless LAN technologies like infrared and spread-spectrum radio.

## 802.12

This is the standard based on 100VG-AnyLAN. This technology uses 100Mbps signaling rate and a special media access method that allows 100Mbps data traffic over voice grade (the VG in 100VG) Category 3 UTP. When a station has data to transmit, it signals a hub. If another station wants to transmit at the same time, the hub allows the highest priority traffic to get transmitted first. This technology is great for maximizing effective use of network bandwidth.

# IEEE Protocols and the OSI Model

Again, the majority of the IEEE standards are used at the lower layers of the OSI model (primarily the Data Link and Physical layers). Figure 6.1 shows how the various 802.$x$ protocols map to the lower layers of the OSI model.

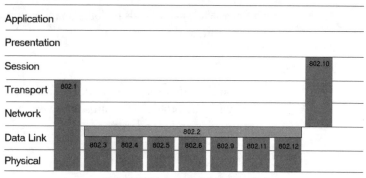

FIGURE 6.1

Mapping the IEEE
protocols to the OSI
model

# IEEE 802.3 and Ethernet

**W**hen PC networks were first developed, three companies came up
with a networking technology known as DIX Ethernet (DIX represents the
three companies that developed it: Digital, Intel, and Xerox), or Ethernet for
short. It used a CSMA/CD media access method, had a 10 Mbps signaling
rate, used thick 50 ohm coaxial cable, and specified a physical bus topology.

When the IEEE 802.3 committee developed its standards, it used Ethernet
as the guideline. From there, it evolved with changes in the Physical layer and
media access methods. Today, these different implementations are given the
generic name of their predecessor, Ethernet.

## IEEE 802.3 and Ethernet Physical Layer Implementations

The original IEEE 10BASE5 implementation is identical to Ethernet. As technologies developed, more Physical layer variations to the 802.3 standard were
developed. Each was basically the same technology as the original Ethernet
with slightly different characteristics. Table 6.1 details the different IEEE
802.3 Physical layer standards as well as the original Ethernet standard.

**T A B L E  6.1:**    Comparing 802.3 and Ethernet Physical Layer Details.

| | Ethernet | 10Base5 | 10Base2 | 10BROAD 36 | 1Base5 | 10BaseT | 10BaseF |
|---|---|---|---|---|---|---|---|
| **Data Rate Mbps** | 10 | 10 | 10 | 10 | 1 | 10 | 10 |
| **Media** | 50 Ohm Coax (Thick) | 50 Ohm Coax (Thick) | 50 Ohm Coax (Thin) | 75 Ohm Coax | Unshielded Twisted Pair | Unshielded Twisted Pair | Fiber-Optic |
| **Topology** | Bus | Bus | Bus | Bus | Star | Star | Star |
| **Max Segment Length (M)** | 500 | 500 | 185 | 1800 | 250 | 100 | 500-2000 |

## IEEE 802.3 and Ethernet Media Access

Ethernet uses the CSMA/CD (carrier sense multiple access with collision detection) media access method, which means that only one workstation can send data across the network at a time. It functions much like the old party line telephone systems used in rural areas. If you wanted to use the telephone, you picked up the line and listened to see if anyone was already using it. If you heard someone on the line, you didn't try to dial or speak; you simply hung up and waited a while before you picked up the phone to listen again.

If you picked up the phone and heard a dial tone, you knew the line was free. You and your phone system operated by *carrier sense*. You sensed the dial tone or carrier and, if it were present, you used it. *Multiple access* means that more than one party shared the line. *Collision detection* means that if two people picked up the phone at the same time and dialed, they would "collide" and both need to hang up the phone and try again. The first one back on the free line would gain control and be able to make a call.

In the case of Ethernet, workstations send signals (packets) across the network. When a collision takes place, the workstations transmitting the packets stop transmitting and wait for a random period of time before retransmitting. Using the rules of this model, the workstations must *contend* for the opportunity to transmit across the network. For this reason, Ethernet is referred to as a *contention-based* system.

Ethernet transfers text a little faster than your voice, at 10Mbps (megabits per second). That translates to about 1.5Mbps if you take overhead into account.

# Ethernet Design Issues

Ethernet is probably the most commonly used networking technology. It is fairly simple to set up, relatively inexpensive, and fairly reliable. It does have its drawbacks, however. The main drawback to Ethernet is that it is contention based. As more people get put on the network segment, traffic increases, and the likelihood of a collision also increases. The more collisions there are, the less data that actually gets transmitted.

For this reason the various design issues that the different types of Ethernet have need to be discussed to minimize the problems that may occur. There are three major types of Ethernet in use today:

- Thick Ethernet
- Thin Ethernet
- Twisted-Pair Ethernet

Each type has its own design issues.

## 10Base5 (ThickNet) Ethernet

The original wiring used for Ethernet is called ThickNet or 10Base5. The 5 stands for its maximum length: 500 meters (1,650 feet). It is named for the size of the wire used, which is about as big around as your thumb. Working with it is like wrestling a boa constrictor. You might say it is not technician-friendly. The coaxial (coax) cable is marked every 2.5 meters (8.25 feet) for connection points, so that you do not try to connect devices closer than 2.5 meters, because a shorter distance degrades the signal.

Most coax is made using PVC coating. If burned, one of the gases it creates is chlorine, which, when inhaled, turns into hydrochloric acid. Teflon-coated cable is much more expensive, but safer to use in ceilings where ventilation systems are located. Some fire codes require the use of plenum-rated cable if the wiring is run through ceilings.

10Base5 (ThickNet) Ethernet has the following specifications:

- Maximum segment length: 500 meters (1,650 feet)

- Maximum taps: 100

- Maximum segments: 5

- Maximum segments with nodes: 3

- Minimum distance between taps: 2.5 meters (8.25 feet)

- Maximum repeaters: 4

- Maximum overall length with repeaters: 2.5 kilometers (1.5 miles)

- Maximum AUI drop cable length: 50 meters (165 feet)

You normally use a device called a *vampire tap* to connect new connections to the ThickNet with a tool that drills a small hole into the coaxial cable. The tap is then attached and tightened down with its connector into the hole. Although in some cases it may be possible to tap coaxial cable with users up and running, you should try to do this after working hours. A mistake can short the center conductor with the shielding and take the entire segment down.

The tap is also a transceiver, a device that handles transmission data signal generation and reception and receives its electrical power through the DIX (Digital, Intel, and Xerox) connector. The DIX connector uses an AUI (Attachment User Interface) cable to connect to the DIX female connector on the LAN card. At both ends of the cable, you must install a terminator to complete the electrical circuit and to cut down on signal reflections. Figure 6.2 shows some components of ThickNet Ethernet, as well as ThinNet Ethernet, which is discussed in the next section.

ThickNet cable has the following disadvantages:

- Large size

- High cost

- Awkward connection method (drilling into the wire)

The advantages of ThickNet cabling are few for today's networks, but many ThickNet networks are still in use and are reliable.

This wiring specification allows you to increase the length of the overall network by using repeaters, which are devices that pick up signals and repeat them to another segment of the cable. You may use a maximum of four

**F I G U R E   6.2**

Some common Thick
and Thin Ethernet
components

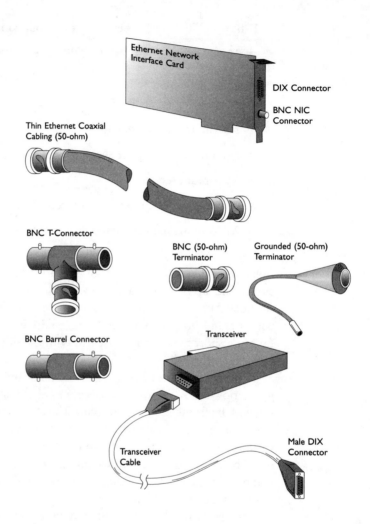

repeaters on one network, with only three of the segments populated with
nodes. Thus the overall length of a network, by implementing repeaters to
extend the length, is 2.5 kilometers (1.5 miles).

## 10Base2 (ThinNet Coax) Ethernet

ThinNet coax quickly became a popular choice of network cabling, because
it costs, appears, and handles just like its affordable and useful cousin—the
75-ohm coaxial cable used for television cable. Because of its low cost, it is
often referred to as *Cheapernet.*

10Base2 (ThinNet) has the following specifications:

- Maximum segment length: 185 meters (610.5 feet)

- Maximum segments: 5

- Maximum segments with nodes: 3

- Maximum repeaters: 4

- Maximum devices per segment: 30

- Minimum distance between nodes: 0.5 meters (1.5 feet)

- Maximum overall length with repeaters: 925 meters (3,052.5 feet)

The term 10Base2 is a little misleading because the maximum length is not actually 200 meters (660 feet) but only 185 meters (610.5 feet). Someone took the liberty of rounding up to make it fit in with the other specifications. Some vendors advertise that by using their hardware you can extend the 185 meters to 300 meters (990 feet). However, if you later mix LAN cards or repeaters from different vendors into your network, you may have problems, because most manufacturers adhere strictly to the IEEE specifications.

The specification for ThinNet is 50-ohm RG-58A/U or RG-58C/U coaxial cable (commonly referred to as *coax*). RG-58A/U is the most widely used type. RG-58A/U has only one shield and does not adhere strictly to the IEEE specification. Although it should not be used, you may still find it in some networks. You should also avoid using RG-59 cable, which is intended for television signals. Another type of cable you may see is RG-58U cable. Installing this type of wiring is a mistake, because it does not meet the IEEE specification for 10Base2.

The connectors used for ThinNet are BNC connectors, along with the T-connectors required to connect to the BNC female connectors on the LAN card. As with 10Base5 (ThickNet), each end of the cable must have a terminator. Only one end of the cable must be grounded.

This wiring specification differs significantly from 10Base5 in that the transceiver is built into the LAN card itself and is not a device that you must attach to the cable. A cable connecting the T-connector to the workstation, called a pigtail, *cannot* be used with this standard. The T-connector must connect directly to the back of the card in a daisy-chain fashion. If it doesn't connect this way, the network connections will fail.

As with 10Base5, you can use up to four repeaters on a network, with only three of the segments populated with nodes. 10Base2 and fiber-optic cabling can be mixed by using a fiber/ThinNet repeater. If you have repeaters on your ThinNet network, be sure that all devices have SQE (Signal Quality Error) or Heart Beat turned off. If SQE is on, the SQE signal will appear as excessive collisions on the network and slow the network down.

To remember what you can put between any two nodes on a coaxial Ethernet network, keep in mind the *5-4-3 rule.* As you may have noticed from the specifications, there is a 5 segment, 4 repeater theme with Ethernet topologies. The 3 part of the rule states that only 3 segments can be populated with nodes. The 5-4-3 rule does not apply directly to UTP or fiber-optic cable segments. With UTP, hubs act as repeaters. You cannot have two devices separated by more than four hubs.

The disadvantages of ThinNet include the high cost compared to UTP cable and the fact that the bus configuration makes the network unreliable. If any node's cable is broken, the entire segment, and probably the entire network, will be affected. Nevertheless, because it was the most economic solution for a long time, ThinNet is used in many existing installations.

## 10BaseT (Twisted-Pair) Ethernet

The use of unshielded twisted-pair (UTP) cable is now a well-established trend in Ethernet network wiring schemes. UTP costs less and is more flexible than 10Base5 or 10Base2 cabling. The specification for UTP was created by the IEEE 802.3 subcommittee in the 1980s. Do not substitute shielded twisted-pair (STP) cable for UTP; the IEEE 10BaseT specification is for UTP only.

10BaseT (Twisted-Pair) Ethernet has the following specifications:

- Maximum segments: 1,024

- Maximum segments with nodes: 1,024

- Maximum segment length: 100 meters (330 feet)

- Maximum nodes per segment: 512

- Maximum nodes per network: 1,024

- Maximum hubs in a chain: 4

10BaseT is wired as a star, which means that each device has its own set of wires connected directly to a hub. Although the physical topology of 10BaseT is a star, its logical topology is a bus, giving you the advantages of a star wiring scheme and a bus in one specification. 10BaseT is easy to troubleshoot, because problems on one segment of wiring usually will not affect the other segments (each node uses its own separate segment).

You can isolate a device that is causing problems by just disconnecting its cable from the hub. Some hubs have built-in management capabilities that will report errors or problems, as well as allow you to disconnect the devices from the hub remotely. These types of hubs are known as *intelligent* hubs. Figure 6.3 shows an Ethernet network with a 10BaseT hub.

**FIGURE 6.3**

An Ethernet network with a 10BaseT hub

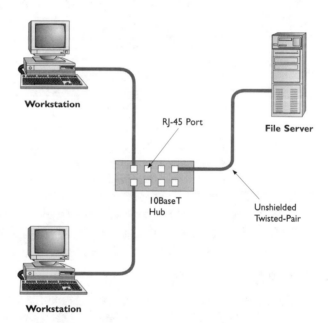

The connection to the hub and the LAN cards is made with an RJ-45 connector. You can also connect 10BaseT to a DIX connector or an AUI connector by using a transceiver or twisted-pair access unit (TPAU). ThinNet connections on LAN cards can also be used with special transceiver devices.

UTP cable is classified in categories defined by the Electrical Industries Association. Categories 1 and 2 are voice-grade cable. Categories 3, 4, and 5 are data-grade. Be sure to ask the vendor for a performance specification sheet when you purchase Category 5 cable to be sure it meets the specifications for your network. (See Chapter 2 for more information about UTP cable categories.)

Some buildings that are wired for telephone service with twisted-pair wires will have extra installed pairs available for your use on your network. If the wiring is Category 3 or better, you can use the existing wiring to add a 10BaseT network inexpensively. You can purchase wall jacks that will have an RJ-45 connector for 10BaseT and an RJ-11 connector for traditional phone lines.

There are also teflon-coated versions of UTP cable for areas that require plenum-rated wire. The cable is light and flexible, which makes it easy to pull through construction. The cable should be 22, 24, or 26 gauge AWG (American Wire Gauge), with an impedance (resistance based on signal frequency) of 85 to 110 ohms at 10MHz.

# IEEE 802.3u and Fast Ethernet

**W**ith emerging technologies such as voice, video, and multimedia, the need for network bandwidth has gone from a murmur to a scream. For this reason, the industry has demanded a faster version of Ethernet. The IEEE 802.3 standard has been modified (IEEE 802.3u) to include a faster version of Ethernet, called simply Fast Ethernet. As you will see, the standard is basically the same as regular Ethernet, but it runs at 100Mbps.

## Topologies

Fast Ethernet is just like the other 802.3 standards in that it uses a physical star topology, which means that each workstation on the network connects to a central hub. In addition to the physical star topology, Fast Ethernet uses a logical bus topology like its 10Mbps counterpart.

See Chapter 3 for more information on physical and logical topologies.

# Media Independent Interface (MII)

The Media Independent Interface (MII) is a new specification for an interface between the Media Access Control (MAC) layer of Fast Ethernet and the three physical layer implementations: 100Base-TX, 100Base-T4, and 100Base-FX. It allows Fast Ethernet to run over any of the three Physical layer implementations (called Physical Layer Devices or PLDs) by simply changing an external transceiver on the network card. You can use a UTP cable up to half a meter in length to connect the NIC to an external transceiver.

# Auto Negotiation

As already mentioned, the need for speed is becoming urgent in many companies. But most companies can't afford to rip out their entire 10Mbps Ethernet network and replace it with 100Mbps Fast Ethernet. For that reason, many Fast Ethernet NICs and hubs are designed as 10/100, which means that they will negotiate speed with the connecting device in order to determine how fast they should run. 10Mbps NICs that connect with 10/100 hubs will run at 10Mbps. If you upgrade the NIC in the computer to a 100 Mbps card, the hub will switch to 100Mbps mode on the same connection. The NIC to hub cable doesn't need to change (assuming it meets the specification for 100Mbps Ethernet).

Upgrading the NIC is good for those companies who have large networks that will be in transition between these standards. The company simply has to replace the hubs, one at time, with 10/100 hubs. Then, as time permits, the company's IS department can replace the Ethernet NICs with Fast Ethernet NICs. The existing 10Mbps cards will run at 10Mbps. The new 100Mbps cards will communicate with the 10/100 hubs at 100Mbps.

In another vein, if the same company were just starting up and weren't sure which standard to use, they could buy and install 10/100 NICs, and 10Mpbs hubs. Then, as their speed requirements increased, they could simply replace the 10Mbps hubs with 100Mbps or 10/100 hubs. The network would then run at 100Mbps.

# Media Access Control (MAC) Specification

For compatibility reasons, the designers of Fast Ethernet decided to leave the media access method the same as the original Ethernet. The media access method for Fast Ethernet is CSMA/CD and, therefore, subjects Fast Ethernet to the same contention limitations as Ethernet.

## Fast Ethernet Network Design Issues

Because Fast Ethernet is somewhat different from regular Ethernet, there is a need to discuss some of the issues involved in designing a network with Fast Ethernet.

Each of the three PLDs has its own design issues.

### 100Base-TX

With the 100Base-TX specification of Fast Ethernet, there are several requirements that must be satisfied when designing a network based on 100Base-TX.

- A 100Mbps transmission speed
- Maximum segment length of 100 meters
- Two pairs of Category 5 UTP or Category 1 STP
- RJ-45 connectors on UTP cabling systems
- DB-9 connectors on STP cabling

### 100Base-T4

100Base-T4 is similar to 100Base-TX in that it can use twisted-pair cabling. However, 100Base-T4 uses all four pairs in an eight-wire UTP cable. 100Base-TX uses only two pairs (same as standard Ethernet). In addition:

- A 100Mbps transmission speed
- RJ-45 connectors
- Maximum segment length of 100 meters
- Category 3, 4, or 5 UTP

### 100Base-FX

The main difference between 100Base-FX and the other Fast Ethernet standards is that it uses fiber-optic cable instead of copper cable as its transmission media. When designing a network using 100Base-FX, the following guidelines must be followed:

- Maximum segment length of 412 meters for a multi-mode fiber running half-duplex

- Maximum segment length of 10,000 meters for a single-mode fiber running full-duplex

- Either two-strand 62.5/125 micro multi-mode or single-mode fiber media

- Either Subscriber Connectors (SC) or Media interface connectors (MIC) specified by ANSI FDDI

### Fast Ethernet Repeaters

Even with the long distances that LANs can cover, there is always that time when you need to extend the network a small amount, say five meters or so. For this situation, you can use repeaters. There are two types of repeaters, Class I and Class II. IEEE 802.3u specifies that Fast Ethernet can use either one Class I or two Class II repeaters in a single collision domain.

In addition to the type of repeater being used, 100BaseT uses two different signal frequencies. 100Base-T4 uses a 25MHz signaling frequency, but both 100Base-TX and 100Base-FX use a 41.6MHz signaling rate. When you use a repeater to connect a 100Base-T4 to 100Base-TX, the repeater must perform signal frequency translation, which can induce latency.

# IEEE 802.5 and Token Ring

IEEE 802.5 is based on work done by IBM and their Token Ring technology. The IEEE 802 committee took IBM's work and pretty much copied it. It is an example of a de facto standard becoming a de jure standard.

## IEEE 802.5 Token Ring Media Access Methods

IEEE 802.5 specifies a token-passing media access method. This media access method uses a special packet called a token. A workstation cannot transmit until it has the token.

A typical IEEE 802.5 communication works approximately like this: The token travels around the ring from workstation to workstation. When a workstation has data to transmit, it removes the token from the ring so no one else can transmit. Then, it transmits its data frames. The data travels to each workstation around the ring. Each workstation examines the destination address and compares it to its own address. If they are the same, the machine copies the data frame into memory. The receiving machine then modifies the frame to indicate that it received the data. The modified frame travels back around the ring until the original sender receives it. The sender then removes the data frame from the ring and generates a new token. The process then begins again.

This process would seem to take a long time, but the entire process happens in milliseconds. With many workstations on the same ring, however, the process could theoretically degrade. For this reason, the designers of Token Ring came up with *early token release*. In this technology, the sending workstation releases the token as soon as it's done sending. This way, many stations can transmit in the same trip around the ring.

Additionally, there is one station on the ring that is known as the *active monitor*. The active monitor is kind of like the hall monitor in a high school. The hall monitor prevents students from roaming the hall unchecked. The active monitor does something similar. It prevents data frames from roaming the ring unchecked. It marks every frame that passes (kind of like a hall pass). If that frame passes the active monitor too many times, it is removed from the ring. The active monitor can perform some other management functions as well.

Any station can be the active monitor. When the current active monitor goes down, an election is forced and another machine becomes the active monitor. On a NetWare network, the server becomes the active monitor eventually because it is usually the machine that is up the longest.

There is more on Token Ring and IEEE 802.5 information later in this book in Chapter 13.

## IEEE 802.5 Network Design Issues

Token Ring (and IEEE 802.5) networks specify a physical star, logical ring topology. In this topology, workstations connect via cables to a central device called a Multistation Access Unit (MAU or MSAU). The MAUs have ports where the cables from the workstations connect. These ports are called *lobe ports*. The MAUs also have special ports that receive signals from one MAU or send them on to other MAUs. These ports are called Ring In and Ring Out, respectively. Figure 6.4 shows a typical Token Ring network.

As you can see, the MAU functions much like a hub, except it uses Ring In and Ring Out ports to connect one MAU to another. Even though it's physically laid out like a star, if you take your finger and trace the path, you will see that the communications happen in a ring.

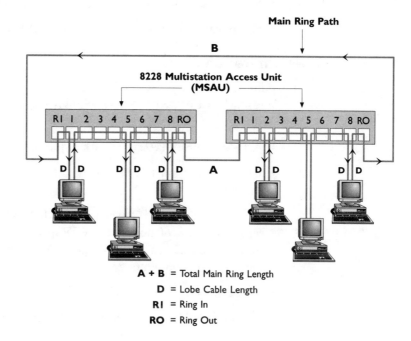

A + B = Total Main Ring Length
D = Lobe Cable Length
RI = Ring In
RO = Ring Out

## Token Ring Restrictions and Limitations

Just like the other IEEE 802 standards, 802.5 has its own set of specifications and limitations.

### Ring Length

The ring length is the distance between Multistation Access Units. The length varies depending on the type of cabling system used between MAUs.

- Type 1 and Type 2 cable, up to 200 meters between MAUs

- Type 3 cable, up to 120 meters between MAUs

- Type 6 cable networks, only 45 meters between units

- Fiber-optic cabling systems, up to 1000 meters (1km)

### Lobe Length

The lobe length of a Token Ring network is the distance between a node and a MAU, the length of which also depends on the type of cable.

- Type 1 and Type 2 cable, up to 100 meters

- Type 3 UTP cable, only 45 meters

- For Type 6 and Type 9 cabling systems, up to 66 meters

- For all cable types, at least 2.5 meters between nodes

### Other Limitations

In addition to the length restrictions, Token Ring specifies many other limitations that must be adhered to. The following list details some of the restrictions.

- A 16Mbps IEEE 802.5 network requires at least Type 4 cabling.

- Each segment must be terminated at both ends and grounded at one end.

- For performance and convenience, the IBM STP specification specifies a maximum of 260 nodes. IBM UTP specifies a maximum of 72 nodes, and IEEE 802.5 has a more limited setup than Token Ring, because it specifies a maximum of 250 nodes.

- You can have up to 33 MAUs on the network.

- All network devices must be operating at the same speed (either 4Mbps or 16Mbps), unless the two different speed networks are connected by a bridge.

## Beaconing

*Beaconing* is a unique function of a Token Ring network. It is the process by which a Token Ring network is able to reconfigure itself in the case of a major failure. Beaconing occurs when there is a problem somewhere on the ring, either a malfunctioning card or a cable fault. When stations detect this problem, they send special frames called *beacons* around the ring continuously. They stop beaconing when they detect a beacon frame from their nearest active upstream neighbor (the workstation immediately before them in the ring, usually called the NAUN).

Sooner or later, the only workstation that will be beaconing is the station immediately downstream of the fault. When it detects that it is the only one sending beacons, it stops and sends a special beacon that contains the reason for the beacon, its own address, the address of the NAUN, and the address of any other station that might be affected. In this manner, the failure point can be isolated and the MAU can automatically reconfigure itself so that the problem lobe is skipped.

# Fiber Distributed Data Interface (FDDI)

**F**iber Distributed Data Interface (FDDI) is an ANSI standard that specifies both the Physical layer and MAC sublayer components of the OSI model. It doesn't, however, specify any of the upper layers, so it is possible to run any of the upper layer protocols over it. It was designed to be a high-speed backbone network specification. It is possible to have all FDDI networks, but they are typically cost prohibitive.

## FDDI and IEEE 802.5

FDDI is very similar to 802.5 and Token Ring, with two major exceptions: it uses two, counter-rotating rings and it can transmit at much higher data rates. It uses the same basic token-passing media access method (except it uses early token release exclusively). It also uses a physical star, logical ring topology. And both can use fiber-optic cable (although FDDI actually specifies it, Token Ring has the option of using it).

## FDDI Network Design Issues

FDDI uses two counter-rotating rings (as opposed to one ring in Token Ring) as shown in Figure 6.5. Only one ring is used for data transfer (called the primary ring). The other ring (the secondary ring) is used for out-of-band management. In the case of a failure, the rings reconfigure and traffic switches to the secondary ring, as necessary.

**FIGURE 6.5**

FDDI uses two counter-rotating rings.

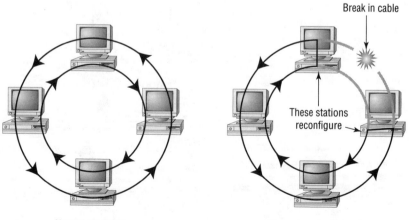

Normal operation                   After auto-reconfiguration

There are some design specifications for FDDI. Each one must be kept in mind when designing a network that is to be based on FDDI.

- FDDI cable is usually multi-mode fiber optic with a core diameter of 62.5 micrometers.

- A repeater is required every 2km or less.

- One ring (primary or secondary) can handle no more than 1000 stations.

- Total ring length (primary or secondary) cannot be longer than 200km.

- For an FDDI network, where all stations are connected to both rings, the maximum cable length is 100km, and only 500 stations can be connected.

## FDDI Station Classes

There are two types of stations that can be connected to an FDDI network, Class A and Class B. *Class A stations* connect to both rings, but *Class B stations* connect only to one of the rings (Figure 6.6). If there is a problem in the ring, Class A stations will be able to reconfigure around the problem area, but Class B stations won't be able to. To realize all the benefits of FDDI, your network should contain only Class A stations.

**FIGURE 6.6**

FDDI station classes

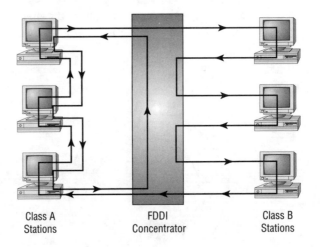

| Class A | FDDI | Class B |
| Stations | Concentrator | Stations |

# WAN Protocols

There are several lower layer protocols that are commonly implemented on Wide Area Networks (WANs). These protocols were designed with efficiency in mind so that the largest amount of data could be transmitted reliably with the least amount of overhead. There are several protocols in use today, including:

- IP over serial lines
- ISDN and B-ISDN
- X.25
- Frame Relay
- ATM

## IP over Serial Lines

One of the most common protocols to run on a WAN today is TCP/IP because of its low overhead, ease of configuration, and its cross-platform nature. There are two major implementations, SLIP and PPP. Both were designed for use over serial lines for point-to-point connections.

### SLIP (Serial Line Internet Protocol)

The SLIP and PPP protocols are used with dial-up connections to the Internet. If you connect to the Internet from your home computer, chances are you're using one or the other of these protocols. SLIP was the first of the two to be developed, and it is the simplest. It functions at the Physical layer only, and does not provide error control or security. Despite these drawbacks, SLIP is still a popular protocol for Internet access. Most users don't need a secure connection, and most high-speed modems provide their own error control.

### PPP (Point-to-Point Protocol)

PPP was developed as an improvement to SLIP, and the functions it provides encompass both the Physical and Data Link layers. PPP's additional functions include error control, security, dynamic IP addressing, and support for multiple protocols. Both SLIP and PPP are point-to-point protocols. PPP provides physical device addressing at the MAC sublayer and LLC-level error control.

Figure 6.7 shows SLIP and PPP mapped to the OSI model.

**FIGURE 6.7**

SLIP and PPP mapped
to the OSI model

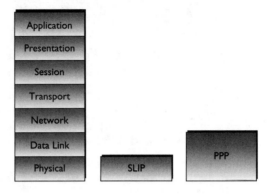

# X.25

The international standards organization CCITT (International Telegraph
and Telephone Consultative Committee), since renamed to the International
Telecommunications Union (ITU), developed X.25 in 1974 as a WAN standard using packet switching.

As you can see in Figure 6.8, X.25 functions at the Network layer. It normally interfaces with a protocol called LAPB (Link Access Procedures—Balanced) at the Data Link layer, which in turn runs over X.21, or another
Physical layer CCITT protocol, such as X.21bis or V.32.

**FIGURE 6.8**

The X.25 protocol
mapped to the OSI
model

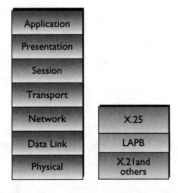

X.25 provides permanent or switched virtual circuits, implying reliable service and end-to-end flow control. However, line speeds used with X.25 are too slow to provide LAN application services on a WAN.

At the Physical layer, X.21 allows for a hybrid mesh topology and a point-to-point connection type.

LAPB is a Data Link layer protocol that provides LLC-level flow control and error control.

At the Network layer, X.25 uses a type of addressing called *channel addressing*, which is similar to logical network addressing except that the address is maintained for each connection.

## Frame Relay

Frame relay is a newer packet-switching technology, similar to X.25, that uses virtual circuits. Like X.25, frame relay is used in WANs. Frame relay assumes that certain error-checking and monitoring tasks will be performed by higher-level protocols, allowing it to be faster than X.25. Frame relay functions at the Physical and Data Link layers of the OSI model, as illustrated in Figure 6.9.

**FIGURE 6.9**

Frame relay mapped to the OSI model

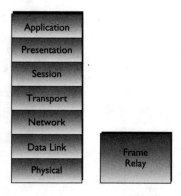

Frame relay is defined by CCITT recommendations I.451/Q.931 and Q.922.

At the Physical layer, frame relay handles point-to-point connections in hybrid mesh physical topologies. At the LLC sublayer of the Data Link layer, frame relay provides error detection but not error recovery.

Frame relay services generally allow customers to specify *committed information rates* according to their bandwidth requirements.

# ISDN (Integrated Services Digital Network) and B-ISDN (Broadband ISDN)

ISDN is a set of standards designed to provide voice, video, and data transmission over a digital telephone network. B-ISDN provides greater bandwidth, which can be used for applications such as video, imaging, and multimedia. B-ISDN can be used with ATM and SONET, which are described in the following sections.

At the Physical layer, ISDN provides time-division multiplexing (TDM). At the Network layer, the ISDN standard is defined by CCITT recommendations I.450/Q.930 and I.451/Q.931.

Figure 6.10 shows ISDN mapped to the OSI model.

**F I G U R E   6.10**

ISDN mapped to the OSI model

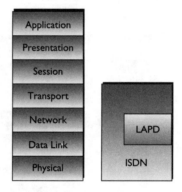

ISDN functions as a transmission media service only. The ISDN specification uses the LAPD (Link Access Procedure, D Channel) protocol at the Data Link layer to provide acknowledged, connectionless, full-duplex service. At the MAC sublayer, LAPD provides physical device addressing. At the LLC sublayer, it handles flow control and frame sequencing.

The ISDN standard for integrating analog and digital transmissions using digital telecommunications networks allows for circuit-switched or packet-switched connections. These connections are provided by means of digital communication channels, or *bit pipes*. Using the ISDN bit pipes, several standard rate multiplexed channels are available. These channels are classified as follows:

Channel A: 4kHz analog channel

Channel B: 64Kbps digital channel

Channel C: 8 or 16 Kbps digital channel (used for out-of-band signaling)

Channel D: 16 or 64 Kbps digital channel (used for out-of-band signaling). This channel includes three subchannels: s for signaling, t for telemetry, and p for low bandwidth packet data.

Channel E: 64Kbps digital channel (for internal ISDN signaling)

Channel H: 384, 1536, or 1920 Kbps digital channel

LAPD operates on the D channel.

The following three channel combinations have been standardized by CCITT as international service offerings:

- Basic rate, which includes two B channels (at 64Kbps) and one D channel (at 16Kbps)

- Primary rate, which includes one D channel (at 64Kbps), 23 B channels in the U.S. and Japan, or 30 B channels in Europe and Australia

- Hybrid, which includes one A channel (4KHz analog) and 1 C channel (8 or 16 Kbps digital)

## ATM (Asynchronous Transfer Mode)

ATM is an emerging standard being developed by the ITU Telecommunications Standards Sector and the ATM Forum. It is most frequently considered for WANs, but it can also be used for LANs and MANs. This protocol covers the functionality of the OSI model's Data Link and Network layers, and can operate over Physical layer protocols such as FDDI and SONET/SDH. Figure 6.11 maps ATM to the OSI model.

A distinguishing feature of ATM is that it uses *cell-switching*. A *cell* is a 53-byte packet that follows a virtual circuit. Its other Network layer function is static route selection.

At the LLC sublayer of the Data Link layer, ATM provides isochronous transmission synchronization and error control.

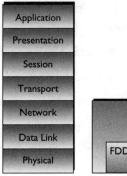

# Review

The following miscellaneous protocol suites were covered in this chapter:

- IEEE 802 Standards
  - IEEE 802.2
  - IEEE 802.3 (Ethernet)
  - IEEE 802.4 (Token Bus)
  - IEEE 802.5 (Token Ring)
  - IEEE 802.6
  - IEEE 802.9
  - IEEE 802.11 (Proposed)
  - IEEE 802.12 (Proposed)
- SLIP (Serial Line Internet Protocol)
- PPP (Point-to-Point Protocol)
- FDDI (Fiber Distributed Data Interface)
- X.25

- Frame relay

- ISDN (Integrated Services Digital Network) and B-ISDN (Broadband ISDN)

- ATM (Asynchronous Transfer Mode)

These protocols function at the layers of the OSI model as shown in Table 6.2.

**T A B L E 6.2:** Miscellaneous Protocol Suite

| Protocol | Layer | Topics & Methods |
|---|---|---|
| IEEE 802.2 | Data Link-LLC | Protocol specific: identification of upper-layer protocols |
| IEEE 802.3 | Physical | Physical topology: 1Base5 (star), 10Base2 (bus), 10Base5 (bus), 10BaseT (star), 10Broad36 (bus), 10BaseF (star)<br>Connection types: multipoint<br>Digital signaling: state-transition<br>Bit synchronization: synchronous<br>Bandwidth use: baseband (except 10Broad36) |
| | Data Link-MAC | Logical topology: bus<br>Media access: contention<br>Addressing: physical device |
| IEEE 802.4 | Physical | Physical topology: bus<br>Connection types: multipoint<br>Digital signaling: state-transition<br>Bit synchronization: synchronous<br>Bandwidth use: baseband |
| | Data Link-MAC | Logical topology: ring<br>Media access: token-passing<br>Addressing: physical device |

**T A B L E 6.2:** Miscellaneous Protocol Suite *(continued)*

| Protocol | Layer | Topics & Methods |
|---|---|---|
| IEEE 802.5 | Physical | Physical topology: star or ring<br>Connection types: point-to-point<br>Digital signaling: state-transition<br>Bit synchronization: synchronous<br>Bandwidth use: baseband |
| | Data Link- MAC | Logical topology: ring<br>Media access: token-passing<br>Addressing: physical device |
| IEEE 802.6 | Physical | Physical topology: ring<br>Connection types: point-to-point<br>Bandwidth use: baseband |
| | Data Link- MAC | Logical topology: ring |
| IEEE 802.11 | Data Link- MAC | Media access: contention |
| IEEE 802.12 | Physical | Physical topology: star<br>Connection types: multipoint<br>Bandwidth use: baseband |
| | Data Link- MAC | Logical topology: bus<br>Media access: contention |
| SLIP | Physical | Connection types: point-to-point |
| PPP | Physical | Connection types: point-to-point |
| | Data Link-MAC | Addressing: physical device |
| | Data Link-LLC | Connection services: error control |
| FDDI | Physical | Physical topology: star or ring (dual)<br>Connection types: point-to-point<br>Digital signaling: state-transition<br>Bandwidth use: baseband |

**T A B L E  6.2:**  Miscellaneous Protocol Suite *(continued)*

| Protocol | Layer | Topics & Methods |
|---|---|---|
| FDDI | Data Link-MAC | Logical topology: ring<br>Media access: token-passing |
| CCITT X.25 | Network | Addressing: channel<br>Switching: packet (virtual circuit)<br>Connection Services: Network layer flow control, error control |
| Frame relay | Physical Data | Physical topology: mesh (hybrid)<br>Connection types: point-to-point<br>Switching: packet (virtual circuit) |
| | Link-LLC | Connection services: LLC-level flow control, error control |
| ISDN | Physical Data Link<br>(see LAPD) Network | Multiplexing: TDM<br>Switching: packet, circuit |
| ATM | Data Link-LLC | Transmission synchronization: isochronous<br>Connection services: error control |
| | Network | Switching: packet (cell)<br>Route selection: static |

# CNE Practice Test Questions

**1.** Which 802.3 standard is the closest to the original Ethernet?

    **A.** 10BaseF

    **B.** 1Base5

    **C.** 10Base5

    **D.** 10Base2

**2.** Which non-IEEE protocol is very similar to IEEE 802.5 Token Ring?

   **A.** SMDS

   **B.** FDDI

   **C.** SONET

   **D.** PAP

**3.** What access control method does IEEE 802.3 use?

   **A.** CSMA/CA

   **B.** Token-passing

   **C.** CSMA/CD

   **D.** 802.3 Enhanced

**4.** Which IEEE 802 standard defines the LLC sublayer functions?

   **A.** 802.3

   **B.** 802.1

   **C.** 802.4

   **D.** 802.2

**5.** Which WAN protocol can support dynamic IP addressing?

   **A.** X.25

   **B.** PPP

   **C.** SLIP

   **D.** ATM

**6.** Which two layers of the OSI model do the IEEE 802.*x* map to primarily?

   **A.** Transport

   **B.** Network

**C.** Data Link

**D.** Physical

**7.** Which IEEE 802.*x* standard is often used concurrently with 802.3, 802.4, 802.5, and 802.6?

**A.** 802.1

**B.** 802.2

**C.** 802.7

**D.** 802.9

**8.** How many Class II Fast Ethernet repeaters can you have in a single collision domain?

**A.** 2

**B.** 3

**C.** 4

**D.** 5

**9.** In an FDDI network where all the workstations are Class A stations, what is the maximum number of stations that can be connected?

**A.** 100

**B.** 250

**C.** 500

**D.** 1000

**10.** Which Fast Ethernet standard uses four pairs of Category 3 UTP cabling?

**A.** 10BaseT

**B.** 100Base-T4

**C.** 100Base-TX

**D.** 100Base-FX

**11.** Fast Ethernet uses which media access method?

 **A.** CSMA/CD

 **B.** CSMA/CA

 **C.** Token-passing

 **D.** Contention

**12.** What is the maximum number of repeaters that can be used on a 10Base2 network?

 **A.** 2

 **B.** 3

 **C.** 4

 **D.** 5

**13.** Which connector is used by 10BaseT Ethernet networks?

 **A.** RJ-11

 **B.** RJ-45

 **C.** RJ-12

 **D.** RJ-36

**14.** What is the maximum segment length for a 100Base-FX Fast Ethernet segment?

 **A.** 100 Meters

 **B.** 185 Meters

 **C.** 412 Meters

 **D.** 500 Meters

**15.** You can have both 4Mbps and 16Mbps Token Ring devices on the same network operating at different speed.

 **A.** True

 **B.** False

# CHAPTER

# 7

Bridging, Switching,
and Routing Concepts

# Roadmap

This chapter covers the various methods of bridging, switching, and routing on an internetwork as well as their associated connectivity devices.

**Topics Covered**

- Why network connectivity devices are used
- Repeaters
- Bridges
- Switches
- Routers
- Unroutable protocols
- Combination devices
- Comparison of bridges, routers, and switches

**Skills You'll Learn**

- List why connectivity devices are used on LANs and WANs
- Describe the differences between Ethernet and Token Ring repeaters
- List the three types of bridges and three of the benefits of bridging
- Describe the operation of a transparent bridge
- Explain the configuration of a spanning tree network
- Describe how a source routing bridge works
- Detail the use of switches
- Differentiate between link state and distance vector route discovery methods
- Define an unroutable protocol and determine how to deal with an unroutable protocol
- Describe the various combination devices
- Outline the use of bridges, switches, and routers in internetworks

**T**his chapter deals with the three main types of connectivity devices used on networks today, how they work, and their operational criteria. You may not have all these devices on your own network, but as internetworking sees more use on today's networks, you will need to know their specifics. This chapter will help you to choose the appropriate device for a specific need on your LAN.

# Why Network Connectivity Devices Are Used

**E**ach LAN is made up of several components, but typically the most prolific is the workstation. Workstations are connected together with other connectivity devices to form a LAN. These connectivity devices are implemented for several reasons:

- To overcome limitations of the network media—Every type of network media (cable or otherwise) has certain limitations, limitations including number of devices on one segment, size of bandwidth, and maximum distance from node to node. Bridges and repeaters are typically used to overcome these limitations.

- To allow transmission of data across networks with different media access methods—LANs today are very fast and efficient at providing communication between workstations. But their very design limits their maximum distances. WAN technologies are great for transmitting data over long distances, but are very difficult to configure. There are devices designed to connect LANs to WANs to facilitate communication between LANs over long distances. Routers are the devices that most often provide the functionality necessary for this procedure.

- To translate between incompatible protocols—In some cases, the need arises to connect networks that have absolutely nothing in common. Everything is different: protocols, physical media, network architecture. In this case, a very complex device is needed to perform multiple translations. Typically, a gateway provides this functionality.

# Repeaters

**R**epeaters are probably the simplest network devices. They are used to extend the maximum distance of a network segment. Because of noise and other factors, some topologies have short maximum distances. As their name suggests, they take whatever comes in on one port, amplify it, and send it out the other port, effectively extending the maximum segment length for the topology.

To ensure performance and reliability, various protocols specify limits on the number of repeaters that can be used with the protocol. Two examples of protocols that limit the use of repeaters are Token Ring and Ethernet.

## Token Ring Repeaters

A Token Ring network is unique with regard to repeaters, because every Token Ring adapter card in each workstation is essentially a repeater. Each workstation receives every packet from the MAU on one set of wires, amplifies it, and retransmits it back to the MAU. In addition to the MAU and the NIC, there are special Token Ring repeaters that are used to extend the maximum lobe length of a ring.

Token Ring specifies a maximum number of repeaters (including any of the above mentioned devices) as well as the lobe length and length of individual cable segments.

## Ethernet Repeaters

As mentioned in the previous chapter, Ethernet has a rule for repeaters called the 5-4-3 rule. This rule states that on an Ethernet network, you can have up to five segments, separated by four repeaters. On these five segments, only three of them can be populated with workstations. The 5-4-3 rule applies to all coaxial cable Ethernet media.

# Bridges

**A**nother type of connectivity device commonly seen on networks is the bridge. A bridge divides a single network segment into two network segments, ultimately dividing the traffic on the larger segment. It increases performance on a network by keeping local traffic local, but letting packets specifically destined for remote segments pass (Figure 7.1). Broadcast traffic on a particular segment is localized to that side of the bridge.

**FIGURE 7.1**

Typical bridge
operation

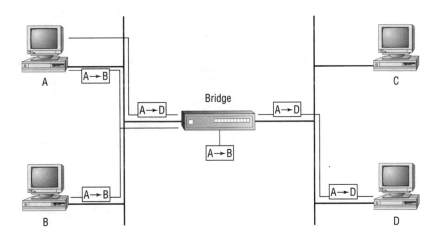

A→ D is allowed to cross bridge

A→ B is not

## Benefits

Bridges have several benefits on a network:

- They function at the Data Link layer of the OSI model, so a large number of protocols can be bridged. Some protocols that cannot be dynamically routed at upper layers of the OSI model can be bridged (like NetBEUI).

- They can function as repeaters, because each packet that is forwarded through a bridge gets amplified and repeated to the destination segment. Therefore, a bridge has all the benefits of a repeater and a few more.

- They increase available bandwidth by dividing a high traffic segment into two (or more) lower traffic segments. They filter traffic based on the hardware addresses of the workstations on a particular segment.

## 80/20 Rule in Bridged Networks

There is a rule that is used when designing bridged networks that says that 80% of the traffic should be local (doesn't need to cross the bridge), and the other 20% should be available for bridged traffic (destined for a computer on the other side of the bridge). Figure 7.2 shows a sample network that should probably be bridged. In this example, the sales department sends e-mail to the research and development department every so often, but they constantly save data to their server. Research and development, on the other hand, use a client-server development application that takes a heavy toll on the network. They also send e-mail to sales.

**FIGURE 7.2**

Sample network before bridging

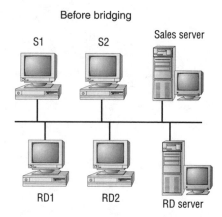

The wrong way to bridge this network would be to put the bridge between the workstations and the servers (Figure 7.3). In this example, both sets of workstations are hitting their respective servers pretty hard, so the bridge is going to work pretty hard, as well. More than 80% of all network traffic will cross the bridge, so this violates the 80/20 rule.

The best way to place the bridge would be to separate the sales and research and development segments with the bridge (Figure 7.4). This way, only the network traffic destined for the other departments would cross the bridge (remember the e-mail they send each other?). No matter how hard one department would hit the network, the excess traffic would not cross the router, and thus would not slow down the other department's segment.

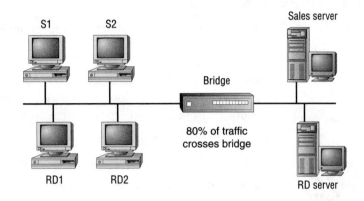

**FIGURE 7.3**

Incorrect bridge placement

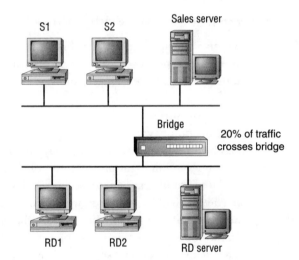

**FIGURE 7.4**

Correct bridge placement

## Types of Bridges

There are three main types of bridges in use today, each with their own use and configuration issues:

- Transparent
- Source-routing transparent
- Source-routing

# Transparent Bridges

A *transparent* bridge is probably the most popular type of bridge because it is very simple to set up and requires very little configuration to function properly. Transparent bridges are often used on IEEE 802.3 (or Ethernet) networks. They are called transparent bridges because the sending device is unaware that the destination device may be on a segment on the other side of a bridge, or that there even is a bridge between them. Hence the bridge is transparent to the sender.

The IEEE 802.1d standard defines transparent bridges.

## How a Transparent Bridge Works

When a transparent bridge is first connected to the network, it forwards all frames, except those that have destination addresses in the bridge's *filtering database* (a database that contains entries for which packet addresses should be forwarded and which should be dropped). By default, there are only a couple of entries (broadcast addresses, for example) hardwired into the database to comply with the various protocol standards. However, this database can be modified either manually by an administrator with the bridge manufacturer's administration software, or dynamically by the bridge itself.

To make filtering database entries dynamically, the bridge learns which hardware (MAC) addresses are on which segments by examining the source addresses of every frame that crosses the bridge. The bridge knows that if a frame comes from a workstation on a particular segment, then that workstation must be on that segment. The bridge then populates its database with this information. After some time, the bridge will only pass frames destined for workstations with remote segments and exclude all other traffic. Because of this ability to learn which nodes are on which segments, transparent bridges are also called *learning bridges*.

## Port States

Every bridge can connect to two or more segments through *bridge ports*. The bridge ports are simply the connectors on a bridge that allow the bridge to connect to two or more segments. Each bridge port is kind of like a network adapter in that it can connect to a single segment.

Each bridge port can be in one of five states at any one instant. Which state it is in depends on either the bridging protocol or the network management program. The states are:

- Disabled
- Blocking
- Listening
- Learning
- Forwarding

The flowchart in Figure 7.5 shows how the bridge switches back and forth between states.

**FIGURE 7.5**

Bridge port states interaction

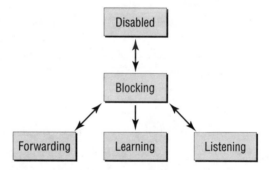

**Disabled**   A bridge port that is in the disabled state doesn't participate in any forwarding or learning. This state is an offline state for that port. This state is controlled primarily by the bridge management software.

**Blocking**   When you bring a new bridge online, it will be in the blocking state (kind of like a standby state) during its initialization. It will only forward data frame addresses to the bridge's multicast address. It will ignore all frames sent to any other destination address. Blocking is also the constant state of the second bridge in a redundant bridge pair.

**Listening**   When a bridge is in the listening state, it is preparing for the learning and forwarding states. A bridge in this state will use its internal timer to wait for the network to settle down between topology changes before enabling the learning and forwarding states. The listening state exists so that incorrect information isn't added to the filtering database, causing bridging loops. Bridging loops are covered later in this section.

**Learning**   During the learning state, a port will not forward frames. It will, instead, try to determine which nodes are on its associated segment. The timer is running during this state as well and is used to specify how much time a port has to learn where nodes are. During this period, the port will populate the filtering database with the source node information it discovers until the timer runs out.

**Forwarding**   This state is considered the normal operating state for a bridge. During this state, a port can perform both forwarding and learning functions. The bridge will forward frames only while in the forwarding state.

## Relay Entities

The entity inside a router that performs the forwarding and filtering services inside a bridge is called the *relay entity*. This entity uses information found in the filtering database to determine whether a packet should be forwarded or dropped.

Based on this information, a relay entity (and thus, a bridge) will only forward a frame if the frame meets all the following criteria:

- It is not addressed to the bridge itself.

- It contains a valid Cyclic Redundancy Check (CRC) value.

- The frame passes the restrictions from the filtering database. That is, the destination address in the frame is on a segment on the other side of the bridge from the sending station.

- The frame contains data from any of the upper layers of the OSI model (any layer above the MAC sublayer of the Data Link layer, including the LLC sublayer of the Data Link layer).

## Store-and-Forward Mode

Transparent bridges use a store-and-forward mechanism when forwarding frames. When a bridge is in the forwarding state, it will receive a packet on one port, read the value of the CRC field and address fields, and store the frame in memory while the CRC and address restrictions from the filtering database are checked for validity. If the frame passes the CRC test and the filtering database restrictions, the frame is forward. If either test fails, the frame is discarded.

The Cyclic Redundancy Check (CRC) test is actually very simple. The entire frame is run through a mathematical calculation, and the result is appended to the frame in the CRC field and placed on the wire. When the receiving station (in this discussion, one of the bridge ports) receives the frame, it reads the CRC field into memory and runs the same mathematical formula against what's left of the frame. If the value of this calculation and the CRC value aren't the same, the receiving data will know that the transmission got changed in some way during transmission and the frame is dropped.

Because this process requires the frame to wait in memory while the checks are performed, a bridge can introduce latency in transmissions that cross a bridge. *Latency* (also called delay) is measured in milliseconds (ms), and its value increases with the size of the frames being forwarded.

Even though it introduces latency, the benefit of the CRC check is that it prevents bad frames from being forwarded. A repeater usually only amplifies the signals it receives and doesn't check for bad data as it passes through.

## Filtering Database Population

The internal filtering database is populated using a three-step process, detailed here. This process repeats itself continuously. The sample network shown in Figure 7.6 illustrates this process.

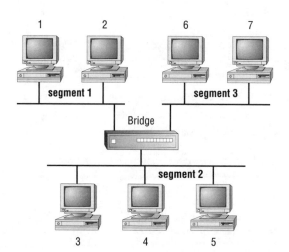

**FIGURE 7.6**

A sample network for illustrating filtering database population

| Filter Database | |
|---|---|
| Segment | Device(s) |
| 1 | |
| 2 | |
| 3 | |

**Step 1**   As soon as the bridge shown in Figure 7.7 is powered up, after a warm-up period specified by its internal timer, the ports will switch to the learning state. During this time, it will examine the source fields of all frames being sent on each segment while it forwards them to all segments. During this time, station 1 sends a frame destined for station 3 on segment 2. The bridge will receive this frame and forward it to all segments. It will also note that station 1 is on segment 1 from its address in the sender field of the data frame.

**FIGURE 7.7**

Populating the filtering database, step 1

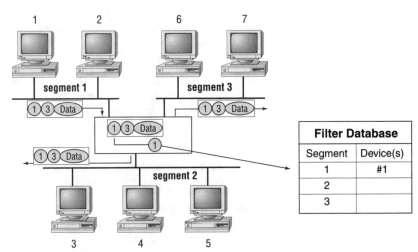

| Filter Database | |
|---|---|
| Segment | Device(s) |
| 1 | #1 |
| 2 | |
| 3 | |

**Step 2**   When station 3 responds to station 1's request, it sends the data frame to all stations on its own network, including the bridge (Figure 7.8). The bridge will forward it only to segment 1 because it has already learned that station 1 is on segment 1, so it doesn't forward it to all segments, only to segment 1. It also notes that station 3 is on segment 2 and adds that information to the filter database.

**Step 3**   The previous two steps show how the filter database is built for stations that communicate with the bridge as the intermediary. As time goes on, more and more traffic will be considered local, and the bridge will discard those frames. For example, if station 2 sends a data frame to station 1, the bridge will read the source and destination fields of the frame and determine that the source address is not in the database, so it is added (Figure 7.9). It also notes that the destination is already on the same segment, because it is in the filter database, so the bridge does not forward it.

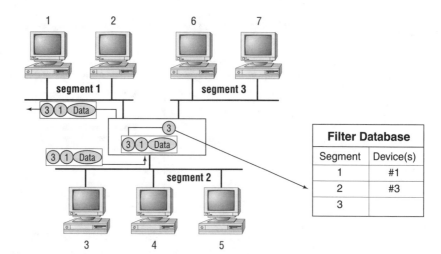

**FIGURE 7.8**

Populating the filtering database, step 2

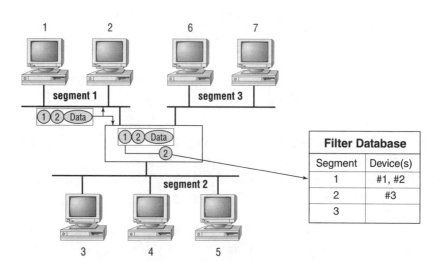

**FIGURE 7.9**

Populating the filtering database, step 3

## Bridging Loops

When connecting multiple segments with a bridge, you are introducing a single point of failure. For this reason, bridges are often implemented in pairs, a primary and a redundant unit. Unfortunately, this has the frequently unwanted side effect of bridging loops.

A *bridging loop* happens when data frames circle endlessly between two redundant bridges. They are primarily caused by bridges that don't use the spanning tree protocol. Figure 7.10 shows a network that might be subject to a bridge loop.

FIGURE 7.10

Possibility of a
bridge loop

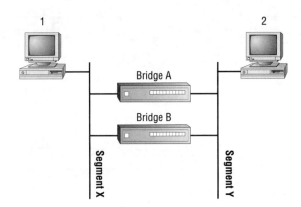

In Figure 7.11, station 1 sends a frame destined for station 2. Both bridges receive it and forward it to segment Y, but because of design and cable length differences, bridge A might forward it to segment Y just slightly ahead of bridge B. Bridge B will then receive the frame sent by bridge A. Because bridge B doesn't know that the frame came from bridge A, it will assume that the frame came from station 1 (because that's the address in the source field). Because a bridge must always use the most current information, bridge B will update its own filter database and forward the frame to segment X (Figure 7.12).

FIGURE 7.11

A data frame is sent
destined for station 2
on segment Y

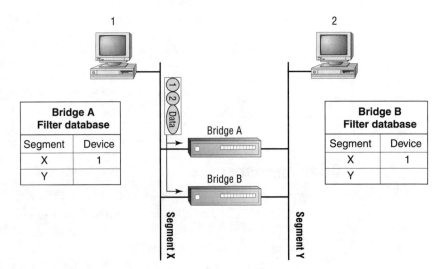

**F I G U R E 7.12**

Bridge A forwards the frame to segment Y slightly before bridge B. Bridge B receives the frame, updates its filter database, and forwards it to segment X.

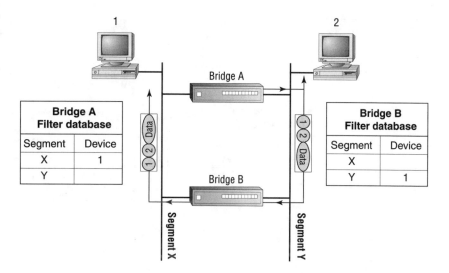

| Bridge A Filter database | |
|---|---|
| Segment | Device |
| X | 1 |
| Y | |

| Bridge B Filter database | |
|---|---|
| Segment | Device |
| X | |
| Y | 1 |

While this is happening, bridge B has forwarded the frame it originally received from station 1 to segment Y. The same process happens. Bridge A receives it, determines it came from station 1 on segment Y, updates its own filter database, and forwards it to segment X (Figure 7.13).

**F I G U R E 7.13**

Bridge B forwards its original frame to segment Y. Bridge A receives the frame, updates its filter database, and forwards it to segment X.

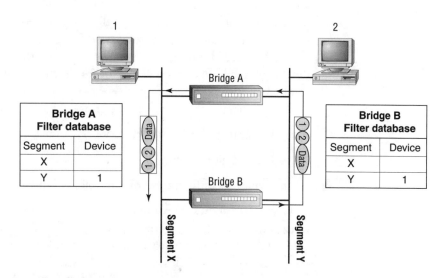

| Bridge A Filter database | |
|---|---|
| Segment | Device |
| X | |
| Y | 1 |

| Bridge B Filter database | |
|---|---|
| Segment | Device |
| X | |
| Y | 1 |

This process leads to an infinite loop and network traffic skyrockets. The same two frames get forwarded over and over again, each time updating the bridge's filter database, ultimately causing network failure (Figure 7.14).

**FIGURE 7.14**

An infinite bridge loop

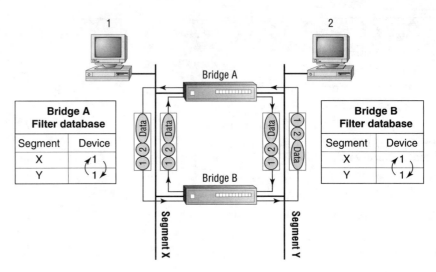

## The Spanning Tree Bridge Protocol

The spanning tree protocol is one way around the bridge loop problem. Specified by the IEEE 802.1, it uses a special packet called the bridge protocol data unit (BPDU) that bridges can use to communicate with one another. The BDPU allows the bridges to elect a bridge called the *root bridge* (kind of like the master bridge) as well as designated and backup bridges for particular segment routes. A *designated bridge* is the bridge that all frames will be forwarded through. The *backup bridge* is the redundant backup for the designated bridge that will take over as the designated bridge in case the original designated bridge fails.

Bridges that use the spanning tree protocol have the following advantages:

- Dynamic failure if the primary bridge fails

- Prevention of bridge loops

- Dynamic configuration of multiple, redundant routes

Figure 7.15 shows an example of a bridge network that uses the spanning tree protocol. At the top of the figure you will find the root bridge. The *root bridge* in a spanning tree network is responsible for initiating configuration messages, which are then sent to all bridges and forwarded by the designated bridges. In this manner, the root bridge can notify all bridges that a change has occurred on the network and the bridges need to reconfigure to adapt to the change.

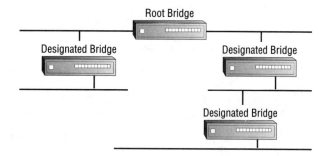

**Bridge IDs**  Each bridge has its own unique identifier called a *bridge ID*. A
bridge ID is an eight-byte, hexadecimal number. The first two bytes make up
the unique identifier assigned by you. The last six bytes are the same as the
hardware (MAC) address for the network interface corresponding to that
port. No matter how many network interfaces the bridge has, the first two
bytes will be the same. The bridge that has the lowest bridge ID will be designated as the root bridge.

You should set the bridge ID manually so that you have control over which
bridge is the root bridge through either manufacturer software or through a
standard interface like Simple Network Management Protocol (SNMP).

**Selecting a Root Bridge**  The first step that bridges perform in a spanning
tree environment is to select which bridge is the root bridge, then determine
designated routes to segments. To start this process, every bridge broadcasts
a frame that contains the fields shown in Figure 7.16.

**F I G U R E  7.16**

Spanning tree bridge
broadcast frame
layout

| DEST ADDR | SRC ADDR | DSAP | SSAP | BPDU | CRC |
|-----------|----------|------|------|------|-----|
| MAC ADDR | | LLC Header | | BPDU | CRC |

If you'll remember, the BDPU is the field that contains the instructions
that allow the switches to send information to one another. This field is
made up of several components, shown in Figure 7.17. The fields of the
BDPU that are used during the initial broadcast are:

- Constants (4 bytes)
  - Protocol ID (2 bytes) = 0

- Message type (1 byte) = 0

- Version (1 byte) = 0

- TCA, TC Flags (2 bytes):

  - TCA (topology change acknowledgement, 1 byte)

  - TC (topology change notification, 1 byte) typically used for adjusting internal timers during bridge reconfiguration

- Root ID (8 bytes)—The bridge ID of the root bridge

- Port Cost (4 bytes)—Cost to the root

- Bridge ID (8 bytes)—The bridge ID of the sending bridge

- Miscellaneous fields (10 bytes)

  - Max Age (2 bytes)—When the message should be deleted (also called TTL Time to Live).

  - Hello Time (2 bytes)—How long since the last configuration message from the root bridge.

  - Forward delay (2 bytes)—How long before proceeding to the next state during a topology change.

  - Port ID (2 bytes)—If two bridges are trying to be the root bridge and they have the same bridge IDs, this value is used to break the tie.

  - Message Age (2 bytes)—Time since last configuration message.

**FIGURE 7.17**

Components of the BDPU configuration message for spanning tree bridges

| Constants | TCA TC | ROOT ID | PORT COST | BRIDGE ID | Misc. |
|-----------|--------|---------|-----------|-----------|-------|

When this process begins, all bridges advertise themselves as the root bridge by putting their bridge ID in the Bridge ID and Root ID fields of the BDPU section of the broadcast frame and broadcasting the frames on every one of their ports (Figure 7.18). The LLC Control field in the message instructs each bridge that receives this frame to forward all BDPUs.

**FIGURE 7.18**

Forwarding all BDPUs
to select a bridge

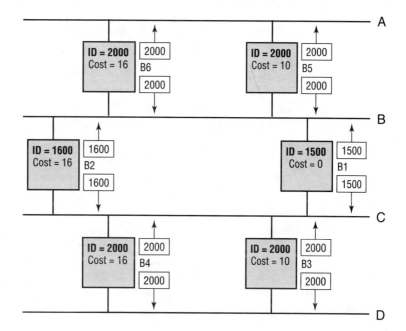

When a bridge receives a BDPU with a bridge ID lower than its own, it stops broadcasting BDPUs, and instead forwards the BDPU from the bridge with the lower bridge ID, replacing the value in the Bridge ID field with its own bridge ID.

Figure 7.18 illustrates how B1 will become the root bridge because it has the lowest bridge ID (1000). Additionally, B2 detects that it is receiving BDPUs from B1 on both ports. It determines that it is in parallel with the root bridge, so it switches both of its ports to the blocking state and, by doing so, becomes the backup for the root bridge.

Once the root bridge has been agreed upon, it starts transmitting BDPUs on all its ports every two seconds (by IEEE default). Because B2's ports are set to blocking, it will not forward these frames, but it will interpret the BDPUs.

**Determining Designated and Backup Bridges**   After the root bridge has been determined, designated routes to the various segments must be determined so that the bridges know how to forward frames. To determine this, the bridges forward the BDPUs from their root ports. A root port is the port on a bridge that is closest to (or faces) the root bridge. The BDPUs sent from the root bridge contain a field called port cost. The BDPUs that the root bridge broadcasts always have a port cost of zero. When the bridges receive these BDPUs, they add their port costs (preconfigured by the administrator at the same time as the bridge ID) to the value of this field and forward it to the next segment. Every bridge that receives this frame from now on will add their port cost to this value. As the BDPU gets farther away from the root, the higher the port cost. Additionally, traveling through a different bridge may have a higher or lower port cost. Figure 7.19 illustrates this process.

Bridges on the same segment (for example B3 and B4 on segment D) will listen for each other's BDPUs and determine who has the higher port cost. The one with the lower port cost (B3) will become the designated bridge for that segment; the other bridge (B4) will set its ports to the blocking state and become the backup bridge for that segment.

**FIGURE 7.19**

Determining a designated bridge using port costs

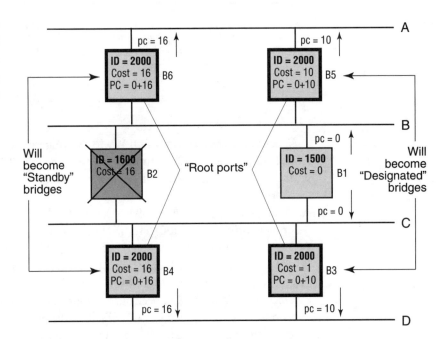

To work correctly with IEEE standards, all BDPUs must be addressed to a multicast address. Unfortunately, not every bridge from every vendor will use the same multicast address. In most cases these addresses are configurable. Check your bridge's documentation to be sure.

**Spanning Tree Layout**  Once the spanning tree bridges (illustrated in the previous figures) have configured themselves, your network might look something like the one in Figure 7.20. Notice that bridges B2, B4, and B6 aren't shown, because they aren't actively forwarding frames, but are in the blocking state.

**FIGURE 7.20**

Tree after root bridge election and route designation

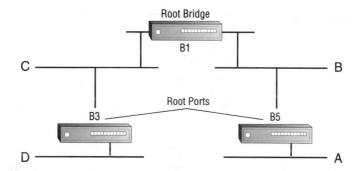

**What Happens If a Network Failure Occurs?**  If a bridge or specific segment fails, a spanning tree allows the bridges to try to reconfigure to take the failure into account. In Figure 7.21, B5 has failed. Bridge B6 detects this because it hasn't received a BPDU from B5 in a specified time period. It then transmits a BPDU frame on its root port with its TCN (topology change notification) byte set, destined for the root bridge.

This is the only time a bridge will transmit a BDPU on its root port after the root bridge has been established.

The B6 bridge will continue to broadcast TCN BDPUs until the designated bridge up the line acknowledges receipt. This process continues until the root bridge receives the notification and acknowledges receipt. When the root bridge receives the TCN, it then broadcasts a BPDU with the TCA (Topology Change Acknowledgement) bit set to all segments (Figure 7.22). This BPDU eventually will make it to all bridges. When a bridge receives this special BPDU, it will stop forwarding frames, clear its database of all non-permanent entries, and revert to the blocked state. It waits in this state for a specified amount of time (specified in the BPDU by the root bridge).

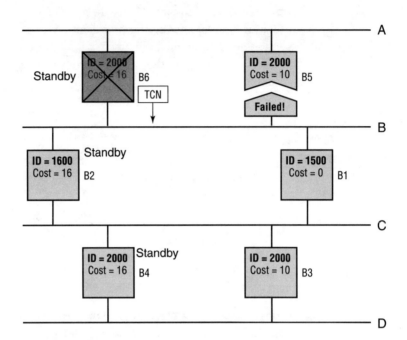

**FIGURE 7.21**

A sample bridge failure. The backup bridge is sending a TCN notification on its root port.

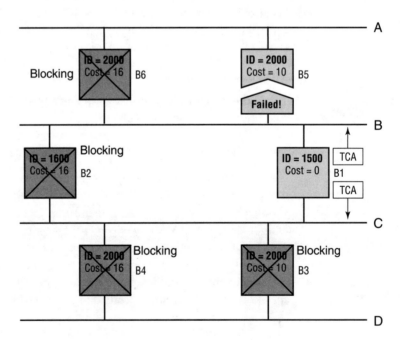

**FIGURE 7.22**

The root bridge sends out a TCA to all bridges, causing them to stop forwarding frames.

After the time to wait has expired, the bridges will start contending to be the designated bridge. Because the values for port cost haven't changed, B3 will again be the designated bridge (just like it was previously in Figure 7.19). But, since B6 is the only bridge on that segment, it will become the designated bridge for that segment (Figure 7.23). The bridges will cycle through all states from blocking to forwarding (as discussed previously) and start forwarding frames again.

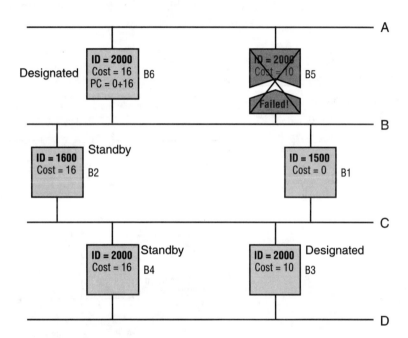

**F I G U R E   7 . 2 3**

The standby bridge B6 now becomes the designated bridge.

**Ideal Spanning Tree Configuration**   There are a few guidelines to consider when configuring a spanning tree environment.

1.  There should be redundant routes to every segment. Instead of implementing one bridge to get to a network segment, install two. When using spanning tree, you don't have to worry so much about bridge loops.

**2.** A frame should never have to be forwarded by more than three bridges after a topology change where a backup bridge becomes the designated one.

**3.** The root bridge should also have a backup.

**4.** There should be no more than one segment between a bridge and the root bridge.

If there is such a thing as an ideal spanning tree bridge configuration, the one in Figure 7.24 is very close to it.

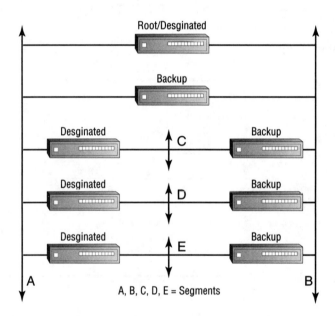

**F I G U R E  7.24**

An ideal spanning tree configuration

A properly designed spanning tree network has the following advantages:

- Minimal latency
- Fast reconfiguration time
- Very fast topology changes

## Source Routing

Whereas transparent bridges are used in IEEE 802.3 networks, source-routing bridges are more commonly found in Token Ring networks. They are called source-routing bridges because they don't contain a filtering database, but rely on the sending devices to include bridging information in the MAC header in the data frame.

When a source-routing device wants to send information to another device over a source-routing bridge, it looks in its table of routes and constructs a frame of addresses to the destination. The frame includes not only the source and destination device, but also all bridges it must pass through on the way there. It then places this information in the MAC header of the frame and places the frame on the network. The bridge picks up the frame and, detecting its own address is the MAC header, forwards it to the specified segment. Figure 7.25 illustrates this concept.

**FIGURE 7.25**

A source-routing network

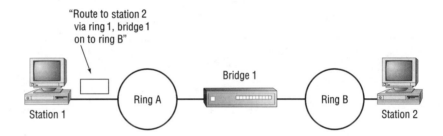

"Route to station 2 via ring 1, bridge 1 on to ring B"

Station 1    Ring A    Bridge 1    Ring B    Station 2

Although the terminology says routing, a source-routing bridge doesn't do any routing, per se. Technically, because the device operates at the Data Link layer and performs a bridging-type process, it is a bridge, by definition.

## Source Route Determination

Because of the way source routing works, each node on a source-routing network must build its own table of routes. This process is called *route determination*. To determine the route to a station, each device sends a special frame called a *hello frame* to the destination device. As it travels toward the destination device, each bridge that it passes through appends its name and route information to the frame and forwards it to the next segment. When the destination station receives the frame, it responds to the source station, sending it back along the same route. When the original sending station receives the frame, it adds that route information to its database.

These operations may seem like a lot of overhead for one frame, but this only happens when the station is not on the local ring. The sending station makes that determination on Token Ring before they transmit the hello frame. It does that by sending a special frame on the local ring without source-routing information. If the frame returns with the Address Recognized Indicator (ARI) set, the sending station knows that the intended destination is on the local ring, and it won't have to use source-routing information to get the packet to its destination.

The routing table is dynamically stored in RAM and is erased every time the station is powered down, or when the time limit for storing those entries has expired.

# Switches

**E**thernet switches are actually a fairly new technology that has enjoyed popularity lately. The main reason why they have become so popular is because of the shortcomings of traditional Ethernet. When Ethernet LAN traffic becomes saturated, you have two choices to solve the problem:

- Segment the network using bridges.
- Replace Ethernet with another network technology.

Neither solution is very cost effective or desirable.

A switching hub (also called a switch) is a better solution for Ethernet network bandwidth problems. It allows you to increase existing bandwidth by simply replacing the hub (and not any of the other components). Hubs are essentially high-speed, multiport bridges, with some operational differences.

First of all, a switch doesn't broadcast a frame to all ports like a true bridge would. Instead, it develops a table of the MAC addresses of connected workstations. Then, when a station on one port wants to send data to a station on another, it sends the data frame. The switch will examine the destination MAC address in the frame and forward the frame to the destination station only (Figure 7.26). For Ethernet, this avoids collisions almost entirely.

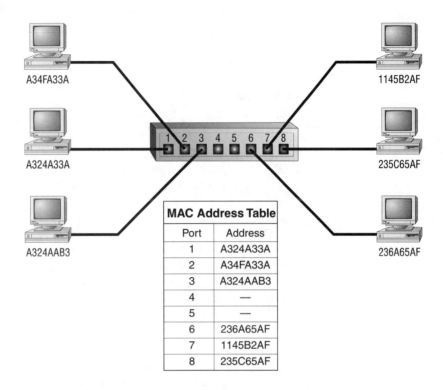

**FIGURE 7.26**

Ethernet switch
functionality

Speaking of collisions, each port on a switch is its own collision domain.
All devices connected to that port (a single workstation or multiple workstation on a 10BaseT hub) compete for bandwidth. The more devices connected
to a port, the more collisions that may occur.

Another difference between a switch and a bridge is a switch can typically
switch among multiple ports simultaneously. It can also monitor traffic
among the different ports. Unfortunately, the monitoring tools that work
with bridges and repeaters don't typically work with switches. A protocol
analyzer will only see what is attached to the same port. There are, however,
tools from the various switch manufactures that can be used to manage
switches as well as other network components.

## Switch Classification

There are many characteristics that separate one vendor's switch from
another. Some of these characteristics include:

- Communication speed (10 or 100Mbps)

- Frame forwarding type (store-and-forward vs. cut-through)
- Full-Duplex ports
- Server connection type

## 10Mbps vs. 100Mbps

Because there are two speeds that Ethernet hubs commonly run at, there are two speeds that switches commonly use. Both hubs and switches can automatically detect the speed and switch between the two. Just as there are 10/100Mbps hubs, there are 10/100Mbps switches. Some switches can even connect different MAC layer protocols like Ethernet and FDDI.

## Store-and-Forward vs. Cut-Through Switches

Store-and-forward switches work very much like bridges in that they copy the entire frame into memory while verifying its CRC (or other integrity checks). Because the frame has to wait in memory, each frame can introduce latency (usually around 1200 microseconds of delay). The amount of latency increases with the size of each frame.

On the other hand, cut-through switches read only the destination address of the frame, then forward the entire frame without examining the rest of it. This greatly improves performance over store-and-forward switches, but it is not without its share of problems. The lack of integrity checking can affect performance as well, because a cut-through switch can inadvertently forward corrupt frames.

On some manufacturer's switches, the forwarding method is configurable. Others take a more advanced approach. The switch operates in cut-through mode, but monitors each port. When the error rate reaches a specified threshold, the switch will fall back to store-and-forward mode.

## Full-Duplex Ports

Switches are designed to be very high-performance network devices. This is especially true when you connect special full-duplex Ethernet NICs to a switch that is capable of full-duplex operation. These NICs are typically found in servers or high-performance workstations. The switch detects that these NICs are attached and, because it's the only NIC attached to that port, allows them to operate in full-duplex mode. This means that incoming and outgoing traffic is perfectly balanced. Whenever you connect a server to a switch in full-duplex mode, you can achieve bandwidths as high as 20Mbps (minus any overhead).

### Multiple Server Connects

NetWare servers can do one very cool thing with a switch. You can place multiple network cards into a server, and the server will connect to the switch using all of them and load balance across them. To do this, you must load a special NLM on the NetWare server and have multiple NICs in the server.

## Virtual LANs

If you connect multiple switches together, you create what is known as a flat architecture. All nodes are essentially on the same level. This architecture cannot scale past a few dozen segments because of large numbers of broadcast propagation and other bridge-type problems.

To get around these problems, switching vendors have come up with a technology known as *Virtual LANs*, or *VLANs*. With a VLAN, you can group a number of stations connected to switches into a logical network segment (see Figure 7.27). Each VLAN is a single broadcast domain, but only stations in a particular VLAN receive those broadcasts.

**FIGURE 7.27**

Virtual LANs within a switched network

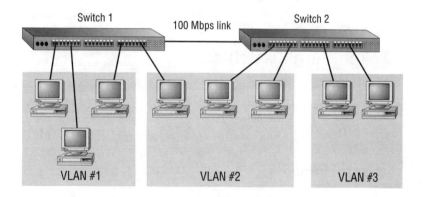

Some switches perform VLAN switching at the Data Link layer, while others perform VLAN switching at the Network layer. The latter switches, in effect, perform some basic routing functions.

### Data Link Layer (Layer 2) VLANs

At the Data Link layer, virtual LANs are defined and maintained by the vendor-supplied switch management software. Traffic within each VLAN is switched using the MAC address. Routers are implemented to handle traffic between VLANs and perform functions like filtering, security, and traffic management. This router can be either a stand-alone router or a router expansion card for the switch. In both cases, the router is outside each Virtual LAN.

### Network Layer (Layer 3) VLANs

The main difference between Data Link layer VLANs and Network layer VLAN switches is that Network layer VLAN switches understand the Network layer addresses of various protocols. Network layer VLAN switches organize stations by subnets that use specific protocols.

The difference between a Network layer switch and a router is that a Network layer switch bridges traffic within each VLAN, at the Data Link layer. When traffic needs to travel between VLANs, a Network layer switch can then perform the routing internally, without needing an external router. A router can only perform routing; it doesn't usually bridge at the lower layers. (There are exceptions, of course.)

Network layer switches can actually perform basic inter-departmental routing and even replace a very low-end router, but it doesn't have the intelligence and software that a full-fledged router has.

## Token Ring Switching

Token Ring switches use technologies similar to Ethernet, including cut-through and store-and-forward frame switching. It hasn't taken off to the same degree as Ethernet switching, because the token-passing technology and bandwidth have usually been sufficient for most users.

### Benefits

Token Ring switching has several benefits over traditional Token Ring. The benefits are similar to the benefits of Ethernet switching.

**Easy Installation**   Installing a Token Ring switch is extremely easy. It is simply a matter of unplugging the dual-port bridge and plugging in the Token Ring switch. In source-routing scenarios, a Token Ring switch can replace the backbone ring and most (if not all) of the source-routing bridges.

**Hop Reduction**   Because of the ability of Token Ring switches to replace multiple source-routing bridges, a Token Ring switch will also reduce the number of hops on a source-routed Token Ring network, because there aren't as many bridges. Additionally, because the number of bridges crossed is reduced, latency (due to these bridges) is also reduced.

**Increased Bandwidth**   When a server is connected directly to a switch, either Token Ring or Ethernet, it provides a virtual pipe between the server and each station. A station doesn't really have to contend for media access between the server and a workstation in a true-switched network (where all network entities are hooked directly to the same switch). It is possible for a workstation to have a full 16Mbps pipe from workstation to server using a Token Ring switch.

**Full-Duplex**   Like Ethernet, Token Ring switches can also provide full-duplex connections to provide better bandwidth use.

**Increased Performance**   All these benefits factor into one major benefit, increased performance. Whether it's speed or efficiency, implementing a Token Ring switch will, in most cases, increase network performance over a standard Token Ring network.

### Disadvantage of Token Ring Switching

The main drawback to using a Token Ring switch is the same as the Ethernet switch, the lack of analysis tools. There are some vendor-specific monitoring tools, and more are appearing all the time.

# Routing Technologies

**M**any networks today are connected to the Internet. It's becoming a very popular thing to do. If your network is connected to the Internet, you will use a router to make the connection. It uses various routing protocols and technologies to connect your network to the thousands of other networks that are on the Internet.

Most routing technologies operate at the Network layer of the OSI model. As such, these technologies use logical network addresses and function independently of the underlying media and protocols. Logical network addresses are often called software addresses because they are typically set by software. They differ from hardware (MAC) addresses in that hardware addresses are set on the hardware at the factory, and they refer to one device only. Network addresses typically identify both the device and the network it resides on.

Each network address can be either a logical address only (it can be dynamically mapped to a particular hardware address) or a combination of the station's hardware address and a logical address. (The logical address is made up of the hardware address of the station plus a software-configured address.) IP is a routable protocol that uses the former addressing scheme, while IPX uses the latter.

Similar to lower-layer forwarding technologies, any packets that are sent with routing technologies must have a destination address and a known path to the destination. That doesn't necessarily mean that the sending station places all this information in the packet itself. Typically, the sending station needs to place only the destination address in the packet; the router will determine the best path and place that information in the packet's header.

## Routing Illustration

To illustrate these routing concepts, examine the internetwork in Figure 7.28. Networks A and C are Ethernet networks, while network B is a Token Ring network. Station 1 on network A is going to transmit data to station 3 on network C. To get the data there, it will have to pass through routers R1 and R2. All stations and routers are running the DLG (a fictitious routable protocol designed for this example) network protocol.

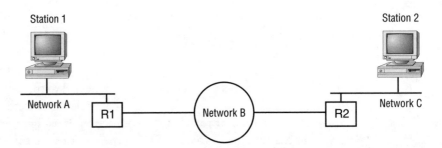

**FIGURE 7.28**

A routing sample network

To send the data over this network, an upper-layer process on station 1 acquires the destination address and queues up the data to be sent. The DLG protocol determines that the destination host logical address is 3.C (station address 3 on network C). The DLG protocol builds a packet with the data and its own error-correcting information and appends its own Network layer header (which includes the source address 1.A, the destination address 3.C, as well as any other Network-layer data). The DLG protocol determines that the destination address is not on the local network because it has a different network address, so it hands the packet to the lower layers with the instruction to transmit the packet to the router R1 for forwarding. Each lower layer adds its own header until the packet is placed on network A, destined for R1 (Figure 7.29).

**FIGURE 7.29**

Beginning the transmission of a packet across the internetwork

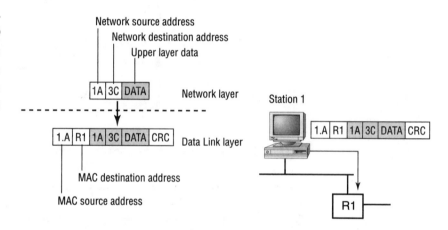

When R1 receives the packet, it copies the frame from network A into its memory at the Physical layer. The Data Link layer verifies the Data Link CRC and passes the remainder to the Network layer (#1, Figure 7.30). At the Network layer, the DLG protocol examines the destination network address of the packet and determines whether the packet is destined for a local or remote network by checking its internal routing information table (#2, Figure 7.30). The DLG protocol determines whether there is a router connected directly to this router that can forward the packet to its destination network address (network C). In this case, R2 is only one hop away, and it has instructions on how to get to network C. So the DLG protocol passes the packet to the Data Link layer with instructions to send it to R2 on the connected Token Ring network (#3, Figure 7.30). The Data Link layer then builds a Token Ring frame with the R1 as the source address and R2 as the destination address. It appends its CRC information and sends it to the Physical layer to be sent on network B to R2.

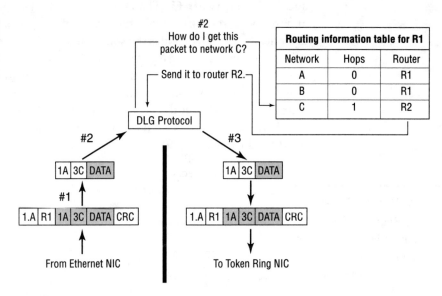

**FIGURE 7.30**

Determining where a
packet should be sent
at router R1

When the frame arrives at R2, the router copies the frame into memory and verifies the CRC at the Data Link layer. The Data Link layer then strips off its header information and passes it to the DLG protocol at the Network layer. The DLG protocol checks its router information table to see if the destination address is directly connected to one of its segments. In this case, the destination network address is network C, which the router knows is directly connected to itself, so it passes the frame to the Data Link layer telling it to send the frame on network C with a source of R2 and a destination of station 3.

Station 3 receives a packet from network C and, when it reads the logical network destination address, determines that the packet is meant for itself (Figure 7.31). Because it was the intended recipient, the DLG protocol strips off its addressing information and passes the data to the upper layers.

**FIGURE 7.31**

Packet reception of a
routed packet

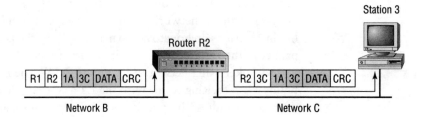

## Routing Database Population

Every router contains a special list or database called a *routing information table*. This table tells a router the location of the network on the internetwork from that router's point of view. The table is used by the network protocols and routing software to determine where to send the various packets they receive. Each table lists network numbers, the routers used to get to those network segments, and how far away they are so the router can make a decision about the best way to send the packet.

Table 7.1 is a sample routing information table for a router designated R2. It says that if it receives a packet with a destination network address of 56, it should send it to router R1. Similarly, if it receives a packet with a destination network address of 24, it should send it to a local segment. Compare the routing table with the sample internetwork diagram in Figure 7.32.

| **TABLE 7.1** | **Network** | **Router** | **Hops** |
|---|---|---|---|
| A Sample Routing Table for Router R2 shown in Figure 7.32 | 56 | R1 | 2 |
| | 24 | R2 | 0* |
| | 36 | R1 | 5 |
| | 78 | R3 | 2 |

\* This number could also be 1, depending on the brand of router or software used.

**FIGURE 7.32**

Internetwork diagram for the routing table in Table 7.1

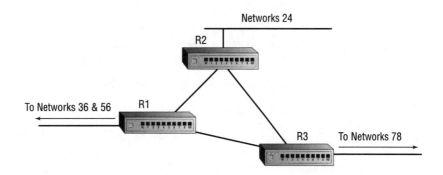

In common routing parlance, every router a packet passes through on its way to its destination is known as a *hop*. The more hops there are to a destination, the longer it will take the packet to get there. Some routing protocols and software allow you to limit the maximum number of hops a packet can take.

The number of hops, the speed of the link between routers, plus a few other factors like latency make up a routing decision factor called *cost*. There may be several different routes to a specific destination, but the route with the lowest cost is the one that a router will usually select when forwarding a packet to its destination.

## Routing Protocols and Route Discovery Methods

The information in these routing tables (including cost, location of segments, and the routers that service them) is discovered by using various route discovery methods. Route discovery is one function of routing protocols. The various routable protocol suites that are commonly found on networks today all have routing protocols to perform functions like:

- Learning the various routes on an internetwork

- Advertising the cost of each route

- Warning routers of down or saturated links

- Updating routing information to keep it as current as possible

Routing protocols operate at the Network layer and work independently of lower layer protocols. They are used primarily to learn how the internetwork is laid out.

The main function of routing protocols for routers is route discovery. *Route discovery* is the process by which the routing tables are built and maintained with information about the various paths to the various segments of an internetwork. There are two main route discovery methods:

- Distance vector route discovery

- Link state route discovery

Most routing protocols used today use one of these two methods for route discovery.

## Distance Vector Route Discovery

In distance vector route discovery, each router tells its neighbors what networks and routes it knows about and how far away they are. Every 60 seconds (this parameter is sometimes configurable), a router using distance vector route discovery will broadcast its entire routing information table to any routers it is directly connected to (Figure 7.33). Each router that receives it adds one to each hop count listed in the routing table it receives. These hop counts are the most valuable statistic used in the calculation of cost. When the router has updated its own routing table, it then can turn around and send its updated routing table to its neighbors.

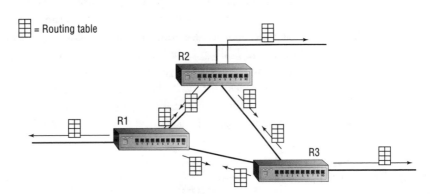

**FIGURE 7.33**

Distance vector route discovery

One point you should remember about distance vector route discovery is that the entries in the routing table have a time-out period, which means that each entry must be updated within a certain time frame, or it is considered out-of-date. If it doesn't receive an update within a specified time-out period, the route information in the table will be deleted. This period can be defined, but it is typically very short (from a few seconds to a couple of minutes).

Some examples of distance vector route discovery protocols are the Routing Information Protocol (RIP) protocol for IPX, RIP for IP (different, even though they share a similar name and acronym), and the Routing Table Maintenance Protocol (RTMP) for Appletalk.

### Advantages and Disadvantages to Distance Vector Route Discovery

There are several advantages and disadvantages to distance vector route discovery when compared to other route discovery methods. There are two major advantages to distance vector. First of all, it's a stout and mature protocol.

Most router manufacturers support distance vector as their default route discovery method (although that is changing). Additionally, it's not a very complex discovery protocol, so there is little impact on a router's processor.

Unfortunately, it does have its drawbacks. Possibly the biggest is the count-to-infinity problem. Figure 7.34 illustrates a sample network that uses a distance vector route discovery method on the routers pictured. If you calculate the number of hops from each router to network 4, following the method of distance vector route discovery, router A would show three hops from network 4, router B – two hops, and router C – one hop. Suppose router C fails. Router B will not realize that router C has gone down and that network 4 is unreachable. It will then only receive routing table updates from router A, which reports that network 4 is three hops away. Router B will add 1 to the hop distance and broadcast to its neighbors (now only router A) that it is positive that network 4 is four hops away. Router A receives this, adds 1 to the hop count, and sends the updates to its neighbors (including router B), saying that network 4 is now five hops away. This process will continue until the hop count reaches infinity. Infinity is an unreachable number, but on routers this number is configurable. It is typically set to 16. When it reaches this point, router B will drop packets destined for network 4.

**FIGURE 7.34**

The count-to-infinity sample network

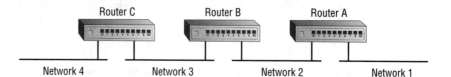

There are two options for distance vector routing software that help reduce (but not completely eliminate) the count-to-infinity problem:

- Split horizon (or *best information*), when enabled, prevents a router from advertising any routes on the network it received them from. In the previous example, if split horizon were enabled on router A, it could transmit updates only on network if it were receiving them from network 2.

- Split horizon with poison reverse is usually called *poison reverse*. When enabled, it determines the hop count of any path it receives updates from to be infinity (usually 16). It performs the same function as split horizon, but with less overhead. Unfortunately, this method causes larger routing updates, because every routing information table must be advertised twice to each network a router is connected to.

## Link State Route Discovery

Link state route discovery is a little more efficient than distance vector. To that end, many network administrators are switching to link state routing protocols on their routers.

The link state discovery method works by transmitting special packets called link state packets (LSPs). These packets contain information about which routers that router is connected to (Figure 7.35). This packet is forwarded to all networks (except the one from which it was sent). Every router will receive multiple LSPs from different sources. When a router has an LSP from every router on the internetwork, it will have an accurate map of the network, gathered first hand from each router.

**FIGURE 7.35**

Link state route
discovery

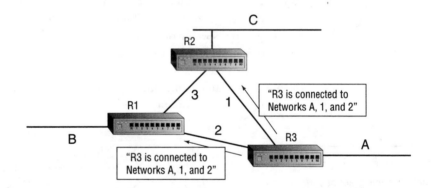

 It may help to think of link state route discovery as trying to figure out one of those word problem games. The ones where "John is sitting next to Mary," "Joe has a blue hat," "Mary is across from John," and so on. You get detailed information about the participants and their immediate neighbors, but not about the entire layout. You (or the router) are left to figure out who (or what router) sits where.

**Advantages and Disadvantages of Link State Route Discovery**    Link state routing definitely has more advantages than disadvantages and is becoming the popular route discovery method on many networks. First of all, the network picture each router has is extremely accurate because it is gathered from each router directly, not from the router's neighbor, routing errors are less likely. Additionally, every router saves a copy of the LSPs it receives. So, if a router wanted more current information, it could query its neighbor and get a copy of the LSPs it had received. Finally, link state routers take less time to converge because they don't suffer from the count-to-infinity problems of distance vector routers.

Unfortunately, the link state route discovery method has one major disadvantage. To perform link state discovery and send out LSPs, it may require more router processor power than distance vector. This disadvantage is becoming more and more slight as processor power on routers increases.

## Load Balancing

Another technology that routers employ is the ability to load balance across multiple routes (Figure 7.36). If a router discovers that there is more than one way to get to a specific destination, it can distribute the load that would normally go on a single route to a destination, over several, redundant routes. This feature makes the use of the available bandwidth more efficient and increases the use of available bandwidth. This feature can be used with both link state and distance vector routing.

**FIGURE 7.36**

Load balancing across multiple routes

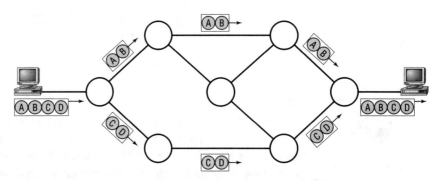

These load-balancing routes can be implemented in a couple of ways. The router can either send packets down each route sequentially in a list or send the packets down each route randomly, gradually phasing out higher-cost or congested routes.

# Unroutable Protocols

The two most popular protocols (IP and IPX) are both routable. Some other protocols are not routable. What distinguishes a routable from an unroutable (also called nonroutable) protocol? The main characteristic of an unroutable protocol is one of two things:

- It uses only static routes that are pre-defined and cannot be updated. Route discovery for these protocols is performed by table lookups only.

- It has no Network layer implementation.

A brief discussion of the more common unroutable protocols follows.

## NetBIOS/NetBEUI

Network Basic Input/Output System (NetBIOS) is a Session layer protocol that opens communication sessions for applications that want to communicate on a LAN. In most occurrences, it runs above a Transport layer protocol called NetBIOS Extended User Interface (NetBEUI). NetBEUI was developed as the transport for NetBIOS. Unfortunately, both protocols were developed only for use on LANs, so neither protocol has a Network layer implementation. Therefore, they are considered unroutable protocols.

While this combination is not routable, it is often bridged on local area networks, especially LAN Manager and Windows NT networks that use these protocols.

## LAT

Digital Equipment Corporation (DEC) designed the Local Area Transport (LAT) protocol to connect terminals to their VAX and other host systems via LAN-attached terminal servers in DECnet environments. Unfortunately it was designed only for LANs and not for WANs. It is an unroutable protocol because it doesn't have a field in any header to indicate the logical network address.

## SNA

IBM's Systems Network Architecture (SNA) protocol was originally designed for host-to-host communication among IBM's mini computers on either twinax or Token Ring networks. Technically, it is unroutable because all its routes are static. Route discovery is performed by table lookup.

IBM has replaced SNA in most cases with Advanced Peer-to-Peer Networking (APPN) for host-to-host communications. It contains a Network layer implementation and is dynamically routable.

# Combination Devices

**W**ith the intricate complexities of modern internetworking, devices have emerged that cannot be classified exactly (bridge, router, or otherwise), so they are classified as combinations of these devices. Unfortunately, they are usually hybrids between two devices, but don't do either job particularly well.

There are two popular examples of these devices, brouters and switching routers.

### Brouters

When you have several different protocols running on several network segments that need to be connected, you may need a router that can bridge the unroutable protocols. Neither a router nor a bridge will work well in this situation, so you need a device that can do both, a brouter.

A *brouter* provides the functionality of both a router and a bridge in the same device. It will try to route the protocol; if it can't, it will forward the packet or frame using bridging technology. It typically costs less than having both devices. If you don't need the functionality of both, however, it may not be a good choice.

### Switching Routers

Lately, router manufacturers have been providing all levels of network interconnectivity with new devices. With the popularity of switches gaining ground in company networks, the router manufacturers didn't want to feel left out. So they developed a switching hub with routing functionality (often called a layer-3 switch). It performs all the functions of a switch, with the ability to provide basic routing services.

# Implementing Internetworking Devices

**W**ith all the different internetworking devices there are to choose from, it is important to be able to choose which device meets a particular need. It is important to understand the differences between bridges, switches, and routers and their effect on the network.

The primary difference between these three devices resides in their implementation of Network and Data Link layer services. The Network layer (as well as routers) has certain functionality that the lower layers do not. For example, the Network layer can break up packets and reassemble them, whereas the Data Link layer cannot.

Each device was designed for a specific purpose. Routers were designed to connect multiple networks into a larger internetwork. Bridges and switches are lower layer devices designed to connect LAN segments to reduce network limitations (for example, length restrictions and bandwidth restrictions).

Another major difference between routers, bridges, and switches is that routers use logical network addresses to tell exactly where a device is on the network. Bridges and switches, because they both primarily use physical (MAC) addresses, can't tell where the device is on the network or how to get there.

Finally, bridges and switches have a flat addressing scheme. All nodes attached to a bridge or switch are considered to be part of the same logical network. Whereas, routers can divide the network into multiple logical networks, each with its own unique identification.

## Router Advantages

A router has several advantages over other internetworking devices, including bridges and switches.

- Routers can handle extremely large packets by fragmenting them into smaller pieces, sending them across the network, and reassembling them. Bridges discard frames that are too large.

- Routers can communicate to warn each other about possible segment overload and failures. Bridges cannot.

- Routers know the layout of the entire internetwork and can determine the optimal route that a packet should take. Bridges only have a general knowledge of the segments they are attached to. They know nothing of other segments.

- Routers recover more quickly from a failure than bridges (especially those using link state routing). They can reconfigure around failed links, if there are redundant backup links, more quickly than bridges. If a bridge fails, all other bridges on the network must stop forwarding frames until a solution is devised.

- Routers can perform packet filtering based on network address. Because bridges can't use network addresses, as long as a frame contains data, it will be forwarded.

- Routers operate independently of the network type. Data can be routed between Ethernet and Token Ring simply. Bridging Ethernet and Token Ring is very complex (and costly for a bridge).

## Bridge and Switch Advantages

Believe it or not, bridges (and switches) do have certain advantages over routers.

- Routers require a great deal of configuration to function properly. Bridges and switches simply plug in and function. (Although each might require some configuration on a large network, the configuration required is still much less than a router in a similar configuration.)

- Bridges operate without the consult of the upper layer protocols, so they can bridge many protocols that aren't routable (such as LAT or NetBEUI/NetBIOS).

- Bridges typically cost less than routers.

- Bridges typically don't have as much complexity and only have to look at the MAC layer address, so they introduce less latency than a router would. A router has to decode frames to the Network layer, so it requires more processing power and takes longer.

## Summary of Bridges and Switches versus Routers

- Use switches to maximize available bandwidth and reduce collisions within a workgroup.

- Use bridges to segment a network and reduce the effect of collisions on an Ethernet network.

- Use routers to connect multiple network segments into an internetwork.

# Summary

## Why Are Connectivity Devices Used?

Connectivity devices are used for three reasons:

- Overcome limitations of the LAN media (distance, bandwidth, and so on)

- Transport data across multiple networks with different media access methods

- Allow communication between different systems with incompatible protocols

## Repeaters

Both Ethernet and Token Ring use repeaters. Ethernet repeaters must follow the 5-4-3 rule. Token Ring repeaters have specifications for lobe length, maximum ring size, and adapter cable length.

## Bridges

- Operate at the Data Link layer to forward packets from one segment to another.

- When placed into an existing network, they can divide the network into two segments, reduce the problems caused by excessive collisions, and still maintain a flat network layout.

- Work independently of upper layer protocols.
- When forwarding, bridges follow the 80/20 rule.
- There are 3 types:
  - Transparent
  - Source-routing transparent
  - Source routing

## Transparent Bridges

- Also called learning bridges because they learn which stations are on which ports.
- Use filtering database to only forward frames destined for a remote segment and keep local traffic from being forwarded.
- Have five bridge port states
  - Disabled—Offline
  - Blocking—Ignores everything but multicast frames
  - Listening—Waiting for the network to settle down
  - Learning—Records source address in the filter database
  - Forwarding—Normal, operating mode
- The relay entity is the entity in the bridge that actually forwards the frames.
- Bridges operate in store-and-forward mode. When forwarding a frame, it is first copied into memory while its CRC is verified. When the CRC has been verified, the frame is copied to the destination segment.

## Building the Filter Database

There are three steps that occur to build the filter database on a bridge. They are, in order:

1. A station transmits a frame to a workstation on a segment on the opposite side of a bridge. The bridge forwards the frame and records the source address and the segment it came from.

2.  The receiving station replies, and the bridge records its address and network segment and forwards the frame to the segment of the original sender. (It had already stored its address information.)

3.  The bridge records source addresses of frames that are transmitted on one side of a bridge to destination addresses on the same segment.

### Bridging Loops

Be aware that bridging loops can occur in networks with redundant bridges that don't use the spanning tree protocol.

### Spanning Tree Protocol

- Specified by 802.1d

- Eliminates bridge loops using designated bridges and backup bridges

- Benefits include:

    - Dynamic configuration of paths between redundant routes

    - Automatic route reconfiguration

    - Prevention of bridge loops

- Uses bridge IDs for identification (lowest ID becomes the root bridge)

- Arranges bridges in a hierarchical tree

### Source Routing

- All bridging information is placed in the header of the frame.

- The sender is responsible for determining the route using hello frames.

- Primarily used on Token Ring networks.

## Switches

- Also known as switching hubs, they function much like multiport bridges to provide a virtual pipe between transmitter and receiver.

- Can be classified as either 10Mbps or 100Mbps, store-and-forward or cut-through.

- Can use full-duplex, if the NIC supports it.

- NetWare servers support multiple, simultaneous connections to a switch to increase throughput.

## Virtual LANs

- One feature of a switch that allows multiple stations connected to a single switch to appear to be on separate, virtual networks (Virtual LANs, or VLANs).

- Can be implemented at either the Data Link layer (requiring an external router) or at the Network layer (includes an internal router).

## Token Ring Switches

- Provide several benefits to Token Ring networks, including:

  - Easy installation

  - Better performance

  - Hop reduction

  - Increased server bandwidth

  - Full duplex capability

# Routers

- Operate at the Network layer to connect multiple networks together to form an internetwork.

- Are intelligent devices capable of selecting from multiple, redundant routes to find the best path to destination, accounting for distance, speed of links, and so on.

- Require both a destination address and route information in the packet when it is sent.

- Use logical network addresses to build routing tables.

- Build routing tables with two different route discovery methods:

  - Distance Vector—All routers broadcast their entire routing table to their neighbors. Each neighbor receives it and adds one to each hop count, updates its own routing table, and retransmits it. This route discovery method is used by RIP for IPX and RIP for IP.

- Link State—All routers broadcast link state packets (LSPs) to tell other routers what routers are directly connected to itself. Upon receiving an LSP, a router will update its own information. This route discovery method is used by NLSP for IPX and OSPF for TCP/IP.

### Defining Unroutable Protocols

A protocol is unroutable (also called nonroutable) if it doesn't have a Network layer implementation or its routes are static and can't be dynamically changed. Some examples of unroutable protocols are:

- LAT
- NetBEUI/NetBIOS
- SNA

Most often, unroutable protocols are bridged or switched instead of routed.

## Comparison between Bridges, Switches, and Routers

- Switches are used to eliminate network congestion within a workgroup.
- Bridges are used to segment the network for increased performance.
- Routers are used to connect multiple networks into an internetwork.

# CNE Practice Test Questions

**1.** A router works at which layer of the OSI model?

**A.** Physical

**B.** Data Link

**C.** Network

**D.** Transport

**2.** A repeater works at which layer of the OSI model?

   **A.** Physical

   **B.** Data Link

   **C.** Network

   **D.** Transport

**3.** A bridge works at which layer of the OSI model?

   **A.** Physical

   **B.** Data Link

   **C.** Network

   **D.** Transport

**4.** A switch can operate at which layers of the OSI model? (Choose all that apply.)

   **A.** Physical

   **B.** Data Link

   **C.** Network

   **D.** Transport

**5.** Which bridging technology organizes bridges into a hierarchy, with designated and backup bridges?

   **A.** Transparent

   **B.** Spanning tree

   **C.** Source routing

   **D.** Distance vector

**6.** Which route discovery algorithm is more efficient in larger networks?

   **A.** Link state

   **B.** Distance vector

**C.** Source routing

**D.** Transparent

**7.** Which is not a routable protocol?

**A.** IPX

**B.** AppleTalk

**C.** IP

**D.** NetBIOS

**8.** Every time a packet crosses a router, the router increments which count?

**A.** Hop

**B.** Router

**C.** Destination

**D.** Hello

**9.** Data Link layer virtual LANs are segmented using which address?

**A.** Hardware (MAC)

**B.** IPX

**C.** TCP/IP

**D.** Network

**10.** Which network device would be the best choice to divide a network with high traffic into two, lower traffic segments?

**A.** Repeater

**B.** Bridge

**C.** Router

**D.** Transceiver

**11.** Which network device will connect multiple networks with different topologies and protocols into an internetwork?

A. Repeater

B. Bridge

C. Router

D. Transceiver

# CHAPTER

# 8

## Internet Addressing Concepts

## Roadmap

This chapter covers the basic TCP/IP addressing concepts you need to understand when hooking a network to the Internet.

### Topics Covered

- IP addressing
- Domain names
- Assigning addresses to hosts
- Using host tables, host names, and domain name services (DNS)

### Skills You'll Learn

- Define the structure of IP addresses
- Describe the process for getting a registered IP address
- Describe IP address classes
- Describe the process for getting a registered domain name
- Assign addresses to IP hosts
- Describe and use host tables, host names, and domain name services (DNS)

# IP Addresses

**E**very entity on a TCP/IP network (called a *host*) must have a network address so that it can be uniquely identified. The addressing format for hosts on a TCP/IP network is a 12-digit dotted decimal number, like the following:

```
xxx.xxx.xxx.xxx (for example, 179.234.29.2)
```

The number is actually 32-bits long and consists of four groups of eight bits called *octets*. The address is assigned by the network administrator and is not hard-wired to the network interface. It can be changed at any time.

Because networks (and all computers, for that matter) work with binary numbers, IP addresses are really collections of binary numbers. For this reason, it is important to understand how to translate binary IP addresses into decimal numbers and vice versa. This technique will also come in handy in understanding the way IP addressing works.

If you can recall basic binary theory, the binary counting system only has two numbers, 0 and 1. Combinations of these numbers represent decimal numbers. It helps to set up a grid of representative numbers. If you look at an eight-bit binary number, it has eight positions. Each position, from right to left, represents a specific power of two (which translates to a specific decimal number). A one in a position means you add the number the position represents to the decimal number you are trying to convert to. Table 8.1 lists the positions, their associated powers of two, and the decimal numbers they translate to.

**T A B L E 8.1:** 8-Bit Binary Positions

| Position | 8 | 7 | 6 | 5 | 4 | 3 | 2 | 1 |
|---|---|---|---|---|---|---|---|---|
| Power of 2 | $2^7$ | $2^6$ | $2^5$ | $2^4$ | $2^3$ | $2^2$ | $2^1$ | $2^0$ |
| Decimal value of a 1 in this position | 128 | 64 | 32 | 16 | 8 | 4 | 2 | 1 |

If you had an eight-bit binary number (or IP octet) of 11010110, that would be 128+64+16+4+2, or 214. To apply this to TCP/IP, if you had a 32-bit TCP/IP address of 11010110.01011010.00001010.00001111, it would translate to an IP address of 214.90.10.15.

Each address consists of two parts, a *network* portion and a *node* portion. When a TCP/IP workstation sends a packet to another workstation over a WAN (like the Internet), the network portion identifies which network segment the receiving workstation is on. Once the packet gets to the network where the receiving workstation is, the node portion of the address identifies which workstation the packet is for. The node portion must be unique within the network. No two nodes on the network can have the same address. Figure 8.1 illustrates this process.

**FIGURE 8.1**

TCP/IP addressing

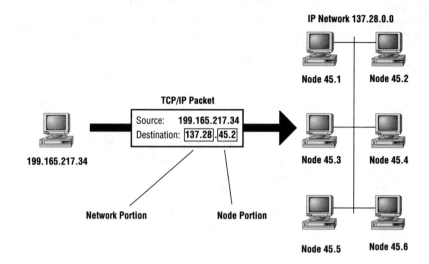

Unfortunately, with the number of hosts on the Internet today, a 32-bit network address limits the number of hosts that can exist on the Internet. So, the next version of TCP/IP, called IPv6 (also called IPng) has a 64-bit addressing length so it can support many more addresses.

Each octet can be a decimal number from 0 to 255, although there are some restrictions on the way these numbers can be used. For example, a network address consisting of all 255's (255.255.255.255) is used for broadcasting to all nodes. Special addresses are covered later in this chapter.

## IP Network Classes

There are many different sizes of TCP/IP networks. Some networks have a limited number of segments, but a large number of nodes. Others have a small number of nodes, but a large number of segments. For this reason, IP addresses are divided into groups called classes. The class of an address specifies which portion of the address is the network and which portion is the node. There are five main classes of addresses, three of which can be assigned to hosts.

- Class A addresses
- Class B addresses

- Class C addresses

- Class D addresses

- Class E addresses

## Class A Addresses

In Class A addresses, the first octet is in the 0-127 range (the first bit of the first octet is 0). That means that an IP address with the first number between 0 and 127 is a Class A address. Another identifying characteristic is that the first octet identifies the network portion of the address and the last three octets identify the node portion.

There are 128 possible Class A networks and each network can have up to 16.78 million hosts.

## Class B Addresses

In Class B addresses, the first octet is in the 128-191 range (the first two bits are 10). The first two octets in a Class B address are the network portion of the address and the last two are the node address.

There are 16,384 possible Class B network addresses available and each network can have up to 65,534 hosts. There are only a few Class B addresses left and they are very hard to get.

## Class C Addresses

Class C addresses are fairly popular, mainly because there are so many of them. There are 2,097,152 possible Class C networks each with up to 255 hosts. Because they are so popular, if a company has enough hosts where they need a Class B address, they may get several Class C addresses instead. Unfortunately, at the rate the Internet is expanding, Class C addresses may eventually run out.

In Class C addresses, the first octet is in the 192-223 range (the first two bits are 110). The first three octets in a Class C address are the network portion and the last octet is the node address.

## Class D Addresses

Class D addresses aren't assigned to hosts. They are normally used for multicast packets. Multicast packets are sent by a host to send messages to a specified group of hosts on a network.

In Class D addresses, the first octet is in the 224-239 range (the first four bits are 1110).

### Class E Addresses

The first octet in a Class E address is in the 240-255 range (the first five bits are 11110). Class E addresses are also not usually assigned to hosts. They are used for some experimental addressing concepts and potential addressing space. They can also be used as broadcast addresses. One special Class E address, 255.255.255.255, is most often used for sending broadcast messages on a local segment. When a packet is sent with a destination of 255.255.255.255, the packet is sent to all workstations on the same segment as the sending workstation. Routers will not forward broadcast packets.

## Special IP Addresses

There are several IP addresses that are commonly used for special purposes. Most implementations of TCP/IP support them in the manner described.

- 0.0.0.0
- 127.0.0.0
- 255.255.255.255
- All zeros in the network portion
- All zeros in the node portion
- Either network or node portion set to all ones

### 0.0.0.0

This address refers to the default route. It is used by the RIP protocol to simplify the IP routing tables. Some older networks use this address as a broadcast address.

### 127.0.0.0

This address (and any address on that network, like 127.0.0.1, 127.0.0.2, and so on) is used to refer to the local TCP/IP interface. It is used by a host to send TCP/IP packets to itself. It is often called the *loopback address*. Using this address, a workstation can send packets to a local address as if it were a remote address.

### 255.255.255.255

This address, as previously discussed, is often called the *broadcast address*. When packets are sent to this address, the packets go to all nodes on the network segment of the sending workstation. Routers won't forward packets that are destined for this address.

## All 0s in the Network Portion

When you have an IP address where the network portion is all zeros (for example, 0.0.0.34 in a Class C address), that address refers to that host on a particular network. For example, if your IP address is 209.67.34.22, 0.0.0.22 would refer to your host on this network only.

## All 0s in the Node Portion

Another special IP address is an address with all its host bits set to 0 (for example, 209.67.34.0 for a Class C network). This address refers a specific IP network (209.67.34). It simply means that all hosts on this network will start with those same numbers.

## Either Network or Node Portion Set to All 1s

When all bits are set to 1, this address works similarly to the 255.255.255.255 address, except the functionality is somewhat split. When the network portion is set to all 1s (for example, 255.255.47.2), it is referring to a specific host on the network (host 47.2 on the network in the previous example). When all the host bits are set to one (for example, 209.67.34.255), it refers to all hosts on that network.

# Obtaining a Registered IP Address from the InterNIC

Assigning IP addresses is somewhat arbitrary. You have complete discretion over which host gets which address. You can even pick the addresses that are used. That is, of course, unless your network is connected to the Internet (and a lot of them are). If everyone chose their own IP addresses, there would be several conflicts as people chose the same addresses.

 If you aren't connected to the Internet and never plan to, you can pick any IP address scheme you want.

For this reason, the Department of Defense (DOD) came up with the concept of registered IP addresses. A central entity would distribute unique addresses to those who requested them.

If you are using Novell's BorderManager Network Address Translation (NAT) feature, you can pick almost any IP addressing scheme for your local network. NAT will translate your IP addressing scheme into one that is valid on the Internet on-the-fly. As you exchange information with the Internet, NAT will translate the sending workstation's IP address into a valid, registered IP address automatically.

## Who is the InterNIC?

The InterNIC is a nonprofit organization tasked by the government with assigning blocks of IP addresses to people who request them. Typically, the InterNIC assigns the blocks to first tier Internet Service Providers (for example, MCI, SPRINT, or USWest). These service providers then assign addresses to other ISPs, who in turn assign them to their clients, as they need them.

The InterNIC is actually part of a company called Network Solutions, Inc., located in Herndon, VA. The actual address is Network Solutions, InterNIC Registration Services, 505 Huntmar Park Drive, Herndon, VA 20170.

For more information about the InterNIC, check InterNIC's website at http://ds.internic.net.

## What Other IP Registries Exist?

Recently, the government has stopped funding the distribution of IP addresses by the InterNIC. For this reason, a non-profit organization called ARIN (American Registry for Internet Numbers) was organized. It now handles the IP assignments formerly handled by InterNIC.

ARIN handles the IP address assignments in North and South America as well as South Africa and the Caribbean. The organization of ARIN was patterned after the European IP registry, Reseaux IP Europeans (RIPE), which is in charge of distributing IP addresses throughout Europe.

In addition to RIPE and ARIN, the Asia Pacific Network Information Center (APNIC) manages IP addresses for Eastern Asia and the Pacific basin.

For information about the other IP registries, check out ARIN's website at http://www.arin.net, RIPE's website at http://www.ripe.net, or APNIC's website at http://www.apnic.net.

## Managing IP Addresses

Because the number of Class C networks is running out, several issues have cropped up within the last few years. For example, any IP addresses you request from your ISP may be non-transferable. That is, they belong to the ISP. If you change ISPs, you must give the addresses back to the ISP you got them from, which means you will have to change all of the IP addresses on your network. No small task on networks with hundreds of hosts.

The shortage of IP addresses becomes more of an issue with the continued massive growth of the Internet. To that end, the next generation of IP is being developed. Called IPv6 (or IPng for IP Next Generation), it should easily alleviate the current shortage of IP addresses. It uses a 64-bit address space instead of the 32-bit address space of traditional IP.

# Domain Names

**D**omain names have become part of popular culture. You can't turn on the TV without seeing an address like www.something.com. Domain names are logical names given to IP hosts. It makes referencing a particular host easier than remembering its dotted decimal IP address.

Domain names can't be just anything. There is a particular format that must be followed. Domain names are laid out in a hierarchical arrangement, often called a tree (Figure 8.2). At the top of the hierarchy is the top of the tree, called the *root*. It is usually indicated with a period (.). Underneath the root are the top-level domains. The domains are like categories that arrange the various domains. Table 8.2 details the various top-level domains and the criteria used to select which domain is assigned.

**FIGURE 8.2**

Domain Name
Hierarchy

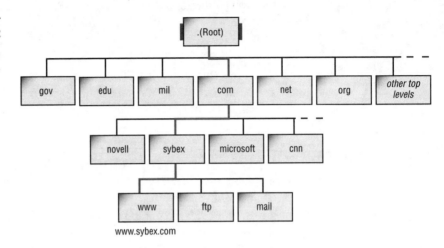

www.sybex.com

**TABLE 8.2**

Top Level Domains

| Domain | Assignment |
| --- | --- |
| GOV | Any department or agency of the United States government |
| EDU | Any educational institution. Within the last few years, this domain is being restricted to only four-year colleges. Other schools use the .US domain. |
| MIL | Divisions of the US military |
| COM | Companies or any commercial venture |
| NET | Primarily used by Internet service providers (ISPs) |
| ORG | Used by nonprofit organizations, primarily. Also used for domains that don't fit anywhere else. |

In addition to these top-level domains, there are domains for other countries as well. Each country has a two-letter country code as specified in the X.500 naming standard. A few of the most common are listed in Table 8.3.

| TABLE 8.3 | Country | Domain |
|---|---|---|
| Examples of International Domains | Australia | AU |
| | Brazil | BR |
| | Canada | CA |
| | France | FR |
| | Germany | DE |
| | Great Britain | UK |
| | Japan | JP |

Companies who have offices in other countries also use these top-level international domains. For example, Novell's main website is www.novell.com, but their website for Germany is www.novell.de.

## Registering a Domain Name

When you connect your network to the Internet and want to set up domain name services (DNS) for your network, you must apply for a domain name. You must register your domain name for the same reasons as registered IP addresses: no two domain names (or addresses) can be the same on the Internet.

When you apply for a domain name, you can choose any name you want, but it should be short, so people can remember it and don't have to type a lot of characters when accessing your Internet servers. Domain names are limited to 255 characters and are not case-sensitive.

The process for registering domain names in the U.S. is different from registering internationally.

### US Domains

The process for obtaining a registered domain name in the U.S. is relatively straightforward. Your ISP can do the work for you, if you want, but it actually isn't that hard. First, pick a name. It should be something that reflects your business or personal name. For example, if your business is called Acme, Inc., you might want to pick acme.com. Unfortunately, you have to make sure that no one else is using that name on the Internet. To do that, you can use an Internet utility called *Whois*. You can find a web interface to Whois at `http://rs.internic.net/cgi-bin/whois`.

When you have determined the name you want to register, you must complete the template from the InterNIC website (located at `http://rs.internic.net/cgi-bin/itts/domain`). There is a wizard that will guide you through the process. You will receive an e-mail stating whether or not the domain name you want is available and if it has been registered. When your name is accepted, it will be released into the DNS zone files and added to the Whois database. After that has been done, you will be billed for the registration. You will have to renew the registration every two years and pay a fee for the continued use of the name.

### International Domains

The process to register a domain name in another country is similar to that in the US, but not as unified. You must contact the top-level domain manager for your country. These individuals (or companies) have applied for that position by contacting the Internet Assigned Numbers Authority (IANA). You can find out who that manager is by going to `http://www.isi.edu/div7/iana/domain-names.html`. From there, it's just a matter of contacting the manager and filling out the appropriate paperwork.

# Assigning Addresses to Hosts

**W**hen implementing TCP/IP networks, you need to assign addresses to each host. Basically, all hosts on the same segment will have the same network portion of their IP address. You simply need to number the hosts on your network uniquely and add that number to the network portion. For example, if the Class C IP address range you were assigned was 209.37.24.0 to 209.37.24.255, all host IP addresses will begin with 209.37.24 and end with a number from 0 to 255 (not including 0 and 255 – they have other, special purposes, as discussed earlier in this chapter).

---

### Special, Reserved IP Addresses

All the discussions so far have been about networks connected to the Internet, because it's the biggest IP-based network. But, what if your network isn't connected to the Internet, and you want to use TCP/IP on it? There are some special IP addresses, reserved by the InterNIC for private use, that you can use that won't be routed on the Internet. They can be used to set up your internal network on TCP/IP, and they won't conflict with anyone else who might be using them on the Internet. The reserved address range for a Class A network is 10.0.0.0 to 10.255.255.255; for a Class B network it's 172.16.0.0 to 172.31.255.255; and for a Class C network it's 192.168.0.0 to 192.168.255.255.

For more information on reserved addresses, you can check out `http://www.nexor.com/public/rfc/index/rfc.html` and search for information on RFC 1918.

---

# Using Host Tables, Host Names, and Domain Name Services (DNS)

In addition to assigning a TCP/IP address to a workstation, you will need to configure some kind of name resolution system to resolve a host name into an IP address. There are two main types of names resolution methods, host tables and domain name services (DNS). Each has its own unique configuration and design issues.

## Host Tables

A host table (also called the HOSTS file) is a text file set up on the local host with the names of the various hosts on the network that are commonly accessed and their associated IP addresses. The file is laid out in three columns. The first column is the IP address of the host; the second is its official host name; and the final column is a list of all the alias names the host has. Figure 8.3 shows an example of a HOSTS file from a NetWare server. The HOSTS file on a NetWare server is located on the server in the SYS:ETC directory. It can also be found on a UNIX machine in the /etc directory.

**F I G U R E  8.3**

A sample HOSTS file from a NetWare server

```
#
# SYS:ETC\HOSTS
#
#                       Mappings of host names and host aliases to IP address.
#
127.0.0.1       loopback lb localhost       # normal loopback address

#
# examples from Novell network
#
130.57.4.2      ta tahiti ta.novell.com loghost
130.57.6.40     osd-frog frog
130.57.6.144    sj-in5 in5
192.67.172.71   sj-in1 in1

#
# interesting addresses on the Internet
#
192.67.67.20    sri-nic.arpa nic.ddn.mil nic
26.2.0.74       wsmr-simtel20.army.mil simtel20
```

## Domain Name Services (DNS)

The other method of resolving host names into addresses, and probably the most commonly used, is domain name services (DNS). DNS is implemented in two parts, a server part and a client part. A DNS server has a list of all the hosts on their networks, their IP addresses, and any aliases for them. The clients (called *resolvers*) are configured with an IP address and the IP address of the DNS server. When you are accessing another host by its host name, the client will ask the DNS server to translate the specified name into an IP address. Figure 8.4 illustrates this process.

FIGURE 8.4

Resolving host names
with DNS

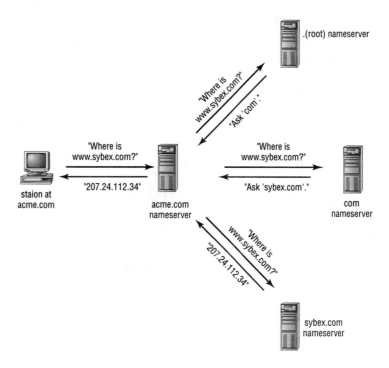

The DNS servers are arranged into a hierarchical structure that follows the domain layout. If your local DNS server doesn't know the IP address of the host name, it can ask its peer server. If the peer server doesn't know, it will ask its peer, and so on back to the root domain.

## DNS Zones

The DNS hierarchy is divided up into areas called zones. A zone begins at a particular domain and extends downward until it reaches a host, or another zone begins. Zones provide logical divisions for the Internet. They may or may not represent physical segments.

Figure 8.5 illustrates an example of a zone setup for a company. Each zone is administrated by an organization. For example, the top-level domains are zones by themselves, administered by InterNIC. Underneath the COM zone is the zone for the Acme Corporation's domain, ACME.COM. If the company is small, the DNS zone is the same as the domain, because there is only one area to manage. But, if Acme happened to be a large corporation, there might be subzones for each division (like SALES.ACME.COM for the sales division, MARKETING.ACME.COM for the marketing division, and so on). Each zone could possibly have its own DNS server, so the zones for the Acme Corporation would be ACME.COM, SALES.ACME.COM, and MARKETING .ACME.COM.

**F I G U R E   8.5**

DNS Zones

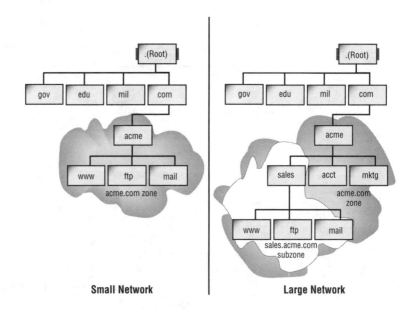

In addition to regular DNS zones, there are two other, special DNS zone types, IN-ADDR.ARPA zones and IP6.INT zone.

**IN-ADDR.ARPA**   The IN-ADDR.ARPA zones provide a mirror image service to DNS. DNS translates names into IP addresses. IN-ADDR.ARPA translates IP addresses into names. The IN-ADDR stands for *inverse address*. IN-ADDR.ARPA addresses are used for services that need to know the specific IP address of a host.

These special IP addresses are entered in the DNS table in reverse. So, if the IP address of a main DNS server for a domain is 129.45.111.34, the IN-ADDR.ARPA entry in the DNS table would be 34.111.45.129.IN-ADDR.ARPA for that domain.

**IP6.INT**   Along with the development of the IPv6 addressing scheme comes the need to modify the existing name resolution schemes to include IPv6 addresses. The IP6.INT zone is used to translate the domain names to IPv6 addresses.

### Master Name Servers

As already mentioned, DNS has two components, the server and the client. The DNS server software can run on almost any server platform, including UNIX (where it was developed), NetWare, and Windows NT. When you set up an IP network, it's a good idea to set up a DNS server designated at the master name server for your DNS domain. The master name server is also called the authoritative server for your domain. It is considered to always have the right information for the domain. It contains information on all the names and addresses of the various IP hosts within your domain, names of any subzones and the addresses of the DNS servers that service them, and the addresses for the root name servers and any other names server addresses required to link your domain to the existing DNS system.

### Replica Name Servers

Replica name servers contain a replica, or copy, of the DNS database. A replica name server simply copies the master DNS database from the master name server to itself. This process is known as *zone transfer*. Replica name servers do not have to belong to the domain they hold replicas for. They can, however, answer DNS queries for information about that domain.

# Review

This chapter covered the basics of Internet addressing, including IP addressing and host names.

- IP addressing
- Domain names
- Assigning addresses to hosts
- Using host tables, host names, and domain name services (DNS)

## IP Addressing

Every computer (called a host) on an IP network must have an IP address. Similar to the address on your house, it allows other computers to find the host on the network. It is composed of four groups of three digit decimal

numbers (or four groups of eight-bit binary numbers) in the format
*xxx.xxx.xxx.xxx*

## Address Classes

There are five main classes of addresses, three of which can be assigned
to hosts.

- Class A addresses start with a number from 1 to 127; the starting bit is
  0, the first octet is the network portion, and the last three are the node.

- Class B addresses start with a number from 128 to 191; the starting
  bits are 10, the first two octets are the network portion, and last two
  are the node.

- Class C addresses start with a number from 192 to 223; the starting
  bits are 110, the first three octets are the network portion, and the last
  is the node.

- Class D and Class E addresses are not typically assigned to hosts, but
  have other uses.

## Special IP Addresses

There are several IP addresses that are reserved for special uses. They are:

- 0.0.0.0 indicates the default route.

- 127.0.0.0 is the loopback address.

- 255.255.255.255 is the broadcast address.

- Network portion of all 0s is used to reference a particular host on this
  network.

- Node portion of all 0s is used to refer to the specified network.

- Network or Node of all 1s functions similarly to 255.255.255.255.
  The decimal 255 in either the entire network or node portion is a
  broadcast address. If the network portion is all 0s, the packets will be
  sent to the specified node on all networks. If the node portion is all 1s,
  the packets will be sent to all nodes on the specified network.

### Other IP Address Considerations

It is necessary to obtain registered IP addresses from the InterNIC if you are connecting your network to the Internet. If you don't, you will receive address conflicts. You can apply for IP addresses from your ISP or from ARIN (American Registries for Internet Numbers). ARIN took over the function of distributing registered IP addresses from InterNIC.

In addition, IP addresses may not be transferable. If you change ISPs, you may have to give all the IP addresses back to the ISP you got them from.

## Domain Names

Domain names are logical names given to IP hosts. They follow a logical hierarchy and organizational structure on the Internet. The top-most levels (top-level domains) separate domain names by type. COM is for companies, EDU for universities and educational institutions, GOV for US government, MIL for US military branches, NET for ISPs, and ORG for non-profit organizations. Additionally, there are top-level domains for each country that follow the X.500 naming convention (CA for Canada, DE for Germany, US for United States, and so on).

Like IP addresses, a domain name for your network must be registered so that conflicts do not occur. US domain names are registered with the InterNIC.

## Using Host Tables, Host Names, and Domain Name Services (DNS)

On a workstation, there are two ways of resolving host names into IP addresses, host tables (also called a HOSTS file) and domain name services (DNS). Host tables contain entries for the name of the host, the IP address of that host, and any alias names for that host. The HOSTS file has the advantage of being local and can be administered simply when there are a small number of hosts. It is typically located in the ETC directory on the SYS volume of a NetWare server.

DNS, on the other hand, is a client-server name resolution system. Each client (called a DNS resolver) that wants to resolve an IP address makes the request of a DNS server. All hosts in a particular domain make up the DNS zone.

There are two types of DNS server, master and replica. A master server contains the host name and IP address information for a particular zone and is considered the authoritative DNS source for a particular DNS zone. A replica server contains the same information, but backs up the master server. The process of transferring DNS information between master and replica DNS servers is called zone transfer.

# CNE Practice Test Questions

**1.** Which IP address is a valid Class C address?

**A.** 204.153.163.67

**B.** 189.45.225.23

**C.** 10.4.2.1

**D.** 245.142.64.15

**2.** Which IP address is a valid Class B address?

**A.** 204.153.163.67

**B.** 189.45.225.23

**C.** 10.4.2.1

**D.** 245.142.64.15

**3.** Which IP address is a valid Class A address?

**A.** 204.153.163.67

**B.** 189.45.225.23

**C.** 10.4.2.1

**D.** 245.142.64.15

**4.** The process of copying host information from a master DNS server to a replica server is called?

**A.** Zone transfer

**B.** DNS copy

**C.** Replication

**D.** Replica updates

5. Which special IP address refers to the local IP interface?

   **A.** 255.255.255.255

   **B.** 197.34.12.255

   **C.** 197.34.12.0

   **D.** 127.0.0.1

   **E.** 172.0.0.1

6. Which domain is NOT considered a common top level domain?

   **A.** COM

   **B.** PRO

   **C.** EDU

   **D.** MIL

   **E.** US

7. Which top-level domain refers to domains located in Germany?

   **A.** DE

   **B.** GE

   **C.** GY

   **D.** GER

8. Where is the HOSTS file located, typically, on a UNIX machine?

   **A.** SYS:ETC

   **B.** /etc

   **C.** C:\ETC

   **D.** \ETC

**9.** What organization is responsible for registering Internet domains?

   **A.** ARIN

   **B.** InterNIC

   **C.** RIPE

   **D.** APNIC

**10.** What organization is currently responsible for keeping track of IP information for Mexico?

   **A.** ARIN

   **B.** InterNIC

   **C.** RIPE

   **D.** APNIC

**11.** What organization is responsible for keeping track of IP information for France?

   **A.** ARIN

   **B.** InterNIC

   **C.** RIPE

   **D.** APNIC

**12.** What organization is responsible for keeping track of IP information for Japan?

   **A.** ARIN

   **B.** InterNIC

   **C.** RIPE

   **D.** APNIC

**13.** How many bytes are there in the network portion of a typical Class B IP address?

   **A.** 1

   **B.** 2

   **C.** 3

   **D.** 4

**14.** Your workstation is trying to access the website www.ebay.com. When your workstation asks the local DNS server, the local DNS server has no entry for www.ebay.com. Which DNS server does your DNS server query next?

   **A.** Root (.)

   **B.** Com

   **C.** Ebay.com

   **D.** www.ebay.com

# CHAPTER

# 9

Subnets and Supernets

## Roadmap

This chapter covers the subnet and supernet concepts you need in order to utilize subnet masking and supernets.

### Topics Covered

- The purpose for using subnets and supernets

- Explain the reason for using subnets

- Describe routing considerations when creating supernets

### Skills You'll Learn

- Assign subnet masks

- Identify the IP address criteria used for supernets

# The Benefit of Using Subnets

When four separate networks are needed within an organization and only one registered IP has been assigned, then four separate subnets must be created by dividing the single registered IP.

The following are reasons a network administrator would create subnets:

- To extend the network: When the maximum physical limitation of the network has been meet, routers may be added and subnets can be created to allow additional hosts.

- To reduce congestion: As the number of hosts on a single network increases, the bandwidth required also grows. By creating subnets, you reduce the number of hosts per network. If traffic consists mainly of communication between hosts on the same subnet, then bandwidth usage is substantially reduced.

- To reduce CPU usage: A high level of broadcasts coincides with a high number of hosts on a given network. All hosts must listen to each broadcast before deciding whether to accept or reject it, regardless of whom it was intended for. Hence, the CPU is accessed, at some level, by each broadcast.

- To isolate network problems: By dividing a network into smaller units, subnets, you reduce the overflow of problems from one segment to the next. Hardware failures and software failures are among the problems that can be reduced to affect smaller portions of the network.

- To improve security: By utilizing subnets, a network administrator can ensure that the internal structure of the network will not be visible from an outside source. Privileged packets will only be broadcast on the subnet it originated from, not throughout the network.

An inbound packet, originating from outside the subnet, may pass through several different subnets before reaching its destination. The same applies for an outbound packet.

- To use multiple media: When using subnets, you have the ability to place different media on separate subnets.

# Subnet Masking

**W**hen connecting to the Internet, a network administrator must ensure that all hosts and networks have unique addresses. An issue arises if more addresses are needed than have been assigned.

Remember that an octet is the same as a byte, and 1 byte = 8 bits.

With TCP/IP, borrowing bits from the host address's bytes to create subnets is possible. This process is called *subnet masking*. A subnet mask is a 4-byte number that is partnered with an IP address to distinguish the network address from the host address.

Within the subnet mask, borrowed bits are set to a value of 1 to differentiate them from the host bits, which are set to a value of 0. TCP/IP states that all IP addresses must have a subnet mask, even if they are not utilizing subnets. Table 9.1 lists the default subnet masks of the various classes of IP addresses in binary and decimal.

**TABLE 9.1:** The Default Subnet Mask

| Class A | | |
|---|---|---|
| **Binary** | 00000000. 00000000. 00000000 | |
| **Decimal** | 255. 0. 0. 0 | |
| Network Address | Subnet Address | Host Address |
| **Class B** | | |
| **Binary** | 11111111. 11111111. 00000000. 00000000 | |
| **Decimal** | 255. 255. 0. 0 | |
| Network Address | Subnet Address | Host Address |
| **Class C** | | |
| **Binary** | 11111111. 11111111. 11111111. 00000000 | |
| **Decimal** | 255. 255. . 255. 0 | |
| Network Address | Subnet Address | Host Address |

## Classful vs. Classless Subnet Hierarchies

There are two types of subnet hierarchies, classful hierarchy and classless subnetted hierarchy.

A classfull IP address hierarchy contains the default number of bits for the network and host addresses. A classless subnetted hierarchy may have a wide variation in the numbers due to the subnet borrowing bits from the host address byte. See Table 9.2 for an example.

**T A B L E 9.2:** Classful Hierarchy—Class B

| 11111111 | 11111111 | 00000000 | 00000000 |
|----------|----------|----------|----------|
| Network  |          | Hosts    |          |

When using a classless subnet hierarchy, a network administrator should keep in mind that there is a balance between the number of subnet addresses and host addresses that will be available (see Table 9.3).

**T A B L E 9.3:** Classless Hierarchy—Class B

| 11111111 | 00000000 | 00000000 | 00000000 |
|----------|----------|----------|----------|
| Network  | Hosts    |          |          |

## Using Subnets

A network administrator must remember the more subnet addresses assigned, the fewer host addresses that will be available (see Table 9.4).

**T A B L E 9.4:** Subnet vs. Host Balance

| 11111111 | 11111111 | 00000000 | 00000000 |
|----------|----------|----------|----------|
| Network  | Subnets  | Hosts    |          |
| 11111111 | 11111111 | 11111111 | 00000000 |
| Network  | Subnets  |          | Hosts    |

When multiple subnets are in use, the duplication of host addresses becomes possible, when the duplicate host addresses are on separate subnets (see Table 9.5).

**T A B L E  9.5:** Duplicate Hosts on Separate Subnets

| 169 | 1 | 118 | 123 |
| --- | --- | --- | --- |
| Network | Subnets | Hosts | |
| 169 | 10 | 118 | 123 |
| Network | Subnets | Hosts | |

External routers, the Internet, use only the network portion of an IP address. For example, on a Class B IP, only 152.151 would be read. Internal routers within a subnetted network use the full IP address—network, subnet, and host. Routers are able to differentiate between the network, subnet, and host portion of an IP address, when the network and subnet bits are set to 1 and the host bits are set to 0.

**Example:**

A corporation has been assigned one Class A IP address (10.0.0.0). They need to create four separate subnets. To create the subnets, the network administrator will set the first byte, the network byte, to 10.*x.x.x* for all hosts on all subnets.

The second byte, the subnet or the segment byte, will be set to a unique value between 0 and 255:

10.0.*x.x* to 10.255.*x.x*

Because the network administrator is using the default subnet mask, 255.255.0.0, a full range of subnets is available.

The third and fourth bytes, the host bytes, will be set to unique numbers on each subnet, between 0 and 254:

10.1.0.1 to 10.1.255.254

10.2.0.1 to 10.2.255.254

10.3.0.1 to 10.3.255.254

10.4.0.1 to 10.4.255.254

# Building the Subnet Addresses from the Subnet Mask

The subnet mask determines how many of the bits in a byte are set aside for use in the subnet address. By using the binary layout of the subnet byte (Table 9.6), a network administrator is able to calculate what the subnet mask needs to be.

**T A B L E  9.6:**  Subnet Addresses

| Bits Used | Binary | Subnet Mask | Subnet Address |
|---|---|---|---|
| 1 | 10000000 | 10000000 | 128 |
|   | 00000000 |  | 0 |
| 2 | 11000000 | 11000000 | 192 |
|   | 10000000 |  | 128 |
|   | 01000000 |  | 64 |
|   | 00000000 |  | 0 |
| 3 | 11100000 | 11100000 | 224 |
|   | 11000000 |  | 192 |
|   | 10100000 |  | 160 |
|   | 10000000 |  | 128 |
|   | 01100000 |  | 96 |
|   | 01000000 |  | 64 |
|   | 00100000 |  | 32 |
|   | 00000000 |  | 0 |

The bit usage continues until the default subnet, all 8 bits, has been reached.

The total number of subnets available can be found by using the formula $2^n-2$, with $n$ being the number of bits available for subnet use.

**NOTE**  Subnets with all bits set to 0 or to 1 are reserved. Some routers and network operating systems will allow these to be used. Standard subnet calculations are done without counting 0 or 1. Check for compatibility before assigning.

## Splitting Bytes

When a Class C IP address has been assigned but subnets are still needed, the partial use of a byte is required. Using a portion of a byte can also be helpful with other IP classes if a large number of host addresses are required per subnet. The balance between the number of subnet addresses and the number of host addresses can be modified to allow fewer or more of either.

When determining the number of subnets based on the number of bits you borrow, the number of subnets available follows the convention $2^h$-2, where $h$ is the number of bits. This is because you can't have a node address with all 1s or all 0s. So, if you borrow one bit, you come up with 2(1)-2=0 subnets. So only borrowing one bit leaves you with no available subnets. Table 9.7 illustrates the number of bits borrowed versus how many subnets are available.

**T A B L E 9.7:** Subnet / Host Balance

| Number of Bits Used | Subnet Mask Byte (Binary) | Number of Subnets | Actual Available Subnets | Number of Hosts on Partial Byte |
|---|---|---|---|---|
| 1 | 10000000 | 2 | 0 | 128 |
| 2 | 11000000 | 4 | 2 | 64 |
| 3 | 11100000 | 8 | 6 | 32 |
| 4 | 11110000 | 16 | 14 | 16 |
| 5 | 11111000 | 32 | 30 | 8 |
| 6 | 11111100 | 64 | 62 | 4 |
| 7 | 11111110 | 128 | 126 | 2 |

After the subnets have been created, the IP addresses can be assigned. When assigning IP addresses there are a few guidelines that must be followed:

- Addresses must have a unique number.

- The network and subnet addresses must not change for any device on their network.

- The host number cannot be set to all 1s or 0s.

## Preparations for Growth

While creating the IP scheme, remember not to use reserved IP addresses and to plan for future growth. To help plan for the future ask yourself the following questions:

- What are our subnet needs today?

  Example: Nine subnets are needed in a network. $2^3$ (8) subnets will not be enough so you must round up to $2^4$ (16) subnets.

- What will our subnet needs be tomorrow?

  Example: Three subnets are needed today. You are currently using $2^2$ (4) subnets, and there is potential for future growth. If possible, it would be advised to use $2^3$ (8) subnets.

- How many hosts are possible on each subnet?

  Example: If 50 hosts are needed on one subnet, you can only use 2 bits for subnetting and still have more than 50 addresses available on that byte.

- What will our host needs be tomorrow?

  When assigning host addresses you must plan with the expectation of future growth.

One strategy that is recommended is to assign IP addresses from the right bit as opposed to the left bit, which will prepare for future growth and smooth the addition of hosts or subnets.

See RFC 1219 at `ftp://nic.ddn.mil/rfc/rfc1219.txt` for more information.

# The Subnet Example

Assigning subnets to a network can be done in three major steps:

1. Determine the number of needed subnets.
2. Determine the subnet mask and subnet addresses.
3. Assign IP addresses to all hosts on all subnets.

# Step 1

The network administrator first needs to determine the number of subnets needed now and in the future. Knowing that they need five subnets now and are planning to grow, the network administrator will use $2^4$-2, or 14, subnets, which will provide adequate space for growth.

# Step 2

The network administrator knows they have been assigned a Class B address of 3.20.0.0 and that the first four bits will be used for the subnet address. Using this information, they can calculate the subnet mask to be 255.255.240.0. With the subnet defined, the network administrator can now calculate the number of host addresses available per subnet (Figure 9.1). To do this, the formula $2^h - 2$ will be used, with $h$ being the number of bits available for host addresses.

**FIGURE 9.1**

Splitting Bytes

255.255.240.0

=

11111111.11111111.1111|0000.00000000

Subnet | Hosts

The network administrator would then obtain the subnet address by calculating the right-most bits from the subnet portion of the subnet mask (Table 9.8).

**T A B L E 9.8:** Finding the Value of the Right-Most Bits

| 1 | 1 | 1 | 1 | 0 | 0 | 0 | 0 |
|---|---|---|---|---|---|---|---|
| 128 | 64 | 32 | 16 | 8 | 4 | 2 | 1 |

They would then take that number, 16, and add it to itself, resulting in the second subnet address, 32. The second subnet address would then be added to the first to calculate the third subnet address, 48. The third subnet address would then be added to the first subnet address which will result in the fourth subnet address, 64. The pattern continues until reaching 255.

If the subnet address is a multiple of the first address, then you can be sure it is a valid subnet address:

32 is a multiple of 16

48 is a multiple of 16

64 is a multiple of 16

Remember that not all software and hardware will support all bits being set to 1 or all bits being set to 0 for a host address.

## Step 3

The next step that would be taken is to assign an IP address to each host (Figure 9.2). In doing this, the network administrator must remember to set the first two bytes to 3.20.$x$.$x$. The first four bits of the third byte must also be set to the binary equivalent of the subnet. It has been decided that the first subnet will be 128. Using this subnet will give a range of 128 (**1000**0000) to 143 (**1000**1111).

**FIGURE 9.2**

Host Address Assignments

3.20.A.B
A = 128 - 143
B = 0 - 255

If the subnet is 160, then the range would be 160 (**1010**0000) to 175 (**1010**1111).
If the subnet is 224, then the range would be 224 (**1110**0000) to 239 (**1110**1111).
If the subnet is 112, then the range would be 112 (**0111**0000) to 127 (**0111**1111).

# Supernets and Their Usefulness

**A** supernet is a group of Class C addresses identified by routers as a single segment. Supernets came into existence in 1993 for the following reasons:

- Few Class C addresses have been assigned.

- Large numbers of Class B addresses have been assigned.

- Internet routing tables have grown too large to be effectively managed.

- Over time, the 32-bit IP addresses will be exhausted.

A subnet will divide bits and create subnets as opposed to combining bits into blocks as supernets do.

A Class C subnet mask at 255.255.255.0 has 24 bits that are used for the network address and 8 bits for the host address (Table 9.9). There are 256 hosts possible on this network when using a supernet mask of 255.255.254.0. When 23 bits are used, the unassigned bit is given to the host address allowing 512 addresses on this network (Table 9.10).

**T A B L E  9.9:**  Subnet

| | | | |
|---|---|---|---|
| 11111111 | 11111111 | 11111111 | 00000000 |
| 255 | 255 | 255 | 0 |

**T A B L E  9.10:**  Supernet

| | | | |
|---|---|---|---|
| 11111111 | 11111111 | 11111110 | 00000000 |
| 255 | 255 | 254 | 0 |

## Supernet Requirements

- Supernets must have successive Class C IP addresses.

    Example: 3.20.99.0 and 3.20.105.0 are not successive;

    3.20.36.0 and 3.20.37.0 are successive.

- The first Class C address's third byte must be evenly divisible by 2.

  Example: 3.20.99.0 is not evenly divisible by 2;

  3.20.36.0 is divisible by 2.

## Supernet Communications

A supernet's routers will broadcast the first Class C IP address along with the subnet mask of 255.255.254.0. The receiving routers will use the subnet mask to detect that one Class C bit has been used to create a supernet with two combined Class C networks. The routers will also know that the first numeric Class C address will be supernet 0 and the next address will be supernet 1.

## Using Multiple Class C Addresses

| Bits Used | 7 | 6 | 5 | 4 | 3 | 2 | 1 | 0 |
|---|---|---|---|---|---|---|---|---|
| Number of Class C Networks | 128 | 64 | 32 | 16 | 8 | 4 | 2 | 0 |
| IP Address Requirements | | >8192 <16384 | >4096 <8192 | >2048 <4096 | >1024 <2048 | >512 <1024 | >256 <512 | |

 See RFC 1338, 1518, and 1519 for more information on supernets.

## CIDR and Supernets

Classless Inter-Domain Routing, or CIDR, is used to enable routers to recognize and translate non-default subnet masks. By using CIDR, all ranges combined under a subnet are broadcast as a single block to Internet routers. By doing this, the amount of traffic and information is greatly reduced.

Routers must be CIDR compliant to allow the creation of supernets.

# Summary

## Benefits of Using Subnets

- To extend the network

- To reduce congestion

- To reduce CPU usage

- To isolate network problems

- To improve security

- To use multiple media

## Subnet Masking

- A subnet mask is a 4-byte number that is partnered with an IP address to distinguish the network address from the host address.

**T A B L E   9.11:**   Default Subnets

| Class A | 255.0.0 |
|---------|---------|
| Class B | 255.255.0.0 |
| Class C | 255.255.255.0 |

## Classful and Classless

- Classful uses the default subnet mask.

- Classless uses a customized subnet mask.

## Using Subnets

When using the default subnet mask, the full range (0–255) of subnet addresses becomes available for assignment.

For example, when a Class B address is subnetted, the available subnets are 0–255, and the available host addresses are 1–254. See Figure 9.3.

**F I G U R E  9.3**

Default subnets

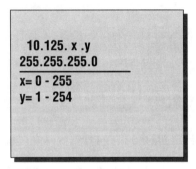

> **10.125. x .y**
> **255.255.255.0**
> _____
> x= 0 - 255
> y= 1 - 254

## Building Subnet Addresses

When building subnets, use the formula $2^n-2$, with $n$ being the number of bits available for subnet use.

## Splitting Bytes

- Addresses must have a unique number.

- The network and subnet addresses must not change for any device on their network.

- The host number cannot be set to all 1s or 0s.

## Preparations for Growth

- What are our subnet needs today?

- What will our subnet needs be tomorrow?

- How many hosts are possible on each subnet?

- What will our host needs be tomorrow?

## Supernets

The following are a few of the reasons supernets came into existence:

- Few Class C addresses have been assigned.

- Large numbers of Class B addresses have been assigned.

- Internet routing tables have grown too large to be effectively managed.

- Over time, the 32-bit IP addresses will be exhausted.

A supernet exists when two or more successive Class C addresses are blocked into one segment. This is accomplished by borrowing the last bit in the third byte and assigning it for use in host addressing.

## Supernet Requirements

- Supernets must have successive Class C IP addresses.

- The first Class C address's third byte must be evenly divisible by 2.

# CNE Practice Test Questions

1. Give two reasons for using subnet masks.

2. What is a subnet mask?

3. If you take a Class B address of 110.132.0.0 and have a subnet mask of 255.255.255.0, what is the range of subnet addresses? Host addresses?

4. What is the subnet mask of a Class C address of 125.152.38.0?

5. Complete the table.

| Subnet Mask | Subnets | Hosts on Partial Byte |
|---|---|---|
| 10000000 | 2 | 128 |
| 11000000 | | |
| 11100000 | | |

| Subnet Mask | Subnets | Hosts on Partial Byte |
|---|---|---|
| 11110000 | | |
| 11111000 | | |
| 11111100 | | |
| 11111110 | 128 | 2 |

6. What is 11111111.11111111.11100000.00000000 in decimal? What class address is it?

7. What is 255.240.0.0 in binary? What class address is it?

8. The second byte of a Class A address has been split, and the first four bits have been used for subnets (**11110000**). The IP address is 138.0.0.0, and the subnet mask is 255.240.0.0. What is the total number of hosts available? (TIP: Don't forget the third and fourth bytes.)

9. The third byte in a Class B address has been split; the first three bits have been used for subnets; the IP address is 152.152.0.0. What is the subnet mask?

10. Using the scenario from question 9, if the first subnet address is 32, then what is the range of host addresses from the third byte? If the subnet address is 140?

# CHAPTER

# 10

The TCP/IP Protocol

# Roadmap

This chapter describes the basic concepts of the TCP/IP protocol suite.

**Topics Covered**

- Comparing TCP/IP to the DOD and OSI model

- TCP/IP routing protocols

- Other TCP/IP protocols

- TCP/IP protocol analysis tools

- The next generation of TCP/IP (IPv6)

**Skills You'll Learn**

- Compare the various parts of the TCP/IP protocols suite to both the DOD and OSI models

- Describe the concepts associated with distance vector routing with IP.

- Describe the concepts associated with link state routing with IP

- Given an error condition or needed function, determine which TCP/IP protocol should be implemented

- Describe the uses of protocol analyzers on a TCP/IP network

- Identify IPv6 concepts

---

The most widely used protocol on networks today is TCP/IP, mainly because of its universal nature. Almost every major network operating system supports it. NetWare 5 supports TCP/IP in what is now called pure IP, in Novell parlance.

*Pure IP* means that no protocols, besides those specified in the TCP/IP RFCs are used in transporting data from client to server. In the past, various vendors advertised that they supported Native IP, which meant different things depending on the vendor and product you were referring to. In Net-Ware 4.*x* NetWare/IP, it meant that you would encapsulate IPX or NCP requests (discussed in Chapter 11) inside TCP/IP packets. It required that both TCP/IP and IPX be loaded. With NetWare 5, however, the clients can talk to NetWare 5 servers using TCP/IP only. All function calls are made with native protocols, like TCP and UDP.

This chapter discusses the details of the TCP/IP protocol suite and the protocols that comprise it.

# Comparing TCP/IP to the OSI and DOD Models

**C**hapters 3, 4, and 5 discussed the OSI model and the functions of each of its layers. However, the OSI model wasn't around when TCP/IP was being developed. As a matter of fact, TCP/IP was around about 10 years before the OSI model. The model that was used to describe the TCP/IP protocol at that time was the US Department of Defense (DOD) networking model.

The DOD model consists of only four layers (as opposed the OSI model's seven). The four layers are, from bottom to top:

- Network Access
- Internet
- Host-to-Host
- Process/Application

Each layer combines the functionality of each of the layers of the OSI model. The components of the TCP/IP protocol suite map very nicely to both the OSI model and the DOD model. Figure 10.1 shows how TCP/IP relates to both the DOD model and the OSI model. Note that the actual TCP/IP protocol suite specification stops at the Internet layer of the DOD model (Network layer for OSI), which means that you can run TCP/IP over any physical media, including Ethernet, Token Ring, and serial lines.

Similar to the OSI model, each layer of the DOD model specifies different functions for the protocols that operate at that layer. Table 10.1 details the layers and their associated functions.

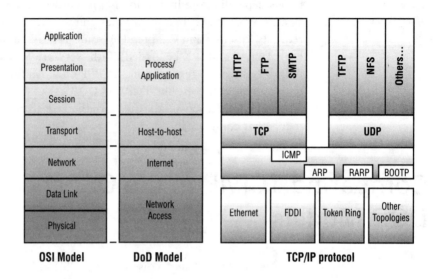

**F I G U R E  10.1**

How TCP/IP relates
to the DOD and OSI
models

| **TABLE 10.1** | **DOD Layer** | **Description** |
|---|---|---|
| DOD layer functions | Network Access | Defines the physical connections between various hosts on the network (for example, cabling systems and network topology). |
| | Internet | Defines routing and internetwork functions. This layer is the foundation of the TCP/IP protocol. |
| | Host-to-Host | Defines host-to-host communications. Responsible for reliable, end-to-end communications and delivery of data. |
| | Process/Application | Provides a user interface to the protocol. Defines data transfer application specifications. |

TCP/IP's popularity has grown mainly because of the Internet. The Internet is based on TCP/IP and many of the protocols with the TCP/IP suite are popular services on the Internet (for example, FTP, HTTP). When networks connect to the Internet, they must implement TCP/IP in order to take advantage of the services offered by the Internet.

# TCP/IP Routing Protocols

The Internet Protocol (IP) is the protocol of the TCP/IP protocol suite responsible for logical addressing and routing. Therefore, it is the protocol most involved in internetworking. IP was originally developed to be a protocol that could use multiple, redundant links to link multiple sites.

IP internetworks are special in that they can be divided into smaller, logical, manageable groups called *autonomous systems*. These systems are administrated as a whole system by a network administrator, yet retain the qualities of an internetwork.

Each of these autonomous systems uses certain protocols, called *interior gateway protocols (IGPs)* to manage routing functions. When these autonomous systems connect to other autonomous systems, they use *exterior gateway protocols (EGPs)* to do so. There are two exterior gateway protocols, Exterior Gateway Protocol (EGP) and Border Gateway Protocol (BGP).

In an autonomous system, the terms *router* and *gateway* are used interchangeably. So, routing protocols are also gateway protocols.

EGP allows routers that lie between the autonomous system and the internetwork to exchange routing information over an internetwork. Unfortunately, EGP wasn't designed for the huge internetworks that are in use today and is not very efficient when used in conjunction with them.

BGP is an improvement over EGP. It scales much better and has more features than EGP. It uses a technology known as interdomain routing to achieve its scalability.

## Routing TCP/IP with Routing Information Protocol (RIP)

TCP/IP can use a distance vector routing protocol called Routing Information Protocol (RIP). A router running RIP will collect information about its neighbor routers and what routes they know about, add that information to its own routing table, record information about its own local routes, then broadcast the entire routing table to all other routers on the network. It is a very simple routing protocol. Figure 10.2 illustrates RIP route discovery.

**F I G U R E  10.2**

RIP route discovery

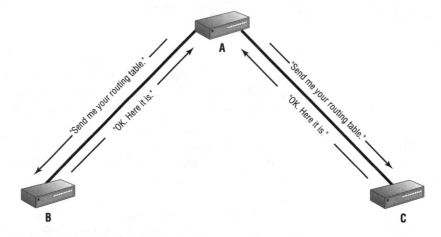

---

### IPv6: How Does it Benefit Me?

Over the last several years, IPv6 has been in development to replace the current version of TCP/IP (called IPv4). It uses a 16-byte address field (instead of the 4-byte address field of IPv4). In addition, IPv6:

- provides for user authentication

- has backward compatibility with IPv4

- has prioritization capability for delay-sensitive data (like network multimedia)

- simplifies association of MAC and IP addresses using autoconfiguration

The main reason driving the development IPv6 is the number of IP addresses available. With IPv6 there are over 1 quintillion (1,000,000,000,000,000,000) addresses available, which should be enough to assign all the PCs in the world an address, at least for now. (Remember, Bill Gates said that 640K should be enough memory for anyone.) IPv6 is discussed in more detail later in this chapter.

RIP forwards packets based on how many hops away a particular network is. If the packet has to pass through two routers on its way to its destination, it is said to have made two hops. If there are two routes to Network A, for example, and route 2 has fewer hops than route 1, the router will route all packets over route 2 because there aren't as many routers to pass through, and the packet will be delivered to its destination sooner.

The number of hops a particular route has is sometimes called that route's *metric*.

You can configure some routers to not necessarily take the route with the fewest number of hops (that is, the lowest metric), but that is usually the default. There are times when you may not want to use the route that has the fewest number of hops. For example, there might be a route that has a high-speed link to the other network, but because it has one more hop in the route, the router may think it's not the best choice. In that case, you would configure the router to take advantage of the higher speed link.

## The Count-to-Infinity Problem of RIP

The main problem of RIP is a problem known as *count-to-infinity*. It happens because RIP gathers routing tables from other routers, adds one to the metric for all routers, then rebroadcasts the routes, causing a major increase in the time required for *convergence* (the time it takes for all routers on a network to know about all routes). In Figure 10.3, if you calculate the number of hops from each router to Network 4, following the method of distance vector route discovery, Router A would show three hops from Network 4, Router B – two hops, and Router C – one hop. Suppose Router C fails. Router B will not realize that Router C has gone down and that Network 4 is unreachable. It will then only receive routing table updates from Router A, who reports that Network 4 is three hops away. Router B will add one to the hop distance and broadcast to its neighbors (now only Router A) that it is positive that Network 4 is four hops away. Router A receives this, adds one to the hop count, and sends the updates to its neighbors (including Router B), saying that Network 4 is now five hops away. This process will continue until the hop count reaches 16. When it reaches this point, Router B will drop packets destined for Network 4.

**FIGURE 10.3**

Count-to-infinity
sample network

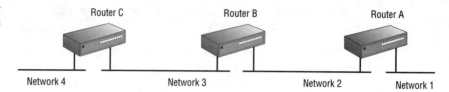

There are two solutions to this problem, enabling split horizon or poison reverse.

**Split Horizon**   With split horizon, all routing tables received on an interface will not be rebroadcast on that interface. So, in Figure 10.4, routes received by R3 from R1 on Network 2 will not be rebroadcast on Network 2. They will be broadcast on Networks A and 1, but not 2. R3 will send updates to R1, but only for networks that R1 didn't send it.

**FIGURE 10.4**

Split horizon

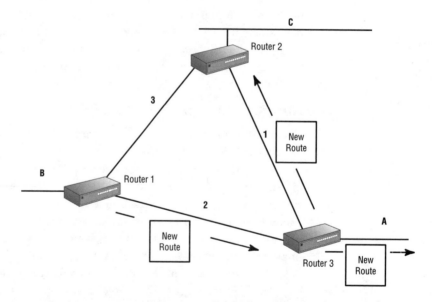

Split horizon, when enabled, will greatly decrease the amount of extra RIP traffic on a network, but because of its additional processing overhead, can increase the time needed for convergence to occur.

**Poison Reverse**   Poison reverse also prevents the count-to-infinity problem, but it does so by broadcasting the routes that it learns from a segment back to the segment as a metric of 16 (unreachable), instead of simply not broadcasting back to the segments. Figure 10.5 shows this option. If Router 3 goes down, users on Segment 2 won't try to send packets to Router 1 to get to Network 3 (as they might if the routers were using RIP without poison reverse).

**FIGURE 10.5**

RIP routing using poison reverse

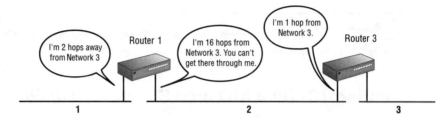

## Using RIP II

The original RIP protocol specification for TCP/IP (also now known as RIP I) was minimalistic. For example, it specified that a router would broadcast a list of all the routes it knew about and each route's associated cost or metric every thirty seconds. RIP I has been in existence so long that most routers (including a NetWare 5 server with multiple NICs acting as a router) support RIP I.

The RIP protocol needed a few updates, so it got them. It was updated to include support for several features. This updated version was designated RIP version 2 (RIP II). The new features it supports include the following:

- Multicast packets allow RIP II routers to talk to each other and reduce the load on non-RIP II routers. These multicast packets are addressed to the IP address 224.0.0.9, typically.

- Subnet masks are included in RIP II packets in the routing information, which allows for the use of variable length subnet masking so more hosts can be used per subnet.

- Next hop addresses allows the sending router to place information in the RIP II packet about which routers it should pass through on its way to its destination network. It prevents packets from being forwarded through unnecessary routers.

- Authentication allows the use of passwords to authenticate to the router for routing information updates.

If you really want to use variable length subnet masks, Open Shortest Path First (OSPF) is a much more efficient choice.

For more information on the RIP II protocol, see the RFC 1387, RFC 1388, and RFC 1389 at http://www.ietf.org.

# Routing TCP/IP with Open Shortest Path First (OSPF)

As with other link state routing protocols, Open Shortest Path First (OSPF) builds its routing information from information (like address and cost) gathered directly from the router attached to the segment in question. It then builds a network map based on this information.

OSPF uses the Hello Protocol to establish and maintain neighbor relationships, which means a router running OSPF will multicast hello packets to all its neighbors. The neighbors will respond to the hello packets detailing the networks and routers they are directly connected to. The router will build a link state database (and thus a logical network map) from this information. The router will use this information to determine the shortest path to each destination on the network.

When a router, routing with OSPF, detects a change, it forwards only the change information to all other routers in a process known as *flooding*. Flooding is when each router forwards any of these packets that it receives to all the segments it is attached to (except the segment the packet came from).

For more information on OSPF, check out RFC #'s 1245, 1246, 1247, and 1253 at http://www.ietf.org/.

## Route Discovery

There are two main steps in the OSPF route discovery process, neighbor discovery and link state database synchronization.

**Neighbor Discovery**   When routers need to discover the available routes (like when they are first brought up), they must first identify their neighbors.

Figure 10.6 shows a router that is just starting up and needs to discover its neighbors. To discover its neighbors, the router sends out hello packets. The packets contain the source router's IP address, subnet mask, priority, and hello interval. These packets are used to find out who the router's neighbors are and establish bi-directional communication between routers. The information discovered by these packets is added to the router's routing table.

**F I G U R E  10.6**

OSPF neighbor
discovery process

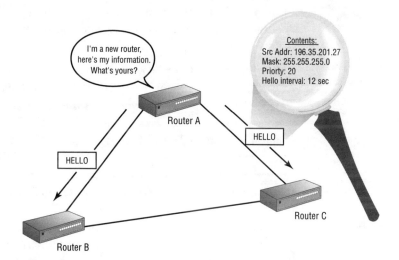

The hello packets perform several functions:

- Determine the router's neighbors

- Tell the source router's neighbors how often it will send hello packets. If a neighbor hasn't received a hello packet in the interval specified, it will determine that the source router is down.

All routers on the same network must have the same hello interval; otherwise they won't see each other as neighbors.

- Help determine the Designated Router (DR) and backup DR. Both entities' information is sent during hello exchanges. OSPF designates the router with the highest priority number assigned will become the DR, and the number with the next highest priority number will become the backup DR (BDR). If a router comes online with a higher priority than either the DR or BDR, then the new router will become the new BDR, if either the DR or existing BDR goes offline. If the existing DR goes down while the new higher priority router is online, the old BDR will become the new DR and the new router will become the BDR.

Router priorities are configurable on most routers. But if you set an OSPF router's priority to zero, it cannot become either a BDR or DR.

**Link State Database Synchronization**  In addition to neighbor discovery, OSPF also takes care of ensuring that all routers have the same link state information. The link state information is used by routers to make a kind of map of the network. All routers on the network have a list of their neighbors and their information. To ensure that all routers have the exact same information (and thus the same map of the internetwork), the DR and BDR must synchronize their link state information with all routers.

When two OSPF routers synchronize, their status changes. Before synchronization, each router is said to be in a *two-way state*. When routers become synchronized, they establish adjacency and enter what is known as the *full neighbor state*. The synchronization process moves the router from the two-way state to the full neighbor state.

The synchronization process is pretty straightforward (Figure 10.7). First, the individual routers exchange database description packets (DDPs) with both the DR and BDR (#1 in Figure 10.7). The DDPs contain a summary of each router's link state database and include the routers and segments that particular router knows about. When each router receives a DDP, it compares the information in the DDP packet with the information it has in its own neighbor's list. If the summary information in the DDP indicates the receiver's information is out of date, the receiver sends a request to the router that has the most current information for a detailed update of the information it has that is out of date. It does this in the form of a *link state request* (LSR) packet. The router that has the information replies with the updated information using a link state update (LSU) packet. When the router that originated the LSR receives the LSU containing the information, it sends a link state acknowledgment (LSA) to the sender of the information to acknowledge that it received it.

**FIGURE 10.7**

OSPF link state data-
base synchronization

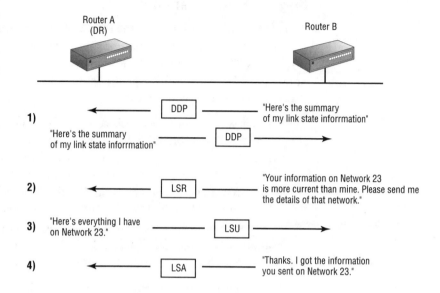

Once the synchronization process has completed for all routers, the DR
and BDR will be in full neighbor state with each router. Each router should
only be in full neighbor state with the DR and BDR.

## Route Selection

As already discussed, the link state database is a logical map of the network.
In order to route packets across an internetwork, an OSPF router must assign
costs to each interface and generate a routing table. This routing table is made
up of a listing of the networks and route the packets must take to get there.
There may be multiple routes to a specific destination and an OSPF router
must determine the best way to get there. It does this using costs. The router
determines all the possible ways a packet could get to a particular network,
calculating the costs involved on each interface, adding those costs together
and coming up with a total cost for the route from end to end. Of multiple
routes, the one with the lowest cost value is the one that is added to the
routers routing database and thus the one most (if not all) packets will take.

The process that builds the routing database only runs when a change
occurs on the network. But, if multiple changes occur to the network in a
short period of time, the router might spend all its time updating the routing
database and not forwarding packets. For this purpose, OSPF includes a
*hold-down interval* that allows a router to wait until a certain number of
changes have occurred and been added to the link state database before calculating cost and updating the routing database.

## Routing Table Maintenance

To ensure that all routers have the most current information, OSPF routers perform route maintenance by sending out LSU packets every so often (every 30 seconds, by default) and when changes occur in the network. OSPF Link State uses LSUs to maintain link state databases when no changes occur. This process uses the following steps:

- Every so often (a time that is configurable on most routers) an OSPF router will flood LSU packets for the entries in its link state database that it is responsible for (not the ones it has received from other routers). *Flooding* is the process in which a router sends link state information to all routers using the DR. To flood an LSU, the router sends the LSU to the DR, then the DR sends the packet to all its routers on the network. The DR can then also send the LSU to another DR on another network. The DR on the other network will continue the process until all routers have received the LSU.

- Whenever a router receives an LSU, it checks the information in the LSU against its link state database. If there is no change, the router simply updates the aging timer (a field indicating how long it's been since the last update to this information). If the router doesn't receive an LSU in a time period four times the router dead interval specified, it purges the corresponding entry, which ensures that the database is always current and also helps each router keep track of the status of its neighbors.

- Whenever a router receives an LSU, it automatically sends an LSA to acknowledge the receipt of the LSU. This ensures that the sending router knows that all routers are receiving their updates. It also helps the sending router determine if a route is invalid.

For all OSPF routing functions to work properly, all routers must be fully synchronized and in a full neighbor state. If something happens to a router, the process of exchanging DDP packets begins again to re-establish adjacencies.

## OSPF Terms

There are a few terms that you must understand before you can configure an OSPF internetwork.

- Autonomous System
- Autonomous System Border Routers
- Areas
- Backbone

**Autonomous System**   An *autonomous system (AS)* is a set of routers that exchange routing information and updates using a common protocol within a single administrative unit. Usually an autonomous system is one network (or internetwork) managed by the company that uses it, connected to the Internet using gateway protocols. Figure 10.8 shows an example of an OSPF autonomous system.

**FIGURE  10.8**

An OSPF autonomous
system

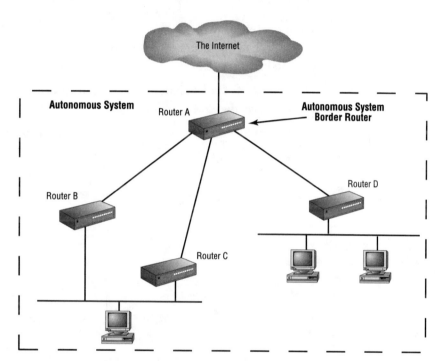

**Autonomous System Border Routers**   When you connect autonomous systems to each other into a very large internetwork (like the Internet), you must use special routing technologies to connect them. Routers that perform this function are called *autonomous system border routers (ASBRs)*.

ASBRs use gateway protocols (like EGP or BGP) to connect their autonomous system to another. As shown in Figure 10.8, Router A is the ASBR.

**Areas**   Maintaining the link state logical map of a network isn't a problem for routers on small or medium sized networks. But, with networks approaching hundreds of routers, this link state map can be huge (several Megabytes) and can take huge amounts of processing power. These factors can ensure that a large, link state internetwork will never converge.

For this reason, OSPF (and some other link state protocols as well) allow an autonomous system to be broken up into areas. OSPF *areas* are logical divisions of the internetwork (usually divided by business group, like department). Dividing an OSPF internetwork into areas reduces the amount of necessary routing table maintenance because each area gets treated like its own autonomous system and doesn't have to worry about link state information from the other areas.

Overall, dividing an OSPF autonomous system into areas provides the following benefits:

- It reduces total amount of link state information sent across the internetwork.

- It reduces the size of the link state database on each router.

- Convergence time takes much less time.

Figure 10.9 shows a network divided into areas.

**F I G U R E   10.9**

An OSPF network
divided into areas

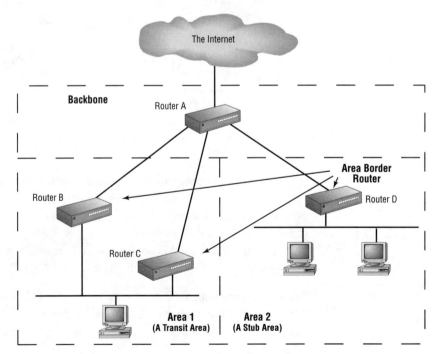

**Backbone**    An OSPF *backbone* is a special OSPF area that all the other areas in an autonomous system connect to. The backbone is illustrated in Figure 10.9.

Any router that connects an area to the OSPF backbone area is known as an area border router (ABR). This router keeps track of the fact that it is responsible for a particular area. It also manages communications between the area and the backbone.

A non-backbone area that contains only one ABR is called a *stub area*. The ABR will broadcast itself to all stations in that area as the default route for all external destinations. Unfortunately, an ASBR cannot be located in a stub area.

A non-backbone area that contains multiple ABRs (meaning there are multiple connections from the area to the OSPF backbone) is called a *transit area*.

## Comparing OSPF to RIP

OSPF has many advantages over RIP and is considered a superior protocol in most respects. Here are a few of the advantages of OSPF over RIP:

- Reduced overhead – Because OSPF only transmits the updated link state information instead of the entire routing table, there is much less extra traffic and thus lower overhead than RIP.

- Variable length subnetting – LSA Packets contain information about the subnet mask for the network. Because of the recent limited availability of IP addresses, it has become necessary to vary the lengths of subnet masks to get more hosts per network. Because of the LSA packet subnet mask field, you can use OSPF to route packets on networks with variable length subnets.

- Supports much larger internetworks – Because of the reduced overhead and variable length subnet capability, OSPF is used on much larger internetworks than RIP. With RIP, as the internetwork gets larger, the internetwork will eventually choke on all the extra routing table updates each router is sending out.

- Much Faster Convergence – Because of the lower overhead, it takes much less time for all routers to have the same routing information. OSPF is a much more efficient routing update protocol.

Using OSPF, the chance that routers will experience the count-to-infinity problem is eliminated.

# Other TCP/IP Protocols

In addition to RIP and OSPF, the TCP/IP protocol suite contains many other protocols with very specific functions. A few of them are:

- The Internet layer protocols (IP and ICMP)
- The Address Resolution protocols (ARP, RARP, BOOTP, and DHCP)
- Host-to-Host layer protocols (TCP and UDP)
- Process/Application layer protocols (FTP, TFTP, HTTP, SMTP, and SNMP)

## Internet Layer Protocols

As mentioned earlier, protocols that correspond to the Internet layer of the DOD model are responsible for routing and logical addressing. They also perform some flow control. Two of the most popular TCP/IP protocols that operate at the Internet layer are the Internet Protocol (IP) and the Internet Control Message Protocol (ICMP).

### IP

The Internet Protocol (IP) provides connectionless, non-guaranteed delivery of Transport layer packets. As these packets (also called transport protocol data units or TPDUs) are delivered to their destinations, IP can fragment them into smaller parts and reassemble them at the destination for easier delivery across internetworks. As the TPDUs are passed from Transport layer to the Network layer, IP places a header on each of the TPDUs for delivery. The header contains information about the source and IP address of the sending station and the destination IP address of the receiving station.

## ICMP

The Internet Control Message Protocol (ICMP) is used to provide error and flow control information to upper layer protocols in the TCP/IP suite. ICMP messages are sent by stations for various reasons, including:

- A packet's time to live (TTL) has expired.

- A packet was sent with a corrupt IP header.

- A packet could not reach its intended destination.

- A sending station wants to determine if a particular station is responding.

- A host needs to notify the network of downed links.

ICMP messages fall into a couple of categories:

- Echo Request and Echo Reply are probably the most popular ICMP messages. A request message is sent to an IP station to see if the station can be reached. Any IP station that receives an Echo Request will send an Echo Reply indicating that it received the request. These ICMP packet types are implemented in every IP stack and are manipulated with the popular UNIX utility PING. This process is known as pinging a station.

There is only one TCP/IP stack that doesn't directly support ICMP functions; the TCP/IP stack in Windows 95 does not have built-in ICMP functionality. The ICMP functionality is part of a separate DLL file (ICMP.DLL). If this file is missing, you cannot ping from that Windows 95 station.

- Source Quench is actually a type of flow control message, a message sent by a destination or intermediate node to the sending station saying, "Hey! Slow down! I can't keep up!" The sending station reduces its sending rate as a result of receiving this packet.

- Redirect is a type of message sent by an intermediary router informing a sending station that there is a better route to the destination. ICMP will automatically add routes to a router's routing table, unless link state routing has been configured.

- Time Exceeded means that a packet has taken too long to be delivered and has been discarded. This packet, when received by the station that originally sent the packet, instructs the station to resend the packet, possibly changing routes or other routing information.

- Destination Unreachable is a message sent to the sending station of a packet indicating that the packet cannot be delivered for any number of reasons, including a link is down or a router is misconfigured.

For more information on ICMP, read RFC 0792 at http://www.ietf.org.

**ICMP Router Discovery**   ICMP can be used by stations to discover routers on a network by transmitting an ICMP packet on the ICMP multicast address, 224.0.0.2. All routers using OSPF on the local segments will respond with their IP addresses. This process does not indicate the best route to use in a particular situation, so it is not often thought of as a route discovery protocol. It simply allows a host to determine the neighboring routers on a segment. But, if a host tries to send a packet over an inefficient route, the router will send an ICMP redirect message telling the sender to use a different route and router.

ICMP route discovery is covered in RFC 1256 at http://www.ietf.org.

## Address Resolution

IP addresses are used to identify a particular host on a network. However, the IP address is a number assigned at the Network layer. There must be a way of associating the IP address with the hardware (MAC) address of the station. For this purpose, there are two major address resolution protocols, ARP and RARP.

### ARP and RARP

The TCP/IP Address Resolution Protocol, or ARP, is used to map the dotted decimal IP address (for example, 204.57.104.23) to the MAC address of a particular host (for example, 00001E4AAA3B). With ARP, you know the IP address of the destination, but not the MAC address. ARP performs the translation and returns the MAC address associated with the provided IP address.

Reverse Address Resolution Protocol (RARP), as its name suggests, performs the exact opposite. RARP is a subset of ARP. Given a particular MAC address, RARP will provide the associated IP address. It is especially useful in determining the IP addresses of diskless workstations.

**ARP Table**   Every host has a table that maps IP addresses to MAC addresses called the ARP table. The ARP protocol is used to create entries in this table as required. If a destination's MAC address is not in the sender's ARP table, it will send a broadcast to the local segment asking all other nodes what the MAC address is for a specific host IP address. When it receives the information, it adds it to its ARP table.

The information requested by the host in response to a particular ARP request may not come from a host on the same network, but from a router on that segment that has the information about the destination MAC addresses.

In some cases, you can manipulate the ARP table yourself. You might do this if ARP is not supported by the destination host.

**Using ARP**   When trying to determine a destination host's MAC address, the sender sends out an ARP packet and waits for the ARP response containing the information (Figure 10.10). If a sender doesn't have the ARP information in its ARP table, the following process occurs:

1. The sender broadcasts an ARP that includes the destination's IP address, but all 0s in the destination's MAC address.

2. All hosts on the segment examine the ARP packet to see if their IP address matches the destination IP address.

3. If the addresses match, the station knows the packet was meant for it. It reads the senders MAC address from the ARP packet and places the address in its own ARP table and adds it own MAC address to the ARP packet. The packet is sent directly back to the original sender using a *unicast* packet (it only goes to the destination, not to every station on the segment).

4. The original sender of the ARP packet reads the reply and adds the MAC information to its ARP table.

5. The original sender can now send the data packet to the MAC address of the intended destination.

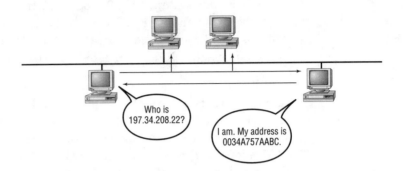

**FIGURE 10.10**

ARP address
resolution process

If the destination host is on a different network across an internetwork, the sender will address the ARP packet to the router. The router will forward the ARP request, and a router on the same segment as the destination will resolve the ARP request using the previous method.

A router can respond to an ARP request on behalf of another host using what is known as *Proxy ARP*.

**RARP and BOOTP**   In some cases, the MAC address is known, but the station needs to know its own IP address. The MAC and IP addresses are kept on a server (called a *BOOTP server*). To get its IP address, a host sends an address request to the BOOTP server. The server looks up the MAC address of the sending host in its tables and assigns it an IP address based on the information found in the table.

RARP is used to accomplish the same thing as BOOTP, but it isn't used to the same extent as BOOTP.

## DHCP

In the past few years, with the increased popularity of TCP/IP on LANs, it has become necessary to assign IP addresses and other TCP/IP parameters to hosts. BOOTP works, but only for IP addresses. Dynamic Host Configuration Protocol (DHCP) can assign a much broader range of host configuration parameters.

DHCP has two major components, a client part and a server process. The DHCP client makes a request and sends it to the server. The server examines the sending address and, using the rules specified by the network administrator, assigns the host an IP address, DNS information, and other host configuration parameters.

IP address assignments are performed in one of three ways:

- Manual Allocation – The network administrator configures the DHCP server with information about each host and which IP address each host should have. DHCP then delivers the IP addresses.

- Automatic Allocation – The network administrator indicates a block of IP addresses. Each workstation that requests an IP address gets one until the block is used up. The workstation keeps the IP address forever (or until the network administrator resets the IP address scheme).

- Dynamic Allocation – With the dwindling number of IP address blocks available, this is the most popular configuration. With this option, a workstation that requests an IP address from a DHCP server is *leased* (loaned) to the IP address for a period of time. After that time (possibly 10 hours), the IP address is considered available and another workstation can request it. Dynamic allocation is useful when not everyone on the network needs one at all times.

## The DHCP Configuration Process

DHCP saves an administrator tons of work when implementing TCP/IP. Specifically in the area of configuring host IP addresses. The network administrator only needs to ensure that the DHCP client is enabled on all hosts (all Windows *9x* stations with TCP/IP have it enabled by default). Then, they must enable the DHCP server for that segment and specify IP configurations for the server to assign. The server will assign the IP configurations to all clients that request one.

The process for address and workstation configuration assignment using DHCP is a simple, two-step process.

1. The workstation broadcasts a DHCP request asking for host configuration information on the local segment to a listening DHCP server.

2. The DHCP server examines the source address of the request to find out which segment the request came from. If the DHCP server is not configured to support that segment, it ignores the request. If it is configured to respond to requests from that segment, it responds with the requested IP configuration information.

### DHCP Relay Agents

Because DHCP uses broadcasts, and routers will not usually forward broadcasts, DHCP requests will not cross a router. So, a DHCP server in most cases would have to be located on the same segments as the hosts it is servicing. Otherwise, all DHCP requests would be dropped by the router and the server wouldn't respond to any DHCP requests because it wouldn't be getting them.

For this reason, if you want DHCP requests to cross a router, you must use a relay agent. A *relay agent* is software that runs on the router and intercepts DHCP broadcasts before they are dropped and forwards them to the DHCP server. In turn, it forwards the response back from the DHCP server to the requesting station.

For information on DHCP and relay agents, see RFC 1531 at `http://www.ietf.org/`.

## Other TCP/IP Protocols

In addition to IP, ICMP, ARP, RARP, BOOTP, and DHCP there are other components of the TCP/IP protocol suite. Some of the most popular protocols at each level of the DOD model are discussed in the following sections.

### Host-to-Host Layer Protocols

Host-to-Host layer protocols are responsible for reliable, end-to-end data communications. These protocols also provide end-to-end flow control. The two most common host-to-host layer protocols are Transmission Control Protocol (TCP) and User Datagram Protocol (UDP).

**TCP**  TCP is the primary transport protocol for TCP/IP. It provides acknowledged, connection-oriented communications from one host to another. It allows for multiple upper-layer protocol (ULP) conversions between hosts. It is a very reliable transport protocol.

**UDP**  User Datagram Protocol provides transport services as well, but it uses connectionless transport instead of connection-oriented. It doesn't have the overhead of acknowledgements. All packets are received with no acknowledgement of receipt. This has the benefit of increased performance, but the downside of possible data loss. UDP is the transport for higher-performance ULPs, like Trivial File Transfer Protocol (TFTP) and Network File System (NFS).

## Process/Application

Apart from TCP and IP, the most well known parts of the TCP/IP protocol suite are those found at the Process/Application layer of the DOD model. This is mainly because the utilities that use these protocols are often called the same name as the protocol.

A few of the most common Process/Application layer protocols and their functions are discussed in the following sections.

**HTTP**  Probably the most popular and well-known Process/Application layer protocol is the Hypertext Transfer Protocol or HTTP. It is the backbone protocol for the World Wide Web on the Internet. It is used to access content on the web servers or other servers.

HTTP uses a client-server architecture. An HTTP client (usually a web browser) contacts an HTTP server (a web server) and makes an HTTP request. This request consists of several informational fields:

- Message Type indicates what type of request is being made, either GET or PUT. This field is almost always set to GET.

- Identifier represents a Uniform Resource Identifier (URI) and indicates which resource gets the request.

- Uniform Resource Locator (URL) is the address of the document being requested (for example: www.tryme.com/index.html) and identifies to the web server which document it should return for the request.

- Protocol Version is the version of HTTP being used to make the request. If no version is specified, HTTP/0.9 is the default.

- Method is the method of information retrieval used in the request.

RFCs 822, 850, 1123, 1590, 1738, 1808, 1945 all have some specifications on HTTP, URLs, or a related topic. They can be found at http://www.ietf.org/.

**FTP**  The File Transfer Protocol (FTP) is used to transfer files between two hosts. FTP provides facilities for login, directory listing, command execution, and file download, regardless of the host operating system.

FTP uses TCP as its transport protocol and, thus, is very reliable. It can require logins before file transfer occurs. Unfortunately, it's not the fastest method of transferring files.

**TFTP**   Trivial File Transfer Protocol (TFTP) can be considered the little brother to FTP. It can do just about everything its big brother can do, but it does it faster. TFTP uses UDP as a transport protocol, so it can transfer files without the overhead of acknowledgements for each packet. It can also transfer files without logins.

It does have its limitations, however. You can't perform directory listings using TFTP. Additionally, most implementations restrict the kind of files that can be transferred using TFTP.

**SMTP**   The Simple Mail Transfer Protocol (SMTP) is almost as popular as HTTP. SMTP is a standard for exchanging electronic mail messages between TCP/IP hosts. It uses TCP as its transfer protocol. It is a common misconception that SMTP is a mail program. It is a mail transport protocol. It is the protocol that simply details how mail messages are transferred.

The nice thing about SMTP is that it is almost a universal mail transport. Almost all mail systems have a gateway (an *SMTP gateway*) that translates mail between the mail system's native format and SMTP so that it can be transmitted over the Internet to any other mail system.

SMTP details are specified in RFC 821 at `http://www.ietf.org/`.

**SNMP**   One protocol that is somewhat less known to the general Internet community, but has extensive use in larger internetwork implementations, is the Simple Network Management Protocol. It lets you request management information (like status, protocol details, and statistics) from any entity running TCP/IP and SNMP including workstations, servers, and routers.

A special station called an *SNMP manager* makes these requests. The SNMP manager sends requests to an SNMP agent running on the IP host. The types of requests you can make and the information you can gather using SNMP is specified in the agents Management Information Base (MIB).

Not all entries in every MIB are supported with a specific implementation of SNMP.

From the SNMP manager, you can request information found in the entity's MIB, or you can change the configuration of the entity. For example, you can view the statistics of how many packets have been forwarded by a particular router.

In addition to viewing and changing information, SNMP allows a device to send an alert, called an *SNMP trap*, to the SNMP console when a specific event occurs. For example, you can set the server to send an SNMP trap when the server's utilization reaches a preset threshold.

There are five main commands defined within SNMP:

- Trap – This command is sent by an SNMP agent to inform an SNMP manager of a special event.

- GetRequest – The SNMP manager uses this command to get information from an SNMP agent.

- SetRequest – The SNMP manager uses this command to change a parameter with a specific agent's MIB.

- GetNextRequest – This command works similarly to GetRequest, but is used when there are several values in a table that must be obtained. This command is issued repeatedly until all the values in the table have been received.

- GetResponse – This command contains the response to a request made by an SNMP manager.

With the size of TCP/IP internetworks and the fact that they are often connected to the Internet, the question of security comes up. With the design of SNMP, there are some basic security features built-in so that not just anyone can use management features of the network. SNMP uses designators called *community names* to establish secure communications between SNMP manager and SNMP agent. To use community names, you specify a special name for each community (listed below). The name must be specified on both the device agent and SNMP manager and can be up to 32 characters of text.

There are three basic communities used in SNMP:

- Trap Community – The trap community name is sent with all SNMP trap messages. An SNMP manager must be set up to accept traps from the same community as the devices you want to monitor. For example, you could set your trap community name on all devices to the name *network-trap*. If the SNMP manager is set to accept SNMP trap packets with the name *networktrap* in them, you can receive all traps for your network (as long as you specify that manager should receive traps for that device). The default community name for the trap community is *public*.

- Monitor Community – The SNMP monitor community name is used to grant access to the MIB of an entity. The default community name is *public*, as well.

- Control Community – If an SNMP manager has the control community name set the same as a device, then the manager can change any of the objects specified in the MIB. The control community is disabled by default, preventing unauthorized people from modifying the MIB.

Whenever configuring SNMP on your network (especially one connected to the Internet), make sure you change the default community names so that unauthorized users are not viewing or changing settings.

# TCP/IP Protocol Analysis Tools

Protocol analyzers help a network administrator gather information about the current state of the network. They can give detailed information about both lower layer protocols like IP and TCP, and upper layer protocols like HTTP and FTP. Protocol analyzers can be either hardware or software. They can monitor traffic, capture packets, and analyze the details of every packet being transmitted on the network. This tool can help you troubleshoot problems that may not be apparent without a detailed view of the network.

There are three main examples of protocol analyzers in use today:

- NetWare LANalyzer Agent in ManageWise

- Network General Sniffer

- NCC LANalyzer

# The Next Generation of TCP/IP (IPv6)

This chapter has discussed TCP/IP (IPv4). A new version of TCP/IP is being designed to overcome the limitations of classic TCP/IP. This new version is called IPv6 (or IPng). This new version will be backward compatible with the current version because of the sheer volume of IP addresses currently in use on the Internet.

IPv6 has several benefits over the current version of TCP/IP, including:

- Quality of Service (QoS) capabilities – This is the ability to reserve part of bandwidth for time-sensitive applications (like video-on-demand).

- Expanded addressing space – The address size will be increased to 128 bits (as opposed to the current 32 bits) to ensure many available IP addresses.

- Anycast address – This address supports addressing a packet to any node on a particular network (like the address *Resident* on a piece of junk mail, send it to whoever is there).

- Simplified header – Redundant header fields in the current IP header will be eliminated.

- Flexible IP header format – This format allows for future expansion of the IP protocol.

- Support for Authentication and Security – This allows TCP/IP to be a much more secure protocol and ensures data integrity.

IPv6 is discussed in more detail at `http://playground.sun.com/pub/ipng/html/ipng-main.html` or in RFC 1883 and 1924 at `http://www.ietf.org/`.

# Summary

**T**his chapter describes the TCP/IP protocol suite and all the protocols that make it up. It is a truly cross-platform protocol as every network operating system includes some functionality for TCP/IP.

## Comparing TCP/IP to the OSI and DOD Models

The DOD model is another networking model that is used to describe the TCP/IP protocol in terms of functionality. There are four layers to the DOD model (from bottom to top):

- Network Access
- Internet

- Host-to-Host

- Process/Application

Each layer corresponds approximately to a layer or two in the OSI model (as shown in Figure 10.1).

Additionally, TCP/IP maps extremely well to the DOD model, mainly because it was designed with the DOD model in mind.

## TCP/IP Routing Protocols

There are two main routing protocols: Router Information Protocol (RIP, I and II) and Open Shortest Path First (OSPF). Both protocols are internal gateway protocols (IGP).

### RIP

The RIP routing protocol has the following features/details:

- Broadcasts its entire routing table every 30 seconds.

- When a router receives routing information, it adds one to the metric of each route, adds the information to its routing table, and rebroadcasts its routing table.

- Is subject to the count-to-infinity problem (unless using split horizon or poison reverse algorithms).

- On large networks RIP can take a long time to converge.

The RIP II protocol supports all the features of RIP I, with the following additional benefits:

- Supports authentication

- Variable length subnet mask

- Next hop address

- Multicast packets

### OSPF

Open Shortest Path First (OSPF) is a link state routing protocol that uses hello packets, link state request (LSR) packets, link state update packets

(LSU), and link state acknowledgement (LSA) packets to build a logical network map of the internetwork.

In order to route packets correctly and accurately, the link state databases must be synchronized. The designated router (DR) and backup designated router (BDR) are responsible for ensuring that all routers are current (said to be in the full-neighbor state). The process involved in synchronizing all routers' link state database is as follows:

1.  The individual routers exchange database description packets (DDPs) with both the DR and BDR.

2.  When each router receives a DDP, it compares the information in the DDP packet with the information it has in its own neighbor's list.

3.  If the summary information in the DDP indicates the receiver's information is out of date, the receiver sends a link state request (LSR) to the router that has the most current information for a detailed update of the information it has that is out of date.

4.  The router that has the information replies with the updated information using a link state update (LSU) packet.

5.  When the router that originated the LSR receives the LSU containing the information, it sends a link state acknowledgment (LSA) to the sender of the information to acknowledge that it received it.

To select which route a packet will take, an OSPF router will contact its routing table, which has been built from its link state database and an algorithm which calculates which route is the most efficient route, based on cost. The routing table is rebuilt only after a certain number of changes have occurred to the network. (A hold-down interval is specified to allow multiple changes to happen after a period of time has elapsed, instead of all at once.)

Route information is maintained using LSUs. A router periodically broadcasts these LSUs to other routers to keep the databases current.

## Other TCP/IP Protocols

There are many other TCP/IP protocols in use today, categorized here by their DOD layer:

Internet layer:

- IP (Internet Protocol) is the protocol that provides routing and logical network station addressing functionality.

- ICMP (Internet Control Message Protocol) is the protocol that provides network control messages for upper layer protocols (ULPs). The most popular are Echo Request and Echo Reply (used with the PING program). It can also be used to identify routers.

- ARP (Address Resolution Protocol) is the protocol that provides a hardware (MAC) address when given an IP address as an input.

- RARP (Reverse Address Resolution Protocol) performs the opposite of ARP. Given a MAC address as an input, it specifies which IP address should be used for that host.

- BOOTP (BOOTable Protocol) performs automatic IP address assignment on a network.

- DHCP (Dynamic Host Configuration Protocol) performs the same function as BOOTP, but with many more options, including the ability to assign subnet mask, DNS information, and other configuration parameters.

Remember that neither BOOTP nor DHCP can cross a router. DHCP requires a relay agent to be able to do this.

Host-to-Host layer:

- TCP (Transport Control Protocol) provides multiple, very secure connections from client to server.

- UDP (User Datagram Protocol) is similar to TCP, but uses connectionless transport services. It has less overhead than TCP and thus has higher performance.

Process/Application layer:

- HTTP (HyperText Transfer Protocol) is the protocol of the World Wide Web. It uses TCP to provide connection-oriented delivery of documents.

- FTP (File Transfer Protocol) provides secure file transfer services using TCP and username and password authentication.

- TFTP (Trivial File Transfer Protocol) provides a similar function (in most cases) to FTP, except that it can't perform directory listings and uses UDP as a transport protocol.

- SMTP (Simple Mail Transfer Protocol) facilitates delivery of e-mail messages between two hosts using TCP as a transport.

- SNMP (Simple Network Management Protocol) allows the viewing and setting of network parameters from a central console. Additionally, it provides for the sending of special messages, called SNMP traps, when a special event occurs.

## TCP/IP Protocol Analysis Tools

TCP/IP protocol issues can be resolved using protocol analyzers. These analyzers are hardware, software, or a combination of both. Some examples of protocol analyzers are:

- Network General Sniffer

- Novell LANalyzer agent for ManageWise

- NCC LANalyzer

## The Next Generation of TCP/IP

There is a new version of TCP/IP being developed that will overcome the shortcomings of the current version of the TCP/IP protocol (IPv4). Some new features of the new version (IPv6) are:

- Anycast addressing

- Expanded addressing

- Quality of Service (QoS) capabilities

- Increased security

- Optimized header format

- Future expandability

# CNE Practice Test Questions

1. Which TCP/IP routing protocols allow for variable length subnet masking?

    **A.** RIP I

    **B.** RIP II

    **C.** OSPF

    **D.** NLSP

2. If an OSPF router is synchronized with a DR or BDR, what is said to exist between the two?

    **A.** Link

    **B.** Imbalance

    **C.** State

    **D.** Adjacency

3. Which IP routing protocol would you choose for a large internetwork with hundreds of routers?

    **A.** RIP I

    **B.** RIP II

    **C.** OSPF

    **D.** NLSP

4. Which component of the TCP/IP protocol suite provides connection-oriented, reliable transport for upper layer protocols?

    **A.** TCP

    **B.** UDP

    **C.** HTTP

    **D.** IP

**5.** Which protocol translates an IP address into a physical (MAC) address?

**A.** HTTP

**B.** TCP

**C.** ARP

**D.** UDP

**6.** Which protocol provides World Wide Web document delivery over the Internet using TCP?

**A.** TCP

**B.** ARP

**C.** RARP

**D.** HTTP

**7.** Which protocol(s) use UDP as a transport protocol?

**A.** TCP

**B.** FTP

**C.** TFTP

**D.** HTTP

**E.** BOOTP

**F.** RIP

**8.** Which protocol is used during an OSPF link state database synchronization?

**A.** RIP

**B.** LSA

**C.** TCP

**D.** HTTP

9. What else must you configure when implementing an OSPF routing environment?

   **A.** Areas

   **B.** Link state synchronization

   **C.** Distance vector table

   **D.** ARP tables

10. Which protocol(s) can gather router address information?

    **A.** ICMP

    **B.** TCP

    **C.** SMTP

    **D.** OSPF

11. What kind(s) of information is/are NOT found in the hello packet used in OSPF route discovery?

    **A.** Route information

    **B.** Neighbor information

    **C.** Hello interval

    **D.** Sender's address

# CHAPTER

# 11

## The IPX Protocol Suite

# Roadmap

This chapter covers the details of the IPX protocol suite and its associated protocols and issues.

## Topics Covered

- Overview of Internetwork Packet Exchange (IPX) and Sequenced Packet Exchange (SPX)

- IPX addressing concepts

- IPX and OSI

- Routing IPX with Router Information Protocol (RIP) and Service Advertising Protocol (SAP)

- Routing IPX with NetWare Link Services Protocol (NLSP)

- Other NetWare protocols and services

- IPX protocol analysis tools

## Skills You'll Learn

- Identify the function of the Internetwork Packet Exchange (IPX) and Sequenced Packet Exchange (SPX)

- Define and describe the use of IPX addresses

- Relate the components of IPX/SPX as they relate to the OSI model

- Describe RIP and SAP and their functions

- Explain IPX link state routing with NLSP

- Compare RIP/SAP, NLSP, and OSPF

- Identify IPX network services

- Explain the types of protocol analyzers

**U**ntil recently, the main protocol that NetWare supported from client to server was the Internetwork Packet Exchange suite, or IPX for short. IPX is based on the old Xerox Networking System (XNS) protocol developed at Xerox's Palo Alto Research Center (PARC) and is made up of several smaller protocols. It is an efficient protocol on LANs and a fairly good protocol for WANs. Most networks that have NetWare servers usually run IPX as their main protocol.

This chapter explains the background information and configuration steps of the IPX protocol. The various protocols that make up IPX are also discussed.

# Overview of Internetwork Packet Exchange (IPX) and Sequenced Packet Exchange (SPX)

**T**he IPX protocol suite is often called by its two major protocol components, *Internetwork Packet Exchange* and *Sequence Packet Exchange (IPX/SPX)*. Before NetWare 5, IPX/SPX was the native protocol for the clients and server. Other protocols were supported, but IPX/SPX had to be implemented. With NetWare 5, either TCP/IP or IPX/SPX can be used as the native protocol.

Each of the two main components provides complimentary functionality. The main function of IPX is to deliver packets across an internetwork. It is the routing component of the pair. It also provides control and file transfer abilities for higher level applications.

If you'll remember, IPX was based on Xerox's XNS. SPX, on the other hand, was based on Xerox's Sequenced Packet Protocol (SPP). SPX is the connection-oriented component of the IPX/SPX suite, meaning that it provides more reliable connections. But, because it is connection-oriented, it doesn't deliver as high a performance as IPX due to the high overhead required in establishing and maintaining the protocol connection.

# IPX Addressing Concepts

Implementing an IPX/SPX-based network requires that you understand the network address concepts that exist for IPX. An IPX network is actually fairly easy to implement because the addressing scheme is fairly easy to understand. There are four types of addresses that exist on an IPX/SPX-based network:

- IPX network address
- Internal IPX address
- Station IPX address
- Socket identifier

## IPX Network Address

*IPX network addresses* are eight-digit hexadecimal numbers (for example, A3F2451B) that uniquely identify the network segment (Figure 11.1). They are used to make IPX internetwork routing possible. When you configure IPX on a NetWare server, you tell the server what IPX network number should be assigned to that network segment. Additionally, each segment's IPX number must be unique on the network. A duplicated network address can cause problems with routing IPX packets.

**FIGURE 11.1**

IPX network number assignments

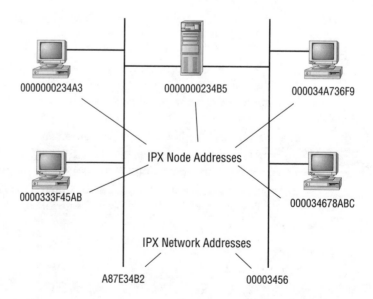

0000000234A3    0000000234B5    000034A736F9

IPX Node Addresses

0000333F45AB    000034678ABC

IPX Network Addresses

A87E34B2    00003456

The addresses 00000000, FFFFFFFF, and FFFFFFFE are reserved for special use on an IPX network and cannot be used for network addresses.

You can pick any eight-digit hexadecimal number for an IPX address. If you want to make sure that the address you are using is globally unique, you can apply for registered IPX network numbers from the Novell Network Registry. Contact them at 1-408-577-7506 or by Internet e-mail at registry@novell.com.

## Internal IPX Address

When installing NetWare 5, you are presented with an eight-digit (four-byte) hexadecimal number (for example, 387F38AB) that is called the *internal IPX address*. The number that appears during installation is a randomly generated number, but you have the option of changing it. The internal IPX address enables the server to perform internal routing to upper layer protocols. It is this address, not the broadcasting name, that is used to uniquely identify a NetWare server on an IPX network.

Even though NetWare 5 can operate completely on TCP/IP, it still requires that an internal IPX network number be assigned.

Each internal IPX address must be unique on an internetwork. If there are duplicates, neither server will be able to be seen on the network, which can create a problem.

## Station (Node) IPX Address

The *station (node) address* is a 12-digit (six-byte) hexadecimal number. To make configuration easy, the node address for IPX was designed to use the hardware (MAC) address of the network interface card as the IPX node address.

Each device on a segment must have a unique node address. If there are duplicates, neither station will be able to communicate with the rest of the network.

When a packet is addressed to the internal network, the node address is always 000000000001.

## Socket Identifiers

Within each server there are several processes running. When a sending workstation is addressing an IPX packet, it needs to specify which service (for example, RIP, NCP, SPX) the packet is destined for on the server. It does this using special addresses called *socket identifiers* (also called socket ID's or socket numbers). Each service is given a unique socket ID. These IDs are usually not assigned by an administrator but by the designers of the various services and protocols.

# IPX and OSI

IPX, like most protocols, is modular and doesn't fit well into any model, including the OSI model. However, there are some generalizations you can make about the mapping of the specific protocols within the IPX protocols suite. Figure 11.2 shows how the IPX protocol suite roughly maps to the OSI model.

**FIGURE 11.2**

Mapping IPX to the OSI model

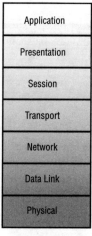

**OSI Model**

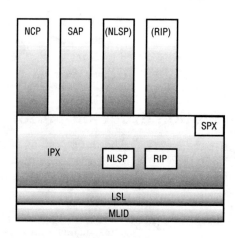

**IPX Protocol Suite**

The following sections cover the specifics of how both IPX and SPX map to the OSI model.

## IPX Mapping to the OSI Model

As you saw in Figure 11.2, IPX maps roughly to the Network and Transport layers of the OSI model. It is a connectionless protocol that performs inter-network routing and logical network addressing. IPX uses protocols such as NetWare Link Services Protocol (NLSP) and Routing Information Protocol (RIP) to compile information about the various networks that exist.

In addition to the network functions of route discovery and logical network addressing, IPX has components for transport reliability and flow control. It is responsible for ensuring that an IPX datagram reaches the intended destination. Figure 11.3 shows the components of an IPX packet.

**FIGURE   11.3**

IPX packet layout

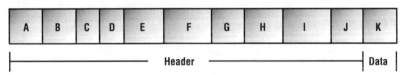

A - (2 bytes) Checksum value
B - (2 bytes) Total Packet length
C - (1 byte)  Transport Control
D - (1 byte)  Packet Type
E - (4 bytes) Destination network address
F - (6 bytes) Destination Host address
G - (2 bytes) Destination Socket Address
H - (4 bytes) Source Network Address
I - (6 bytes) Source Host Address
J - (2 bytes) Source Socket Address
K - Data

## SPX Mapping to the OSI Model

The main transport layer functionality of the IPX protocol suite is handled by SPX. It provides the connection-oriented packet delivery for IPX. It also provides packet fragmentation, sequencing, and reassembly for packets that are too big for the Data Link layer.

SPX provides its connection-oriented services by using connection identifiers (connection IDs). Connection IDs allow for virtual circuits between sending and receiving processes. Figure 11.4 shows the components of an SPX packet.

**FIGURE 11.4**

SPX packet layout

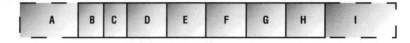

A - (30 bytes) IPX Header information
B - (1 byte)   Connection Control
C - (1 byte)   Datastream Type
D - (2 bytes)  Source Connection ID
E - (2 bytes)  Destination Connection ID
F - (2 bytes)  Packet Sequence Number
G - (2 bytes)  Acknowledgement Number
H - (2 bytes)  Allocation Number
I - (Variable) Data

# Routing IPX with Router Information Protocol (RIP) and Service Advertising Protocol (SAP)

**E**very protocol has to have a method of discovering what services are available on the network. IPX uses two protocols, *Router Information Protocol* (RIP) and *Service Advertising Protocol* (SAP), to aid in the discovery of network services. When a client wants to exchange information with a server, it has to know where all the services are on the network. IPX performs that function with RIP and SAP.

## Distance Vector Routing with IPX

RIP and SAP work together to discover where all the network services are. When IPX needs to learn routes on an internetwork using distance vector route discovery methods, it uses RIP to determine the routes and SAP to advertise them to the network. Both protocols are used for both router updates and client to server communications.

### Router Information Protocol (RIP)

Router Information Protocol is the distance vector route discovery protocol that IPX uses. It uses hops and ticks to determine the cost for a particular route. It is implemented as a network service, but performs Network layer routing functionality.

IPX RIP and TCP/IP RIP (discussed in Chapter 10) are not the same, even though they use the same acronym. Both are mutually exclusive to their respective protocol suites.

**RIP Use**   If you'll remember from Chapter 7, because RIP is a distance vector route discovery protocol, all routers that use it must transmit their entire routing tables to their local neighbors. Each neighbor then adds one to the hop count, updates the local routing tables, and transmits them to their neighbors.

Routers will transmit their routing tables on five specific occasions:

1. When a request is received from another router requesting routing updates, the entire routing table is transmitted to the requesting station.

2. When RIP detects a change in any route, the router detecting the change will broadcast its routing table to the network.

3. When a router is brought offline, it broadcasts the fact that all routes directly on the other side of it are now unreachable. It accomplishes this by broadcasting its routing table with all hops to reach destination fields set to 16 (or whatever the current routing software allows as the maximum number of hops).

4. When a router is brought online, it reports the segments it knows about and announces its availability by broadcasting its routing table.

5. To ensure that all routers have the most current information, all routers broadcast their entire routing table every 60 seconds.

**RIP Packet Construction**   The RIP protocol has two types of packets, requests and responses. Both packets have a similar construction. Each packet consists of several fields. Some of the fields are:

- Network Address contains the address of the network that is being reported.

- Hops Away contains the number of routes between the router and the network being reported.

- Packet Type indicates which type of packet is being sent, a request or response.

- Time (in ticks) indicates how long (in 1/18ths of a second) it takes to reach the network being reported.

Each RIP packet can contain information on up to 50 different networks.

**Route Discovery Process** Every IPX router that uses RIP to discover routes follows the same process to discover them. Each router first advertises its own local segments and routes. Then it broadcasts a route request to its local neighbors, asking for their routing information tables. When a neighboring router receives a request, it replies with the information it knows about the entire internetwork. The router that made the original request receives the routing tables from the other router and incorporates the information into its own routing table, after adjusting the hop count. Finally, the router is ready to advertise the information it has learned, minus any split horizon exclusions. Figure 11.5 illustrates this process.

**FIGURE 11.5**
IPX RIP route
discovery

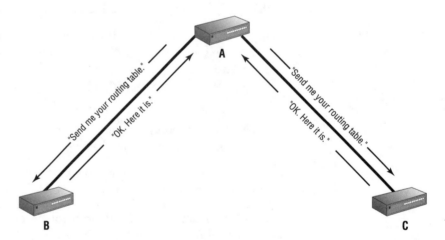

## Service Advertising Protocol (SAP)

SAP is used to advertise the existence of services on an IPX network. All servers on a network will send out SAP packets for the different services hosted on that server: services like file services, print services, and remote console services.

Each router has an agent for SAP packets that maintains a table of all the services on the network. This table is known as a *server* (or services) *information table*. Every client that needs to find a service will contact the nearest SAP agent to find out where to locate the server that is hosting the service.

Every so often, the routers will broadcast their server information to the other routers so that all the routers have current information about which services are on the network. In that respect, SAP is a lot like RIP in that it periodically sends out the information it knows about.

There are three types of SAP packets sent out on a network to broadcast the existence of specific services:

- SAP service queries are sent by a client to determine the names and services located on specific server.

- SAP service responses are the packets that are sent in response to SAP service queries. There are two types, general service and nearest service. General service responses are sent in response to broadcasts, and nearest service responses are sent in reply to specific queries.

- Every server broadcasts SAP packets when it is brought online. During these broadcasts, the server sends information about itself to everyone on the network. Additionally, the server will re-identify itself every so often (every 60 seconds, by default) using a service identification packet.

**Service Discovery with SAP**   Service information tables are updated in much the same way that routing information tables are updated. First, the router advertises its own services, if any. Then the router broadcasts a request (using a service request packet) to all connected segments. The neighboring routers (and servers) will respond with the information they have about the services they know about on the network. The originating router records the information in its own tables, then turns around and advertises the new services it knows about along with its own information.

You can use the NetWare console command TRACK ON to track RIP and SAP traffic on a NetWare server.

**Filtering SAP on WAN Links**   SAP traffic can become unwieldy in an IPX-based WAN environment. Because of the sheer number of SAP broadcasts that occur (every server, every 60 seconds), it sometimes becomes necessary to filter unnecessary SAP traffic from the WAN. This can be done at the router. You can set the router to filter all SAP traffic from the WAN, or at least reduce it to inbound or outbound only.

NetWare 5 includes a new feature, WAN Traffic Manager, that, when installed on a server acting as a WAN router, can be used to schedule WAN traffic. This has the benefit of reducing total WAN traffic. This functionality can also be found in some routers.

# Routing IPX with NetWare Link Services Protocol (NLSP)

**N**LSP is the link-state routing protocol used by IPX. It replaces the RIP/ SAP communication between IPX routers. It is used most often in IPX internetworks to increase performance. It has advantages over IPX similar to OSPF over IP RIP; for example, it uses less bandwidth and is quicker to converge.

There are three terms you must understand when discussing NLSP.

- *Link* is the connection between two routers. A link is made when both routers on each side of the connection recognize each other.

- *Adjacency* refers to a router's immediate neighbors.

- *Designated router* (DR) is a router elected to speak for all other routers on a network. It performs special functions and has special responsibilities on a network. Every NLSP network has a DR.

## Learning Services and Routes

Like RIP routers, NLSP routers must learn their routes before they can forward packets. This section describes the method used by NLSP to discover routers and services on the network.

### Step 1: Learning the Adjacency Database

Every NLSP router must learn about its immediate neighbors before routing can take place. It does this by exchanging *hello* packets. Hello packets allow an NLSP router to inform other routers of its status, the routers it knows about, and its priority (discussed later).

When a hello packet is received, the information contained in that packet is added to the adjacency database, so the router knows about its neighbors. The adjacency database is a link state packet. There are four main fields in the adjacency database:

- Priority is the value used by routers to determine which router is the DR. The highest value in this field indicates the DR.

- System Identification (ID) indicates the internal IPX address of the designated router.

- Physical (MAC) Address indicates the MAC address of the specified router.

- Holding Time is how long before this router should expect to wait before receiving another hello packet from the specified router. It is also used to tell if a router is no longer available. If a packet is not received from the specified router in the specified time, this router will know that the specified router is probably down.

## Step 2: Automatically Electing a Designated Router (DR)

The designated router is the router responsible for creating a pseudonode, managing database synchronization, and translating information from RIP/SAP routers (all discussed later in this section). A DR is selected using the priority number contained in the hello packet. Each NLSP router is configured with a priority number. The router with the highest priority value will become the DR. If two routers have the same priority, the tie is broken by examining the MAC address of both routers. The one with the highest MAC address becomes the DR.

## Step 3: Creating a Pseudonode

After each router has an adjacency database and the DR has been elected, a link state database must be created for each router. The *link state database* is the router's own map of the internetwork. In order for packet forwarding to occur successfully, each router must have the same link state database. But, before a link state database can be created for each router, the DR needs to create a pseudonode.

The *pseudonode* is an imaginary node that all routers on the network connect to. All routers think they are directly connected to the pseudonode, and the pseudonode is represented as being connected directly on all routers on the network. The reason for the pseudonode is so that link state information does not have to be kept for all nodes on the internetwork. Figure 11.6 illustrates a sample internetwork and the pseudonode layout for it.

The DR is responsible for maintaining and acting on behalf of the pseudonode. It sends out link state packets including the links from each router to the pseudonode. The DR also can send packets as the pseudonode. It represents the pseudonode until the DR is removed from the network.

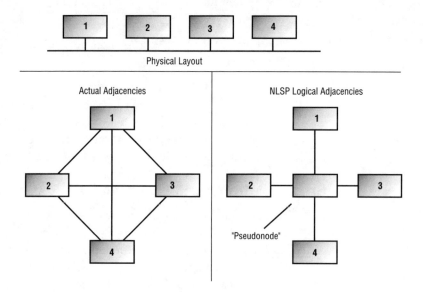

If a new DR is elected, several things happen:

1. The outgoing DR sends a link state packet (LSP) that indicates it is no longer representing the pseudonode. It purges all pseudonode LSPs.

2. The new DR purges the old DR's pseudonode link state packets from the link state database. It then creates new LSPs for the new pseudonode.

3. The old DR and all the other routers broadcast and forward new LSPs that indicate the link to the new pseudonode.

## Step 4: Building the Internetwork Map

When a router has connected to the pseudonode, it is ready to begin exchanging link state information to help all routers create an internetwork map. It exchanges information with other routers using LSPs. LSPs contain information about the router such as its name, network number, links it is connected to, and other management information.

After a router has made several LSPs, it floods them to the network. Each router that receives an LSP adds the LSP to its link state database. Eventually, all routers on the network will have the same link state database. With the information contained in this database, a router can build a logical map of the internetwork, including routers and their connected segments.

# Route Selection

When the router knows about all the other routers, the internetwork can make determinations about the best route for packets to take. NLSP routers use a forwarding database for route selection. It works similarly to the RIP routing information table. There are a couple of differences, however:

- The forwarding database is a result of a calculation performed on the link state database.

- Routes are selected by cost, not hops or ticks. Cost is a special number assigned to each network interface that includes those factors, plus others like line speed. The best route is the one with the lowest cost.

- The forwarding database is separate from the link state database, which has the advantage of improved performance, because the router doesn't have to run the route calculation before it floods new information.

- The forwarding database can store up to eight routes that are of equal cost for a given network. This information is used in case there isn't one single route with a lowest cost. In the case of multiple same-cost routes, each route (up to eight) is stored in the database so that the sending router can perform load balancing across them. If a new, lower cost route is discovered, all same-cost route entries are replaced in the database with the newer, low-cost route information.

- The forwarding database gets rebuilt every time a change occurs in the link state database.

To prevent the continuous recalculation of the forwarding database information, the router waits a specified time (called the *hold-down interval*) between calculations of the forwarding database information.

When creating the forwarding database, the NLSP router must first initiate the calculation algorithm (after first making sure the link state database is created). Then, it calculates the cost for each path to a specific network across the internetwork and prioritizes the ones with the lowest total cost.

Total cost is determined for the route between destinations by adding the costs for each route it travels over. For example, if a router had to send a packet to a network, and that network was connected by three other networks to this network, each with a cost of 25, the total cost would then be 75 for that particular route. But, if there were a different route between here and there with a cost of 80, the multi-hop route would still be the best choice, according to the rules of NLSP routing.

NLSP allows a maximum path cost of 1023. Each interface can have a cost value between 1 and 63.

The final step in rebuilding the forwarding database is to enter the results of the cost calculation into the forwarding database. Each entry contains the route (network number), next hop, and cost for each route. The router will now use this information to route packets.

## Maintaining Routes

In addition to learning and selecting routes, NLSP must also be able to make sure that each router has the most current link state database entries. NLSP performs the following functions when maintaining routes:

- Synchronizing router information across the network

- Notifying routers of a change

## Synchronizing Router Information across the Network

If you'll recall, the designated router (DR) is responsible for ensuring that all routers on the same internetwork are synchronized to the same link state database. It uses packets called *complete sequence number packets* (CSNPs) to send all routers a summary of its link state database. When a router compares the CSNP to its own internal link state database, it can do one of several things:

- If the CSNP contains information that is the same as the router's link state database, the router does nothing.

- If the CSNP contains information about a route that the receiving router doesn't have, the receiving router will send the DR a *packet sequence number packet* (PSNP) to request the full copy of the route information for the route it doesn't have in its link state database.

- If the CSNP information is out of date, or routes are missing that the receiving router knows about, the receiving router will send all routers on the network the updated link state packets (LSPs).

Sometimes, multiple routers flood information about the same route. However, one router will typically have started transmitting before the rest. If a router is flooding LSPs and receives LSPs that have been marked as being flooded from another router with the same information, it will stop flooding its own LSPs.

Figure 11.7 summarizes the link state database synchronization process.

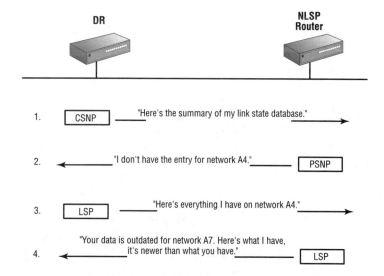

**F I G U R E   11.7**

Link state database synchronization

## Notifying Routers of a Change

Network changes happen constantly. Like RIP/SAP, NLSP must have a way of notifying all routers of these network changes. While RIP/SAP simply broadcasts the entire routing table and every router updates the information and rebroadcasts the information, NLSP uses link state packets (LSPs), which every router will flood (forward without updating the packet). So, all routing change information is firsthand from the router that detected the change. In addition, only the change is sent, not the entire database.

When a change occurs, the router that detects it will send out an LSP with the change to all routers. All routers will receive the information, read the information, update their own link state database, and flood it out each interface (except the one it received it on). Additionally, each packet has a sequence number. If a router receives an LSP and compares the sequence number to the LSPs it has received and if the LSP has already been received by that router, the router will discard it. Figure 11.8 illustrates this process.

**FIGURE 11.8**

Change notification
with NLSP

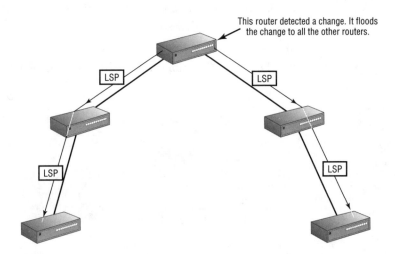

Using this method, both the count-to-infinity and the slow convergence (how long it takes for all routers to know about new information) problems of RIP/SAP are overcome.

Also, the link state database uses an aging time to indicate when a specific LSP entry is outdated. To ensure that the LSPs don't expire often, each router broadcasts all the LSPs it is responsible for during an LSP change or every two hours, which keeps the LSPs current.

When a link goes down, a router floods an LSP indicating that the specified link is down. Any routers that receive this packet don't immediately delete unreachable routes from their link state database. Instead, they flag these LSPs as unreachable. The LSPs will expire eventually if the link is not brought back up before the aging time expires the entry, preventing massive reconfiguration traffic if a link is down for only a few moments (for example, during routine maintenance).

## DR and IPX RIP/SAP Routers

NLSP is backward compatible with RIP/SAP through a gateway of sorts. The DR in an NLSP environment performs RIP/SAP to NLSP translation so that RIP/SAP information can be propagated throughout and NLSP network. It does this using pseudonode LSPs.

## Comparing NLSP and RIP

There are two main similarities between NLSP and RIP. They are both routing information protocols, and they both use a hop and tick count in determining the best route for a packet. From there, the differences begin. One of the biggest differences between them is that RIP uses broadcasts and second-hand information from its neighbors to update its routing tables. NLSP, on the other hand, uses first-hand information from the router that has the routing information.

Additionally, RIP has a maximum hop count of 15 hops before a destination is considered unreachable (a hop count of 16 is considered unreachable). NLSP has a maximum hop count of 126 (127 is considered unreachable).

Finally, a RIP router will update other routers by broadcasting its entire routing table. Whereas, an NLSP router will only send out the change; thus, it has less overhead.

Because of these benefits, NLSP makes a much better choice for routing IPX in a WAN environment. It's more efficient and eliminates the need for constant SAP broadcasts for routing information. It also makes much more intelligent decisions about the routes for specific packets.

## Comparing OSPF and NLSP

As discussed in Chapter 10, Open Shortest Path First (OSPF) is commonly implemented in very large WAN environments (primarily those running TCP/IP). It is also a link state protocol that functions similarly to NLSP. Table 11.1 shows the OSPF packet types and their corresponding NLSP packet types. Table 11.2 shows the different database types of OSPF and NLSP.

| T A B L E  11.1 | OSPF Packet | NLSP Packet | Information |
|---|---|---|---|
| Comparing OSPF and NLSP Packets | Hello | Hello | OSPF hello packet—includes the subnet mask |
| | LSU | LSP | Link state update packet—includes all link state advertisements |
| | DDP | CSNP | Database description packet—not sent periodically like CSNPs are |
| | LSR | PSNP | Link state request |
| | LSA | - | Link state acknowledgement—special reply packet used when an LSU or DDRP is received |

| T A B L E  11.2 | NLSP Database | OSPF Database |
|---|---|---|
| Comparing OSPF and NLSP Databases | Adjacencies database | Neighbors list |
| | Forwarding database | Routing table |
| | Link state database | Link state advertisement database |
| | - - - - | Interfaces list—includes cost, hello interval time, and DR/BDR flag |

# Other NetWare Protocols and Services

NetWare supports many protocols and services. Each of them resides above the Network layer and provides functionality for clients. A few of the most common protocols and services are:

- Application services
- NetWare Core Protocol (NCP)

- Multiple Link Interface Driver (MLID)
- Link Support Layer (LSL)

## Application Services

*Application services* are the upper-layer processes that provide network functionality to clients. The functionality includes file services, print services, mail services, communication services, and database services. These application services are typically implemented as NetWare Loadable Modules (NLMs). They can use many lower-layer protocols (for example, the Transport layer) including NCP, TCP/IP, SPX, and IPX.

## NetWare Core Protocol

The *NetWare Core Protocol* (NWCP) is the core protocol for the functionality of NetWare. NetWare client software make NCP requests (calls) to the basic functions and services of a NetWare server. The services respond with NCP replies.

NCP can run over IPX (its standard configuration) or TCP/IP (an optional configuration).

Each NCP request contains a function code that tells the receiving server which server the request is meant for.

Since the development of NetWare 5, TCP/IP is the default protocol. NCP has been redesigned to work with TCP/IP.

## Multiple Link Interface Driver (MLID)

The Multiple Link Interface Driver (MLID) is a piece of software that controls and understands a network card. It is simply a network card driver made by the NIC's manufacturer that complies with Novell's Open Data Link Interface (ODI) specifications. An MLID allows multiple protocols to run over a single network interface.

### Link Support Layer (LSL)

The *Link Support Layer* is a component of the Open Data Link Interface specification that allows communication between the MLID and upper-layer protocols. It acts as a switchboard to enable multiple protocols over a single network board.

# IPX Protocol Analysis Tools

There are many tools used to analyze protocols at the various OSI model layers. The following sections cover the details of a few of them and their relationship to the OSI model.

## Time Domain Reflectometer

This tool is commonly used by cabling technicians to troubleshoot Physical layer problems, like cable breaks and wrongly configured plugs. A Time Domain Reflectometer (also called TDR) sends out signals to a responder device and record the details of the return signal. It is sometimes sold as a separate device or incorporated into other, more complex protocol analyzers.

## LANalyzer for Windows

Novell sells a software protocol analyzer that can analyze protocols from the Application layer down to the Physical layer. It runs under Windows 3.*x*, Windows 9*x*, and Windows NT. It can be used to perform packet analysis at multiple layers, as well as to provide performance analysis and trend information.

## ManageWise

ManageWise, made and distributed by Novell, is a comprehensive network management system. It includes components for server management, protocol analysis, network trend tracking, segment monitoring, and centralized workstation and network management. It uses server-based agents and a centralized management console to provide a total network management package. It also has functions for snap-in components from other network management suites (SNMP, for example).

### Network General Sniffer

The first, and best, protocol analyzer is probably the Sniffer, made by Network General. It is a hardware and software solution that can detect, decode, and analyze almost any protocol. It is so good and so widely used that almost any protocol analyzer became known as a network sniffer.

# Summary

This chapter describes the details of the Internetwork Packet Exchange protocol and its related protocols.

## Overview of Internetwork Packet Exchange (IPX) and Sequenced Packet Exchange (SPX)

- The IPX/SPX protocol suite is based on Xerox's Xerox Network Systems (XNS) network protocol. The subset protocol SPX is based on the Xerox protocol SPP (Sequenced Packet Protocol).

- The IPX protocol's functions include:

  - Logical network addressing

  - Routing

  - Connectionless information transfer

- The SPX protocol's functions include connection-oriented information transfer.

## IPX Addressing Concepts

- An IPX network address is an eight-digit (four-byte) hexadecimal number assigned to a particular network segment. There cannot be duplicate numbers on the same network.

- An internal IPX address is an eight-digit (four-byte) hexadecimal number assigned to an IPX server and used to uniquely identify a server on the network. Duplicated addresses will hide both servers from the network.

- A station (node) IPX address is a 12-digit (six-byte) address used to uniquely identify the node on the network. The node IPX address is actually the same as the hardware (MAC) address of the network interface card IPX is bound to.

- A socket identifier (also called a socket number) uniquely identifies the sending and receiving service.

 Remember that IPX addresses 00000000, FFFFFFFF, and FFFFFFFE are reserved for special uses.

## IPX and OSI

- IPX roughly maps to the Network layer of the OSI model, because it performs functions like routing and logical network addressing.

- SPX is a Transport layer protocol that performs connected-oriented datagram delivery. It also performs message segmentation, sequencing, and reassembly for messages too large to fit in the Data Link layer frame size.

## Routing IPX with Router Information Protocol (RIP) and Service Advertising Protocol (SAP)

- RIP (Router Information Protocol) is a distance vector routing protocol that IPX uses to perform the function of route discovery.

- SAP (Service Advertising Protocol) is a broadcast protocol used to advertise various network services to the rest of the network.

- RIP and SAP work together to route client messages around the network.

- RIP and SAP are used for both client to server and client to router communications.

## RIP

- RIP is implemented as a service and has its own socket address.

- IPX routers transmit routing information on five occasions:

  - When a request is received from another router requesting routing updates

  - When RIP detects a change in any route

  - When a router is brought offline

  - When a router is brought online

  - Every 60 seconds

- RIP uses requests and responses to exchange information between routers. Each packet contains information about the network address of the route in questions, how far away it is, and how long it takes to reach the network.

- A RIP router follows this process to discover routes:

  1. Each router first advertises its own local segments and routes.

  2. A router broadcasts a route request to its local neighbors, asking for their routing information tables.

  3. When a neighboring router receives a request, it replies with the information it knows about the entire internetwork.

  4. The router that made the original request receives the routing tables from the other routers and incorporates the information into its own routing table, after adjusting the hop count.

  5. The router is ready to advertise the information it has learned, minus any split horizon exclusions.

## SAP

- SAP packets advertise services on the network.

- Services that are found are recorded in a server information table, also called a services table.

- There are three types of SAP packets found on an IPX network:

  - SAP service queries

  - SAP service responses

  - Periodic SAP information broadcasts

- SAP uses the following steps to learn about services on a network:

  1. A router advertises its own services, if any.

  2. A router broadcasts a request (using a service request packet) to all connected segments.

  3. The neighboring routers (and servers) respond with the information they have about the services they know about on the network.

  4. The originating router records the information in its own tables then turns around and advertises the new services it knows about along with its own information.

- It is beneficial to filter SAP in a WAN environment.

# Routing IPX with NetWare Link Services Protocol (NLSP)

NetWare Link Services Protocol (NLSP) is the link state routing protocol that IPX uses. It has many advantages over RIP/SAP and is much more scalable. Three terms for link state routing you must know:

- Link is a connection between routers.

- Adjacency means a router's immediate neighbors.

- Designated Router (DR) is a router that represents and manages all other routers on an NLSP network.

## Learning Services and Routes

There are four steps to learning routes on an NLSP-based IPX network:

1. Send hello packets to learn your adjacent neighbors and build the adjacency database (link state packet).

   - Hello packets from each router contain information about the segments that router knows about.

   - During the exchange, each router creates an adjacency database (a link state packet, or LSP).

- Each LSP contains system ID, priority, physical address, and holding time.

2. Elect a designated router (DR).

- The router with the lowest advertised priority value in its hello packet becomes the DR.

- The DR has three responsibilities:

  - Creating a pseudonode

  - Managing database synchronization

  - Translating RIP/SAP transmissions into NLSP routing information

3. Create a pseudonode.

- The pseudonode is an imaginary node that represents all the routers on the network. All the routers logically connect to the pseudonode.

- The pseudonode is used to reduce the size of most link state packets.

- The DR sends packets on behalf of the pseudonode.

4. Build a map of the network using link state packets.

- Each router sends LSPs with information about the links it and its neighbors have.

- The LSPs are flooded to the entire internetwork.

- Flooding is the process the routers perform when a packet (in this case an LSP) is received, read, and interpreted, then forwarded without modification.

- Each router that receives an LSP adds the information to its link state database.

## Route Selection

- A forwarding database contains information about the best route to take when reaching a particular segment.

- The best route is chosen using the idea of lowest cost. Cost is determined by the speed of links between routers, the number of hops to the segment, and the number of ticks it takes to reach the segment.

- The forwarding database is rebuilt when there is a change. It will, however, wait for a specified amount of time (called the hold-down interval) before recalculating costs.

- NLSP has the capability of load balancing across multiple routes, if their costs are the same.

## Maintaining Routes

To synchronize link state databases between the DR and other routers:

- Every so often the DR sends complete sequence number packets (CSNPs) with a summary of the link state database to other routers.

- The routers compare their link state database to the CSNP and send a request to the DR for information if their link state database has an entry that is out of date. This is accomplished using a partial sequence number packet (PSNP). The DR then floods an LSP to the network that includes the new information.

- If the information in the DR's link state database is out of date, the router will send out new LSPs with the new information.

To notify all routers on an internetwork of a network change:

- Routers will flood LSP packets containing only the change onto the network to all routers.

- Changes are received by all routers very quickly because all routers receive change information from the router that discovered it, not second-hand.

- The link state databases use an aging timer to note when an LSP entry has expired.

## DR and IPX RIP/SAP Routers

Networks that use NLSP can communicate with networks that use RIP/SAP by using the DR as a kind of gateway. The DR translates RIP/SAP routing information into NLSP format. RIP routes are known to NLSP routers as external routes.

## Comparing NLSP and RIP

RIP:

- Uses hops and tick counts to determine best route

- Has a maximum of 15 hops (16 is unreachable)

- Gets updates second-hand from other routers

- Broadcasts its entire routing table every 60 seconds

NLSP:

- Uses hops and tick counts to determine best route

- Has a maximum of 126 hops (127 is unreachable)

- Gets updates first-hand from the router that finds the change

- Floods only the changes

- Is better for use on a WAN than RIP/SAP

- Stores a complete map of the network

### Comparing OSPF and NLSP

(See Figure 11.2 earlier in this chapter.)

## Other NetWare Protocols and Services

In addition to the routing protocols, IPX has several other protocols and services that run with it. Some of them include:

- Application services

- NetWare Core Protocol (NCP)

- Multiple Link Interface Driver (MLID)

- Link Support Layer (LSL)

## IPX Protocol Analysis Tools

There are several protocol analysis tools commonly used on NetWare networks:

- Time Domain Reflectometers

- LANalyzer for Windows

- ManageWise

- Network General Sniffer

# CNE Practice Test Questions

1. Which of the following apply to IPX routers that use RIP?

   A. They are not reliable.

   B. They suffer from the count-to-infinity problem.

   C. They are used most often on a WAN link.

   D. They support up to 126 hops.

2. Which of the following apply to IPX routers that use NLSP? (Choose all that apply.)

   A. They are not reliable.

   B. They suffer from the count-to-infinity problem.

   C. They are used most often on a WAN link.

   D. They support up to 126 hops.

3. IPX corresponds closely to which layer of the OSI model?

   A. Network

   B. Transport

   C. Data Link

   D. Physical

4. SPX corresponds closely to which layer of the OSI model?

   A. Network

   B. Transport

   C. Data Link

   D. Physical

5. Which routing protocol is based on link state route discovery?

   A. IPX

   B. SPX

**C.** RIP

**D.** NLSP

6. Which routing technology uses SAP for service discovery?

**A.** IPX

**B.** SPX

**C.** RIP

**D.** NLSP

7. Which is NOT a function of the DR in an NLSP network?

**A.** Create a pseudonode

**B.** Remain offline until a router malfunctions, then take over the function of that router

**C.** Transmit, receive, and convert information to and from RIP/SAP routers to allow NLSP and RIP networks to communicate

**D.** Manage the synchronization between the DR and individual routers on a particular network

8. When a RIP router is brought offline, it broadcasts its routing information and the fact that routes it provides are unavailable.

**A.** True

**B.** False

9. What protocol should be filtered on a WAN link to decrease broadcast traffic across the link?

**A.** SAP

**B.** RIP

**C.** NLSP

**D.** LSP

**10.** Which protocol provides NetWare clients with access to various services on a NetWare server?

**A.** RIP

**B.** NLSP

**C.** NCP

**D.** CNSP

# CHAPTER

# 12

## Directory Services

## Roadmap

This chapter provides an overview of the basic features and benefits of Directory Services' standards and protocols.

### Topics Covered

- X.500

- Lightweight Directory Access Protocol (LDAP)

### Skills You'll Learn

- Explain the features, benefits, and directory structure of X.500

- Explain the features and benefits of LDAP

---

T his chapter will introduce the X.500 Directory Services naming standard and the LDAP protocol, which together form a means of creating a global, hierarchical database and providing client access to the database.

# X.500

A directory, as defined by Merriam Webster, is an "alphabetical or classified list (as of names and addresses)." One example of a traditional, printed directory is the telephone book. It provides you with the names, addresses, and telephone numbers of the people who live in a city or otherwise defined area. Sometimes, a telephone book directory entry also provides further identifying information, such as a fax number, and in the case of the yellow pages, further information about a company's products and services offered, opening hours, and so on.

This concept has been applied to the creation of electronic directories, which hold the names and other identifying information about people and resources of an organization or otherwise organized group or entity. Electronic directories are distributed, global databases.

X.500 is a standard that was developed to enable the creation of such electronic directories using standard terminology to represent, gain access to, and use resources in each directory database. The standard terminology for a resource in a directory is *object*. If so desired, objects stored in a local directory can become globally available to all users of the Internet through integration into a global directory.

Using X.500, all directory information is stored in what is considered a single, global, logical database called the *Directory Information Base (DIB)*. Despite its identification as a single database, it can be distributed over a network. Each individual entry in a DIB provides information about an object (also called node).

Novell Directory Services (NDS) and the Domain Name System (DNS) are two examples of directories that are based on the X.500 standard. An example of an organization that provides Directory Services is an organization called InterNIC, which manages U.S. domain name registrations.

## Services

Directories provide the following:

- Unified (standard) naming service
- Name and address resolution
- Unique object naming scheme
- Object description capabilities

The X.500 standard defines processes at the Application layer of the OSI model. It was first approved in 1988 to handle e-mail address management together with the X.400 standard and has since been expanded and enhanced to describe the current standard.

The complete X.500 standard ISO/IEC 9594: Information Technology — Open Systems Interconnection — The Directory can be ordered from the ISO at http://www.iso.ch.

Refer to Chapters 3, 4, and 5 for information on the OSI model and the Application layer.

X.500 provides directory security through two authentication methods, *Simple* and *Strong*. The Simple method requires a valid password for authentication. The Strong method requires the use of encryption and a public key for authentication.

# Directory Structure

Directories using the X.500 standard are hierarchical in nature and use a structure called the *Directory Information Tree (DIT)*. In a DIT, the top level of the structure is called the *[Root]*, which leads to the fact that the DIT is commonly referred to as an *inverted tree*.

Making up the structure below the [Root] are *intermediate objects* and *leaf objects*. Leaf objects are also called terminating objects.

## Intermediate and Leaf Objects

To easily find objects in the Directory, it must be further organized through the use of intermediate objects. They can be likened to alphabetized subsections of a telephone book (A, B, C, and so on).

Finally, leaf objects represent resources in your organization (such as people, devices, applications, services, and so on) and can be likened to each name in a telephone book (Smith, Chang, Moreau, and so on).

Each object in the tree has *attributes,* which are properties that define the object. Information stored in an attribute is called a *value*. An example of an attribute in a telephone book is a phone number, and the value is the number itself. Objects can have many different attributes.

### Object Labels and Graphical Object Representation in the Tree   Each object (depending on its type) can be located only in certain places within the DIT. Labels are used to identify object types and thus their possible locations in the tree. Each label is a one- or two-character abbreviation of the object type or of an object attribute. Each object is also graphically represented in the tree. A leaf object's graphical representation varies depending on the type of leaf object (for example, user, printer, and application).

Object types, where in the tree an object is allowed to reside, and object attributes follow rules called the *schema*.

The following table describes each of the possible object labels in an X.500 DIT, the associated object type, and the possible location of the object in the tree.

**T A B L E  12.1:**   Labels, Object Types, and Object Locations in the Tree

| Label | Object Type | Location in the Tree |
|-------|-------------|----------------------|
| C | Country | Below [Root] |
| O | Organization | Below [Root] or below Country objects |
| OU | Organizational Unit | Below Organization or Organizational Unit objects (Intermediate grouping object) |
| CN | Leaf (CN is an abbreviation for Common Name, a leaf object attribute.) | Below Organization or Organizational Unit objects |

### Distinguished Names (DN) and Relative Distinguished Names (RDN)

When accessing an object located in a DIT, you must specify either its *distinguished name (DN)* or its *relative distinguished name (RDN)*.

The DN is a unique name for each object and consists of the entire path from the [Root] to the object. It is built by stringing RDNs together from the [Root] to the object. Thus, no two objects can have the same DN. An example of a DN for a leaf object called MARY is MARY.ACCTG.ORG.

The RDN is an object's local name and may or may not be unique. An example of an RDN is MARY. Multiple leaf objects could have this local name but be located in different O or OU objects. This means that each MARY has a unique DN (full path from [Root] to object with varying O or OU objects in the path), but not a unique RDN (local name is MARY).

## Agents and Agent Communication

X.500 uses *Directory System Agents (DSA)* to provide easier access to and more efficient management of the directory database. It uses *directory user agents (DUA)* to give users (people or processes) access to the Directory.

### Directory System Agents (DSA)

Directory System Agents (DSA) are divisions of the directory database and can be distributed across a network, providing easier access to resources (resources can be placed closer to users of those resources).

Although distributing the database means that portions of the database are placed on multiple servers (possibly in multiple locations), the structure of the Directory does not change, and information can continue to be shared throughout heterogeneous environments. Each database division (DSA) can encompass one or more organizations. Once divided, the directory database still appears as a single database to users and services.

This ability to divide the database into smaller portions, and distribute these portions across a network, provides one of the key features of X.500 to an organization's network environment: scalability.

## Directory User Agents (DUA)

Directory User Agents (DUA) enable users to access information in the DIB by allowing communication with DSAs though the *Directory Access Protocol (DAP)*. (See Figure 12.1.) The following outlines the process of information retrieval:

1.  The user sends a request to the DSA over DAP using a DUA.

2.  The DSA accesses the DIB, retrieves the information, and returns it to the DUA over DAP.

3.  The DUA forwards the information to the user.

**F I G U R E  12.1**

Requesting DIB information using a DUA

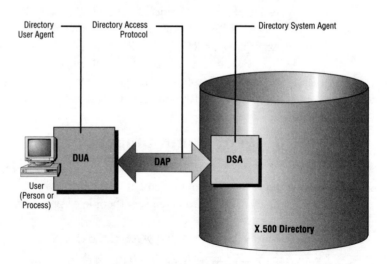

Users can use one of three types of DUAs to communicate with DSAs and access information in the DIB: command line, forms-based, or browser.

Communication between DUAs and DSAs occurs over the Read, Search, and Modify ports. The following table lists these three ports and the functions they provide:

| | Port | Function |
|---|---|---|
| **T A B L E  12.2**<br>DUA to DSA communications ports and their functions | Read | Read, compare, and abandon |
| | Search | List and search |
| | Modify | Add, remove, and modify entries<br>Modify RDN |

## Agent-Communication Protocols

Because a Directory can have multiple DSAs, it is necessary to enable DSAs to communicate with each other. (See Figure 12.2.) Three protocols are available for this purpose:

- Directory System Protocol (DSP)

- Directory Information Shadowing Protocol (DISP)

- Directory Operational Binding Management Protocol (DOP)

**F I G U R E  12.2**

Communication using multiple DSAs

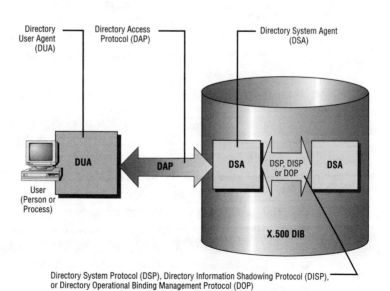

Directory System Protocol (DSP), Directory Information Shadowing Protocol (DISP), or Directory Operational Binding Management Protocol (DOP)

# Additional Main Features of X.500

In addition to scalability (mentioned earlier in this chapter), replication and synchronization are two other main features of X.500.

## Replication

The replication feature enables you to make copies of the directory database and store them across the network, providing fault tolerance. All copies (replicas) of the database are identical, which leads to faster access speeds when retrieving information from the database.

## Synchronization

It is very important that all replicas of the database are updated regularly so that the information in all replicas is identical and up-to-date through synchronization. When synchronization occurs, updates are sent to servers that contain replicas of the database. Synchronization can be accomplished through the following methods:

1. Master/Shadow Arrangement

2. Changes are made in the original database and sent to replicas at certain intervals.

3. Peer-to-Peer Update Mechanism

4. Changes are made either in the original database or in replicas and are sent to replicas and the master copy at certain, pre-defined intervals.

5. No changes

6. Changes to the database are not allowed.

# X.500-Related RFCs

In-depth information on the X.500 standard has been available since 1988 in several RFCs (also called ITU-T Recommendations). These recommendations were developed by the CCITT (Consultative Committee for International Telegraphy and Telephony), a part of the International Telecommunications Union (ITU). It is available in what is called the Blue Book in Volume III: Fascicle VIII.8, Data Communication Networks Directory, Recommendations X.500-X.521. You can also find this information on the Web at http://www.itu.int/publications/, through e-mail by sending the command GET ITU-5233 to itudoc@itu.ch, or through gopher by accessing gopher.itu.ch.

**NOTE** The CCITT has recently undergone a name change to Telecommunication Standardization Sector.

**T A B L E  12.3:**  ITU-T RFC Numbers and Titles

| RFC # | Title |
| --- | --- |
| 1309 | Technical Overview of Directory Services Using the X.500 Protocol |
| 1308 | Executive Introduction to Directory Services Using the X.500 Protocol |
| 1292 | A Catalog of Available X.500 Implementations |
| 1632 | A Revised Catalog of Available X.500 Implementations |
| 1943 | Building an X.500 Directory in the US |
| 2294 | Representing the O/R Address Hierarchy In the X.500 Directory Information Tree |
| 2293 | Representing Tables and Subtrees in the X.500 Directory |

# Lightweight Directory Access Protocol (LDAP)

To make the information in an X.500 Directory useful, users need access to the Directory database. Users can be either people or processes. Earlier, this chapter covered using the Directory Access Protocol (DAP) for this purpose. This protocol can be used; however, it has a lot of overhead. Much more common is the use of the *Lightweight Directory Access Protocol (LDAP)*. This protocol is designed for use with simple management and browser applications for read/write access to the DIB.

Using LDAP eliminates most of the overhead incurred at the Session and Presentation layers of the OSI model, which means faster, more efficient handling of client queries. It runs over connection-oriented, reliable transport protocols, such as TCP/IP. When a client sends a request to a server via LDAP, it is sent to a server who receives the request, queries the Directory, retrieves the information, and returns the response to the client. If errors occur, then the error is returned to the client.

Additional information on LDAP is available in RFC 1777 – Lightweight Directory Access Protocol

## Connectionless Lightweight Directory Access Protocol (CLDAP)

The *Connectionless Lightweight Directory Access Protocol (CLDAP)* is derived from LDAP and is able to perform only a limited set of operations, which further reduces overhead. It is intended for use with applications that perform simple lookup functions and send only small read requests to the server to query the Directory. CLDAP runs over connectionless transport protocols such as UDP.

 Additional information on LDAP is available in RFC 1798 – Connectionless Lightweight X.500 Directory Access Protocol.

# CNE Practice Test Questions

1. What are the services offered by X.500?

    A. Unified (standard) naming service

    B. Name and address resolution

    C. Private key encryption

    D. Unique object naming scheme

    E. Object description capabilities

2. What are the main features of X.500?

    A. Scalability

    B. Simplicity

   **C.** Replication

   **D.** Connectivity

   **E.** Synchronization

**3.** At what level of the OSI model are X.500 Directory Services processes defined?

   **A.** Application

   **B.** Session

   **C.** Presentation

   **D.** Network

**4.** LDAP runs over

   **A.** IPX/SPX

   **B.** UDP

   **C.** TCP/IP

   **D.** PBX

**5.** LDAP is used for

   **A.** User access to the X.500 Directory

   **B.** Server access to the X.500 Directory

# PART

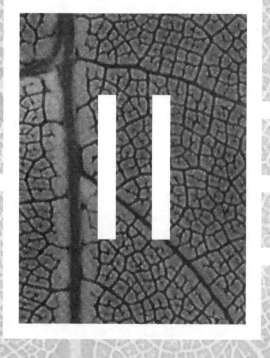

# II

## Service and Support

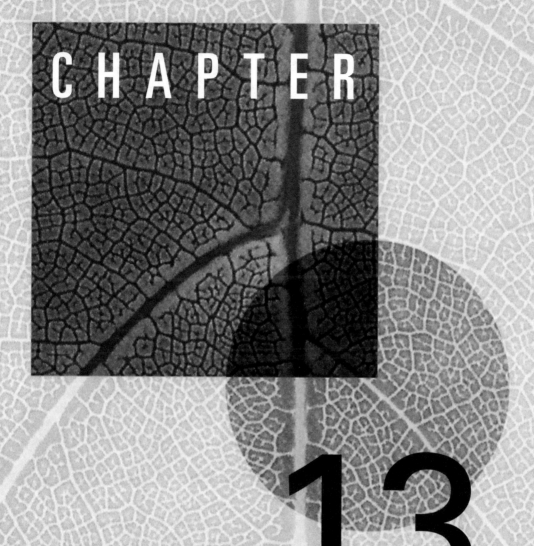

# CHAPTER

# 13

## The Basics of Network Troubleshooting

## Roadmap

This chapter covers the basics of network troubleshooting.

**Topics Covered**

- Preventative maintenance procedures
- Network troubleshooting
- Troubleshooting references

**Skills You'll Learn**

- Explain the process of providing service and support on a network
- Explain the six-step Novell Troubleshooting Model
- Explain the types of system diagnostics
- Explain anti-static measures
- Explain common documentation practices
- Use the Support Connection website to find technical support information
- Use Support Source and Microhouse Technical Library to find hardware configuration settings
- Determine which research tool to use to find the answer to a problem

As a network administrator, one of the major tasks that you have after the network is up and running is to keep it that way. And the best way to keep the network productive is to avoid potential problems.

You probably already know that preventing problems is a lot easier than troubleshooting them. With a little effort, you can minimize the number and kinds of problems that occur. But no matter how diligent you are, problems will occasionally happen. The information in this chapter should help you prevent some of the most common problems and develop a strategy for troubleshooting problems when they do happen.

# Preventing Problems

The first step in problem prevention is to set up the network carefully. Viruses and electrical problems can wreak havoc on a network, but they are almost entirely preventable. Other risks can be minimized by taking care of the network's physical environment.

Your job is to protect the network from accidental or deliberate acts that threaten the security, reliability, and availability of data. Most people know that you need to take care of your hardware—the machines that make up the network. They also know that you must take care of your data if you don't want to lose it. But not many people give enough thought to the other component, the people. Remember that keeping your data safe means considering all threats.

Network problems can be placed in four general categories:

- Problems with the physical environment, such as temperature and air quality
- Electrical problems, such as static and power surges
- Viruses
- Security issues

## Problems in the Physical Environment

Although today's computers are not especially sensitive to their environment, their physical surroundings do have an impact on them. A good rule of thumb might be that if you feel comfortable in a room, the computers probably do, too. However, a few general areas where you can protect your network include temperature, air quality, and magnetism.

### Temperature

Temperature has a definite effect on your computer. When components get hot, they expand; when they get cold, they contract. This can cause what is known as *chip creep*, which means that integrated circuits gradually lose contact with their sockets. This lack of contact can cause problems, because the chip won't send or receive signals as necessary. It doesn't take a heat wave to make this happen—the temperature inside a working computer can be as much as 40 degrees higher than the temperature outside the computer. The extra heat is generated by the computer's components. Check your fans periodically to make sure they are working correctly.

Whenever you receive new equipment, let it adjust to room temperature before using it. Remember, the equipment may have been somewhere cold while you were in the warm building. Taking an hour or two to let the equipment slowly warm to room temperature might increase the lifetime of your new, and probably expensive, equipment.

## Air Quality

To cool the computer, a fan circulates air through the case of the CPU. The question is: What is in the air that is being circulated? Dust, smoke particles, thermal insulation, and hair can damage hard disks and other components inside the CPU. All these environmental pollutants can affect the workings of a computer. Don't underestimate these factors. A workstation's life can be cut in half by the kind of air found in some offices—not to mention industrial sites. You should use appropriate filtration devices to filter out the pollutants in the air.

## Magnetism

Magnetism poses a problem for computers. Magnetism can corrupt computer data on magnetic storage devices (such as tapes, floppy disks, and hard disks). You should ensure that magnetic objects are removed from proximity to devices or storage media that they might affect. Remember that telephones, stereo speakers, electric motors, and anything with a magnet can adversely affect the computer. Take care of the potential threats of magnetism before your network loses data or has damaged equipment.

# Electrical Problems

Most of the physical conditions that cause problems happen over an extended period of time. Electrical problems occur quickly and often without warning. Problem prevention here has more to do with careful planning and taking precautionary actions during installation and maintenance. Crosstalk, noise, static, and transients are the four main types of electrical problems and are described in the following sections.

## Crosstalk

When two wires are close to each other, the magnetic fields each wire generates can interfere with normal transmission. Crosstalk can result in data loss or corruption. There are two ways to combat crosstalk, space and shielding. If one cable is affecting another cable, you can try to increase the distance between the cables. The other solution is shielding. Unshielded twisted-pair (UTP) cable is the medium most affected by crosstalk. Shielded twisted-pair (STP) cable is better because the shielding provides some protection from interference. Fiber-optic cable is the best medium; it uses light rather than electricity and is completely immune to crosstalk.

## Noise

Does anyone really like noise? Not sound, *noise*. In electrical terms, noise is defined as a low-voltage, low-current, high-frequency signal that interferes with normal network transmissions, often creating bad data. Noise normally occurs in observable patterns, such as static on a television screen. An oscilloscope can be used to check for the presence of noise.

There are two kinds of noise when talking about computer networks, *electromagnetic interference* (EMI) and *radio frequency interference* (RFI). EMI is the most common type of computer noise. Possible sources of EMI include lights, engines, industrial tools, and radar. Possible RFI sources include microwaves, appliances, and furnaces.

**WARNING**  Noise can distort signals with random fuzziness, preventing the hardware from properly detecting data.

To minimize noise, you may want to take some of the following precautions:

- Properly ground equipment.
- Avoid placing cables close to possible EMI and RFI sources.
- Use shielded cables whenever possible.
- Check the FCC noise emission rating of your equipment.

## Static

The buildup of static electricity doesn't usually damage computer components, but the sudden discharge of static can. Static electricity can build up to dangerous levels before discharging all at once.

Most people are familiar with static electricity. You build up a charge by dragging your feet on a dry, brittle carpet so that you can shock a friend. This discharge, called *electrostatic discharge* (ESD), must be close to 3,000 volts for a person to feel it. By contrast, computer components such as microchips can be damaged by charges of 20 to 30 volts. To make matters worse, about 90 percent of the time, ESD will not affect equipment immediately. Instead, components tend to degrade over time and eventually fail.

Here are a few ways to avoid static:

- Always ground yourself and any equipment you will be working on. Use antistatic matting and wrist straps.

- Never let anyone touch you while you are working on sensitive equipment. It is silly to go to the effort of grounding yourself, just to let someone else deliver the ESD by touching you while you work on sensitive equipment.

- Never directly touch electrical leads of components or integrated circuits.

- Always use antistatic bags to transport and store components with integrated circuits, such as network cards.

- Keep ambient humidity at 70 to 90 percent. Low humidity makes static problems worse.

Some materials carry static charges easier than others. Styrofoam is one common material that carries static buildup. Make sure styrofoam cups and packing material are not left near devices with integrated circuits. Polyester ties and other types of synthetic clothing can also carry static buildup.

## Transients

A *transient* is a high-voltage burst of current. Transients rise and decay quickly, usually lasting less than one second, and occur randomly. They are commonly called *spikes*. Their random nature means that you cannot predict them. A transient could be caused by trouble somewhere down the power line, such as a blackout or lightning strike.

Transients can seriously damage network components. To protect your equipment from power spikes, you should take some of the following precautions:

- Put the computers on their own circuit with a separate circuit breaker, and avoid placing too much equipment on that circuit.

- Ensure that the computer is properly grounded. Check that no one has put in a two-prong adapter on a three-prong plug, which would disconnect the ground.

- Use a surge protecting power strip or adapter.

The flip side of transients is a *brownout*, also called a *sag*. When you see the lights flicker in a room, it is usually caused by a brownout, which is a temporary decrease in voltage level. Systems can crash, and data can be corrupted, as a result of a brownout. The best solution to this problem is to use an uninterruptible power supply (UPS).

## Viruses

A computer *virus* is a pernicious computer program that alters stored files or system configuration and copies itself onto external disks or other computers. Viruses cause problems by altering files and configurations or by growing exponentially, which can consume hard disk space and network bandwidth.

Viruses require an action of some sort to activate them. To achieve this, they often attach themselves to executable files. Executable files have the file name extensions EXE, BAT, or COM. Other opportunities are provided by overlays (OVL), file allocation tables (FATs), boot sectors, and memory. A virus can attack immediately or wait until a specific action, such as a warm boot, triggers it.

*Worms* are another form of a destructive or dangerous program. Unlike viruses, worms do not reproduce themselves. Instead, they fulfill a specific function at a specific location. For example, a worm may be set up to penetrate a database and transfer information to an unauthorized individual. They are called worms because they move across a network without leaving detectable signs.

A *Trojan horse* is a program that is designed to hide in the disguise of something harmless, waiting for the right moment to do its deed. For example, a Trojan horse could capture a user ID or password by pretending to be the LOGIN program on a network.

Networks are a frequent target for virus programmers because they provide the chance to simultaneously infect a number of workstations. Fortunately, because NetWare works differently than DOS, the server is immune to most viruses. Workstations are still vulnerable, however, and a virus can spread between workstations when executable programs are transferred across the network.

Any place at which data enters a computer—a floppy drive, modem, network interface card, and so on—offers a point of entry for a virus. These are the areas that you must strive to control. For the most part, viruses do not come with retail software from a reputable dealer. Most of the time, viruses come from software obtained in some other way, such as with programs that are downloaded or copied from home computers.

Unlike the NetWare servers, most workstations use Windows 95/98, the most popular platform for viruses. Some viruses can even affect the server. Here are some strategies for protecting the network against viruses:

- Teach network users about viruses and how to prevent them. Most workstations have at least one vulnerable point of entry. If users are aware of the threat of viruses, they can help to combat it. If they must install any programs, teach them how to check the program for viruses first. Tell them to avoid downloading untested programs from the Internet or bulletin board services if possible.

- Perform regular backups on servers and workstations, and check the backups.

- Clean the workstation's Master Boot Record using the FDISK /MBR command.

- Regularly scan your workstations and servers with a reputable anti-virus package. For network virus scanning, some of the best third-party programs are Central Point Anti-Virus for NetWare, NetShield from McAfee Associates, LAN Protect from Intel, and InocuLAN from Cheyenne Software. You can set up login scripts to launch these types of programs to automate the process for both workstations and the server.

- Control entry points on workstations and servers.

- Flag all EXE and COM files on the server as read-only.

- In the SYS:PUBLIC, LOGIN, and application directories, grant users Read and File Scan rights only.

# Security

True network security means protecting network data from both deliberate and accidental threats. A network is no good without the data it can send, manipulate, and receive.

Although NetWare provides some powerful security features, it offers only a small portion of the defense needed for a truly secure network. One of the main causes of network problems, for example, is the user. Although some users may wish to deliberately harm the network and server, problems caused by users are usually accidental. Users can do damage simply by trying a command that they don't understand or turning off something they shouldn't.

Threats to the network can be classified into several general categories:

- Destruction:   Data and hardware can be destroyed by deliberate or negligent acts.

- Corruption:   Data that has been corrupted is untrustworthy and often worthless.

- Disclosure:   Data of a confidential nature could be intercepted. Passwords and other confidential data must be protected vigorously.

- Interruption:   If the network goes down, you can't use the resources you need. Downtime means unavailable data, which means loss of money.

## Your Security Plan

Problems caused by negligence are bad enough, but if someone is actively and maliciously trying to cause problems, you have a greater threat. In order to deal with these possible threats, you need to come up with a security plan. Your plan should have the following steps:

1. Examine and analyze each segment of the network for possible security breaches.

2.  If you find alarming threats, consider various responses in terms of their cost and how important they may be.

3.  Make the affordable changes as needed.

4.  Check and maintain your controls to keep them working and protecting the network.

As a general rule, if someone can get to the server and spend a few minutes unnoticed, he or she can access the data—or at the very least, cause damage. If you are concerned about security, keep servers locked away.

## Security Controls

You can use security controls that will minimize threats to data, software, and hardware. Some controls that you can implement include the following:

- Require unique passwords.

- Require regular, frequent password changes.

- Restrict login times.

- Require adequate security on dial-up telephone lines (modems).

- Limit access to network resources to a need-to-know (and need-to-change) basis.

- Use software that employs encryption.

- Use data redundancy on the server (RAID, disk mirroring, and duplexing).

- Develop contingency plans for vital services in case of natural disaster (earthquake, flood, fire, and so on).

- Keep the server in a locked room.

Encryption is standard on NetWare 3.1*x*, 4, and 5. To take advantage of this feature, make sure the Allow Unencrypted Passwords SET parameter is set to OFF.

# Troubleshooting the Network

**Y**ou can use the problem prevention techniques discussed here to reduce the number and types of problems that occur, but things will still go wrong with the network. When they do, it's time to do some troubleshooting. Troubleshooting usually involves a combination of knowledge and experience.

## Isolating the Problem

Troubleshooting requires the ability to separate a problem into smaller parts and see how all the parts relate to one another. Breaking a problem down allows you to test individual guesses at what went wrong. To help you isolate a problem, you can take the following steps:

- Eliminate the possibility of user error.

- Check the physical site. Is everything that should be there present and connected correctly?

- Back up data if there is a question that storage media (hard drive or disk drives) may be the problem.

- Turn everything off and back on again. This action solves a number of problems.

- Simplify the system. Remove unnecessary elements, which might include some TSR (terminate and stay resident) programs and AUTOEXEC.BAT and CONFIG.SYS file parameters. Try pulling out expansion cards. Isolate the problem by involving a minimum number of factors.

These steps can be useful for solving a number of network problems. However, for more complex and persistent problems, you should turn to the Novell troubleshooting model, which is described in the next section.

# The Novell Troubleshooting Model

The Novell troubleshooting model has six steps:

1. Try a quick fix.

2. Gather basic information.

3. Develop a plan of attack.

4. Execute the plan.

5. Ensure user satisfaction.

6. Document the solution.

## Try a Quick Fix

There's a saying that applies to the first step of the troubleshooting model, "K.I.S.S." or "Keep it short and simple." The first step when troubleshooting a network problem is to try a quick fix. In other words, look for the simple stuff before breaking out the big guns. Some examples of K.I.S.S. procedures are:

- Check that all cables are plugged in.

- Determine if it was a user error.

- Turn the computer off and back on again.

- In the startup files (that is, AUTOEXEC.BAT, CONFIG.SYS on the workstation and AUTOEXEC.NCF & STARTUP.NCF on the server), remove any lines that are not required for system startup.

- Verify security rights.

- Remove unnecessary hardware expansion cards (sound cards, scanner cards, and so on).

- Check operating system patch level. Some patches solve problems while others conflict with new software. Usually when you call technical support, they will ask you if you have the most current patches applied.

If none of these examples works, you can certainly try some of your own that you have gathered. If this step doesn't work, it's time to move on to the next step.

## Gathering Basic Information

The next step is to discover what you can through communication with the users and other sources of information. You need to find out what problems the end user is experiencing and what the computer was doing when the problem occurred.

You should ask network users experiencing the problem several questions as you begin the troubleshooting process. For example, the following questions may provide a wealth of information:

- When was the last time it worked? Have they used it recently or has it sat dormant for a period of time? This question is particularly pertinent to hardware problems. If the last time they used this modem was two years ago, it can make a difference in how you approach the problem.

- What changes have been made since the last time it was used? Have there been new hardware additions? Software additions? Has anything on the network been rearranged?

After you have talked to the users, check your documentation to find out how the network usually operates. When you know what is normal for the network you can compare that performance with what is occurring now.

As you can see, communication with the user is a major part of this step. You need to be calm and a good listener. The better you communicate with the people who use the network, the easier troubleshooting will be. Also, remember that they are going to be nervous. They probably have deadlines and responsibilities; some may even feel their jobs are on the line. Be reassuring, but take what they tell you with a grain of salt. Sometimes end users give very inaccurate information.

## Developing a Plan of Attack

After you have gathered some basic information, use that information and your own knowledge to diagnose the most likely problem. Break the problem into smaller parts. Is the problem in the area of user error, application software, operating system software, or equipment? Then prioritize your hypotheses according to their chance of success and the cost of attempting the solution. Remember that cost involves more than hardware; you must factor in network downtime and technician time as well. This prioritization will help you to decide which solution to work on first.

Approaching a network problem in this way is similar to how you might go about repairing your car. When you take it to a mechanic, he asks what the problem is, looks at the car himself, and then tries to analyze probable causes. If you are having trouble starting the car, the mechanic may look at the battery, battery cables, starter, and ignition switch (breaking the problem into smaller parts). You want to start with the most likely and least expensive fix, don't you? Taking a wrench to tighten battery cables might not cost you more than a few minutes of time. Replacing the starter motor will be more expensive.

## Executing the Plan

When you have a plan of attack, you are ready to test your hypotheses. You should know which hypothesis is most likely to be successful and cost the least. Then test each part of your hypothesis, one element at a time.

In order to fix the problem as efficiently as possible, make only one change at a time. Making several at once won't help you determine the exact problem. Would you want the mechanic in the car repair example to replace the starter motor and your battery before knowing which was faulty?

Be sure to use reliable procedures, checking equipment and software when you are testing. Otherwise, you may become confused trying to determine what the original problem was and what new problems have been introduced.

It may be best to begin testing your hypothesis using *forward chaining*, which is the technique of beginning with the source device and moving toward the destination device. Investigating in the reverse fashion, from the destination device to the source device, is called *reverse chaining*.

## Ensure User Satisfaction

After you have fixed the problem and tested the solution, you must make sure that the solution is agreeable and understood by the user (or at least the user's manager). It is sometimes the case that you have solved the problem, but the user can't tell because they weren't performing the procedure correctly in the first place. For this reason, you want to make sure you contact the person who reported the problem and show them that the problem is resolved.

## Documenting the Solution

Enough of the right kind of documentation will save hours in trouble-shooting time for any size network. With detailed, up-to-date documentation, system administrators can predict possible network problems and take precautionary measures to avoid them. Also, if a similar problem occurred in the past, you may find the answer in the documentation without needing to go through the process again.

Three kinds of records compose troubleshooting documentation:

- The LAN system
- History
- Resources available

**The LAN System**    Troubleshooting documentation starts with the LAN system. Your LAN system documentation should include a detailed map that identifies the locations of all users and user groups, as well as all hardware components: printers, workstations, cabling, routers, and so on. You should also have an inventory of all components on the system.

A record of the jumper and DIP-switch settings for network components can be very helpful.

**History**    Network history documentation can help you with current problems and prevent even larger problems in the future. The history should include a description of the purpose the LAN serves for the organization that uses it, who the end users are, which workstations and other equipment each user employs, and the training background of the end users. The LAN history should also include a detailed log of past problems, so that recurrent problems can be isolated and corrected.

Another part of LAN history is a record of normal LAN operation. Baseline statistics might include traffic, CPU usage, errors, bandwidth utilization, and other relevant information. When a problem occurs, you can compare the network's current operation with the records of its normal operation.

**Available Resources**    There are a number of resources that can help you find the solution you are looking for. Choose the one that is best for you. You probably won't want to call Novell's technical support division and pay an arm and a leg to find answers to technical questions. But you may need to use tools such as the Microhouse Technical Library or the Network Support Encyclopedia.

# Using System Diagnostic Software

**E**very technician has a bag of tricks that they can use to solve a problem. This bag may contain items like screwdrivers, a multimeter, as well as other tools. But some of the tools used most often are software tools called system diagnostics. There are several products available for use on a NetWare network to help in troubleshooting problems.

- CheckIT Diagnostic

- LANalyzer for Windows

- Ontrack Data Recovery for NetWare

## CheckIT Diagnostic

This product, made by TouchStone Software, has long been used for diagnosing and reporting on DOS and Windows workstations. It has gone from Check It, to WIN Check It, to Check It Pro in various versions and iterations. It has features for reporting system configuration (including memory, processor, hard disk and network statistics) as well as problem detection (like I/O, memory address and IRQ conflicts). It also lets you run tests on the various hardware components, either once or in a continuous loop.

## LANalyzer for Windows

LANalyzer is a Windows program, made by Novell, that allows you to view network packets as they pass your workstation. It can display network bandwidth use in a graphical format as well as collisions per second and errors per second. But, the most valuable feature of LANalyzer is the ability to capture packets your workstation receives. You can then view the details of the packet, including source and destination address, source and destination port, and the actual data being sent.

In order to use LANalyzer to report errors, you must have a network card that supports "promiscuous mode." Promiscuous mode lets a network card pass network errors to the software above it, instead of simply discarding the packet. Only a few network cards support this feature. Novell recommends an actual NE2000 network card (NOT an NE2000-compatible) for use with this feature.

## Ontrack Data Recovery for NetWare (ODRN)

Ontrack is a company that performs data recovery on various types of hard disks. Their services are used when the data on the disk is absolutely irreplaceable. They have their own bag of tricks that they can employ to recover data from a badly damaged disk.

They also have developed software called Ontrack Data Recovery for NetWare (ODRN). This software, when loaded on a server, can aid in the recovery of data from a damaged disk. However, it is still best to have backup methods employed instead of relying on software that might be able to recover your data in case of a failure. This software is just another tool in your bag of tricks.

# Reference Sources for Troubleshooting

Fortunately, you *aren't* left alone in the troubleshooting battle. There are several reference sources that can help you in your quest for information about the problems on your network or server. The following are some tools that can provide valuable data about hardware and software problems:

- The Novell Support Connection is a World Wide Web site or CD-ROM that contains Technical Information Documents (TIDs), software updates, and patches in a searchable format.

- The SupportSource available from Microhouse Corporation is an interface to several technical databases called Knowledge Modules. The most popular of these modules is call the Microhouse Technical Library (MTL).

## The Novell Support Connection

Assuming you have a connection to the Internet, you can access most (if not all) of the technical support information you will need directly from Novell's Support Connection website at `http://support.novell.com`. The website is the most current source for TIDs, file updates, patches, and technical support options. Figure 13.1 shows a typical screen you would see when accessing the main menu of the Support Connection website.

**FIGURE 13.3**

Novell Support Connection website main menu

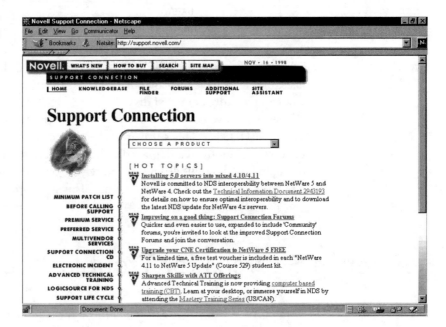

In addition, Novell distributes information monthly on a CD called the Novell Support Connection CD. In addition to the information found on the website, the CD provides technical support information, like a complete set of AppNotes (a Novell publication that contains lots of how-to information in a magazine format).

There are six major areas to the Support Connection website. They are accessed by clicking on the words under the toolbar at the top of the page. Each area has a different function. The areas are:

- Home
- Knowledgebase

- File Finder
- Forums
- Additional Support
- Site Assistant

Because websites in general change daily, no one can guarantee that each page will look exactly like the screenshots. But the areas should remain pretty close to the same. Check the website if you are unsure what these areas are called.

**Home**   This area is the main screen or home page of the Support Connection website, as seen previously in Figure 13.1. It allows you to navigate to the other areas. Additionally, it contains hotlinks to the latest Novell support news and product releases.

**Knowledgebase**   This area is probably the most valuable to a technician looking for an obscure problem. Simply click in the "Enter word or phrase" box shown in Figure 13.2 and type in the key words that describe your problem. For example, if you were having problems with your NetWare 5 server hanging periodically, you would probably type in **NetWare 5 hang** and the knowledgebase would return all entries that contained all those words, in order of likeliness. The responses will be listed as hyperlinks to their subjects. In the previous example, you might receive 100 responses, but the one you are looking for should be at or near the top with a "100%" next to it, and it might be called "NetWare 5 server hangs periodically." Knowledgebase is updated daily as Novell support technicians get answers for new technical issues.

**File Finder**   This hot link will bring you to the area of the Support Connection website that lets you search for downloadable files (Figure 13.3). If technical support gives you the name of a file to download, this is the area you use to search for it. You can also view the most commonly downloaded files, look at the support files for a particular product, as well as view all the downloadable software. The Support Connection is also the quickest way to get the newest Novell Client software.

**FIGURE 13.4**

The Knowledgebase
area of the Support
Connection website

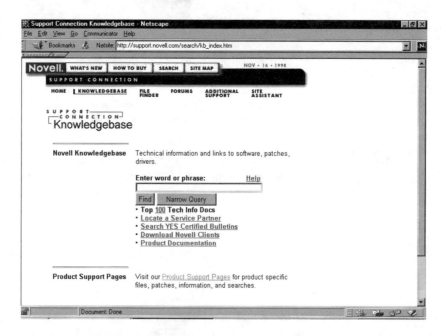

**FIGURE 13.5**

The File Finder area of
the Support Connec-
tion website

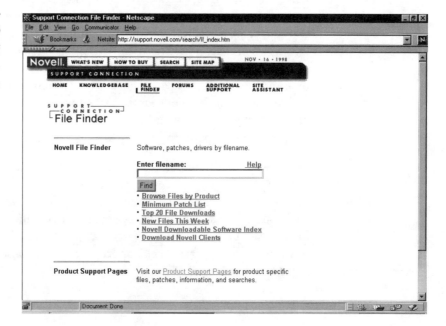

**Forums**   The Forums area (Figure 13.4) is the area you go to when you've exhausted all the quick fix options and you want to ask your peers what they think. From this page you can access the various discussion groups that Novell mediates. Many of your colleagues may have had the same problem as you and may have found a solution. You can discuss these issues and hopefully find resolution.

**FIGURE 13.6**

The Forums area of the Support Connection website

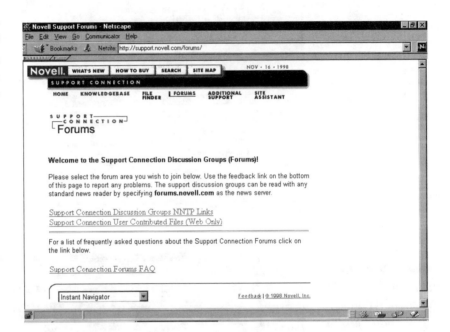

**Additional Support**   This area could be considered a last resort. If you can't find the answer elsewhere, this area (Figure 13.5) tells you how to contact Novell and use their expertise to help solve the problem. Of course, the various support options don't come for free. This area also details how much each option costs and which is the best solution for your company.

**Site Assistant**   This area can be considered the manual for the Support Connection website. The page in Figure 13.6 lists several frequently asked questions (FAQs) on how the website works and where you can go for specific information.

**FIGURE 13.7**

Additional Support
area of the Support
Connection website

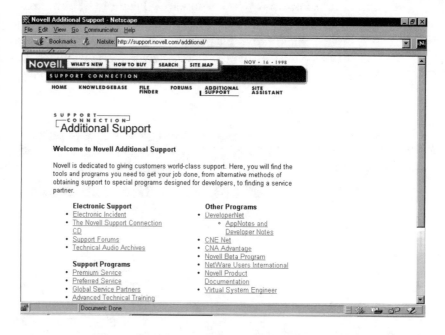

**FIGURE 13.7**

Additional Support
area of the Support
Connection website

**FIGURE 13.8**

Site Assistant area of
the Support Connec-
tion website

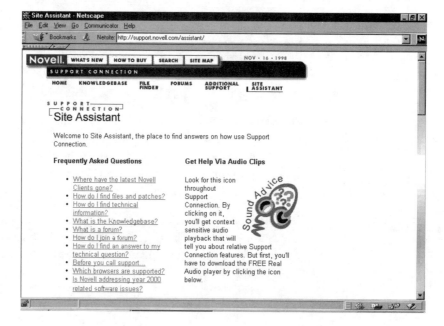

**FIGURE 13.8**

Site Assistant area of
the Support Connec-
tion website

## SupportSource and the Microhouse Technical Library

SupportSource is a CD-ROM–based program that accesses many technical databases (called Knowledge Modules). It provides a single screen interface (Figure 13.7) for these databases that allows them to be searched for specific technical information.

**FIGURE 13.9**

SupportSource main screen

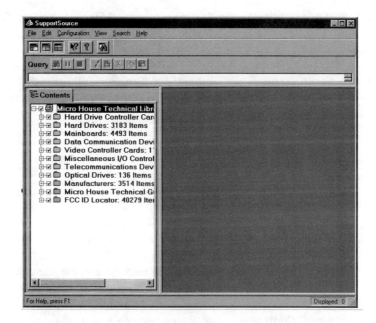

SupportSource has several hardware and software requirements:

- Windows 3.1*x* (preferably Windows 95/98) with Win32 for 32-bit support
- 8MB of RAM (16 recommended)
- 10MB free hard disk space (50 recommended)
- CD-ROM drive (4× or faster)
- 486 or faster CPU (Pentium recommended)
- Mouse
- VGA or better video display capable of 800 x 600 resolution

As with any software, it is better to adhere to the recommended requirements than the minimum, because the software will run better.

The most popular Knowledge Module is the Microhouse Technical Library (MTL). The Microhouse Technical Library is a searchable database on several categories of information. These categories and what they cover are listed in Table 13.1.

**T A B L E  13.4:**   Microhouse Technical Library (MTL) Information Categories and Descriptions

| Category | Description |
| --- | --- |
| Hard Drive Controllers | Contains the specifications, jumper settings, component locations and diagrams of various hard disk controllers |
| Hard Drives | Contains the specifications, geometry, and settings for over 3000 hard drives |
| Mainboards | Details over 4400 different mainboards and their memory configurations, jumper settings, and layouts. |
| Data Communications Devices | Details the settings and configurations of over 2000 different LAN and WAN network cards |
| Video Controller Cards | Contains the settings and diagrams for over 1000 different video adapters |
| Miscellaneous I/O Controller Cards | Details the settings and configurations for over 1000 different I/O cards (like parallel, serial, and multimedia expansion cards) |
| Telecommunication Devices | Contains the settings for over 1000 different modems and other telecommunications devices (like ISDN adapters) |
| Optical Drives | Details over 100 different CD-ROM and CD-WO drives and their specifications |
| Manufacturers | Details over 3500 companies including telephone numbers, contacts, and website addresses |
| Microhouse Technical Guide Series | Contains the text from several of the Microhouse Technical books providing information on hard disks, modems, and networks |
| FCC ID Locator | If you know the product's FCC ID, you can use it to find the product's manufacturer. |

At this writing, the retail price for the MTL CD (a single copy) is $395. New updates are released regularly, and you can subscribe to receive the latest versions.

## Using the MTL

There are three ways of using the MTL, once you have installed it. You can either search for what you are looking for, or you can use the screens to navigate to what you are looking for. The easiest way to find information is with the search function. At the top of the main screen you will see a field underneath the word *Query*. If you type in what you are looking for and press ENTER, the window at the bottom will show you a list of the items it finds in the Result list window.

For example, if you search on *NE2000* (Figure 13.8), MTL will return a list of all the documents it found that term in. The list will be ordered with the most relevant (most occurrences of the query word) to least relevant (least number of occurrences).

**FIGURE 13.10**

Finding the term *NE2000* in MTL

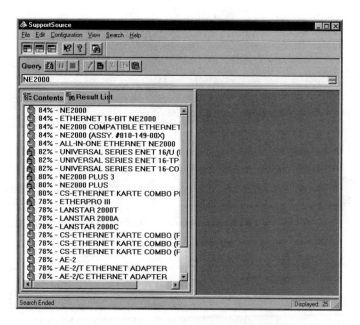

If you double-click an entry in the list, the document will display on the right side with several tabs (Figure 13.9). The Document tab comes up by default. It shows the settings and the connectors of the device in question, as well as any text documentation. Any pictures will show up in the Diagram tabs, any driver files will show up on the Driver tabs, and manufacturer information will be shown in the Company tab. The Summary tab details all the database information relevant to the document selected.

**FIGURE 13.11**

Viewing a Document

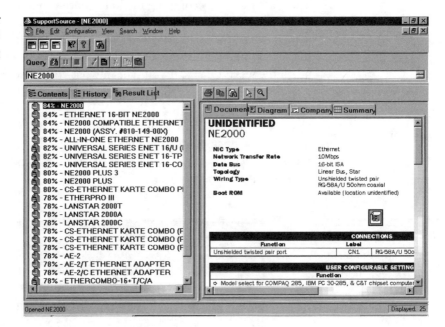

On some systems, you won't be able to see the text or details because the monitor is set to a low resolution. If you want to zoom in, click the magnifying glass above the Document tab then click in the image. To zoom in, click the magnifying glass, hold down the CTRL key and click in the image.

The other way to search is to use the Query Assistant (Figure 13.10). To access the assistant, choose Query Assistant from the View menu. The Query Assistant provides a graphical interface to the query language used by the

Query feature. You simply fill out the query using the drop down lists and checkboxes in the assistant. When you have selected all the options you want, click on the Copy query text button (the leftmost button on the toolbar). Then, click the Close Query Assistant button (the button with the X on the toolbar). Notice that the Query field now has text in it. To perform the Query, simply press ENTER or click the Start search button (the one with the magnifying glass icon.

# Choosing a Research Tool

There's an old saying, "Choose the right tool for the right job." Each tool has its own advantages and disadvantages that make that particular tool good for that particular job. Sometimes tool uses overlap, but, for the most part, the software tools discussed here have advantages that suit them for a particular troubleshooting job. Table 13.2 sums up the different tools and their advantages and disadvantages.

**T A B L E  13.5:**   Software Troubleshooting Tool Comparison

| Tool | Advantages | Disadvantages |
|---|---|---|
| SupportSource CD with MTL | • Comprehensive hardware documentation<br>• Excellent diagrams | • Must have a CD-ROM drive, which might be difficult in the field |
| Novell Support Connection website | • Most current information<br>• Comprehensive information<br>• Discussion groups available<br>• Easy to use, web-based format | • Requires a modem and ISP connection |
| Novell Support Connection CD-ROM | • Comprehensive information<br>• No modem required<br>• Can be used as an archive of older documents and drivers | • No discussion groups<br>• Never 100% current<br>• Requires CD-ROM drive |

# Review

This chapter explored the process of troubleshooting the network. In addition, it suggested several tools that can help make the troubleshooting process easier. By understanding these techniques and services, you can solve most network problems.

## Problem Prevention

The best way to keep the network productive is to avoid potential problems. The first step is to set up the network carefully. There are four general categories of network problems:

- Physical problems are related to the environment and include temperature, air quality, and magnetism.

- Electrical problems in networks usually stem from four main sources: crosstalk, noise, static, and transients.

- Viruses can change files and configurations and may grow exponentially, which interrupts the data flow.

- Security threats can be classified into the general categories of destruction, corruption, disclosure, and interruption. You can avoid security problems by having a security plan and using security controls.

## Network Troubleshooting

To troubleshoot problems when they do arise, you need to isolate the problem. You can do this by checking for user errors and examining the physical site. Also, try turning everything off and then on again and removing unnecessary system elements.

The Novell troubleshooting model has six steps:

- Try a quick fix. Use your knowledge of computers and networks to determine if it's something that can be fixed simply (like an unplugged cable).

- Gather basic information. Talk to the users to get information about the problem. Then check the network logs and record keeping devices to find out what is normal operation for the network.

- Develop a plan of attack. Formulate an idea about what the problem is most likely to be, and then divide the problem into smaller parts. Prioritize your hypotheses according to their chance of success and the cost of the solution.

- Execute the plan. Break down the problem into individual elements that can be tested. Then test each element individually.

- Ensure user satisfaction. Make sure that all people involved in this problem are satisfied that the problem has been solved.

- Document the solution. Keep records on the LAN system, history, and available resources.

## Troubleshooting Reference Sources

Several troubleshooting tools are available. This chapter introduced the following:

- Novell Support Connection website
- The Microhouse Technical Library (MTL)
- Novell Support Connection CD

## Choosing a Research Tool

Use the best tool for the job. Remember that the Support Connection website is probably the best support tool because it has the most current information and most companies now have an Internet connection.

# CNE Practice Test Questions

**1.** Which is NOT a category of network problems?

   **A.** Physical problems

   **B.** Electrical problems

   **C.** Network design problems

   **D.** Viruses

**2.** Which problem is most likely to cause corruption of data?

   **A.** Static

   **B.** Magnetism

   **C.** Crosstalk

   **D.** Transients

**3.** What is the most likely cause of a network problem?

   **A.** Viruses

   **B.** User error

   **C.** Static

   **D.** Transients

**4.** Which term describes a surge of voltage?

   **A.** Virus

   **B.** Transient

   **C.** Static

   **D.** Noise

**5.** Which technique will NOT reduce the possibility of noise?

   **A.** Proper grounding

   **B.** Use of shielding

   **C.** Avoiding interference sources

   **D.** Proper user training

**6.** If you handle the internal parts of a computer, what can cause damage?

   **A.** Viruses

   **B.** Noise

**C.** Static

**D.** Crosstalk

**7.** Which of the following best describes computer viruses?

   **A.** They are a myth.

   **B.** They are usually created accidentally.

   **C.** They cannot affect networks.

   **D.** None of the above

**8.** Which source is most likely to have the latest driver for a network card for NetWare?

   **A.** The Microhouse Technical Library (MTL)

   **B.** The Novell Support Connection website

   **C.** The NetWare Support Encyclopedia (NSEPRO)

   **D.** The Encyclopedia of Hard Drives

**9.** Which source would you look in for the latest Novell news?

   **A.** The NSEPRO

   **B.** The Novell Support Connection website

   **C.** The MTL

   **D.** None of the above

**10.** Which MTL category would show the jumper settings for a hard drive interface card?

   **A.** Hard Drive Controllers

   **B.** Hard Drives

   **C.** Miscellaneous I/O Controller Cards

   **D.** Manufacturers

# CHAPTER

# 14

Connections: Network
Interface Cards and Cables

# Roadmap

This chapter describes the installation and troubleshooting process for Network Interface Cards (NICs) and their cables.

## Topics Covered

- The different types of network media
- Installing and configuring the different types of Network Interface Cards (NICs)
- Installing and configuring an Ethernet network
- Installing and configuring a Token Ring network
- Fiber Distributed Data Interface (FDDI) network description
- Asynchronous Transfer Mode (ATM) network description

## Skills You'll Learn

- Explain the various types of network cables
- Install, configure, and troubleshoot an Ethernet network
- Install, configure, and troubleshoot a Token Ring network
- Explain FDDI
- Explain ATM

---

This chapter covers the components that hold the network together: network cabling, network interface cards (NICs), and associated supporting components. It discusses these components in the context of four common network topologies: Ethernet, Token Ring, FDDI, and ATM.

You'll find that a clear understanding of NICs and cabling will give you an edge when choosing fast and reliable network components, as well as when you are troubleshooting those components that turn out to be not so fast and reliable. Your network plan is your guide to selecting the components for your new network.

# Planning a Network

The first thing a network administrator or network design engineer must do when designing a network is research. Too many networks are the results of magazine ad design engineering—building a network based on questionable information. Unfortunately, this method produces about the same results you would have if you let the marketing department design your network. Be careful where and how you acquire your information.

You should prepare for designing your network by following these steps:

1. Understand the jobs of the network users.

2. Create a list of requirements.

3. Create a list of components that meet the requirements.

## Understanding Users' Jobs

When you understand the jobs of your users, you'll know which features your future network implementation must have in order to provide the correct services for the users.

For example, if your users work with graphics or document imaging, they will require a network with lots of bandwidth to accommodate the high amounts of network traffic. If the users will use the network mostly for text documents, the network won't need a lot of bandwidth.

*Bandwidth* refers to the range of frequencies a medium (such as cable) can accommodate. In networking, bandwidth is measured in terms of the number of bits that can be transmitted across a given medium per second. Generally, a high bandwidth increases throughput and performance.

## Listing Network Requirements

When you have a good understanding of what the network will be used for, you should create a document listing requirements. In this document, detail the specific functions the network will fulfill.

For example, if your users fax a lot of documents to customers, the list of requirements might include:

- Ability to fax from Windows applications

- Fax success notification
- Fax failure notification

## Listing Network Components

A list of network components is critical to network planning. Make sure that the components you are considering have been tested and approved to operate with NetWare and particularly with the version of NetWare you are planning to use. Don't forget to specify the version of NetWare and the DOS Requester (or shell) that you will be installing. Some applications work only with a certain version.

Novell tests hundreds of network components each year, and it publishes the results as Novell Labs Bulletins. Novell has two levels of certification for hardware and software products. The first level, "It runs with NetWare," does not require any testing by Novell—vendors test their own products in labs of their choosing under Novell-specified test conditions. Only products that carry the NetWare Tested and Approved label have been tested in Novell's labs. Bear in mind that even if a product is "Tested and Approved," it doesn't mean it will work perfectly with your configuration. It's impossible for vendors or Novell to test every possible circumstance. You should test any new product carefully.

You can find Novell Labs Bulletins on Novell's NSEPRO CD-ROM, Compu-Serve's NetWire forum, or the Novell Support Connection website (http://support.novell.com). These resources are described in Chapter 13. If you do not have access to these sources, try calling Novell at 1-800-NETWARE (1-800-638-9273) to find these publications. This number also provides access to Novell's fax-back document service, which allows you to request faxed documents about products and general Novell information.

You also need to be sure that the cabling you plan to use will work at your site and with your system. If you plan to run the cables through your ceiling, be sure to check to see if fire codes in your area require plenum-rated wire. Wire demolition (the removal of old wire) and reinstallation can triple the cost of a cabling project. Also, be sure the cable meets the specifications of the LAN cards you are installing and the hubs or MSAUs (multi-station access units) you are planning to use.

You must take your entire system into consideration when acquiring products for your LAN or WAN. For example, you may purchase a Novell-approved, LAN-based remote control program (a program that allows you to control a workstation across a LAN connection), only to find that it will not reach workstations installed on segments on the other side of your network's routers. If you had checked with the manufacturer, you would have learned that it worked with NetWare, but it didn't work across routers.

## Installing the Network

After you have planned your network and verified that the products are tested and approved to work with NetWare, you are ready to start your installation. The easiest part of the installation is loading the operating system. (Configuring the operating system and installing the equipment is another story.)

NetWare 3.*x*, 4.*x*, and 5 all come with installation programs that virtually run themselves, a great leap forward from the old NetWare 2.15, which required a minimum of 45 disk exchanges in order to set up the operating system.

A good installation strategy is to begin by installing the NICs in the workstations. If possible, use the default interrupt of the NIC you have chosen to install. Also, try to standardize all the NIC settings—port settings, interrupts, memory addresses, and DMA channels—to be the same in all workstations. Standardization can eliminate complicated problems and, in most cases, will even work with workstations that come from different vendors.

For example, your organization may have purchased various PC clones that run at different speeds and have various types of motherboards. When you install the network, try to configure all the workstations with the same brand and model of card. Most of the machines will probably be able to use identical settings, making it fast and trouble free to install those workstations. If you are lucky, there won't be hardware conflict problems with any of the machines.

# Ethernet Networks

**E**thernet, the most popular network specification, was originally the brainchild of Xerox Corporation. Introduced in 1976, it quickly became the network of choice for small LANs. The UNIX market was the first to embrace this easy-to-install network.

## How Ethernet Works

Ethernet uses the CSMA/CD (carrier sense multiple access with collision detection) media access method, which means that only one workstation can send data across the network at a time. It functions much like the old party line telephone systems used in rural areas. If you wanted to use the telephone, you picked up the line and listened to see if anyone was already using it. If you heard someone on the line, you didn't try to dial or speak; you simply hung up and waited a while before you picked up the phone to listen again.

If you picked up the phone and heard a dial tone, you knew the line was free. You and your phone system operated by *carrier sense*. You sensed the dial tone or carrier and, if it was present, you used it. *Multiple access* means that more than one party shared the line. *Collision detection* means that if two people picked up the phone at the same time and dialed, they would "collide" and both need to hang up the phone and try again. The first one back on the free line gains control and is able to make a call.

In the case of Ethernet, workstations send signals (packets) across the network. When a collision takes place, the workstations transmitting the packets stop transmitting and wait for a random period of time before retransmitting. Using the rules of this model, the workstations must *contend* for the opportunity to transmit across the network. For this reason, Ethernet is referred to as a *contention-based* system.

## 10Base5 (ThickNet) Ethernet

The original wiring used for Ethernet is called ThickNet or 10Base5. The 5 stands for its maximum length, 500 meters (1,650 feet). It is named for the size of the wire used, which is about as big around as your thumb. Working with it is like wrestling a boa constrictor. You might say it is not technician-friendly. The coaxial (coax) cable is marked every 2.5 meters (8.25 feet) for connection points, so that you do not try to connect devices closer than 2.5 meters, because a shorter distance degrades the signal.

Most coax is made using PVC coating. If burned, one of the gases it creates is chlorine which, when inhaled, turns into hydrochloric acid. Teflon-coated cable is much more expensive, but safer to use in ceilings where ventilation systems are located. Some fire codes require the use of plenum-rated cable if the wiring is run through ceilings.

10Base5 (ThickNet) Ethernet has the following specifications:

- Maximum segment length: 500 meters (1,650 feet)

- Maximum taps: 100

- Maximum segments: 5

- Maximum segments with nodes: 3

- Minimum distance between taps: 2.5 meters (8.25 feet)

- Maximum repeaters: 4

- Maximum overall length with repeaters: 2.5 kilometers (1.5 miles)

- Maximum AUI drop cable length: 50 meters (165 feet)

You normally use a device called a *vampire tap* to connect new connections to the ThickNet with a tool that drills a small hole into the coaxial cable. The tap is then attached and tightened down with its connector into the hole. Although in some cases it may be possible to tap coaxial cable with users up and running, you should try to do this after working hours. A mistake can short the center conductor with the shielding and take the entire segment down.

The tap is also a *transceiver*, a device that handles transmission data signal generation and reception, and receives its electrical power through the DIX (Digital, Intel, and Xerox) connector. The DIX connector uses an AUI (Attachment Universal Interface) cable to connect to the DIX female connector on the LAN card. At both ends of the cable, you must install a terminator to complete the electrical circuit and to cut down on signal reflections. Figure 14.1 shows some components of ThickNet Ethernet, as well as ThinNet Ethernet, which is discussed in the next section.

ThickNet cable has the following disadvantages:

- Large size

- High cost

- Awkward connection method (drilling into the wire)

The advantages of ThickNet cabling are few for today's networks, but many ThickNet networks are still in use and are reliable.

This wiring specification allows you to increase the length of the overall network by using repeaters, which are devices that pick up signals and repeat them to another segment of the cable. You may use a maximum of four repeaters on one network, with only three of the segments populated with nodes. Thus the overall length of a network, by implementing repeaters to extend the length, is 2.5 kilometers (1.5 miles).

**F I G U R E 14.1**

Some common Thick
and Thin Ethernet
components

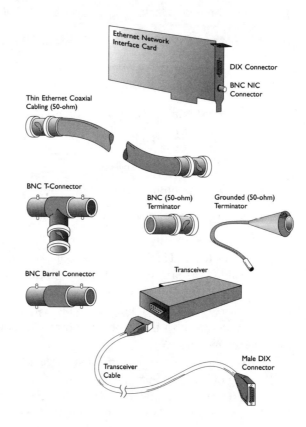

## 10Base2 (ThinNet Coax) Ethernet

ThinNet coax quickly became a popular choice of network cabling, because it costs, appears, and handles just like its affordable and useful cousin—the 75-ohm coaxial cable used for television cable. Because of its low cost, it is often referred to as *Cheapernet*.

10Base2 (ThinNet) has the following specifications:

- Maximum segment length: 185 meters (610.5 feet)
- Maximum segments: 5
- Maximum segments with nodes: 3
- Maximum repeaters: 4
- Maximum devices per segment: 30

- Minimum distance between nodes: 0.5 meters (1.5 feet)
- Maximum overall length with repeaters: 925 meters (3,052.5 feet)

The term 10Base2 is a little misleading because the maximum length is not actually 200 meters (660 feet) but only 185 meters (610.5 feet). Someone took the liberty of rounding up to make it fit in with the other specifications. Some vendors advertise that by using their hardware you can extend the 185 meters to 300 meters (990 feet). However, if you later mix LAN cards or repeaters from different vendors into your network, you may have problems, because most manufacturers adhere strictly to the IEEE specifications.

The specification for ThinNet is 50-ohm RG-58A/U or RG-58C/U coaxial cable . RG-58A/U is the most widely used type. RG-58A/U has only one shield and does not adhere strictly to the IEEE specification. Although it is not used much anymore (often replaced by 10BaseT technologies), you may still find it in some networks. You should also avoid using RG-59 cable, which is intended for television signals. Another type of cable you may see is RG-58U cable. Installing this type of wiring is a mistake, because it does not meet the IEEE specification for 10Base2.

The connectors used for ThinNet are BNC connectors, along with the T-connectors required to connect to the BNC female connectors on the LAN card. As with 10Base5 (ThickNet), each end of the cable must have a terminator. Only one end of the cable must be grounded.

This wiring specification differs significantly from 10Base5 in that the transceiver is built into the LAN card itself and is not a device that you must attach to the cable. A cable connecting the T-connector to the workstation, called a *pigtail,* cannot be used with this standard. The T-connector must connect directly to the back of the card in a daisy-chain fashion. If it doesn't connect this way, the network connections will fail.

As with 10Base5, you can use up to four repeaters on a network, with only three of the segments populated with nodes. 10Base2 and fiber-optic cabling can be mixed by using a fiber/ThinNet repeater. If you have repeaters on your ThinNet network, be sure that all devices have SQE (Signal Quality Error) or Heart Beat turned off. If SQE is on, the SQE signal will appear as excessive collisions on the network and slow the network down.

To remember what you can put between any two nodes on a coaxial Ethernet network, keep in mind the *5-4-3 rule.* As you may have noticed from the specifications, there is a five segment, four repeater theme with Ethernet topologies. The 3 part of the rule states that only three segments can be populated with nodes. The 5-4-3 rule does not apply to UTP or fiber-optic cable segments. With UTP, hubs act as repeaters. You cannot have two devices separated by more than four hubs.

The disadvantages of ThinNet include the high cost compared to UTP cable and the fact that the bus configuration makes the network unreliable. If any node's cable is broken, the entire segment, and probably the entire network, will be affected. Nevertheless, because it was the most economic solution for a long time, ThinNet is used in many existing installations.

## 10BaseT (Twisted-Pair) Ethernet

The use of unshielded twisted-pair (UTP) cable is now a well-established trend in Ethernet network wiring schemes. UTP costs less and is more flexible than 10Base5 or 10Base2 cabling. The specification for UTP was created by the IEEE 802.3 subcommittee in the 1980s. Do not substitute shielded twisted-pair (STP) cable for UTP; the IEEE 10BaseT specification is for UTP only.

10BaseT (Twisted-Pair) Ethernet has the following specifications:

- Maximum segments: 1,024

- Maximum segments with nodes: 1,024

- Maximum segment length: 100 meters (330 feet)

- Maximum nodes per segment: 512

- Maximum nodes per network: 1,024

- Maximum hubs in a chain: 4

10BaseT is wired as a star, which means that each device has its own set of wires connected directly to a hub. Although the physical topology of 10BaseT is a star, its logical topology is a bus, giving you the advantages of a star wiring scheme and a bus in one specification. 10BaseT is easy to troubleshoot, because problems on one segment of wiring usually will not affect the other segments (each node uses its own separate segment).

You can isolate a device that is causing problems simply by disconnecting its cable from the hub. Some hubs have built-in management capabilities that will report errors or problems, as well as allow you to disconnect the devices from the hub remotely. These types of hubs are known as *intelligent* hubs. Figure 14.2 shows an Ethernet network with a 10BaseT hub.

**FIGURE 14.2**

An Ethernet network with a 10BaseT hub

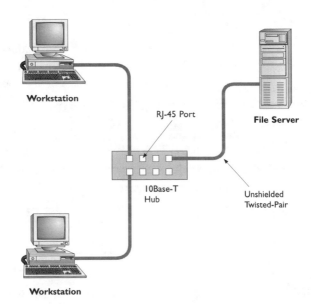

The connection to the hub and the LAN cards is made with an RJ-45 connector. You can also connect 10BaseT to a DIX connector or an AUI connector by using a transceiver or twisted-pair access unit (TPAU). ThinNet connections on LAN cards can also be used with special transceiver devices.

UTP cable is classified in categories defined by the Electrical Industries Association. Categories 1 and 2 are voice-grade cable. Categories 3, 4, and 5 are data-grade. Be sure to ask the vendor for a performance specification sheet when you purchase Category 5 cable to be sure it meets the specifications for your network. (See Chapter 2 for more information about UTP cable categories.)

Some buildings that are wired for telephone service with twisted-pair wires will have extra installed pairs available for your use on your network. If the wiring is Category 3 or better, you can use the existing wiring to add a 10BaseT network inexpensively. You can purchase wall jacks that will have an RJ-45 connector for 10BaseT and an RJ-11 connector for traditional phone lines.

There are also Teflon-coated versions of UTP cable for areas that require plenum-rated wire. The cable is light and flexible, which makes it easy to pull through construction. The cable should be 22, 24, or 26 gauge AWG (American Wire Gauge), with an impedance (resistance based on signal frequency) of 85 to 110 ohms at 10MHz.

## 10BaseF

10BaseF is another implementation of Ethernet that has become popular lately. It is designed to use the 10Mbps standard signaling rate of Ethernet, but take advantage of the new features of fiber-optic cable. The unique thing about 10BaseF is that fiber-optic cable can handle so much more bandwidth, but the designers of 10BaseF chose to use the fiber-optic technology to increase the distance between workstation and concentrator to a maximum of 2,000 meters.

In addition to the workstation-to-hub distance increase, the standard uses two 62.5 micron fiber optic strands with 125 micron cladding instead of a single copper cable. Additionally, regular Ethernet NICs are typically used with 10BaseF media adapters to connect workstations to a 10BaseF concentrator. These media adapters attach to the 15-pin AUI connector commonly found on Ethernet NICs.

Some hubs can use 10BaseF technology to connect to each other. Some of these hubs have AUI ports that can use the aforementioned media adapter. On the other hand, some hubs use a modular design with a replaceable media adapter module.

## 100BaseT

100BaseT (also referred to as Fast Ethernet) is a standard that is rapidly gaining acceptance in the industry. It is based on some of the same technologies as 10BaseT (particularly the CSMA/CD media access method) but can use data transmissions rates of up to 100Mbps.

There are three main implementations of 100BaseT in use today:

- 100BaseT4
- 100BaseTX
- 100BaseFX

Each has its own specific configuration issues. But they all use a network layout similar to 10BaseT (a NIC in each workstation, cables run from each device to a concentrator or hub, physical star, logical bus topology, and CSMA/CD media access). The specifications differ mainly in the type and number of cables used from workstation to hub.

### 100BaseT4

100BaseT4 is designed to run over either Category 3 or Category 4 cabling. It is popular because some older buildings don't have the capability of upgrading their cabling systems to Category 5. You do not have to have Category 3 or Category 4 cable; it will run on Category 5 as well.

The main disadvantage is that because of the poorer cable quality, all four pairs in an eight-wire cable must be used. The signal is divided among the wires for more resistance to noise.

### 100BaseTX

100BaseTX is the closest 100Mbps standard to 10BaseT. In this implementation, only four wires are required, two for transmission and two for reception. But, unlike 10BaseT, 100BaseTX *requires* Category 5 cabling. All connectors and cable in the cabling system must be rated at Category 5.

### 100BaseFX

100BaseFX is the only implementation of 100BaseT that uses fiber-optic cabling. It still uses a hub, but instead of a single, copper cable, it uses two strands of multimode fiber-optic cable for each connection from workstation to hub. Typically, this cable is a 62.5 micron fiber-optic core with a 125 micron outer cladding. One strand of cable is used for transmitting, the other is used for receiving.

Another difference between 10BaseT and 100BaseFX is the distance between workstation and concentrator. In 100BaseFX, the maximum distance is 412 meters, allowing the network to span much greater distances.

## Gigabit Ethernet

Of all the types of Ethernet, none has been more eagerly anticipated than the one known as *Gigabit Ethernet*. It still uses the same CSMA/CD media access method that the other types use, as well as the physical star topology, but Gigabit Ethernet, as its name suggests, will transfer data at 1000Mbps or

1Gbps. Just like other types of Ethernet, not everyone can agree on the specifics of the standards, so there are two proposed major standards:

- IEEE 802.3ab (also known as 1000BaseT)
- IEEE 802.3z (also known as 1000BaseX)

### 1000BaseT

1000BaseT is based on the proposed IEEE 802.3ab standard that defines 1000Mbps transmissions over Category 5 copper cable for segments up to 100 meters. There are plans to develop the standard so that it uses the same RJ-45 connector as 10BaseT and 100BaseT implementations of Ethernet.

### 1000BaseX

1000BaseX is actually a group of 1Gigabit standards that are based on the 8B/10B encoding scheme developed by IBM. There are many subsets of the 1000BaseX standard that specify the different physical media and topologies. There are three major Gigabit Ethernet standards:

- 1000BaseLX specifies fiber-optic backbone media
- 1000BaseCX specifies short distance copper media
- 1000BaseSX specifies fiber-optic media

## Troubleshooting Ethernet Networks

The best tool for troubleshooting Ethernet is common sense, along with a bit of knowledge. Protocol analyzers will fill in vital gaps by giving you trend and error information that otherwise cannot be detected.

If your network is larger than 30 to 50 workstations, a *protocol analyzer*, such as Novell's LANalyzer for Windows, can be a wise investment. Troubleshooting these networks without one can be like a doctor trying to diagnose a heart problem without a stethoscope. See Chapter 18 for more information about LANalyzer.

### Ethernet Card Problems

When a workstation's NIC goes out and begins to talk consistently and incoherently on the network, it will create packets that are larger than 1,518 bytes and have CRC errors. This type of packet is called a *jabber packet*. To find the faulty card, disconnect workstations or hubs one at a time until you narrow it down to the rogue card.

In some cases, resource conflicts can cause network communications problems. You may need to take all the boards out of your system except the network adapter. When you have it working again, add one board at a time until you find the board that has the conflicts. Reconfigure and continue adding cards till the system is up and running.

Remember that COM1 uses IRQ 4 and COM2 uses IRQ 3. Try avoiding these when configuring IRQs because they are commonly used by a serial mouse and modem. Sometimes, just the presence of the serial port will interfere with these IRQs. You can usually disable a serial port you're not using.

Check for the common error of not having common frame types (ETHERNET_802.2, ETHERNET_802.3, ETHERNET_II and ETHERNET_SNAP) bound to the workstation and the file server. If they are not bound correctly, your workstation will respond with a File-Server-Not-Found message.

Be sure to use the diagnostics program that ships with the LAN card. You will be able to test and configure the card in the machine rather than removing it. If you use a card that has two or more ports, you will want to be sure you have set the jumpers or configuration to use the correct port on the card.

Some network adapter cards do not make connection very well in the card socket. Cleaning its connector and resetting can usually solve this. (Don't be tempted to use an eraser to clean the connector, because it will leave that nasty grit on the card.) If you have checked the settings and cleaned the card, and it still doesn't work, replace it with a spare that you know is functional.

## 10Base2 Problems

If your 10Base2 network goes down, it is likely that the bus continuity has been damaged. Someone may have damaged or disconnected one of the connectors while moving a PC around.

Check terminators at both ends of the cable with a volt-ohm meter to be sure they still read 50 ohms resistance. Check resistance of the entire segment of cable by using the center conductor of a T and the outside shield of the T. It should measure 25 ohms or slightly above. If it measures closer to 50 ohms, you may have a faulty terminator, a missing terminator, a break in the wire, or a missing T-connector. Also, check that one end of the cable is still grounded.

If you are working with 10Base2, make sure the cable has not grown too long by the consistent addition of users without considering wiring lengths, a very common problem with bus topology networks.

Because some people see little difference between RG-59, RG-58A/C, and RG-62, you may need to make sure someone did not just add a black piece of coax to extend or repair the cable. Also check for the wrong connector types on your cable, as well as pigtails on ThinNet networks.

If only one workstation is having a problem on a **10Base2** or **10Base5** network, you can be sure it is not the cabling but rather the LAN card, the transceiver, or AUI cable if 10Base5. You will more than likely need to swap out the card to nail this one down, so make sure you have a spare. Don't forget to configure it before you attempt this solution.

## Cable Problems and Cable Testing Tools

Check to make sure the cabling does not run near high voltage and that it isn't wrapped in cable trays. Florescent light ballast can also cause electromagnetic interference (EMI). Check that the wires are not run against or across these. Electrical motors will also cause EMI if wires are run across them.

Network cable testing equipment can locate wiring faults quickly. If you suspect you may be doing troubleshooting on a regular basis, a network cable tester is a good investment. Novell also provides a utility called COMCHECK that you can get from the NSEPRO or through The Novell Support Connection website. (See Chapter 13 for more information about these resources.)

A time-domain reflectometer is a cable-testing device that you can use to tell if the cable is shorted, broken, or crimped. The device sends a signal down the wire and listens for what type of signal reflects back. From the reflection, it can determine the type of problem with the cable; this method is much like throwing a rock down a well and listening for how long it takes to hear it hit the bottom, as well as sensing if it hit water, dirt, or other rocks.

# Token Ring Networks

Token ring was developed by IBM as a robust, highly reliable network. It is more complex than Ethernet because it has self-healing properties. Token Ring is an IEEE 802.5 standard whose topology is physically a star but logically a ring.

Workstations connect to the bus by means of individual cables that connect to an MSAU or controlled-access unit (CAU). This type of topology is illustrated in Figure 14.3.

**FIGURE 14.3**
A Token Ring network
is a physical star and a
logical ring.

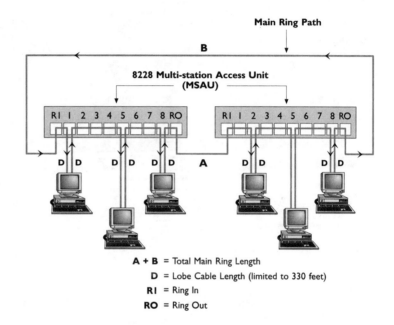

A + B = Total Main Ring Length
D = Lobe Cable Length (limited to 330 feet)
RI = Ring In
RO = Ring Out

The difference between an MSAU and a CAU is that an MSAU is a passive device that has no power plug and no intelligence, while a CAU has intelligence and a power plug. A CAU can perform physical network management operations.

The original Token Ring cards were 4Mbps. These were later replaced by 16Mbps cards. The 16Mbps cards are manufactured to work at 4Mbps, for compatibility purposes, but the 4Mbps cards only run at 4Mbps. The 4Mbps version will allow only one token on the ring at a time. The 16Mbps version will allow a card to retransmit a new free token immediately after the last bit of a frame. The term for this is *early token release*.

When configuring a Token Ring network, you must remember that all Token Ring cards must be set to either 4Mbps or 16Mbps. You cannot mix the speeds on the same segment.

Some typical Token Ring components are illustrated in Figure 14.4.

**FIGURE 14.4**

Token Ring
components

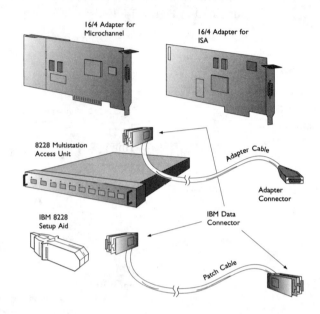

Token Ring has the following basic specifications:

- Cable type:   UTP, STP, or fiber-optic

- Maximum MSAUs:   33

- Maximum nodes:   260

- Maximum distance between node and MSAU:   45.5 meters (150 feet) for UTP cable; up to 100 meters (330 feet) for STP or fiber-optic cable

- Maximum patch cable distance connecting MSAUs:   45.5 meters with UTP cable; 200 meters (660 feet) with STP; 1 kilometer (.6 mile) with fiber-optic cable

- Minimum patch cable distance connecting MSAUs:   2.5 meters (8 feet)

- Maximum cumulative patch cable distance connecting all MSAUs: 121.2 meters (400 feet) with UTP cable; fiber-optic cabling can span several kilometers

A *patch cable* is a cable that connects two MSAUs.

# How Token Ring Works

In a Token Ring, although the cards attach like a star to the MSAU or CAU, they function logically in a ring. The ring passes a *free token* (a small frame with a special format) around the ring in one consistent direction. A node receives the token from its *nearest active upstream neighbor* (NAUN) and passes it to its *nearest active downstream neighbor* (NADN). If a station receives a free token, it knows that it can attach data and send it on down the ring. This is called *media access*. Each station is given an equal chance to have the token and take control in order to pass data.

Each station in the ring receives the data from the busy token and repeats the data, exactly as it received it, on to the next active downstream neighbor on the ring. The addressed station (the station the data is intended for) keeps the data and passes it on up to its upper-layer protocols. It then switches two bits of the frame before it retransmits the information back on to the ring to indicate that it received the data. The data is sent repeatedly, until it reaches the source workstation, and the process begins again.

Each station in the ring basically acts as a repeater. The data is received and retransmitted by each node on the network until it has gone full circle. This is something like the party game called Rumor or Telephone, in which one person whispers something into one player's ear, who in turn repeats it in someone else's ear, and so on, until it has gone full circle. The only difference is that, in the party game, when the person who initiated the message receives it back, it has usually undergone substantial permutations. When the originating node on the network receives the message, it is normally intact except that two bits have been flipped, to show that the message made it to its intended destination.

## Active Monitors and Standby Monitors

The station that has been up the longest normally will become the *active monitor*. Token Ring allows only one active monitor on a ring at a time. All other stations on the ring become *standby monitors*. They wait in the wings in case the active monitor bites the dust, in which case a new active monitor is negotiated. Minor errors, such as the active monitor being turned off, are dealt with by the active monitor and standby monitors.

On a NetWare-based Token Ring network, the file server eventually ends up as the active monitor, because it is usually up for the longest continuous period of time.

The active monitor does a sort of system check every seven seconds. In this check, the active monitor sends out a token to the next station on the ring. This token informs the station of the active monitor's address. This station also lists the active monitor as its upstream neighbor. The station then informs the station next in the ring of the active monitor's address. This process proceeds around the ring until the token returns to the active monitor. Through this process, each station learns three pieces of information: the address of the active monitor, who its upstream neighbor is, and who its downstream neighbor is.

## Beaconing

If a station does not hear from its upstream neighbor within seven seconds, it assumes something bad has happened and acts on its own. It sends a message down the ring announcing three basic pieces of information: who it is (its network address), its NAUN's address (the station it has not heard from in the allotted time), and the type of beacon (the condition being indicated, such as no response from the node). This action is called *beaconing*. It occurs when the Nearest Active Upstream Neighbor Notification fails, as illustrated in Figure 14.5.

**FIGURE 14.5**

Beaconing points out breaks on a Token Ring network.

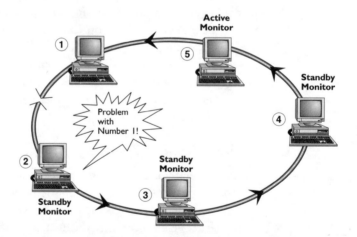

The beaconing process serves to identify any area on the ring where there is a problem. (A problem area on the ring is called the *fault domain*.) Once the fault domain is located, the workstation that reported the problem—the downstream neighbor of the faulty workstation—has the job of removing the faulty station's packets from the network, ensuring that the network remains stable.

During the beaconing process, each Token Ring card takes itself out of the ring and does an internal diagnostic to determine if it has a problem. If it can, it will repair itself without administrator intervention. The automatic corrective action process of the card is called *auto-reconfiguration.* If it finds an error during auto-reconfiguration, it will not attempt to re-enter the ring. With this information, the ring can repair itself without the network falling apart. This is sort of a built-in self-diagnostics and repair program.

 If for some reason the card fails to correct itself so that it can get back on the ring safely, you must manually reconfigure the card or physically remove the card and replace it with a hot (functioning) spare.

## Advantages and Disadvantages of Token Ring

Like other network standards, Token Ring has unique features and its own list of advantages. Here are some of the advantages:

- Unlike Ethernet, Token Ring shows little or no degradation in performance under heavy loads.

- Built-in diagnostic and recovery mechanisms, such as beaconing and auto-reconfiguration, make the protocol more reliable.

- Token Ring makes connecting a LAN to an IBM mainframe easier because IBM created it and supports it.

- Fault-tolerance features are provided through ring reconfiguration, called ring-wrap. A single cable can create a ring when attached to two MSAUs.

Some of the disadvantages of Token Ring are as follows:

- Token Ring cards and equipment are more expensive than Ethernet or ARCnet systems.

- Token Ring can be very difficult to troubleshoot and requires considerable expertise.

## Token Ring Card Addressing and Settings

A Token Ring card has a unique address created and stored on each card during its manufacturing process. Some cards allow you to change this by using special configuration software that is provided by the card manufacturer.

A single workstation can have a maximum of two cards installed. One is designated as the primary card and the other as the alternate.

A Token Ring card normally uses DIP switch settings to configure the card, as shown in Figure 14.6. The connector to which the cable connects is a 9-pin female connector. A Token Ring network uses four wires to make the connection to each card, similar to UTP cable connections. Token Ring can also use STP cable.

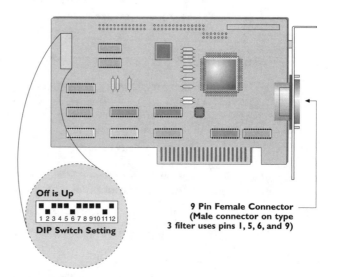

**F I G U R E  14.6**

Token Ring NIC DIP switches

Off is Up

1 2 3 4 5 6 7 8 9 10 11 12

DIP Switch Setting

9 Pin Female Connector
(Male connector on type
3 filter uses pins 1, 5, 6, and 9)

## Cabling for Token Ring

The main purpose of Token Ring cabling is to connect the workstation's LAN card to the MSAU and connect other MSAUs together.

Here is a list of IBM standard cable types that can be used with Token Ring:

- Type 1 is STP cable and is used to connect terminals and distribution panels and to run through walls to wiring closets in the same building. It is made of two twisted pairs of solid core 22 gauge AWG copper wire that is surrounded with a braided shield. It can be run through conduit, inside walls, or in wireways for short distances.

- Type 2 is also STP cable and is used for connecting terminals located in the same physical area or room and distribution panels in wiring closets. It is made just like Type 1 cable with the exception that it incorporates four twisted pairs of telephone wires, so that, with one wire run, you can hook up both data and telephone equipment.

- Type 3 is UTP cable with four pairs, each twisted two times for every 3.6 meters (12 feet) of length. It is used because it is cheaper than Type 1 or 2 cable. The downside of Type 3 is that it is subject to crosstalk and noise and cannot be used for runs as long as possible with Type 1 and 2 cable. It is made of either 22 or 24 gauge wire.

- Type 5 optical cable is used only on the main ring path. It consists of 62.5 micron diameter or 100 micron diameter fiber-optic cable.

- Type 6 is STP cable that does not carry signals as far as Type 1 and 2 cable. It is generally used only as patch cable or extensions in wiring closets. It is made with two 26 gauge AWG stranded core copper wires twisted together in a shielded jacket. Type 6 is much easier to work with than Type 1 because it is more flexible; it consists of stranded copper wire rather than solid core.

- Type 8 cable is used for runs under carpets. Like Type 6 cable, it is made of two 26 gauge AWG stranded core wires twisted together.

- Type 9 cable is basically the fire-retarding version of Type 6 cable. It is plenum-rated and used for runs in ceilings where ventilation systems exist. It is made with two 26 gauge AWG stranded core copper wires twisted together in a shielded jacket.

The IEEE standards committee has developed a UTP/TR specification that replaces the old 4Mbps standard. Consequently, Token Ring networks that incorporate UTP are quickly becoming popular alternatives. You can now buy MSAUs that are designed for both Type 1 and Type 3 UTP cable. The UTP/TR standard uses Category 5 UTP cable, the same type used for Ethernet 10BaseT networks. Category 5 cable (not to be confused with Type 5 fiber-optic cable) has many more twists per foot than its cousin Category 3 and so is less suscep-tible to crosstalk and signal loss (attenuation) at 16Mbps speeds. You will also find it can handle distances that are close to the capabilities of Type 1 cable.

In noisy industrial situations, Type 1 cable is still preferred because STP cable is less susceptible to noise. Large network systems also still use Type 1 cable because it is very reliable.

## The IBM 8228 MSAU

IBM's Token Ring implementation has been the most popular implementation of the IEEE 802.5 standard. For this reason, when looking at Token Ring cabling and hardware, it is important to consider IBM's 8228 MSAU.

There are some differences between IBM's specifications for Token Ring and those of the IEEE 802.5. For example, each allows a different number of stations on an STP ring.

The IBM 8228 MSAU can connect up to eight workstations. It has a Ring In (RI) and a Ring Out (RO) connector for connecting to other MSAUs by means of a patch cable. The patch cable has an IBM Data Connector at both ends of the cable and is used to connect MSAUs, repeaters, and other IBM equipment.

Token Ring adapter cables are used to connect a workstation's Token Ring LAN adapter to an MSAU. It has a 9-pin male connector on one end and an IBM Data Connector on the other end. You will find the 9-pin connector only on the Token Ring LAN cards. All other equipment uses the IBM Data Connector.

When you first receive an MSAU, you will need to set it up using the port reset tool that comes with the MSAU and inserts into the IBM data port on the MSAU. This tool is also handy when you are troubleshooting and need to initialize a port by hand. When the port is initialized, you will see the light on the MSAU, representing the port.

## Troubleshooting Token Ring Networks

Most Token Ring problems come from very obvious and easy-to-find mistakes. You can begin by asking questions such as these:

- Are the patch cables and adapter cables to the workstations of the correct specifications?

- Are the correct types of cables in the right places?

- Are the connectors tight and properly secured?

## Token Ring Card Problems

Start your troubleshooting by confirming that there are no resource conflicts with the Token Ring NIC and other devices installed in the workstation. This is especially true if you are adding a card or have recently added other devices to the workstation.

Check the Token Ring card's custom statistics to see if there are any internal errors listed. If there are internal errors, this is usually a sign that the card has malfunctioned and should be replaced. Token Ring card addresses are hard-coded into the ROMs, but some cards allow you to override this address with a custom address. Be sure to check that you do not have two cards with exactly the same node address, which has been known to happen with Ethernet, Token Ring, and ARCnet networks.

Be sure that all Token Ring cards are configured for the same speed. In other words, if a network is set for 16Mbps, make sure that the card you are troubleshooting is configured for 16Mbps as well. One way to verify this is to watch the Token Ring MLID (Multiple Link Interface Driver) as it loads. It will display the configured Token Ring speed of the card. If the system is an IBM/PS2 and the user used the IBM reference disk to set up a new or existing piece of hardware in the machine, the Token Ring card will be automatically reset to the 4Mbps speed. If you do happen to place a card in the network that is configured with the inappropriate Token Ring speed, it will cause the network traffic to halt temporarily while the ring beacons.

You can specify three different settings for a Token Ring card merely by using the device drivers supplied with the card:

- The adapter address, which can be changed to override the internal address built-in by the manufacturer

- Shared RAM locations the card uses

- Activation of the early token release feature (but only with 16Mbps Token Ring cards set to 16Mbps)

## Cabling and MSAU Problems

Be sure that your network cabling and associated hardware have been documented well to make it possible for you to quickly identify the cable and MSAU of a malfunctioning station. This type of information is critical when isolating a hardware-related problem.

Do not mix MSAUs from different vendors. Internal electrical characteristics, such as impedance, can cause problems with Token Ring networks.

If your network does not have bridges or routers, you can try a trouble-shooting fix that is often used to reset the Token Ring network:

1. Disconnect all the patch cables from the MSAUs.

2. With the setup tool, reset each port.

3. Reconnect each port one at a time with the patch cables.

It's also a good idea to have special cable testers and equipment built specifically for troubleshooting a Token Ring on hand.

# FDDI Networks

**F**DDI (Fiber Distributed Data Interface) is a topology standard that transmits information packets using light produced by a laser or LED (light-emitting diode) and offers incredible speed. FDDI uses fiber-optic cable and equipment to transmit data packets. It has a data rate of up to 100Mbps and allows very long cable distances.

TP-PMD (Twisted Pair-Physical Medium Dependent), also known as CDDI (Copper Distributed Data Interface), is a variation of FDDI that uses copper cable for transmission over short distances.

This topology manages access to the network using IEEE 802.5, like Token Ring. But it also has many improvements over Token Ring, including a system fault-tolerance strategy that employs two rings instead of one and a technique called *wrapping*.

## How FDDI Works

With FDDI, a station must have a token before it can transmit frames. The size of FDDI frames can be between 17 and 4,500 bytes. Stations on the network read the messages that travel around the ring from NIC to NIC. When a station reads a frame that matches its address, it copies the frame and creates an acknowledgment frame. Then it transfers the token to the next attached network node.

FDDI uses the primary ring to move data and a second ring to provide system fault tolerance and backup. The two rings rotate (send messages) in opposite directions, so they are called *dual counter-rotating rings*. The second ring is inactive until needed. Figure 14.7 shows the design of an FDDI topology.

**FIGURE 14.7**

FDDI topology design

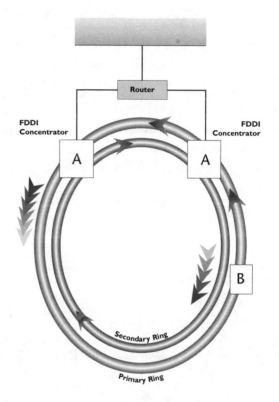

Devices such as workstations, bridges, and routers can be attached to the rings. There are two types of stations, Class A and Class B. Class A stations are also called *dual-attached stations* (DASs) because they can be attached to both rings at the same time. Class A stations are extremely stable. They can survive a break in one or both rings. The only time a Class A station will be isolated from the network is if there are two breaks in both rings on both sides of one workstation.

Class B stations are called *single-attached stations* (SASs) because they only attach to one ring. Class B workstations are not as fault-tolerant as Class A workstations, because they cannot use wrapping, the strategy that takes advantage of the dual-ring system if a break occurs in one or both of the rings. A break in the ring on which a Class B station is attached will probably isolate a Class B workstation.

Wiring concentrators can also be used to provide protection against breaking the rings. FDDI concentrators function much like Token Ring MSAUs, but they are more intelligent than MSAUs. FDDI concentrators can communicate with stations to verify the integrity of the station-to-concentrator connection, and they can reroute packets instantaneously.

*Wrapping* is the system fault-tolerance feature that takes effect when a break occurs on one or both of the rings. When a break occurs in a ring, the first step is the identification of a failure domain (the area affected by the break that cannot carry data). The failure domain includes the machine closest to the cable break and its nearest upstream neighbor. Wrapping reroutes the packets around the two workstations bordering that failure domain. Two Class A machines can then use the second ring to route packets around the failure domain. Class B workstations cannot take advantage of wrapping because they are only connected to one ring. During this time, FDDI concentrators have an important role and must be able to reroute information instantaneously. Figure 14.8 shows how FDDI wrapping works.

**F I G U R E   14.8**

FDDI wrapping

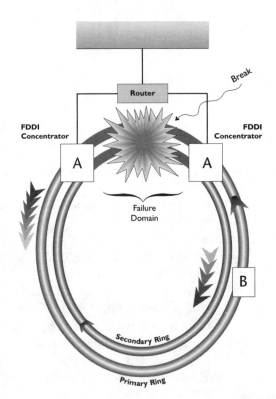

FDDI also has three network management functions built in:

- Connection Management (CMT) assigns connections to workstations that wish to attach to the network and removes them when unattached.

- Ring Management (RMT) is the system for finding and resolving problems in the ring.

- Station Management (SMT) provides the auto-reconfiguration feature and allows the monitoring of the ring's status using specialized software.

## Advantages and Disadvantages of FDDI

FDDI has some great advantages. Advantages due to the use of fiber-optic cable (described in the next section) include the following:

- High bandwidth:   Using light provides enormous bandwidth, as high as nearly 250Gbps. High bandwidth allows for great speed. As stated earlier, most FDDI implementations can handle data rates of 100Mbps.

- Security:   It is difficult to eavesdrop on fiber-optic cable transmissions.

- Physical durability:   Fiber-optic cable doesn't break as easily as other kinds of cable.

- Resistance to EMI:   Fiber-optic cable is not susceptible to EMI.

- Cable distance:   Fiber-optic cable can transmit signals well over two kilometers. Under experimental conditions, distances of hundreds of kilometers are possible.

- Weight:   Fiber-optic cable weighs a lot less than copper wire with similar bandwidth.

In addition to those resulting from the use of fiber-optic cable, FDDI has other advantages:

- Use of multiple tokens:   FDDI uses multiple tokens to improve network speed.

- Ability to prioritize workstations:   FDDI can designate some workstations as low-priority workstations, which allows FDDI to bypass low-priority workstations when necessary, providing faster service to high-priority stations.

- System fault tolerance:   FDDI can isolate faulty nodes with the use of wiring concentrators for instantaneous rerouting. Wiring concentrators function as centralized cabling connection devices for workstations. The other big advantage is wrapping.

As you can see, there are a number of advantages to FDDI. As with all topologies and systems, there are also some disadvantages. FDDI is a complex technology. Installation and maintenance require a great deal of expertise. However, this is a new technology and there should be advancements coming.

The other disadvantage of FDDI is cost. Fiber-optic cable itself is becoming more inexpensive. However, other equipment, such as adapters and concentrators, can be very expensive. With some of this core equipment costing a great deal of money (a typical FDDI concentrator might run more than a thousand dollars per network node), costs for even a small network add up quickly.

## Cabling for FDDI

Rings in FDDI are made of fiber-optic cables. Fiber-optic cable consists of optical fibers made from glass (or plastic). The fiber consists of an inner glass core surrounded by more glass called *cladding*. Light is flashed at either end of the cabling by LEDs or ILDs (injection laser diodes). The signals are then sent through the core, and the cladding acts like a mirror reflecting light back into the core. Fibers are often bundled together to allow multiple signals to be sent at one time. Each fiber can carry signals in only one direction. Figure 14.9 shows two fiber-optic cables.

**FIGURE 14.9**

Two fiber-optic cables

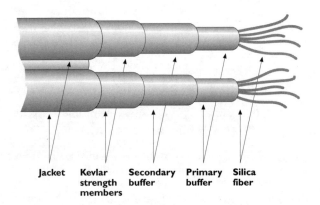

Jacket    Kevlar        Secondary    Primary    Silica
          strength      buffer       buffer     fiber
          members

Today, many fiber-optics manufacturers are working to improve fiber-optic cable so that it will be less expensive and easier to use. Some manufacturers have begun to offer cable with plastic rather than glass. Plastic typically does not have the purity to allow long cable runs or high throughput.

A second improvement has been more successful, snap-in connectors. Formerly, fiber-optic termination included using epoxy preparation and polishing of the glass; it was an involved process. Snap-in connectors have simplified the connection process greatly.

Fiber-optic cable comes in various types and wavelengths. To make the best selection, choose a fiber-optic cable based on its intended use. Then be careful to match the cable to its appropriate connectors.

## Troubleshooting FDDI Networks

The common problems that occur on FDDI networks involve connectors, cabling, and communication delays.

### Connector Problems

Dirty connectors can cause problems in FDDI networks. To allow clear communication, the connector must be free from dirt or dust. Remember that the signals are being transmitted using light. If the connectors are dirty, you can clear them using a lint-free cloth and alcohol (you should only use alcohol to clean connectors).

Another problem may be a bad connector or an open segment of cable. A loss of optical power over 11 decibels may indicate a problem of this nature. Faulty connectors, bad connections, or open segments (segments that are incorrectly terminated) may be responsible for this loss.

### Cable Problems

If you use the wrong type of cable between nodes, you will experience problems. Multimode fiber is good for distances up to two kilometers (1.2 miles). Use single-mode fiber for longer distances.

The type of fiber-optic cable you use can affect network speed. You should probably replace any plastic fiber-optic cable if you want throughput of more than 10Mbps. Glass fiber-optic cable is the preferable alternative. Plastic should not be used on runs longer than 50 meters (165 feet).

There are several ways to find cable problems. If a complete break occurs in a cable segment, you can find the break using a flashlight. For small breaks, you can use an optical power meter and a source of light energy to test the cable. You can also use an optical time-domain reflectometer (OTDR), although this is the most expensive option.

### Communication Delays

FDDI always has communication delays of up to 4 milliseconds. Novell's Packet Burst Protocol, which will send multiple frames, can help you minimize the effect of this delay. See Chapter 18 for more information about the Packet Burst Protocol.

Inefficient path selection may also be a problem. Source routing, in which the entire route is included in the transmission, offers the best option for path selection on a NetWare FDDI network.

# ATM Networks

There have been a lot of discussions lately about a new packet-switching technology known as *Asynchronous Transfer Mode (ATM)*. It is great for high-speed, dedicated bandwidth applications like CAD, video conferencing, and network video-on-demand. It can take advantage of bandwidths anywhere from 25 to 2488 Mbps over existing UTP or fiber-optic cabling.

It works by establishing a virtual circuit from source to destination using special ATM switches and keeping it open until the communication is finished. These switches are currently available, but are used primarily for backbone applications. The cost of the switches makes an ATM-only network currently impractical.

## Advantages and Disadvantages of ATM

There are several advantages and disadvantages of ATM. The advantages are:

- It uses special fixed-length 53 byte packets called *cells.* Their size makes it easy for them to be switched and routed.

- Because it uses switching technology, a dedicated connection is established between sender and receiver.

- It can operate at maximum bandwidth for long periods of time.

- It can use both fiber-optic and copper media.

- The supporting hardware can do both routing and error correction.

- Because of the switching architecture, load balancing across virtual circuits is possible.

- It is probably the best choice for on-demand, real-time network video and audio because it doesn't have timing variations.

There are many advantages of ATM, and only a few disadvantages:

- The cost of ATM switches is currently higher than other fast networking technologies.

- Most WAN technologies don't have the bandwidth to support ATM.

# Review

This chapter covered planning a network and the components of common network topologies. In addition, it explained the concepts, usage, and advantages and disadvantages of these network topologies.

## Network Planning

Planning the network is the first step. You should follow these rules when planning:

- Understand the jobs of the network users.

- Create a list of requirements.

- Create a list of components that meet the requirements.

- Be sure the wire meets the specifications of the LAN cards you are installing and the hubs or MSAUs you are planning to use.

- Make sure the software you plan to install on your NetWare server is tested and approved by the manufacturer to operate with the version of NetWare you are planning to use.

## Ethernet

Ethernet is still the most popular network specification. It uses the media access method of CSMA/CD (carrier sense multiple access with collision detection), which means that only one workstation can use the network at a time.

The original wiring used for Ethernet is called ThickNet or 10Base5. ThinNet or 10Base2 is another choice. Because of its similarity to the coaxial (coax) cable used for cable television, it is economical and easy to work with. 10BaseT or Unshielded Twisted-Pair (UTP) is now a well-established trend in Ethernet network wiring schemes and gives you the advantages of a star wiring scheme and a bus logical topology in one specification. 100BaseT is becoming the standard for high speed networking in networks where 10BaseT was popular. It is virtually the same as 10BaseT, except that it runs at higher speed.

The 5-4-3 rule is used to determine the limits of Ethernet systems. The 5 is for the maximum of five segments, and the 4 is for the maximum number of repeaters. The 3 part of the rule states that only three segments may actually be populated with nodes. This rule does not apply to UTP or fiber-optic cabling. The complete 5-4-3 rule applies to coax segments only. With UTP, hubs act as repeaters. You may not have two devices separated by more than four hubs.

Ethernet comes in four basic frame types: Ethernet_II, Ethernet_802.3, Ethernet_802.2, and Ethernet_SNAP. In order for computers to communicate, they must use the same frame type. A common error is to have different frame types bound to the workstation and the file server.

To troubleshoot Ethernet networks, check for faulty NICs and be sure NICs are connected properly. To look for cable problems, use cable testing tools, such as a time-domain reflectometer. Check for incorrect cable types. Also check for the wrong connector types on your cable, as well as pigtails on ThinNet networks.

## Token Ring

Token Ring is an IEEE 802.5 standard whose topology is physically a star but logically a ring. Workstations connect to the bus by means of individual cables connected to a multi-station access unit (MSAU) or controlled-access unit (CAU). The ring passes a *token* (a small frame with a special format) around the ring. Each station in the ring receives the data from the busy token and repeats the data exactly as it received it onto its next active downstream neighbor on the ring.

Token Ring has the advantages of built-in diagnostic and recovery mechanisms and fault-tolerance features, such as beaconing, auto-reconfiguration, and ring-wrap. Its disadvantages are that it is more expensive than Ethernet or ARCnet and it can be difficult to troubleshoot.

Token Ring generally uses shielded twisted-pair (STP) cable, but can also use UTP and fiber-optic cable in some cases. IBM standard cable Types 1, 2, 3, 5, 6, 8, and 9 can be used with Token Ring.

When troubleshooting a Token Ring system, start by confirming that there are no resource conflicts with the Token Ring NIC and other devices installed in the workstation. Then you can check the Token Ring card (such as its custom statistics for internal errors, which indicate a faulty NIC, and for duplicate node addresses) and your network cabling. Be sure that all Token Ring cards are configured for the same speed (4Mbps or 16Mbps).

# FDDI

FDDI (Fiber Distributed Data Interface) uses fiber-optic cable and equipment to transmit data packets. This topology manages access to the network following the IEEE 802.5 standard, like Token Ring. Unlike Token Ring, it employs two rings instead of one and a methodology called wrapping. It has a data rate of 100Mbps and can transmit well over a mile.

Many of FDDI's advantages are due to its use of fiber-optic cable, which gives it a high bandwidth, improves security, adds physical durability, increases resistance to EMI, and extends cable transmission distance. Other advantages of FDDI include its use of multiple tokens, ability to prioritize workstations, and system fault tolerance. Using FDDI has two main disadvantages, installation and maintenance requirements and high cost.

Some common problems in an FDDI network are dirty connectors, bad connectors or open segments of cable, inappropriate cable usage, cable problems, communication delays, inefficient transmission handling, and inefficient path selection.

# ATM

ATM is a new, high-speed technology that utilizes packet-switching technology and special 53-byte packets called cells. It runs at speeds from 25 to 2488 Mbps, and it is most often used in either backbone applications or on-demand video and audio applications.

# CNE Practice Test Questions

**1.** Which of these technologies is typically the most expensive?

   **A.** Ethernet

   **B.** ATM

   **C.** Token Ring

   **D.** FDDI

**2.** What is the most commonly used topology?

   **A.** Ethernet

   **B.** ATM

   **C.** Token Ring

   **D.** FDDI

**3.** Which device is used to add connections to ThickNet cabling?

   **A.** A repeater

   **B.** A hub

   **C.** A vampire tap

   **D.** A pigtail

**4.** Which of the following is NOT a disadvantage of ThickNet?

   **A.** High cost

   **B.** Large size

   **C.** Reliability

   **D.** Connection method

**5.** Which device allows you to increase the network's overall length?

   **A.** A repeater

   **B.** A passive hub

**C.** An active hub

**D.** A vampire tap

**6.** What is the maximum length allowed for ThickNet cable?

    **A.** 100 meters (330 feet)

    **B.** 100 feet (30.3 meters)

    **C.** 300 feet (90.9 meters)

    **D.** 1,650 feet (500 meters)

**7.** What is the maximum number of segments on a ThinNet network?

    **A.** 5

    **B.** 4

    **C.** 30

    **D.** 100

**8.** What is the maximum length of a ThinNet segment?

    **A.** 925 meters (3,052.5 feet)

    **B.** 200 meters (660 feet)

    **C.** 185 meters (610.5 feet)

    **D.** 100 feet (30 meters)

**9.** What other name is used for ThinNet?

    **A.** 10BaseT

    **B.** 10Base2

    **C.** Ethernet

    **D.** Ethernet_SNAP

**10.** What is the maximum length for an Ethernet UTP (unshielded twisted-pair) connection?

**A.** 100 meters (330 feet)

**B.** 200 meters (660 feet)

**C.** 185 meters (610.5 feet)

**D.** 500 feet (151.5 meters)

**11.** What is the speed of a Token Ring network?

**A.** 10 Mbps

**B.** 4/16 Mbps

**C.** 100 Mbps

**D.** 2.5 Mbps

**12.** What is the speed of a 100BaseT network?

**A.** 10Mbps

**B.** 4Mbps

**C.** 100Mbps

**D.** 2.5Mbps

**13.** Which types of cable can be used with 100BaseT4?

**A.** Category 3 UTP

**B.** Category 5 UTP

**C.** Fiber-optic cable

**D.** Coax cable

**14.** What is the most expensive type of cable?

**A.** Fiber-optic

**B.** 10Base2 coaxial

**C.** UTP

**D.** ThickNet

# CHAPTER

# 15

## Working with Storage Devices on the Network

## Roadmap

This chapter describes the skills needed to install and troubleshoot storage devices on the network.

### Topics Covered

- Basic hard disk theory

- Hard disk configuration

- CD-ROMs with NetWare

### Skills You'll Learn

- Explain hard disk types and their different interfaces

- Explain how to install and configure SCSI and IDE hard disks on workstations and a NetWare server

- Explain how to create partitions and volumes on hard disk in a NetWare server

- Explain how to configure CD-ROMs on a NetWare server as a volume

One of the most unpleasant tasks you will face as a network administrator is to inform a network user that his or her data has been lost—particularly when that user is your boss. To avoid this uncomfortable situation, you should invest your time wisely in building and maintaining a dependable network storage system.

Network storage devices are to a network what a vault is to a bank. Without a solid, secure vault, the bank is vulnerable to losing money and valuables; without a reliable, fault-tolerant method of storing information, your network is vulnerable to losing its precious data.

This chapter surveys the field of network storage options, including hard drives, tape drives, CD-ROMs, and magneto-optical drives. A solid understanding of network storage systems can help you avoid some real network tragedies—or at least recover from them quickly when they happen.

# Hard Drives

**I**n many respects the hard drive is the most crucial component on your network. It is the basis of the file server, because the operating system of the network resides on it. It also holds the most current files on the network. As a network administrator, you must be able to maintain this foundation for the entire network. You must carefully plan fault tolerance and frequently back up the data stored on the hard drive.

A storage system using hard drives is composed of two major components:

- The hard drive itself
- The disk controller

The hard drive is composed of fixed disks (as opposed to removable floppy disks) that are contained in a sealed casing. These disks, often referred to as *platters*, are made of aluminum coated with magnetic recording material on which data is stored.

Opening the vacuum-sealed hard drive casing exposes the platters to dust. This dust can scratch the platter and destroy data.

The *disk controller* provides the interface between the hard drive and the motherboard of the server. The disk controller communicates commands from the CPU to seek, read, or write data to the hard drive.

## How Hard Drives Work

Most hard drives contain a number of two-sided platters on which data is stored. Data is read from and written to the platters by what is called the *read/write head*. Read/write heads reside on arms, the *head arms*, which move the heads across the platters. As a head is drawn across a platter surface, the data stored on that surface is read.

Within the drive casing is a small spindle motor that rotates the platters inside the drive casing at speeds of 3,600 to 7,200 revolutions per minute (rpm). The read/write heads are held above the platters by a *head carriage*, which floats the heads on a cushion of air. Figure 15.1 illustrates the components of a hard drive.

**FIGURE 15.1**

The parts of a hard drive

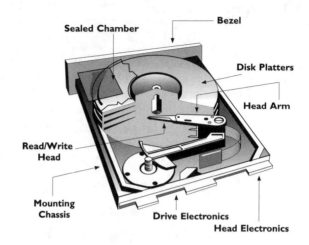

 Read/write heads normally never actually touch the platter. When a read/write head does touch the platter, destroying data, you have what is called a head crash.

A new hard disk must be *partitioned* and *formatted* before it is possible to store files on it. Partitioning prepares platters for formatting, which is the process of setting up the disk for the use of the operating system.

 In NetWare 5, the NWCONFIG.NLM file server utility is used to partition and format the server hard drive.

Data is stored on the disk under a system composed of three main divisions:

- *Tracks* are concentric rings into which platters are divided when the hard disk is formatted. The platter is also divided into *sectors* that resemble the slices of a pie. Figure 15.2 illustrates a segmented platter.

- Data is organized on a platter in the areas formed by the cross-sections of tracks, sectors, and cylinders. The multiple platters of a hard drive, stacked on top of each other, create cylinders. The corresponding cross-sections on all platters are called cylinders.

**F I G U R E   15.2**

The segmentation of a
hard disk platter

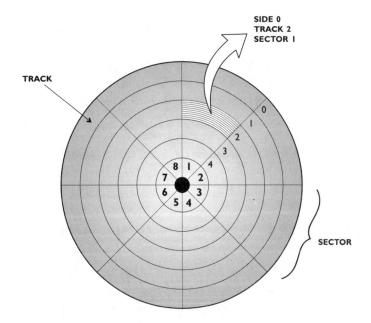

- Within these cross-sections are minimum units of data storage. In Net-Ware, these minimum units are called *blocks*.

In NetWare, the minimum unit of storage in a hard drive is a block. DOS uses clusters as its minimum unit of storage.

After data is requested by the CPU, it takes a brief amount of time (called the *seek time*) for the read/write head to reach the track on which the data is stored. Once the track is reached, the platter must be rotated until the correct data is under the read/write head. The time it takes for this to happen is called *drive latency*. The combination of drive latency and seek time compose what is called *access time*.

When the read/write head reaches the correct position on the platter, it reads the magnetically encoded data stored on the disk surface, which the disk controller interface transfers back to the CPU. The rate at which this data is transferred is called the *data transfer rate*. It is measured in megabytes per second.

# Hard Drive Interface Types

Hard drive interfaces are the means by which hard disk controllers transfer data between the hard drive and the data bus. The interface is the method that determines how data is transferred in terms of speed, which components are utilized, and compatibility with different operating systems.

NetWare is compatible with three main hard drive interfaces:

- Integrated Drive Electronics (IDE) and Enhanced IDE (EIDE)
- Small Computer Systems Interface (SCSI)

Because familiarity with these hard drive interfaces can come in handy on occasion, the following sections examine them in detail.

## Integrated Drive Electronics (IDE)

Western Digital Corporation developed the IDE interface in the mid-1980s, using a variation of the RLL encoding scheme. What was new with this interface was that more intelligence was built into the hard drive. With IDE, the intelligence of the interface is centered on the drive itself, instead of on the controller interface, producing a shorter data path and protecting the communication from external electrical noise. (Although it does still require a controller, an IDE controller is a simple device.)

IDE has replaced ST-506 in most of today's PCs. Drive sizes range from 340MB to 12GB, and larger sizes are always being developed. The IDE interface has several limitations, including:

- A maximum drive capacity of 528MB using a standard BIOS. Newer BIOS versions support drives larger than 1GB. Software included with some large-capacity drives allows them to work with any BIOS, but this requires a TSR program and will not work for a NetWare server.

- It does not support optical or tape drives. However, CD-ROM drives using the IDE interface can be used.

- Because IDE controllers do not support multitasking, they can slow the speed at which the network operating system issues commands to other types of drives. The IDE drive must finish its current operation before another drive can be accessed.

A new version of the IDE standard, EIDE or Enhanced IDE, is becoming popular. EIDE removes many of the disadvantages of IDE drives and supports higher capacities and multitasking. It also supports optical drives.

Finally, the speed of EIDE drives is much faster (up to 16.6MBps) and comparable to SCSI. In order to use EIDE, both the drive and the controller must support it.

## Small Computer Systems Interface (SCSI)

The SCSI interface is known for more than its peculiar name (pronounced *scuzzy*). Beyond being just a disk interface, SCSI provides a complete expansion bus capable of connecting other SCSI-type devices, (such as tape backup drives, CD-ROMs, magneto-optical devices, and so on).

SCSI allows up to eight devices to be connected to the SCSI bus, including one host bus adapter and up to seven drive controllers. Usually, this means seven drives, but it's possible to control two drives using a single SCSI address. You must assign an address, or LUN (logical unit number), to each device. Typically the controller uses ID 7, and the drives are assigned 0–6. The first drive is usually ID 0, but you can actually use any number as long as it's unique.

You can use all the same type devices, different combinations of devices, or only one device on one bus slot. A cable attaches the devices in a chain to the SCSI controller card installed in a server or client. Internally installed devices, those within the CPU, are attached with ribbon cables designed for SCSI. External devices are attached with cables that have the appropriate connectors for that type of device.

SCSI data rates are faster than IDE and EIDE because SCSI uses a parallel data communication system. SCSI supports a total of nine data lines and nine control lines. Standard SCSI will transfer data at 5MBps over its eight-bit bus.

A SCSI controller usually has a built-in BIOS. This BIOS loads into the upper memory area of the PC and controls all the operations on the SCSI bus. The SCSI controller uses a DMA channel, a hardware port address, and a memory address. You must be careful to assign unique numbers to avoid a conflict with other devices in the system. Figure 15.3 illustrates a chain of devices and their addresses.

SCSI controllers usually include floppy disk controllers. If your system uses a separate floppy controller, you should disable floppy support on the SCSI controller. Many new SCSI controllers also include serial and parallel ports; the same warning to disable support on the SCSI applies in this instance also.

**FIGURE 15.3**

SCSI devices in a chain

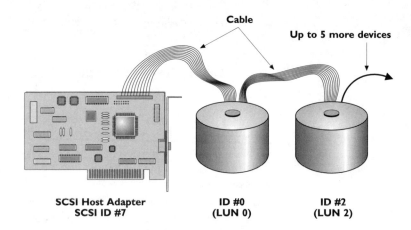

A terminating resistor, or *terminator*, is used at each end of the SCSI bus to absorb the signal and prevent it from reflecting back through the bus. Terminators are usually small devices that plug into sockets near the SCSI connector on the controller and on the last drive in the chain. Many SCSI controllers and drives have built-in control over termination, and you simply have to change a jumper setting to turn termination on or off. Figure 15.4 shows how SCSI devices must be terminated.

SCSI uses an *advanced SCSI programming interface* (ASPI) device driver, provided by the manufacturer. NetWare includes drivers for many popular SCSI drives and controllers, but you should use the driver provided by the manufacturer if possible. It is usually a more recent version.

Because drives, CPUs, and data buses are getting faster, there has recently been a need for faster versions of the SCSI standard. Several new standards with enhanced features have been created.

Standards for the SCSI interface are set by the American National Standards Institute (ANSI) X3T9.2 committee. The committee has created a new version of the SCSI standard, simply called SCSI-2. SCSI-2 goes beyond running hard drives by defining the protocols, hardware, and command set to run other devices. Most modern drives and controllers support the SCSI-2 standard.

FIGURE  15.4

Examples of SCSI
termination

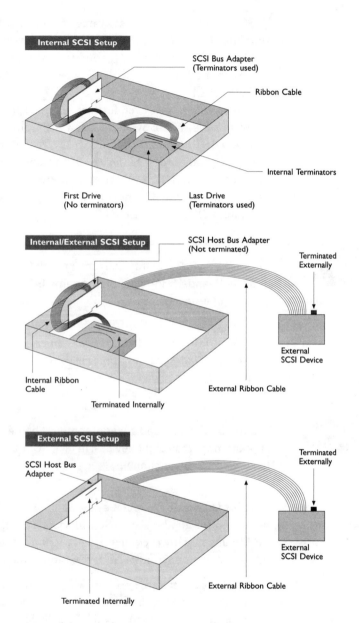

**F I G U R E   15.4**

Examples of SCSI
termination

Mixing SCSI-1, SCSI-2, or SCSI-3 on the same host is not recommended
unless the SCSI adapter has a method of handling both standards.

SCSI-2 has improved data rates of up to 10MBbps. Another improved standard, FAST SCSI-2, supports data rates as high as 10Mbps. For FAST SCSI-2 to operate efficiently, you need to use the appropriate SCSI interface card with the MCA, EISA, VESA, or PCI bus. The speed of SCSI-2 requires a high-speed bus.

WIDE SCSI-2 goes even further, making speeds of 20 to 40MBps theoretically possible. WIDE SCSI-2 is a new technology and is not yet as commonly used as FAST SCSI-2. WIDE SCSI-2 increases speed by providing a second data path. Standard SCSI devices use a single-ended signaling process and a 50-pin cable. WIDE SCSI-2 uses a differential signaling process and 68-pin cable. Some newer SCSI host adapters include connectors for both the regular and WIDE SCSI formats.

Because they are electronically incompatible, you cannot mix differential and single-ended signaling on the same SCSI bus. If you need to support both regular and WIDE SCSI, you need two controllers.

Finally, fairly recently SCSI-3 has emerged as the new SCSI standard. Known as Ultra-SCSI, it is capable of transfer rates up to 40MBps over a 32-bit bus.

In addition to increased speeds, some of the newer SCSI standards can support more than eight devices. In fact, SCSI-2 and SCSI-3 can support up to 15 devices on a channel.

**Tips for Using SCSI Devices**   SCSI is a popular format for NetWare server disks, and for good reason—SCSI devices are flexible, affordable, and fairly easy to install. However, they are not without their problems. The following tips will help you set up SCSI devices and avoid common problems.

- Choose software and hardware carefully. Ensure that version numbers are current and that each device can work with the other devices on the same bus. If possible, use SCSI host adapters with a software setup program for jumper and termination settings, which allows you to configure the card and correct problems without disassembling the computer.

- Use SCSI-2 devices. If you are designing a new network, use the equipment that offers the best performance, which probably means SCSI-2. If you are adding to an existing system, use SCSI-2 only if the controller supports both types of drives.

- Check connections. As with all devices, proper connections for SCSI devices are important. You must use the correct pin number and connector size for all devices on the bus and the SCSI host bus adapter. The cables shipped with the hard drive or controller are not always the right ones for your system; in addition, some systems, such as SCSI and FAST SCSI-2, use similar cables that are not compatible. Also check that the maximum length for the SCSI bus (19 feet, 10 inches) has not been exceeded and that all connectors fit properly.

- Check for proper LUNs. As discussed earlier in this chapter, each SCSI device must have a unique logical unit number (LUN) for identification. The addresses range from 0 to 7. If two devices are set to the same number, at best only one of them will work.

- Check termination. Check that the SCSI bus is terminated properly on both ends. You may have to install terminating resistors, change a jumper setting, or use the software configuration program to turn on termination.

- Check power levels. For signals to function correctly, the SCSI bus requires a stable source of power. The SCSI devices and the host bus adapter must supply the necessary terminating power.

- Check for hardware conflicts. The disk controller's BIOS memory address, port address, IRQ (Interrupt), and DMA channel must not conflict with those of other components in the computer.

- Do not mix models of SCSI adapters on the same computer. Mixing ASPI managers can cause operating conflicts. The ASPI software manager is written specifically for an adapter card.

## Disk Coprocessor Boards

A *disk coprocessor board* (DCB) is a type of hard drive controller that uses its own coprocessor chip to offload the I/O from the CPU. Because more of the work is performed by the controller, the NetWare server is free to do other things, which improves server performance. DCBs are also called *host bus adapters* (HBAs).

Novell developed the original DCBs, which had an 80188 on-board processor. DCBs were developed for the ISA (AT bus), EISA, and microchannel architectures. Novell no longer develops hardware products, but several types of DCBs are available from third parties.

Today's high-performance SCSI, IDE, and EIDE controllers include the same features found in a DCB. The easiest solution for a high-performance NetWare server is to use a reliable, high-end SCSI controller. Because of this, DCBs are largely outdated.

A file server can support up to four *disk channels*. A disk channel consists of a DCB and its disk subsystems. Each DCB can support up to eight SCSI units, which can each support up to two disk drives. External disk subsystems can be daisy-chained off the port on the end of the card. Figure 15.5 shows a typical DCB configuration.

**FIGURE 15.5**

A typical Disk Coprocessor Board (DCB) configuration

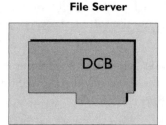

Controller 0     Controller I

# Configuring Hard Drives

**H**ard drives are an important part of your network—possibly the most important. The data and applications on the network depend on properly configured hard drive storage. This section describes the techniques you can use to configure the hard drive and controller, and discusses some common problems you may encounter both during the installation and afterward.

# Setting Jumpers on the Hard Drive and Controller Card

When a hard drive arrives from the manufacturer, you need to check the jumper settings. The manufacturer usually ships hard drives with default jumper settings, which may or may not work with your particular needs. Depending on the drive type, you may need to set the following jumpers directly on the drive:

- C/D or DS: IDE drives use this setting to identify whether the drive is to be a C or a D drive.

- Drive Type: Drive type settings apply only to ESDI, RLL, and MFM drives. The drive type setting identifies the number of drives and indicates whether flat or twisted cable is being used.

- SCSI ID: As you read earlier, SCSI supports eight devices with addresses 0 through 7. You will need to set this address, or LUN, for each device in the system. You usually set it with three jumpers that define a binary number. Hard drives typically ship with a LUN setting of 0. Usually, the SCSI host bus adapter (HBA) gets number 7, and other devices get numbers that start with 0 and go up through 6. Figure 15.6 shows a typical SCSI host bus adapter.

**F I G U R E   15.6**

A typical SCSI host bus adapter

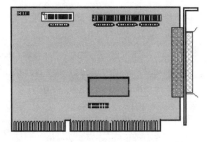

 Check the documentation for all SCSI drives. The settings may vary with each vendor!

- Master/Slave: If two drives share the same IDE cable, the DSP jumper indicates which drive is the master and which drive is the slave. In ESDI, the master is 0, and the slave is 1.

- ACT: This jumper defines the status of an LED on the front of the computer. The LED lights up when the computer is active. Network administrators can use the drive light as a troubleshooting tool. The ACT jumper is used to activate the LED.

The hard drive may come with a controller card. If it does, you may need to set the following jumpers on the card:

- Interrupt (IRQ): The controller interrupt defines a unique path between the server CPU and disk controller. The interrupt and I/O addresses serve to distinguish the disk from any other internal component. A typical hard drive controller interrupt is 14, which is often the default setting and will work unless you have another drive controller in the machine.

The controller interrupt and I/O addresses must be specified in the command that loads the disk driver in the STARTUP.NCF file. These addresses are used to uniquely identify each disk.

- Base I/O: The base I/O address defines an area of memory used to store data being sent between the server CPU and disk controller. The base I/O address is set by the manufacturer and usually does not need to be changed. You may need to change this address to avoid a conflict with another device.

- DMA Channel: Direct memory access (DMA) creates a dedicated memory circuit between disk controller and server memory. Some SCSI and ESDI devices require their own DMA channel.

- Base BIOS Address: If the controller card uses a built-in BIOS, you may need to set this address. Set the address so as to avoid a conflict with other devices, such as video cards and network interface cards (NICs).

These setting are very important. If any setting is incorrect, the drive may not work at all or may not perform optimally. Follow the documentation provided with the disk drive and controller to be sure you are configuring everything correctly.

## Hard Drive Cabling

Hard drive cables provide the connection between the disk controller and the hard drive. Hard drive cables must be installed correctly so that the pins in the connectors can receive and transmit the proper signals for data transfer. Improper installation can cause data loss and potential damage to drive components.

Two common mistakes made when installing cables are using the wrong cables and reversing the pins.

To avoid the most common problems, do the following:

- Ensure that the colored stripe, usually red, attaches to pin 1 on the disk controller and the hard drive. Pin 1 will be marked with the number 1 or a square.

If you are unsure how to position the connector, don't guess. Reversing the cable can cause major damage to all components that are involved.

- Make sure you have the right cable. Floppy drive cables and hard drive cables look similar, but they have different connections. Using the wrong cable can have disastrous results.

MFM and RLL drives use two cables, one for control and the other for data.

- Check the cable distance. The maximum distance for an IDE cable or a single SCSI cable is 18 inches.

By making sure you have the right cables and that the stripe is on the side where pin 1 is on both connections, you can correctly install the hard drive cable. Figure 15.7 shows the hard drive cables for each type of drive interface.

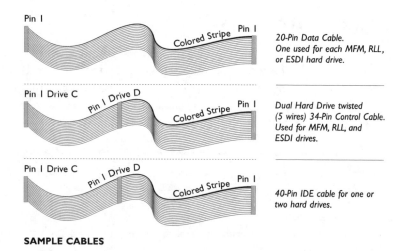

**F I G U R E  15.7**

Three examples of hard drive cables

Pin I

Colored Stripe   Pin I

20-Pin Data Cable. One used for each MFM, RLL, or ESDI hard drive.

Pin I Drive C

Pin I Drive D

Colored Stripe   Pin I

Dual Hard Drive twisted (5 wires) 34-Pin Control Cable. Used for MFM, RLL, and ESDI drives.

Pin I Drive C

Pin I Drive D

Colored Stripe   Pin I

40-Pin IDE cable for one or two hard drives.

**SAMPLE CABLES**

## Formatting the Hard Drive

At this point, the hard drive is physically installed in the computer, its jumpers are set, and the cables are connected. There is still another step before you can access the drive: You must format the drive so that it can store data. Drive preparation includes the following four steps:

1. Choose the CMOS drive type.

2. Low-level format the drive (usually not needed).

3. Partition the drive.

4. Perform the high-level format.

### Choosing a CMOS Drive Type

The *complementary metal-oxide semiconductor* (CMOS) memory is a battery-operated chip found on the computer's motherboard. Found in almost every personal computer today, the CMOS contains critical system parameters: time, floppy drive configurations, adapter, memory, and hard drive settings. The CMOS hard drive settings specify the information the computer needs to access the drive, including the following:

- Number of cylinders

- Number of heads

- Capacity

- Write pre-compensation

You must set all these parameters before the computer can access the drive. You should document the settings so that you can refer to them later. If your documentation has been misplaced, some troubleshooting tools, such as the Microhouse Technical Library, can help you. This library contains a database of disk drives and is fully described in Chapter 13.

Keep in mind the following while choosing the right CMOS drive type:

- SCSI: Most SCSI drives use the Type 0 or Not Installed parameter. The disk controller's BIOS overwrites the settings during power-up. Refer to the controller's documentation for the correct setting.

- IDE: Most IDE drives use user-definable settings (often drive Type 47). When you define drive Type 47, you must then manually define the drive's cylinders, heads, sectors, and capacity. Many BIOSs include an *auto-detect* option that reads the parameters of an IDE drive; most new IDE drives support this feature.

The last parameter in this section is *write pre-compensation*. Write pre-compensation refers to the fact that cylinders toward the center of the drive have shorter tracks than those farther away from the center. The magnetic field passed through the read/write heads is strengthened as the head moves closer to the center of the drive to handle the shorter tracks. If used, the write pre-compensation is determined by the maximum number of cylinders on the drive divided by two. Write pre-compensation is used mostly with older drives.

To modify the CMOS parameters, you must access the Setup program provided with your PC. This is accessed in the following ways:

- Some systems require you to press a key just after turning the computer on. This key is the Del key in the majority of PCs currently available. Some use the Esc key.

- Some computers use a keystroke to activate Setup at any time. This is often Ctrl+Alt+Esc but varies with different systems.

- Some systems include a Setup program on floppy disk.

To find out how to access the Setup program on your PC, check the documentation that came with your PC. You can also use a third-party utility, such as CheckIt Pro, to view the CMOS information.

## Low-Level Formatting

The basic structure of the hard disk is defined by the *low-level format*. The low-level formatting process is usually performed at the factory before the drive is shipped, so you rarely have to worry about it. If you do need to do a low-level format, check with the disk manufacturer for the best method to accomplish the task. If you are not careful, you may damage the drive.

Low-level formatting defines sectors and bad spots on the hard drive. The tracks on the disk are marked into sectors. Each sector is assigned a number, or sector ID. A low-level format also identifies bad sectors on the disk. A hard drive from the factory already has the bad sectors marked as unusable. NetWare then passes over the bad sectors when reading or writing data.

Hard drives are not perfect—most disks have bad sectors. A hard drive is considered okay to ship by the manufacturer if the bad sectors constitute less than one percent of the total size of the drive. Because the low-level format marks the bad sectors, they are ignored when the drive is used.

After the initial low-level formatting at the factory, you might use a low-level format to re-mark the previously used sectors of a hard drive, to try to repair a disk that shows a high number of errors, or to change the *interleave ratio*.

Do not attempt to low-level format an IDE drive. This action is rarely supported and can damage the drive.

The sectors on the disk aren't always read in their physical order. The interleave ratio controls where the next logical sector should be located on the hard disk. The interleave ratio plays a more important role with slower CPUs. Machines with fast processors can use a 1:1 interleave ratio, assigning every contiguous sector in order. Slower CPUs need more time to process information. To give the processor more time, the interleave ratio might be set at 2:1. With a 2:1 interleave ratio, the CPU skips every other sector, giving the processor more time to digest the information from a sector. The interleave ratio can alleviate bottlenecks if it is properly set. Figure 15.8 shows a hard drive with a 2:1 interleave ratio.

**FIGURE 15.8**

A hard drive with an interleave ratio of 2:1

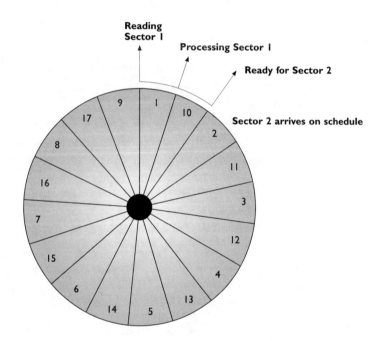

As mentioned at the beginning of this section, you will probably not need to bother with a low-level format because it is performed at the factory. If the interleave ratio is incorrect, you will need to intervene. Setting the interleave ratio too high or too low affects the speed of the drive. Utilities are available to monitor interleave ratios.

IDE drives don't use an interleave setting; the storage of data is managed by the on-board controller. Older MFM and RLL drives have interleave settings, as do some current SCSI drives.

If you are getting a large number of disk errors, you may want to set the interleave ratio. Recommendations for interleave ratios are as follows:

- 1:1 interleave ratio for all 486 machines, DOS machines running at 20MHz or faster with 286 or 386 motherboards, and machines running NetWare that are 10MHz or faster with 286 or 386 system boards

- 2:1 interleave ratio for machines running DOS at between 10 and 16MHz and are using 286 or 386 motherboards

- 3:1 interleave ratio for AT class computers running at 6 to 8 MHz and for XT class machines running DOS applications

- 4:1 interleave ratio for XT machines running at 4.77MHz

## Partitioning

*Partitioning* a drive divides the drive into allocation units, creating a logical structure. Partitioning defines what type of data each section of the disk will store. Most commonly, you will use DOS partitions and NetWare partitions. The DOS partition structure can be created with a DOS program called FDISK. FDISK sets the partitions on a hard drive. Figure 15.9 shows the FDISK Options screen.

**F I G U R E  15.9**

The DOS FDISK utility allows you to partition a disk drive.

```
                       MS-DOS Version 6
                     Fixed Disk Setup Program
              (C)Copyright Microsoft Corp. 1983 - 1993

                         FDISK Options

    Current fixed disk drive: 1

    Choose one of the following:

    1. Create DOS partition or Logical DOS Drive
    2. Set active partition
    3. Delete partition or Logical DOS Drive
    4. Display partition information
    5. Change current fixed disk drive


    Enter choice: [1]




    Press Esc to exit FDISK
```

For NetWare 5 and above, the recommended size of the DOS partition is 50MB. The minimum is about 25MB. DOS must be installed in a primary DOS partition, and that partition must be configured as the drive's active partition.

When the DOS partition is created, DOS recognizes the rest of the system as a non-DOS partition. NetWare recognizes primary and extended DOS and NetWare partitions. Partitions for operating systems other than NetWare, such as DOS, UNIX, and OS/2, are displayed as non-NetWare partitions. The DOS partition is used for booting the server. When SERVER.EXE has been activated and the NetWare disk drivers are loaded, the NetWare partition can be accessed. Figure 15.10 shows how a disk drive is partitioned.

**FIGURE 15.10**

A hard disk is divided into partitions for DOS and NetWare.

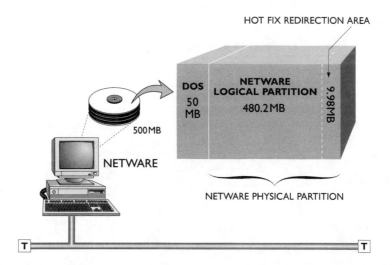

You can have only one NetWare partition per drive. The NetWare partition has a physical partition and a logical partition. NetWare identifies the DOS physical partition as physical partition 0 and the NetWare partition as physical partition 1. NetWare reserves an area within its partition as the *hot fix redirection area*. This area is used to compensate for bad sectors. The hot fix redirection area is not included in the NetWare data area because data files cannot be stored in this area without specific action being taken.

The remaining portion of the NetWare partition (98 percent) is called a *logical partition* because it is the only area of the NetWare disk that can store user data files. Each logical partition has a unique logical ID number. You use this ID number when referring to the logical partition. You will need it when configuring disk mirroring, which is discussed later in this chapter.

## High-Level Formatting

The last step in preparing a hard disk is high-level formatting. You will usually format the DOS partition and create volumes in the NetWare partition. Formatting in DOS accomplishes the following:

- Scans the disk and notes bad sectors
- Creates the DOS boot sector
- Creates a DOS File Allocation Table (FAT)
- Creates a blank root directory

To format the disk in drive C: and copy hidden DOS system files and the COMMAND.COM file to the root directory, you can use the following command:

```
FORMAT C: /S
```

There is a definite advantage to including a bootable DOS partition on your server's hard disk. It will boot faster than with a floppy disk, and you can be sure that it will automatically restart the server after a power outage.

Before you format a drive that has data on it, make sure you back up all necessary data. The format destroys the existing data.

Some third-party utilities allow recovery of data from a disk that has been inadvertently formatted, if the hard drive has not been written to since the format. Even if the data has been overwritten, there is still hope. Professional data recovery services can often recover data that has been overwritten several times. These services are extremely expensive and should be considered only if the data is very important.

High-level formatting on a NetWare server involves creating volumes. To know which volumes are occupying which partitions, NetWare uses a *volume definition table*. Four copies of the volume definition table are kept at different locations on each NetWare partition.

You create volumes on a NetWare partition using the NWCONFIG.NLM utility. In a default environment, a single volume (the SYS volume) occupies the entire NetWare partition. NetWare 5 allows *spanning*. Spanning refers to volumes that extend across multiple drives. Parts of the same volume on separate disks are called *volume segments*. There can be up to eight segments on each hard drive and 32 segments per volume.

You can use spanning to improve performance, because data on two drives can be read at the same time. Also, spanning allows you to increase volume size without re-creating a volume and is an easy way to increase the size of the SYS volume without re-installing NetWare.

Spanning does have the disadvantage that when one drive and its volume segment are lost, you can lose access to the entire volume. Techniques to keep from losing the entire volume in this way include RAID (*redundant array of inexpensive disks*), mirroring, or duplexing, which are discussed in the next sections.

## Using RAID Drives

RAID is a standard for data integrity and reliability. As the name implies, it uses multiple disks and often stores data in more than one of them for redundancy. RAID's popularity is growing as a result of the need for more drive speed and data availability. In a network environment, RAID can work with NetWare's *System Fault Tolerance* (SFT) to protect data. In general, RAID is defined as any disk subsystem architecture that combines two or more physical disk drives to create a larger logical disk structure. Two major goals are achieved by using RAID, data redundancy and increased capacity.

The use of RAID lets you set up the best disk array to protect your system. In a disk array, the drives are coordinated into different levels of RAID. Redundancy is achieved by storing the same data on multiple disks. Alternatively, RAID may split the data among drives on the bit, byte, or block level. The capability to split data into different sequences across drives is called *data striping*. Figure 15.11 shows basic data striping.

Your choices when setting up the drive for the network are important. You must choose the best RAID level, balancing the requirement for data redundancy and capacity against the cost. Using RAID provides not only NetWare fault tolerance but increased data capacity as well. When you use two 1.6GB drives with RAID, you can create a 3.2GB logical drive (twice the size) or use the drives as a 1.6GB mirrored pair. Figure 15.12 shows an example of redundant data striping.

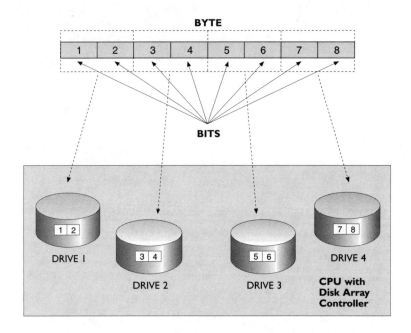

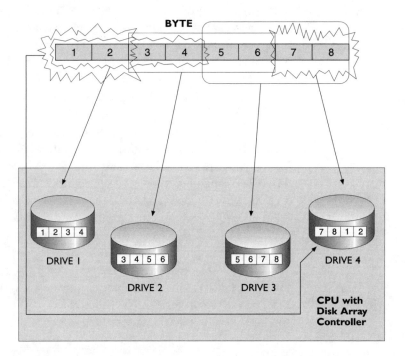

Currently, there are seven levels of RAID technology, numbered 0, 1, 2, 3, 4, 5, and 10. Each RAID level has advantages and disadvantages. A higher level does not necessarily mean a better RAID implementation. You must make the best choice for your particular situation. Each of the levels is discussed below.

### RAID Level 0

Level 0 begins with an array of disks. The system distributes blocks of data to each drive (data striping) in succession, which improves performance by avoiding the build up of many I/O requests behind one busy disk. Also, it provides much larger volume sizes. The failure of a single disk, however, can bring down the system, and redundancy of data is not provided. Figure 15.13 shows an example of data striping using bytes.

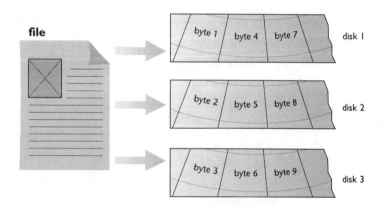

**FIGURE 15.13**

Data striping using bytes

*Data spanning* (a variation of data striping) incorporates another strategy by writing data to the next *available* disk. If the next disk in the array is busy, data spanning skips it and tries the following disk until it finds an available disk. Because all the drives are kept busy, performance improves.

### RAID Level 1

Level 1 involves disk mirroring or duplexing. In *disk mirroring*, drives are paired and mirrored (each byte is written to both drives). The drives can be *duplexed* by adding a separate host adapter for each one. The benefit in both cases is data redundancy. If something happens and one of the drives crashes, the other drive can take over without any interruption.

Although an extra host adapter adds cost to the system, duplexing will make your system much more reliable than mirroring alone. There are two main reasons to choose duplexing:

- The controller card or cable might be the source of a problem. Duplexing provides redundancy for these components.

- In many hard disk crashes, the controller locks up, making the other drive in the mirrored pair useless and defeating the purpose of mirroring.

One disadvantage with RAID Level 1 is that it requires twice the disk space. No extra capacity is created by having more than one drive. However, the current low cost of disk drives makes the redundancy worthwhile in most cases. You must also make sure your power source can handle the demands of the additional devices.

NetWare 5 supports disk mirroring or duplexing internally. You do not need to use a dedicated RAID solution.

## RAID Level 2

This level uses data striping similar to that used in Level 0, writing the data to each drive in succession. However, instead of writing the data in blocks, Level 2 writes the data a bit at a time to each drive. This strategy makes data transfers extremely fast because all the drives are transmitting in parallel. Data integrity is insured using a separate *check sum* drive to isolate faulty bits. This level does not require total data redundancy.

Because each drive is working on every write attempt, the write mode can be agonizingly slow. Check sum information is redundant. Level 2 is not efficient or economical for personal computers. Level 2 is more common with mainframes.

## RAID Level 3

Think of this level as Level 2 for personal computers. RAID Level 3 uses bit-level data striping. At this level, four or five drives are used. One of the drives is dedicated to parity information to ensure the data integrity for the other drives. As with Level 2, Level 3 has a high transfer rate because all the drives are transmitting at once. It can also handle long data transfers. If one drive fails, the system is not affected. The array controller uses the parity drive to reconstruct the contents of the defective disk, and the defective disk is skipped on writes.

As with Level 2, write attempts with Level 3 can be extremely slow because the parity drive is accessed for every write. Also, computer overhead can be very high as a result of calculating parity. The failure of any two drives causes problems with the system. In addition, NetWare cannot use RAID Level 3 because NetWare reads and writes data in 4KB blocks rather than in long streams of bits.

## RAID Level 4

RAID Level 4 integrates the strengths of Levels 0 and 3. This RAID implementation performs data striping in blocks instead of bits. Using block interleave provides better access to NetWare data. Similar to Level 3, this level uses a drive for parity checking. As you remember, using a single parity drive increases fault tolerance and keeps the system up if one drive crashes. Level 4 provides the ability to do multiple simultaneous reads because each drive can read a block of data.

The downside to RAID Level 4 is that writes are very slow and computer overhead is raised by parity calculations. Additionally, if the array controller fails, the entire array cannot function.

## RAID Level 5

Level 5 has some of the elements and advantages of all the proceeding four levels. Level 5 uses block data striping and distributed check data on all drives. Reads and writes can happen in parallel for fast transfer rates. It efficiently handles small blocks of data, which allows it to work well with NetWare. Also, Level 5 uses a unique parity scheme called distributed check data, which means that the algorithm that checks parity exists in part on every drive. Because the parity algorithm is on all drives, efficiency increases as the number of drives increases. RAID Level 5 implementation provides virtual redundancy at a low cost. Level 5 also provides for the use of *hot spares*.

Hot spares, or hot swappable drives, are drives that can be mounted in the array cabinet and left dormant. If a drive in the array fails, the spare can be picked up by the array to replace the failed drive. The data is then rebuilt on the spare drive, and the spare drive functions with the array, which provides a method of replacing the damaged drive without taking down the system.

RAID Level 5 is not as fast as Level 0 or Level 1 because of the overhead required for parity calculations. Also, because large file transfers are done in blocks, Level 5 can be slower than Level 3, which uses parallel bytes.

## RAID Level 10

Level 10 duplicates data across two identical RAID 0 or hard disk drives. You can think of this as not only mirroring a single drive, but also mirroring an entire array of disk drives. All data on one array is mirrored on the second array. The idea of Level 10 is similar to Novell's StandbyServer, which mirrors the data on file servers.

## Choosing a RAID Implementation

When choosing RAID for an organization or a customer, you need to consider the following:

- Weigh the importance of data and applications to the cost of downtime and lost business.

- Consider the number of users and the required drive capacity.

- Consider the size of data blocks and type of access (direct or sequential) needed.

- Consider the proportion of reads and writes to I/O activity and what transfer rate is needed.

Many vendors support RAID in software or hardware. Hardware implementations are usually faster. It is your job to find out what the best implementation is and who provides that implementation. Be sure that the vendor's solution fully supports NetWare (most do) and supports the level of RAID you wish to implement. Level 5 is the most commonly used with NetWare networks.

# Disk Mirroring and Disk Duplexing

Disk mirroring and disk duplexing are two System Fault Tolerance (SFT) strategies that protect the network if you experience hard disk crashes. The aim of these strategies is to protect data and keep the network up and running or, at least, to minimize downtime. Both strategies utilize an additional hard drive to serve as a backup. All data written to one disk is written to the second disk also, allowing little or no data loss if one disk fails.

## Disk Mirroring

As already stated, *disk mirroring* writes data to two hard drives through the same disk channel. Both hard drives are connected to the same disk controller and cable. Figure 15.14 shows how disk mirroring works.

**F I G U R E   15.14**

Disk mirroring stores data on two identical drives.

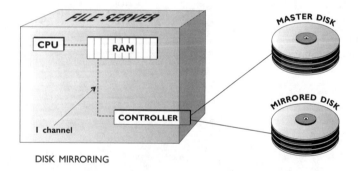

Everything written to one disk is written to the other. Any changes to the primary drive affect the secondary drive as well. The hard drives should therefore mirror each other exactly. If something happens to the primary drive, the secondary drive can immediately take over, allowing network users to continue accessing data with little or no downtime.

If a server has enough drive and card slots available, the mirroring can be internal. If not, an external drive subsystem can be used. In order to use disk mirroring, the drives must have logical partitions of identical sizes. Ideally, the drives should be identical, but it is possible to use different capacities of drives in a mirrored pair if the logical partition sizes are the same.

Disk mirroring provides a high level of data reliability because it mirrors the information on the disk. Disk mirroring also has an SFT weakness, the disk channel. If a piece of hardware in the disk channel other than the disk fails, the disk—and the data it contains—will be inaccessible. Disk duplexing addresses this problem.

## Disk Duplexing

If the disk controller fails, you cannot access the data even on mirrored disks. *Disk duplexing* provides another level of SFT, or protection, by writing to disks located on different hard disk channels. Providing entirely separate hard disk channels adds another layer of protection because any part of one channel can fail, but the other channel is unaffected. Disk duplexing can be expensive, but it is a means of ensuring data reliability. Figure 15.15 shows an example of disk duplexing.

**FIGURE 15.15**
Disk duplexing uses redundant drives and drive controllers.

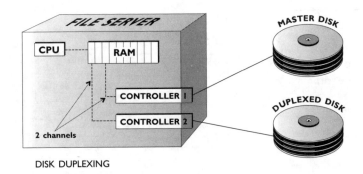

DISK DUPLEXING

The hard disk channel may consist of a host bus adapter, disk controller, cabling, and server disks. In Figure 15.15, each channel has a separate power supply, adding another layer of protection. If one power supply fails, the second channel continues to work without interruption, and the server stays up and running. Also, this figure shows a situation in which each controller has two disks attached to it.

Because duplexing uses two disks on separate channels, NetWare can read and write to both disks at the same time, which allows NetWare to perform *split seeks*. NetWare performs a split seek by accessing both disks at the same time and retrieving data from the first disk it finds the data on. Split seeks allow faster access time, especially when many reads are being performed. Disk duplexing can provide added data reliability and access speeds.

Disk mirroring is similar to a single train track. There is only one way to go on the track. If the track is broken or damaged, trains cannot move in either direction to transport their freight. Traffic stops. Duplexing most resembles the traffic on roads: If one lane is blocked, you simply change lanes and keep right on going.

## Implementing Disk Mirroring and Duplexing

Mirroring and duplexing are considered the same thing by NetWare. To NetWare, all you are doing is writing the same information to different logical partitions. Logical partitions were discussed earlier in this chapter and are the area of the NetWare partition where user files can be stored. Although mirroring and duplexing write their data to different partitions, the process is the same as far as NetWare is concerned.

The difference, of course, involves hardware. Mirroring uses the same disk channel (host bus adapter, disk controller, and cabling) for both hard disks. Duplexing uses a different channel for each hard disk providing hardware redundancy.

In NetWare 5, you use NWCONFIG.NLM to mirror or duplex. The following example assumes you have already installed the operating system and are working from and on a network drive. You should perform this procedure during off hours when no one is using the network.

The process of installing a mirrored or duplex disk pair destroys any existing data on the disks. Disk mirroring or duplexing should be performed when you are formatting the hard disk before it has data on it. Otherwise, you should back up all necessary data.

To install a disk pair as mirrored or duplexed, follow the steps below.

1. Install the necessary hardware, using correct termination and addressing. Document the model numbers of the drives and the disk controller card.

2. Bring the server up, and load NWCONFIG.NLM. From the Installation Options menu, select Disk Options, and press Enter. The Available Disk Options menu is displayed (see Figure 15.16).

**F I G U R E  15.16**

The Available Disk
Options menu of the
NWCONFIG utility
allows you to config-
ure disk mirroring.

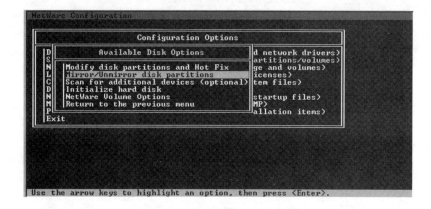

3. Select Mirror/unmirror disk partitions, and press Enter. The Disk Partition Mirroring Status screen appears (see Figure 15.17), displaying
   the status of all drives in the file server.

**F I G U R E  15.17**

The Disk Partition Mir-
roring Status screen
displays the status of
mirrored drives.

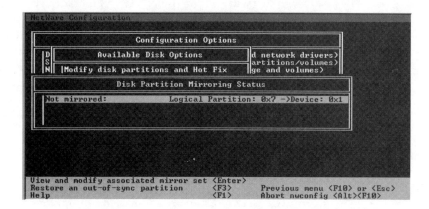

4. Select the drive designated Logical Partition #1 to be the primary
   drive, and press Enter. The Mirrored Disk Partitions screen appears.
   Figure 15.18 shows the Mirrored Disk Partitions screen.

FIGURE 15.18

The Mirrored Disk Partitions screen lists partitions that are mirrored.

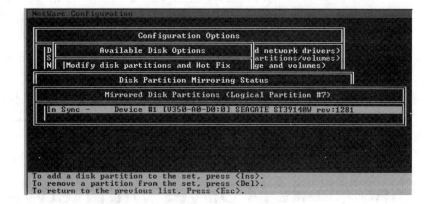

FIGURE 15.18

The Mirrored Disk Partitions screen lists partitions that are mirrored.

5. To add another logical partition, press Insert. The available partitions you can choose from are then displayed in the Available Partitions screen.

6. Highlight an available partition, and press Enter. The Mirrored Net-Ware Partitions screen displays the In Sync status of the partitions. Partition 1 should be In Sync. Partition 2 shows an Out of Sync status. After a few seconds, Partition 2 begins synchronizing with Partition 1.

7. When the synchronization process from step 6 is complete, the Partition Mirroring Status screen indicates that the partitions are mirrored.

## Tips for Working with Mirrored or Duplexed Drives

Disk mirroring and duplexing is complex. Using them correctly can provide added data reliability, but you must not simply mirror or duplex the drives and then forget about them. Below are some tips to help you work with disk mirroring and duplexing:

- Mirroring and duplexing do not take the place of backups! You must continue to perform regular system backups.

- Always load the disk drivers in the same order. Start with the first internal disk driver and continue in the order they are addressed.

- Remember that to NetWare, mirroring and duplexing are the same. System messages do not differentiate between the two.

- Periodically check the status of your mirrored drives. Using NWCONFIG.NLM or the MONITOR utility, check that the partitions are still In Sync.

- Periodically check the error logs. Make sure that none of the mirrored drives has been deactivated.

- Document thoroughly. Keep track of which drives are primary and which are secondary for each channel. Also, keep a record of the size and configuration for the drives.

# Using CD-ROM Drives with NetWare

**C**ompact disk read-only memory (CD-ROM) drives have been an exciting enhancement to NetWare networks. They can hold text, programs, audio, video, audio/video information (AVI), and graphics. You might say there is no form of computer data that cannot be stored on a CD-ROM.

CD-ROMs are quickly becoming the media of choice for software distribution. Many commercial packages, such as encyclopedias, are now available only on CD-ROM. Because of the large amount of data required for encyclopedias, those purchased for a personal computer are available only on CD-ROM.

Several methods are used to connect a CD-ROM to a computer system. Some CD-ROMs use a proprietary controller or interface. These proprietary interfaces are often used with sound cards that also support the CD-ROMs. These types of interface cannot be used on a NetWare server.

Some CD-ROMs can be connected to a parallel port and, with special drivers, function quite well. Another popular method is to use an IDE (Integrated Drive Electronics) controller.

If you are planning to use a CD-ROM with your file server and wish to mount CD-ROMs for network access, you should use a SCSI controller and a matching SCSI CD-ROM, because NetWare provides full support for SCSI devices as CD-ROMs. A new driver also allows IDE CD-ROM drives to be used with NetWare servers.

## Advantages of CD-ROMs

CD-ROMs have several important advantages on a network:

- CD-ROMs provide quick access to large volumes of data. Current CD-ROMs, using only one side of a CD, hold up to 682MB of data.

- CD-ROM is a light-weight media that is inexpensive to reproduce.

- Nearly all CD-ROMs are compatible. Many text-based databases are stored on CD-ROMs allowing keyword searches.

- Unlike floppy disks or hard drives, CD-ROMs are not damaged by humidity or magnetic fields.

Many unwary floppy disk users have lost all the data on their floppy disks by placing them on top of stereo speakers. Because today's multimedia PCs often include speakers, this is becoming more common. Speakers have magnetic fields that can make a mess of the magnetic charges on floppy disks. CD-ROMs are immune to this because they do not use magnetism to store information.

## Disadvantages of CD-ROMs

CD-ROMs are not always the best network storage devices. Their disadvantages include the following:

- CD-ROMs are considerably slower than hard disk drives. A typical CD-ROM has access times of 200 milliseconds or slower, while hard drives typically have an access time of about 10 milliseconds.

- Although their prices are dropping, CD-ROM drives and their media are still expensive compared to floppy disk drives. However, the large capacity of CD-ROM disks makes them far superior to floppies for software distribution.

You can put most any PC-formatted CD-ROM into a CD-ROM drive on a NetWare 3.12, 4.x, or 5 server and mount it as a volume. (Audio CD-ROMs do not mount on Novell servers.)

NetWare is compatible with the ISO (International Standards Organization) 9660 standard, or a subset called the High Sierra Standard. Almost every CD-ROM now available uses one of these compatibility standards.

> If you are installing a CD-ROM on your system, you must have the correct drivers for the SCSI adapter in your system. Remember that you must have both the *.HAM file for the host adapter and the *.CDM file for the drive.

## Working with CD-ROM Drives

Because a CD-ROM is just about the fastest way to add 628MB of organized data to a network, its use is highly recommended. Remember to carefully plan your system before you add a CD-ROM to your network. Improper planning is a sure ticket to spending all night trying to get your system to work. As with all network equipment, poor planning can lead to unnecessary downtime and frustration for a network administrator. A specific type of knowledge is required for successfully adding a CD-ROM to your network. The following information will be helpful to an alert administrator.

- Do not install a CD-ROM in a drive bay in a system where it is directly above a hard disk drive. The magnetic fields generated by a CD-ROM player are strong enough in this position to damage data stored on the drive.

- If you plan to use the CD-ROM on the same controller as the hard drives in your system, make sure that the controller is the proper type, because some controllers and drives do not function correctly with a CD-ROM.

- Some CD-ROM drives use what is called a *caddie* to hold the CD-ROM when it is inserted into the drive. Be sure to use these correctly because improper use of the caddie damages the CD-ROM permanently. If a caddie type CD-ROM drive is being used, a caddie should be purchased for each CD-ROM. Using a caddie for each CD-ROM disk eliminates the need to handle the CDs, and the CDs last longer.

NetWare 3.12 was the first version of NetWare to ship with CDROM.NLM (although an update available from Novell did allow 3.11 file servers to support CD-ROMs). The first versions of NetWare, up to 4.02, mounted the CD-ROM as a Read Write volume and displayed countless write error messages when the system attempted to write to the CD-ROM. NetWare 4.1 corrected this problem. With NetWare 5, in most cases, you simply insert the CD and it mounts as a volume automatically.

# Review

This chapter examined network storage devices. A solid understanding of network storage systems can help you avoid some of the many pitfalls of network administration.

## Hard Drives

Hard drives are an integral part of any network and require careful setup in order to function properly. You must carefully plan fault tolerance and frequently back up the data stored on the hard drive.

A storage system using hard drives is composed of the hard drive itself and the disk controller. The disk controller provides the interface between the hard drive and motherboard of the server.

There are four main hard drive interface types:

- ST-506: Originally designed in the 1970s to deal with 5MB hard drives, the ST-506 uses both MFM and RLL encoding schemes. No current models are available. However, you may find the ST-506 on some older workstations, especially those with hard drives smaller than 80MB.

- Integrated Drive Electronics (IDE): Developed in the mid-1980s, the IDE interface has replaced ST-506 on most of today's PCs. Drive sizes range from 340MB to 1.6GB.

- Enhanced Small Device Interface (ESDI): The ESDI is a more powerful version of the ST-506 standard, and while it uses the same cabling system as the ST-506, the two are not interchangeable.

- Small Computer Systems Interface (SCSI): Pronounced *scuzzy*, SCSI goes beyond a simple disk interface, as it provides a complete expansion bus capable of connecting other SCSI-type devices (such as tape backup drives, CD-ROMs, magneto-optical drives, and so on). SCSI data rates are faster than IDE and ESDI because SCSI uses a parallel data communication system.

## Hard Drive Cabling

Hard drive cables provide the connection between the disk controller and the hard drive. Hard drive cables must be installed correctly so that the pins in the connectors can receive and transmit the proper signals for data transfer. To avoid the most common cabling problems, do the following:

- Ensure that the colored stripe, usually red, attaches to pin 1 on the disk controller and the hard drive.

- Make sure you have the right cable. Floppy drive cables and hard drive cables look similar, but they have different connections.

- Check the cable distance. The maximum distance for an IDE cable or a single SCSI cable is 18 inches.

## Formatting the Hard Drive

The final step before you can access the hard drive is to format the drive so that it can store data. Drive preparation includes the following four steps:

- Choose the CMOS drive type.

- Perform the low-level format (usually not needed).

- Partition the drive.

- Perform the high-level format.

## Using RAID Drives

RAID, which stands for *redundant array of inexpensive disks,* is a standard for data integrity. The two major goals achieved by using RAID are data redundancy and increased capacity.

Currently, there are seven levels of RAID technology, numbered 0, 1, 2, 3, 4, 5, and 10. Each RAID level has advantages and disadvantages. A higher level does not necessarily mean a better RAID implementation for your situation.

### Disk Mirroring and Disk Duplexing

Disk mirroring and disk duplexing are two System Fault Tolerance (SFT) strategies that protect the network if you experience a hard disk crash. Both strategies utilize an additional hard drive to serve as a backup. All data written to one disk is written to the second disk also, allowing little or no data loss if one disk fails.

# CD-ROMs

Compact disk read-only memory (CD-ROM) drives have been an exciting enhancement to NetWare networks.

If you are planning to use a CD-ROM with your file server and wish to mount CD-ROMs for network access, you should use a SCSI controller and a matching SCSI CD-ROM, because NetWare provides full support for SCSI devices as CD-ROMs. A new driver also allows IDE CD-ROM drives to be used with NetWare servers. However, if you use SCSI disks, don't attempt to use an IDE CD-ROM, and vice versa; it is nearly impossible to run both types of drives in a PC without conflicts.

The main advantages of CD-ROMs include the following:

- CD-ROMs provide quick access to large volumes of data. Current CD-ROM technology holds up to 682MB of data.

- CD-ROM is a light-weight media that is inexpensive to reproduce.

- Because CD-ROMs use a standardized formatting, nearly all CD-ROMs are compatible.

- Unlike floppy disks or hard drives, CD-ROMs are not damaged by humidity or magnetic fields.

# CNE Practice Test Questions

**1.** Which is NOT a division of a hard disk?

   **A.** Tracks

   **B.** Cylinders

   **C.** Pages

   **D.** Sectors

**2.** What is the minimum unit of storage on a NetWare 5 volume?

   **A.** A cluster

   **B.** A cylinder

   **C.** A block

   **D.** A track

**3.** What is the time required for the read/write head of a disk drive to reach the data called?

   **A.** Drive latency

   **B.** Seek time

   **C.** Transfer time

   **D.** Access time

**4.** What are the most common hard drive interfaces today?

   **A.** ST-506 and IDE

   **B.** IDE and SCSI

   **C.** IDE and ESDI

   **D.** MFM and RLL

**5.** What is the range of Standard SCSI device numbers?

    **A.** 0 to 7

    **B.** 1 to 7

    **C.** 1 to 16

    **D.** 0 to 6

**6.** What does the stripe on one side of a disk cable typically mean?

    **A.** The cable is faulty.

    **B.** Pin 1 is on that side.

    **C.** Pin 36 is on that side.

    **D.** This is a floppy disk cable.

**7.** Which drive standard uses two cables per drive?

    **A.** ESDI

    **B.** SCSI

    **C.** IDE

    **D.** ST-506

**8.** Which DOS program is used to partition hard disks?

    **A.** FORMAT

    **B.** FDISK

    **C.** SYS

    **D.** PARTMAN

**9.** Which step do you usually NOT have to perform to prepare a disk?

   **A.** Partitioning

   **B.** Low-level formatting

   **C.** High-level formatting

   **D.** Setting CMOS drive type

**10.** What do you call two drives using the same controller and containing identical data?

   **A.** Duplexed

   **B.** Mirrored

   **C.** Matched

   **D.** RAID 7

**11.** Which is NOT an advantage of disk duplexing?

   **A.** Faster disk read access

   **B.** Fault tolerance

   **C.** Backups are no longer necessary

   **D.** One drive still works if the other fails

**12.** What is the NetWare 5 utility used to manage mirrored drives?

   **A.** DISKMAN

   **B.** PARTMAN

   **C.** NWCONFIG

   **D.** SERVMAN

**13.** What are the advantages of CD-ROM storage?

   **A.** Faster access than hard disks

   **B.** Light weight and portability

   **C.** Cheaper than floppy disk drives

   **D.** All of the above

**14.** Which NLM must you load on a NetWare server to enable a CD-ROM to be used as a NetWare volume?

**A.** NWCONFIG

**B.** MONITOR

**C.** Volumes

**D.** CD-ROM

# CHAPTER

# 16

Troubleshooting the Novell
Client for Windows 95/NT

## Roadmap

This section describes the issues in troubleshooting the Novell Windows 95 and NT Clients.

### Topics Covered

- The architecture of the Windows 95 and NT clients
- Novell client troubleshooting techniques

### Skills You'll Learn

- Describe the architecture of the Novell Client for Windows 95
- Describe the architecture of the Novell Client for Windows NT
- How to troubleshoot the Novell Client on a Windows 95 workstation
- How to troubleshoot the Novell Client on a Windows NT workstation

The Novell Client for Windows 95 and the Novell Client for Windows NT are the method by which Windows 95 and Windows NT, respectively, can connect to a NetWare network. Each client has its own configuration and troubleshooting issues. This chapter examines those issues in detail.

# Novell Client for Windows 95

The Novell Client for Windows 95 has been around since Windows 95 was developed, although when it was first released it was called Client32. The Novell Client for Windows gives local applications access to the network. Windows 95 does have built-in network access functionality, but the Novell Client gives *complete* access to all NetWare features, including NDS and Z.E.N.Works.

The Novell Client has a number of features:

- It allows files with long filenames to be stored on the server.

- It is fully integrated with the Network Neighborhood and Explorer utilities.

- It is loaded automatically during Windows 95 startup.

- Its parameters can be managed by the Windows 95 System Policy Editor.

- It supports NetWare login scripts.

- It can be automatically upgraded to a newer version through a login script using the Automatic Client Upgrade (ACU) feature.

- It can coexist with the Microsoft Client for Microsoft Networks for simultaneous access to Microsoft networks and Novell networks.

- It supports multiple protocols including TCP/IP, IPX/SPX, SNMP, Named Pipes, and NetBIOS.

- It can be installed at the same time as Windows 95 using the Windows 95 Unattended Install feature (UNATTEND.TXT).

- Unlike some previous versions, it can connect to multiple NDS trees simultaneously.

- It supports automatic reconnection to network resources after an interruption of service.

For the most part, the Novell Client for Windows 95 works with Windows 98 as well. For the rest of this chapter, you can assume that anything that refers to Windows 95 will also apply to Windows 98 as well.

## Windows 95 Client Components

From the beginning, the Novell Client for Windows 95 was designed to be a modular system. This approach makes the client more efficient because unneeded components aren't loaded, conserving memory.

There are four main components to the Novell Client for Windows 95 and each component performs a specific function.

- The NetWare I/O Subsystem (NIOS)

- LAN drivers

- Communications protocols

- NetWare Client Requester

## The NetWare I/O Subsystem (NIOS)

The Novell Client for Windows 95 was designed similar to the NetWare server in that there is a central core piece that manages the resources and several loadable pieces that provide additional functionality. In the Novell Client for Windows 95, these pieces are called the NetWare I/O Subsystem (NIOS) and NetWare Loadable Modules (NLMs), respectively.

NIOS performs the same functions as the NetWare core operating system in that it manages all the resources, including memory. As a matter of fact, NIOS performs memory management on the memory it is given, which has the benefit of not requiring a reboot every time a client parameter is changed.

NIOS is actually implemented in Windows 95 as a virtual device driver (VXD). NIOS.VXD is the core part of the Novell Client for Windows 95. The other components are loaded by the Registry as Windows 95 boots.

## LAN Drivers

Probably the most important component of the Novell Client for Windows 95 is the LAN driver. The LAN driver is the software component that provides an interface between the Novell Client and the network interface card (NIC).

There are two types of LAN drivers that the Novel Client can use. It can use drivers that adhere to Microsoft's Network Device Interface Specification (NDIS). Most network cards have an NDIS driver that comes with Windows 95. In addition, the Novell Client can use the 32-bit Open Data Link Interface (ODI) drivers provided by Novell. Figure 16.1 shows the protocol stack that the Novell Client uses and how the two types of LAN drivers interface with the upper level protocols.

If you want to use Microsoft networking components as well as ODI LAN drivers, you can. You need to have a driver called ODINSUP (<u>ODI</u> <u>N</u>DIS <u>Sup</u>port) installed. ODINSUP translates NDIS network calls into ODI network calls.

## Communication Protocols

As discussed previously in Chapter 6, a *communication protocol* is a set of rules that govern communication. The Novell Client for Windows 95 can use either or both of two protocols to communicate with a NetWare 5 server. It can use either TCP/IP or IPX.

**TCP/IP**   TCP/IP is a suite of protocols developed for use with the Internet. It is a very efficient protocol on a WAN (fairly efficient on a LAN) and fairly easy to configure. Lately, it has seen an explosion of use on LANs because of

**FIGURE 16.1**

Novell Client for Windows 95 LAN driver configurations

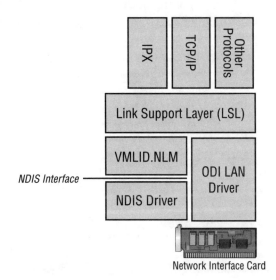

IPX

TCP/IP

Other Protocols

Link Support Layer (LSL)

VMLID.NLM

ODI LAN Driver

*NDIS Interface* ———

NDIS Driver

Network Interface Card

the popularity of the Internet and the tendency of network administrators to want to standardize on one protocol. To that end, when Novell was developing NetWare 5, they decided to make it 100% pure IP, which means that the only protocols running on the network are those related to the TCP/IP specification. Different companies have advertised (Novell included) that they were running native IP, but, in fact, they were usually encapsulating some other protocol inside of TCP/IP. Pure IP uses only protocols specified in an RFC. No IPX or NetBIOS encapsulation occurs. As a matter of fact, even if you do not load the IPX protocol on the server, it will work fine. This was not possible in previous versions.

One major advantage to using TCP/IP on the client side is that most companies today already have some connection to the Internet at the desktop, which means that they already have TCP/IP loaded at the workstation. To connect to a NetWare server, they only have to add the client software; they don't have to run multiple protocols. Also, many companies have a WAN that connects all the different sites together. Because TCP/IP is very efficient in a WAN environment, it is usually the default protocol used on them. Additionally, the same companies will specify only that TCP/IP be used on the WAN. If you wanted to use IPX on the WAN, you had to encapsulate IPX inside of TCP/IP, which is very inefficient. Now, because both the LAN and the WAN are using TCP/IP, the encapsulation can go away.

**IPX**    The Internetwork Packet Exchange (IPX) protocol was developed at the same time as NetWare. It is based on the Xerox Networking System

(XNS) protocol developed by Xerox in the 1980s. It is a very efficient protocol in a LAN environment and is easy to configure. It does have some limitations in a WAN environment, but it was the only choice on versions of NetWare before 5.

Because of NetWare's popularity it became the de facto standard protocol for smaller networks. However, lately TCP/IP has been replacing IPX as the LAN standard. It has the capability of being used on a WAN, but it isn't as efficient as TCP/IP.

### NetWare Client Requester

The NetWare Client Requester portion of the Novell Client for Windows 95 is the component that most users don't see. They do, however, know it's there because they can access the services and resources of the network. The Client Requester does most of the higher level functions for the Novell Client software, including redirecting file and print requests and caching files for network transmission and reception.

As a loadable module (CLIENT32.NLM), the Client Requester provides functionality similar to the NetWare DOS requester that was used under DOS. Fortunately, it is also backward compatible with the DOS requester, so any programs that made API calls to the DOS requester should function under the Novell Client.

## Windows 95 Client Troubleshooting

The Novell Client for Windows 95 is just like any other piece of software. It will have problems. When it does, you need to know the best ways to solve them. There are a few things to know in order to help you troubleshoot efficiently.

### Troubleshooting Resources

The first thing any good technician has is a good set of tools. There are several tools you can use to troubleshoot the Novell Client on a Windows 95 workstation. Some of the most common tools are:

- Network Control Panel
- REGEDIT
- LANalyzer

- The Novell Client log file (NIOS.LOG)

- The MODULES command

**Network Control Panel**   The Network Control Panel is used to configure the various networking components for Windows 95. To access the Network control panel, click Start ➤ Settings ➤ Control Panel and double-click the Network control panel to bring up a screen similar to the one in Figure 16.2.

F I G U R E  16.2

The Network Control
Panel

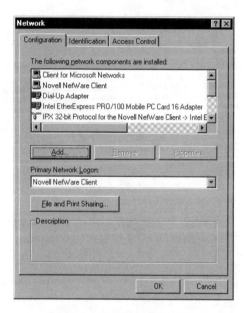

From this screen you can see which network components are installed, add or remove components, as well as configure existing network components.

**REGEDIT**   Windows 95 comes with a very powerful tool for configuring itself, the Registry Editor or REGEDIT. It allows you to view and change all the settings in the Windows 95 Registry (the database that contains all the settings for Windows 95 and its applications).

Normally, changes to the Registry are made using the Control Panels, the options menu in an application, or other utilities. Sometimes, though, you may need to make changes to the Registry manually. To start up the Registry Editor, click Start ➤ Run and type in REGEDIT. Click OK and REGEDIT will start. (See Figure 16.3.)

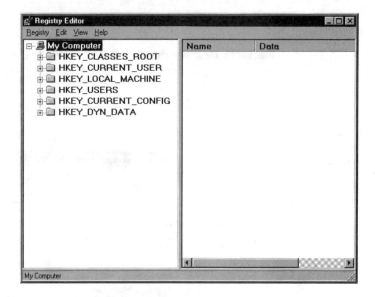

You can use the Find option on the Edit menu in REGEDIT to find the value of the setting you need to change.

**LANalyzer**  LANalyzer is a tool in the family of products known as protocol analyzers. A *protocol analyzer* uses a network card to examine packets as they cross the network. The analyzer is used to monitor network segment performance, troubleshoot errors, view specific packets, and monitor traffic levels over time.

Protocol analyzers work by translating the raw packets it receives on its network cards into descriptions of what's going on. Most human beings can't read binary information, so the protocol analyzer translates the packets into a logical stream of network information and statistics.

Novell makes two types of protocol analyzers, the LANalyzer Agent for the ManageWise console and LANalyzer for Windows. The former is an NLM that runs on one or more NetWare servers and can monitor multiple segments simultaneously. The latter is a program that runs on Windows (see Figure 16.4) and can view detailed information about a single segment. In addition, it is portable and can be taken to whichever segment requires it.

**FIGURE 16.4**

LANalyzer for Windows main window

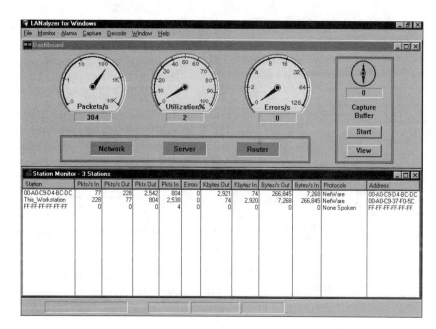

**FIGURE 16.4**

LANalyzer for Windows main window

There are several problems that LANalyzer can detect, including:

- "Chattering" or defective network cards
- Too much traffic
- Address conflicts
- Invalid addresses
- Routing problems

**The Novell Client Log File (NIOS.LOG)**    When the Novell Client starts up, it loads several NLMs. It has the capability of logging all the settings it reads and the diagnostic information to a special log file. That log file is the NIOS.LOG file in the C:\NOVELL\CLIENT32 directory. To create it, you must enable it by putting the NWEnablelogging=True entry in the [386Enh] section of the SYSTEM.INI file. Once enabled, the Novell Client will create the file and start logging to it.

You can change the location of the log file. To do this, you must open the Network Control Panel, select the Novell NetWare Client, select Properties then Advanced Settings. Scroll down to the Log File property. You can then change the location by typing in the name and path in the Setting box.

You can also change the maximum log file size. To change it, simply return to the Advanced Settings area of the Novell NetWare Client Properties screen and click the Log File Size property. You can then change the value from 65535 bytes (the default setting) to any value from 0 to 1048576 bytes.

The log file is important because, if there is an error during login, you can examine the file to get a clue as to a possible cause. If a particular module doesn't load, you'll be able to tell which module didn't load and conditions under which the problem occurred.

> If you enable the log file, remember that because the Novell Client has written everything to the NIOS.LOG file, the boot process may take longer. So, it may not be the best idea to have this enabled at all times.

**The MODULES Command**   The MODULES command (a command line command, part of the Novell Client Requester), when executed at a Windows 95 command prompt, will display a list of the Novell Client for Windows 95 modules that are loaded currently (Figure 16.5). It can be executed by typing the word **MODULES** at any Windows 95 command prompt.

This command is useful in helping to determine what parts of the Novell Client are at what versions and to determine if the problem is caused by an old version of one of the modules of the client.

## Troubleshooting Steps

There is a standard set of steps used to troubleshoot Novell Client for Windows 95 problems. Novell recommends the following five steps when trying to troubleshoot these problems.

**Step 1: List the Symptoms of the Problem.**   More than one technician has been in the position of frantically trying to fix a problem with a network and getting nowhere. When they finally ask for a second opinion, it is commonly, "What are the symptoms of the problem?" Usually the response is something like ,"The customer said such-and-such doesn't work, so I'm fixing it." They never bother to examine the symptoms of the problem.

The first step, then, is to determine the symptoms of the problem, then you can work on solving the problem.

**F I G U R E  16.5**

A sample output from
the MODULES
command

```
List of installed NetWare Loadable Modules (NLMs).

LZFW, Lanalyzer for Windows, NIOS Interface  v2.20  (960226)
(C) Copyright 1996 Novell Inc. All rights reserved
C:\LZFW\LZFW.NLM

Novell NDPS Prgm Event Notification Module  v1.00  (970623)
CoPyRiGhT = (c)Copyright 1995-1997 Novell, Inc. All rights
reserved.
C:\NOVELL\CLIENT32\NDPS\DPLSNCLI.NLM

Novell NDPS Print Redirection Module  v1.00  (970623)
CoPyRiGhT = (c)Copyright 1995-1997 Novell, Inc. All rights
reserved.
C:\NOVELL\CLIENT32\NDPS\DPRNTCLI.NLM

Novell NDPS RPC Library Module  v1.00  (970623)
CoPyRiGhT = (c)Copyright 1995-1997 Novell, Inc. All rights
reserved.
C:\NOVELL\CLIENT32\NDPS\DPRPCCLI.NLM

Novell NDPS C Library Module  v1.00  (970623)
CoPyRiGhT = (c)Copyright 1995-1997 Novell, Inc. All rights
reserved.
C:\NOVELL\CLIENT32\NDPS\DPLIBCLI.NLM

Novell NWSIPX API NLM for Client 32
```

**Step 2: Rule Out Hardware Issues.**   The Novell Client software is like other software in that it has certain hardware requirements. Some of those requirements are listed here and should be checked to make sure that hardware isn't causing the problem.

- Does the workstation meet the hardware requirements for the Novell Client for Windows 95, including 486 or higher processor and 16MB of RAM?

- Have there been any hardware changes, including additions or removals?

- If there is a Link Status light on the workstation and hub, does it indicate that there is a connection between workstation and hub?

- Are all the workstations experiencing this problem, or is the problem unique to this workstation?

- Is the NIC installed properly?

- Is the rest of the cabling system installed properly?

**Step 3: Rule Out LAN Driver Problems.**   In order for the Novell Client to function properly, it must have the proper version of the LAN driver. Remember that the Novell Client can use either Novell's 32-bit ODI drivers or Microsoft's NDIS driver. To see which you are using, open the Network Control Panel, click your network card driver, then click Properties. If the screen displays Enhanced mode (32-bit and 16-bit NDIS) selected, then you are using NDIS LAN drivers. If, in addition to the LAN driver for your network card, you see a LAN driver for ODINSUP, you are using the 32-bit Novell ODI drivers.

To determine which version of a 32-bit ODI LAN driver you are using, type **MODULES** at a command prompt and press ENTER. On the screen that appears, note the version and date of the LAN driver (typically it has an extension of .LAN, making it easy to identify). Then, check the version and date against the ones on either the Novell Support Connection website (http://support.novell.com/) or on the manufacturer's support website. If the versions are different, make sure the most current one is installed.

To determine which version of an NDIS driver you are using, run Windows Explorer and navigate to the Windows directory (typically C:\WINDOWS). Once you are there, look for a file with the .DOS extension. Typically it has a name similar to your network card. For example, a National Semiconductor NE2000 card might have a NDIS driver file called NE2000.DOS. Right click the file and look at the modified date. Compare this date with the date of the driver file on either Microsoft's support website (http://www.microsoft.com/support/) or on the manufacturer's support website.

Another way to find the most current version of the NDIS driver quickly, is to use the Find command under the Start menu and type in **\*.DOS**. This will find any files with the extension .DOS. Additionally, it will show the location and last date modified. Plus, you can see if you have a more current driver somewhere else on your system.

**Step 4: Check Client Software Version.**   Some features of NetWare (particularly Z.E.N.Works) don't work properly without the correct version of the client software. For this reason, you must be able to determine exactly which version of the Novell Client software the computer is running.

The best way to determine which version of client software your computer is running is to use the Registry Editor to view the Client Version setting in the Registry. To access this setting, run REGEDIT and navigate to HKEY_LOCAL_MACHINE ➤ Network ➤ Novell ➤ System Config ➤ Install ➤ Client Version. There you will find four settings: MAJOR_VERSION, MINOR_VERSION, Revision, and Level (Figure 16.6). If you put them together in that order, separated by periods, you will get a version of something like 2.5.0.0 (using the numbers from Figure 16.6).

**FIGURE 16.6**

Using REGEDIT to determine client version

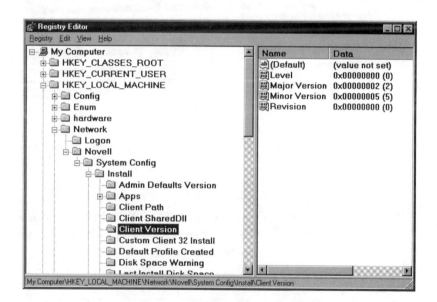

Another way to find the client version, if you have a fairly new version of the client, is to use the properties of the Novell NetWare Client in the Network Control Panel. To access this information, open the Network Control Panel, select the Novell NetWare Client and click the Properties button. A screen will appear that has the information you need on it (Figure 16.7). The numbers represent, in order, major version, minor version, revision, and level.

FIGURE 16.7

Using the Network
Control Panel to deter-
mine client software
version

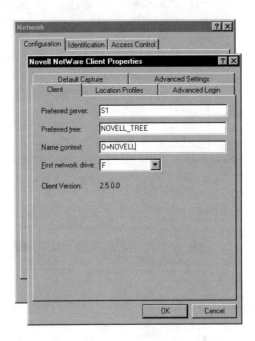

If you find that the client is out of date, you can upgrade it by downloading the newest client or patches from the Novell Support Connection
website http://support.novell.com and running the client installation
program at the workstation. If you want the upgrade to happen automatically, you can place the SETUP.EXE with the /ACU switch in the login script
for all the users. When the users login, if the client version of the SETUP program is newer than the version of software they are running, it will automatically upgrade the users' client software.

Before you install Novell Client Software or patches, it is always a good
idea to back up the Registry. You can use either commercial backup software or the Windows 95 Emergency Recovery Utility (found on the
Windows 95 installation CD).

**Step 5: Rule Out Configuration Issues.**    In addition to checking the
hardware and client software, you should check to see that the client has
the correct configuration parameters. To access these parameters, open the
Network control panel, select Novell NetWare Client, and click Properties. The tabs at the top of the screen shown previously in Figure 16.7 will

allow you to configure the connection parameters for the client. If these aren't configured correctly, the client may not connect to the server correctly, if at all.

It is especially important to configure the Preferred Tree and Name Context parameters. Without them, the workstation can't figure out where to look for the user object it is using to log in with. You may get "The user does not exist in the specified context" error if these parameters aren't configured correctly.

# Novell Client for Windows NT

**W**indows NT is gaining ground in the corporate world as the operating system of choice for the desktop. To that end, Novell has developed client software for Windows NT that enables Windows NT users to access a Novell NetWare network. It has several features, including:

- Fully integrated into Windows Explorer and Network Neighborhood

- Supports long filenames for files stored on server

- Supports upgrading clients using the Automatic Client Upgrade (ACU)

- Is loaded at startup

- Allows parameters to be managed using the Windows NT System Policy Editor

- Allows Windows NT users to run Novell NetWare login scripts

- Can be installed at the same time as Windows NT using the Windows NT unattended install (UNATTEND.TXT)

- Supports multiple protocols, including IPX/SPX, TCP/IP, Named Pipes, NetBIOS, Winsock, and Simple Network Management Protocol (SNMP)

- Provides simultaneous access to multiple NDS trees

- Coexists with other network clients, including Microsoft Client for Microsoft networks

- Provides automatic reconnection to network files and services

The Novell Client for Windows NT works on both Windows NT Workstation and Windows NT Server.

# Windows NT Client Components

The Novell Client for Windows NT is very similar to the Novell Client for Windows 95 in that it is modular and has multiple components. However, Windows NT is a more secure desktop environment and has its own login procedure that must be accounted for. For this reason, the Novell Client for Windows NT supports simultaneous login to NetWare and Windows NT.

There are five main components that make up the Novell Client for Windows NT. They are:

- The NetWare Client Requester

- LAN Drivers

- Communications Protocols

- NWFS.SYS

- Graphical Identification and Authentication (GINA) Module

## The NetWare Client Requester

The NetWare Client Requester is basically the same component as its Windows 95 counterpart. It connects the local Windows NT resources to the various NetWare services, like file and print services. In addition, it provides integration with NDS to allow management of Windows NT without having to implement Windows NT domains.

The file that provides the NetWare Client Requester function is CLIENT32 .NLM. It should be noted that any applications that require NETX or Net-Ware DOS Requester support are compatible with the NetWare Client Requester.

## LAN Drivers

Just like the Novell Client for Windows 95, the Novell Client for Windows NT can use either NDIS or 32-bit ODI drivers. If you choose to use the 32-bit ODI drivers, the ODI NDIS Support module (ODINSUP) allows Microsoft protocols and networking components to work with Novell 32-bit ODI drivers.

## Communications Protocols

Another similarity between the Novell Client for Windows 95 and the Novell Client for Windows NT is that both can use either TCP/IP or IPX/SPX as their transport protocol when accessing NetWare servers. But, with TCP/IP becoming more prevalent in networks, you can choose to standardize on TCP/IP for both NetWare and Windows NT servers.

## NWFS.SYS

NWFS.SYS is much like the NIOS.VXD component of the Novell Client for Window 95 in that it provides the core component of the client. All other client modules are loaded after this driver. It is implemented as a file system driver/redirector. It provides the backward-compatibility with software written for older Novell APIs.

## Graphical Identification and Authentication (GINA) Module

The last component of the Novell Client for Windows NT is one that has caused much controversy lately. Microsoft provides an interface for the logon procedure called WinLogon. The WinLogon component of Windows NT has several pieces to it, some of which are replaceable. One of these components is the Graphical Identification and Authentication (GINA) module. Some developers (including Novell) replace this component with their own version of the GINA.

Microsoft's GINA implementation is known as MSGINA.DLL and comes with Windows NT. Novell's GINA module is called NWGINA.DLL which takes over the authentication and user interaction from MSGINA.DLL. Fortunately for Windows NT users, NWGINA.DLL can also perform authentication to the local Windows NT workstation.

When you install the Novell Client for Windows NT, the Registry is modified so that the NWGINA module replaces the MSGINA module.

# Windows NT Client Troubleshooting

Troubleshooting a Windows NT workstation is very similar to troubleshooting a Windows 95 workstation. As a matter of fact, similar tools are used. The operating system is different, however, so some of the uses will be different.

### Troubleshooting Resources

There are several tools you can use when troubleshooting the Novell Client for Windows NT. Each tool is used differently. The most commonly used troubleshooting tools are:

- The Network Control Panel
- REGEDIT
- LANalyzer for Windows
- The MODULES command

The tools work the same way as they do under Windows 95.

### Troubleshooting Steps

The troubleshooting steps for Novell Client for Windows NT are basically the same as those for Windows 95, except the minimum requirements for the Novell Client for Windows NT are higher than those for the Windows 95 client (32 MB of RAM, 486 required, Pentium or higher recommended).

# Review

In this chapter you learned the basic components of the Novell Client for Windows 95:

- Netware I/O Subsystem (NIOS)
- LAN Drivers
- Communication Protocols
- NetWare Client Requester

Additionally, you learned that the Novell Client for Windows NT has some similar components:

- The NetWare Client Requester
- LAN Drivers
- Communications Protocols

- NWFS.SYS
- Graphical Identification and Authentication (GINA) Module

This chapter explained some details about the troubleshooting tools you have at your disposal for troubleshooting the Novell Client for Windows 95 and for Windows NT, including:

- The Network Control Panel
- The REGEDIT program
- LANalyzer for Windows
- The NIOS.LOG log file
- MODULES

# CNE Practice Test Questions

1. Which line, when placed in the SYSTEM.INI file, will enable the Novell Client log file?

    **A.** Logging=True

    **B.** NWEnablelogging=True

    **C.** Startlog=True

    **D.** NCStartlogging=True

2. What is the minimum amount of RAM required for the Novell Client for Windows 95?

    **A.** 8

    **B.** 16

    **C.** 32

    **D.** 64

**3.** What is the minimum amount of RAM required for the Novell Client for Windows NT?

   **A.** 8

   **B.** 16

   **C.** 32

   **D.** 64

**4.** Where do you change the size of the log file?

   **A.** HKEY_LOCAL_MACHINE/Network/Client32/LogSize

   **B.** Properties of Novell Client for Windows 95 in Network Control Panel

   **C.** Properties of Novell Client for Windows NT in Network Control Panel

   **D.** My computer ➤ logfiles

**5.** Which component of both Novell Clients allows support of Microsoft components and protocols when using the 32-bit ODI modules?

   **A.** LSL

   **B.** ODI

   **C.** TCP/IP

   **D.** ODINSUP

**6.** LANalyzer for Windows is an example of which of the following?

   **A.** Protocol Analyzer

   **B.** Internet Protocol

   **C.** Control Panel

   **D.** Registry Entry

**7.** Which component of the Novell Client for Windows 95 acts much like the SERVER.EXE component of a NetWare server, providing an interface between the Windows 95 and network services?

   **A.** NWFS.SYS

   **B.** LAN Driver

   **C.** LSL

   **D.** NIOS.VXD

**8.** Which component of the Novell Client for Windows NT provides an interface between Windows NT and network services?

   **A.** NWFS.SYS

   **B.** LAN Driver

   **C.** GINA

   **D.** NIOS.VXD

**9.** What is the name of the Graphical Identification and Authentication (GINA) file that the Novell Client replaces MSGINA.DLL with?

   **A.** NIOX.VXD

   **B.** NWGINA.DLL

   **C.** NCGINA.DLL

   **D.** GINA.DLL

**10.** What is the location in the Windows 95 Registry, of the version of the Novell Client for Windows 95?

   **A.** HKEY_LOCAL_MACHINE/Novell/Network/Version

   **B.** HKEY_LOCAL_MACHINE/Network/System Config/Install/ Novell/Version

   **C.** HKEY_LOCAL_MACHINE/Novell/Install/System Config/ Version

   **D.** HKEY_LOCAL_MACHINE/Network/Novell/System Config/ Install/Version

# CHAPTER

# 17

Troubleshooting Printing Systems

# Roadmap

This chapter describes the details of the various types of network printing systems available under NetWare and how to troubleshoot them.

**Topics Covered**

- Overview of NDPS concepts
- How to troubleshoot NDPS
- Overview of queue-based printing
- Troubleshooting queue-based printing

**Skills You'll Learn**

- How to troubleshoot NDPS printing problems
- Describe the steps for troubleshooting queue-based printing
- Diagnose queue-based printing problems at the workstation
- Diagnose queue-based printing problems at the print queue
- Diagnose queue-based printing problems at the print server
- Diagnose queue-based printing problems at the remote printer workstation
- Diagnose queue-based printing problems at the printer

I f you've spent an entire day troubleshooting a problem with a network, there's a good chance it involved printing. Printing is one of the most complicated network services provided by NetWare 5 and probably the most prone to problems. This chapter contains information that can help you face even the toughest of printer problems: the printer itself, the connections, print queues, print servers, and, most problematic of all, workstation printers.

To understand printing with NetWare 5 printing, you must first understand queue-based printing.

# An Overview of Queue-Based Printing

**N**etWare originally used a technology known as queue-based printing to provide shared printer access to its users. NetWare 5 has this same technology available. If you don't remember the details of queue-based printing, here is a quick summary of the objects involved in the printing process. Not surprisingly, this is also a list of the possible causes of printing problems.

- In order to print to a network printer, you must first send the data to a *print queue*. The print queue stores each set of data, or *print job*, that it receives. The jobs are then sent, one at a time, to the print server. The Print Queue NDS object controls the print queue. You change the properties of this object to control the queue. The NetWare Administrator dialog box for a Print Queue object's properties is shown in Figure 17.1.

**FIGURE  17.1**

The Print Queue object's properties, displayed by NetWare Administrator

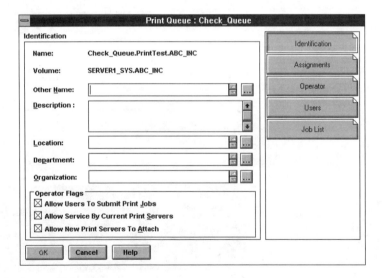

- The *print server* accepts print jobs from print queues and sends them to the appropriate printer. In NetWare 3.1*x*, print servers were limited to 16 printers; in NetWare 4.1 this limit was increased to 256, which allows you to easily use a single print server for the entire network.

- You create the Print Server object in NDS. The properties of the Print Server object provide identification information and define the list of printers the server can send jobs to. You can control these properties using NetWare Administrator. The Print Server dialog box in NetWare Administrator is shown in Figure 17.2. PSERVER.NLM is the program that runs the print server. Figure 17.3 shows the first screen you see when you load PSERVER.NLM.

**F I G U R E  17.2**

The Print Server object's properties, as shown in NetWare Administrator

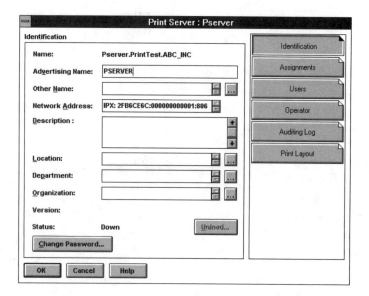

**F I G U R E  17.3**

The PSERVER NLM runs the print server.

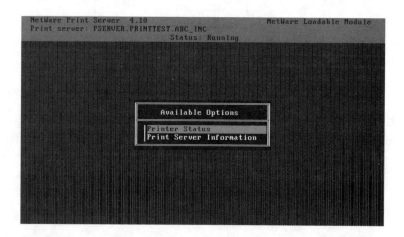

- You must create a *Printer object* to represent each network printer. The properties of the Printer object identify the printer and list the print queues that the printer accepts jobs from. Other properties define the type of printer and how it is accessed. Printers can be attached to a server, to a workstation, or directly to the network.

- CAPTURE is a TSR (terminate and stay resident) program that allows you to *redirect* printing to a network printer. You specify a local printer port (usually LPT1, LPT2, or LPT3) in the CAPTURE command line. After the CAPTURE command is executed, any printing that your workstation sends to this port is redirected to the network queue specified.

- The *port driver* is a piece of software that transfers data between the print queue and the printer. The port driver program is NPRINTER .NLM for server printers, NPRINTER.EXE for DOS workstation printers, or NPRINTER Manager for Windows 95 workstation printers. Printers that are directly connected to the network don't require this software.

The Print Queue, Print Server, and Printer objects handle a typical print job in this order:

**1.** The application sends the data to the CAPTURE program.

**2.** When the application is finished sending the print job, CAPTURE sends it to the print queue.

**3.** The print server takes the job from the top of the print queue and sends it to the port driver.

**4.** The port driver (NPRINTER) receives the job and sends it to the printer.

**5.** Finally, the printer prints the job.

Figure 17.4 illustrates the printing process.

**FIGURE 17.4**

Several components are involved in the printing process.

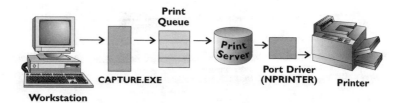

Print Queue

Print Server

Port Driver (NPRINTER)

Printer

CAPTURE.EXE

Workstation

For more detailed information on NetWare printing, see *NetWare 5: CNA/ CNE Administrator and Design Study Guide* by Michael Moncur et al.

# The Troubleshooting Process

The following sections describe some of the problems that can occur with printers. By following the steps below, you should be able to narrow down the cause of the printer problem. Next, look at the specific section in this chapter for further information about the type of problem.

1. Run the printer's self-test. Refer to the manual to see how to do the self-test; it usually involves holding down one of the buttons on the printer while turning the power off and on.

2. If the self-test doesn't work, turn the power off and on, and then try the self-test again.

3. If the self-test still doesn't work, the problem must be with the printer itself. Refer to the sections on troubleshooting printer problems in this chapter.

4. If the self-test works, try printing a screen next. If the printer is attached to a workstation, you can press Print Screen from any DOS application. If the printer is attached to a server, you can either take the server down and try a print screen from Windows 95 or connect the printer to a workstation temporarily.

5. If printing a screen doesn't work, the problem is between the printer and the workstation or server—most likely the cable. Refer to the section on troubleshooting printer connections in this chapter.

6. If printing a screen worked, use PCONSOLE or NetWare Administrator to determine whether jobs are entering the print queue.

7. If jobs are in the queue, the problem must be with the print server or printer.

8. If no jobs are in the queue, the CAPTURE command is not set correctly, or an application is sending data to the wrong port in Windows 95.

9. Check all connections and cables.

10. Static may cause printers to fail or to go offline. Position the printer on a hard wood surface, or purchase an anti-static mat to place under it.

11. If the printer is a remote printer, make sure the workstation is on, attached to the network, and running the NPRINTER.EXE (DOS) or NPRINTER Manager (Windows 95) program.

12. If printing is slow, you may be using a serial printer. Serial printing is much slower than printing with parallel connections. Also, remote printers are slower than server printers. Directly connected network printers are usually the fastest.

13. Be sure that you have the latest version of all software drivers.

Read the following sections for detailed information about the many things that can go wrong in the printing process.

# Troubleshooting Printers and Connections

Once you've set up network printing, all the components generally work unless you change something. Thus, the most common problems are with the physical components—the printer and the physical connections between the printer and the server, workstation, or print server. Each of the several types of printers has its own set of problem areas:

- A dot matrix printer uses a set of pins that move forward and press a ribbon against the paper, making a dot. These printers are commonly used for invoices, checks, and continuous forms. They are loud and prone to problems, but they do work with multi-part forms.

- An ink jet printer is a more modern version of the dot matrix printer. It uses a similar dot pattern, but liquid ink is forced through tiny nozzles to create the dots on the paper. These printers are typically faster than dot matrix printers, which print by making an impact on the paper, and much quieter. Because there's no impact in ink jet printing, they won't work with multi-part forms; but the paper jams much less frequently. Another advantage of an ink jet printer is that the print head generates virtually no heat.

- A laser printer uses a laser (or a matrix of LEDs, in some cases) to fuse toner particles onto the paper. Laser printers are usually the most expensive and produce the highest quality printing. In addition, high-speed models are available. They do have their share of problems, which are discussed later in this chapter.

- Other printers include daisy-wheel, band printers, and other types. Most of these types of printers are now antiques, but they're still used in many companies. Because of the variety of types of printers, all of their specific problems cannot be covered here.

If you're having a printer problem, first follow the general guidelines provided in the next section. Then move on to the specific section for your type of printer.

Printers are incredibly complicated devices. The tips in this chapter are for user-level troubleshooting and are by no means a guide for printer service technicians. If these tips don't help, call a dealer or other service company and arrange for service.

## General Printer Troubleshooting

Most of the problems you encounter with printers will be simple ones. So, check the simple things first:

- If the printer has LEDs, LCDs or other diagnostic indicators, check them to determine the source of the problem.

- Is the printer out of paper?

- Is the ribbon, ink cartridge, or toner running low?

- Is the printer unplugged, turned off, or set to offline?

- Is the connection between the printer and the workstation or server in place?

- Have you created the NDS objects needed for printing and configured them correctly? See NetWare 5: CNA/CNE Administrator and Design Study Guide for the details of how to do this.

These solutions sound obvious, but they correct problems that do occur. If you're helping someone troubleshoot a problem over the phone, be extra sure he or she has checked these items. You would be surprised how many people don't.

When you've eliminated the obvious, move on to the less obvious solutions:

- Check the *paper path*, the path the paper travels as it enters and exits the printer. Look for any obstruction—usually a torn piece of paper.

- Clean the printer, and see if that fixes the problem. Vacuum dust from all areas, and remove any paper fragments. Clean ink-covered surfaces carefully, using a cotton swab dipped in alcohol.

- Check the printer's environment. High humidity, heat, cold, or even a leaky roof could cause problems. Moist paper can cause feed problems.

Don't try lubricating moving parts, unless your printer's manual instructs you to do so. You can damage the apparatus, and all you'll get for your trouble is a lecture from the technician when you call for repairs.

After you've tried these solutions, check the connections, as described in the next section, and then move on to the specific section in this chapter for your printer. You should also check the troubleshooting section of the printer's manual.

If you have to troubleshoot printers frequently, you'll probably get ink or toner on your hands. A supply of disposable plastic gloves is definitely a good investment.

# Troubleshooting Network Printer Connections

After you've eliminated a printer problem, check the connection to the printer. There are three possible ways a printer can be connected:

- Server printers are attached directly to a file server.

- Workstation printers, or remote printers, are attached to a network workstation.

- Directly connected network printers are attached to the network directly, using a hardware device or a card within the printer.

## Understanding Serial and Parallel Connections

There are two common interfaces for printers, serial and parallel. The interface you use depends on the interface supported by the printer and the port available on the workstation or server. Parallel connections are the most common, but serial connections are still used on many printers.

**Serial Connections**   A serial connection sends data to the printer one bit at a time, which is not an efficient arrangement. In addition, a serial connection must be configured carefully. Here are some of the parameters associated with serial printing. In all cases, the same parameters must be set at the printer and at the workstation or server.

- Baud rate is the rate at which data is sent. Speeds range from 1,200 baud to 57,600 baud.

- Parity specifies whether extra bits of data are sent for error checking. Options include even, odd, mark, space, and none.

- Data bits are the number of bits used to represent a character, usually seven or eight.

- Stop bits are the number of bits sent between characters, usually ranges from zero to two.

- Flow control is the method used for the printer to tell the host to slow down to allow it to print the data it has received. Values are typically XON/XOFF (software), DTR/RTS (hardware), or none.

The main advantage of serial printing is the distance that a serial connection can extend. While a parallel printer cable can typically extend no more than 15 feet, a serial connection can reach as far as 300 feet. Serial data can be transmitted through a modem for virtually unlimited distances. However, parallel printing is more commonly used because it is faster and more reliable.

**Parallel Connections**   A parallel printer connection sends eight bits of data at once. Because the speed, flow control, and other parameters are standard, there are no parameters to set for a parallel connection. Simply run a parallel cable from the workstation or server to the printer, and you're set.

Although you can purchase parallel printer extension cables, you should avoid increasing the distance beyond the limits. The official limit for a parallel cable is 15 feet, but you can usually get away with 20. If you need to run the cable a greater distance, do one of the following:

- Consider attaching the printer to a workstation that is nearer to the desired location.

- You can buy *parallel extenders*, which can extend the reach of a parallel cable to 300 feet or more. These consist of two devices, which are attached to the printer and to the workstation or server. Parallel extenders typically cost about $150 for the pair.

## Checking the Connections

Printer problems can be hard to diagnose because so many different systems interact in the process of printing. By following the steps below, you should be able to determine where the problem is—in the printer itself, the workstation, or the network.

1. Try the printer's self-test. Refer to the manual to see how to perform the self-test; it usually involves holding down one of the buttons while turning the power off and on.

2. If the self-test doesn't work, turn the power off and on, and then try the self-test again.

3. If the self-test still doesn't work, the problem must be with the printer itself. Refer to the section on troubleshooting printer problems later in this chapter.

4. If the self-test worked, try printing a screen next. If the printer is attached to a workstation, you can press Shift+Print Screen from any application. Then you can go into Paint, paste the image from the clipboard and print it out. If the printer is attached to the server, you can either take the server down and try a print screen from DOS or connect the printer to another workstation.

5. If printing a screen doesn't work, the problem is between the printer and the workstation or server—most likely the cable. Try a different cable or a different LPT port.

6. If printing a screen works, move on to the Troubleshooting Print Queues section for more instructions.

# Troubleshooting Dot Matrix Printers

This section covers some details related to impact dot matrix printers. These printers use a *print head* that moves across the paper. Pins within the print head move out to strike the ribbon and press ink onto the paper. Common configurations use either 9 or 24 of these pins. These printers typically use a tractor-feed system to pull continuous paper into the printer.

## Maintenance Tips

If you are using dot matrix printers, follow these tips to keep them running in top shape and avoid problems.

- The print head generates a lot of heat. Be sure that the printer is not covered during use and is placed in a well-ventilated area.

- Use high-quality ribbons, preferably direct from the manufacturer of the printer. Cheap ribbons are often unreliable and can damage the print head. Also, if a ribbon has not been used for a long time it may dry out. A dried-out ribbon won't work very well and may damage the print head.

- Don't try to move the platen knob (the knob that advances the paper) while the printer is on or running. Also do not move the print head. If you need to move these to fix a paper jam, turn off the printer first.

- Be sure the printer is compatible with the paper you are using. Some types of thicker paper, such as multi-part forms and card stock, may be too thick for some printers. You also may need to adjust the print head distance to make these types of paper work.

- Be sure the paper source is positioned so that paper feeds easily into the printer, and position the printer so that the output paper stacks itself neatly. This can be tricky using an ordinary table or desk; printer stands, made for the purpose of supporting printers, are available.

## Diagnosing a Problem

The most common problem with dot matrix printers is a simple paper jam. You'll find that the paper stopped moving and the last 30 pages of your report have been printed on a single line, burning a hole in the paper. In this case, simply clear the paper out as best you can and reload it. You may also need to clean excess ink off the print head and platen.

Other common problems possible with dot matrix printers are listed in the following sections.

### Does Not Print, Prints Partial Data, or Prints Garbled Characters

Check these items if the printer doesn't print at all:

- Check for a bad connection or a disconnected cable.

- Your printer may have DIP switches, which you can use to set options. Check the manual for their location, and be sure they are set correctly.

- Be sure you are using the correct driver for your printer and that the correct printer type is selected in the application, especially for Windows applications.

- Be sure you have used a long enough timeout value in the CAPTURE command. With low timeout values and a slow computer, the data may be sent to the printer before it's finished, resulting in partial printing and garbage characters.

- If the printer uses a serial connection, make sure the baud rate and other settings of the printer match those of the workstation. You may need to add a MODE command to the workstation's AUTOEXEC.BAT file to set the communication settings. Here's a typical command that sets the printer on COM2 to 2400 baud, eight bits, one stop bit, and no parity:

```
MODE COM2: 2400, N, 8, 1, P
```

**Poor Print Quality or Incorrect Formatting**   If the printer prints, but the print job is formatted incorrectly or is of poor quality, try these solutions:

- Check the ribbon; poor quality is usually a symptom of a worn ribbon. Replace the ribbon and see if the problem is solved.

- You may need to adjust the print head's distance from the paper. If it's too far away, printing may be faded. If it's too close, the ribbon brushing against the paper may cause streaking.

- If neither of those helped, try cleaning the print head carefully.

- Be sure you are using the correct driver for your printer and that the correct printer type is selected in the application, especially for Windows applications.

- If the output is double-spaced (and you weren't expecting it to be), check the DIP switch settings.

- Check for a broken or stuck pin.

**Printing Stops in the Middle of a Job**   Try these solutions if the printer works but stops while printing:

- Most likely, the paper is jammed. Carefully remove the damaged paper, reload the paper on a new sheet, and continue.

- Check for a jammed ribbon. Try replacing the ribbon if possible.

- If the printer stopped printing after printing for a long time, it may be overheating. Most dot matrix printers include a device called a *thermistor*, which detects high temperatures and shuts down printing. This may happen occasionally with no ill effects, and most printers resume printing automatically when they cool. If it happens frequently, the thermistor or another circuit may be defective.

# Troubleshooting Ink Jet Printers

Ink jet printers have emerged in the last five years as a very popular alternative to conventional dot matrix printers. They are equally inexpensive, are quieter, and produce higher print quality. In addition, print jobs don't suffer from the fading of a ribbon as it is worn out. However, ink jet printers do have their share of problems—including a few that can leave you wishing for a simple ribbon tangle.

## Maintenance Tips

Although ink jet printers function similarly to dot matrix printers, they follow completely different rules for maintenance. Here's a list of items to keep the printer running smoothly:

- Printing doesn't fade when the ink runs out in an ink jet, unlike a dot matrix printer. Printing usually stops entirely, and most printers are smart enough to stop printing when this happens. When it does, replace the cartridge immediately. Although you can often continue printing or shake the cartridge to get the last drop out of it, you can damage the printer by doing so.

- Avoid refilling ink cartridges, particularly doing so yourself. Although many people successfully do this, many printers die early deaths because of poor-quality ink. If you must try it, consider it carefully, and be sure to purchase a tried-and-true product.

- Position the printer on a completely level surface. This is even worth checking with a carpenter's level. Many printers can dry out if positioned incorrectly.

- Use high-quality paper. Some cheap papers leave fragments in the printer's works and damage the print head.

## Diagnosing a Problem

Ink jets aren't quite as easy to diagnose and maintain as dot matrix printers. In many cases, you are better off going to an authorized repair technician. The following sections describe some problems you may be able to correct.

**Printing Fades or Starts and Stops**   Try replacing the ink cartridge. If you are using a refilled or third-party cartridge, try the manufacturer's model, and see if it helps.

- Check to see if the printer is tilted. Level it if necessary.

- Most ink jet printers have a cleaning feature that you can activate with one of the switches on the printer or through the properties of the print driver. Check the manual, and try this. You may need to perform the cleaning several times before it helps.

**Printer Stops Entirely**   Check the basics—is the printer unplugged, turned off, or offline?

- Try replacing the ink cartridge. Most printers go offline when they detect that the ink supply is low.

- Check for a paper jam or for any object that may be restricting the movement of the print head.

- If the printer flashes a light or displays an error code, check the manual.

# Troubleshooting Laser Printers

Laser printers are the highest quality printers available. Not coincidentally, they are also the most expensive and the most complicated. Laser printers have their share of problems. They are best maintained by an authorized service technician; however, you can perform several simple maintenance tasks that can help you avoid trouble.

## Maintenance Tips

- When the toner cartridge is low, replace it as soon as possible. When you do, clean the inside of the printer following the instructions in the manual.

- Be extra careful of the corona wires (tiny wires near the fuser) when cleaning. They can break and are quite expensive to replace.

- Replace the fuser bar (a long, rectangular piece of cotton or fabric) when you replace the cartridge.

- Laser printers generate quite a bit of heat. Keep them in a well-ventilated room.

- Avoid refilled or remanufactured toner cartridges if at all possible. They are usually poor quality and can damage the printer. If you do try them, be sure they are from a reputable company that remanufactures all the parts.

Toner is very messy. Be careful when handling toner cartridges. If you ship them, be sure they are sealed in plastic bags. If you get toner on your hands or clothing, rinse immediately with *cold water*; warm or hot water may fuse the toner and make it harder to remove.

- Be careful with envelopes or labels that aren't certified for use with laser printers. They may come unglued in the printer and cause damage.

- Check the printer's manual for any other routine maintenance procedures.

The inside of a laser printer is very hot. Be careful, and avoid touching any parts with bare hands. Turn the printer off, and allow it to cool for several minutes before handling any components of the printer.

## Diagnosing a Problem

The following sections contain possible solutions to some of the common symptoms suffered by laser printers. Because laser printers that are used often require frequent maintenance, you may wish to purchase a service contract or extended warranty.

**Printing Fades or Streaks**   Try replacing the toner cartridge. If you are using a refilled or third-party cartridge, try the manufacturer's model, and see if it helps.

- If the output is blurred, clean the corona wires and drum.

- Horizontal lines or spots that occur a fixed distance apart may be caused by damage to the roller. If you see these spots or lines in print jobs, call a service center.

- If the output is completely black, check for a broken corona wire or a bad cartridge.

- Try removing the toner cartridge, and carefully shaking it to redistribute the toner.

- If the output is compressed or stretched, you may have a motor problem. Also, the paper may not be feeding correctly. Check the paper tray.

- Some papers, especially high-gloss papers and card stock, don't accept toner very well. Be sure to use paper approved for laser printers.

- If you are using high-quality paper but the toner flakes off the page, the fuser is probably not getting hot enough. Call a service center.

**Printer Stops Entirely**  Check the basics—is it unplugged, turned off, or offline?

- Check for a bad cable or bad connection, and be sure you are running the correct software drivers.

- Try replacing the toner cartridge. Most printers go offline when they detect that the toner supply is low.

- Check for a paper jam, particularly where the paper enters and exits.

- If the printer flashes a light or displays an error code, check the manual.

## Troubleshooting PostScript Printers

PostScript is a page description language used in many high-end laser printers. It is typically not seen in other types of printers. PostScript allows for complicated formatting and compatibility with many high-end software packages. Here are some tips for troubleshooting PostScript printers.

- Be sure you are using the correct PostScript version of the driver software, particularly if you are using Windows.

- Be sure that the PostScript mode is enabled on the printer. Many printers have an alternate mode, such as PCL, that may be the default.

- PostScript printers don't recognize the regular form-feed, tab, or alphanumeric characters. Because of this, be sure to use the NFF (No form feed), NB (No banner), and NT (No tabs) options with the CAPTURE command.

# Troubleshooting Print Queues

**W**hen you have eliminated the printer itself as a cause of problems, you can move on to the other parts of the network printing system, starting with the print queue. In theory, the CAPTURE program on the workstation should send data to the print queue. As a first step, find out whether capturing is successful. Type this command: **CAPTURE SH.**

This command shows you which port is captured to each print queue. Next, run the PCONSOLE utility. Select Print Queue Options, then select Current Print Jobs. PCONSOLE displays a list of the jobs in the queue. Read the following sections to diagnose the problem.

## Jobs Are Not Listed in the Queue

Try sending several print jobs. If they are not listed in the print queue, check the following:

- The CAPTURE command may not be executing. Type **CAPTURE SH** to view settings and be sure they are correct.

- Be sure your application is sending data to the correct port, as listed in the CAPTURE command.

- Check that the CAPTURE command includes either the timeout (TI) or autoendcap (AE) options. Try typing **CAPTURE /EC** to end the capture manually. If that works, you need to add a timeout or autoendcap to the command.

- Check the available disk storage on the volume where the print queue is stored—usually the SYS volume. If the volume is almost out of space, queue files will not be created.

If none of these solutions is effective, the print queue files may be corrupt. Print queue files are stored in the QUEUES directory, usually under the SYS volume. Delete all the files in this directory, and then send another job.

## Jobs Never Leave the Queue

If the print jobs keep piling up in the queue, the problem is with the print server or printer. Do the following:

- Check the printer itself, as described earlier in this chapter.

- Make sure PSERVER.NLM is running on a server.

- Make sure that the port driver (either NPRINTER.NLM or NPRINTER. EXE) is running on the server or workstation to which the printer is attached.

If none of these solutions fixes the problem, move on to the following section on print servers.

# Troubleshooting Print Servers and Printer Objects

**F**ollow these steps to diagnose a print server problem:

- Be sure the print server is running on a server. You can load it by typing this command: **LOAD PSERVER** *name* (where *name* is the name of the Print Server object).

- In the PCONSOLE utility, select Print Server Information and then Print Server Information and Status. Be sure the print server is running. Figure 17.5 shows the Print Server Information and Status window in PCONSOLE.

**FIGURE 17.5**

The Print Server Information and Status window in the PCONSOLE indicates if the print server is running.

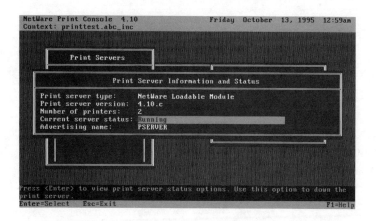

- Take the print server down using PCONSOLE, and reload it using the LOAD PSERVER command shown previously to stop jobs that are currently printing.

- Make sure that you have created a Print Server object to handle printing and that you have configured it correctly.

- Be sure that each user has rights to the Print Server object. Placing the Print Server object in the same context as the users who use it is a good way to ensure that each user has rights to the Print Server object.

- Check whether the server is low on RAM. If there is insufficient memory, PSERVER.NLM may not run properly.

- Check the Queues Serviced by Printer option in PCONSOLE (see Figure 17.6) or in the Printer object's properties (see Figure 17.7). Be sure the correct queue or queues are listed.

**F I G U R E  17.6**

The Queues Serviced by Printer screen in PCONSOLE lists queues for the printer.

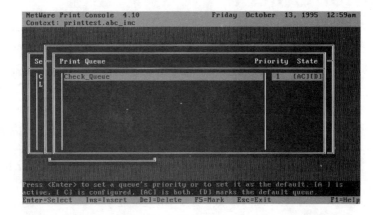

**F I G U R E  17.7**

The Printer object's Print Queues property shows that the Check_ Queue queue is the only queue serviced by the Check_Printer printer.

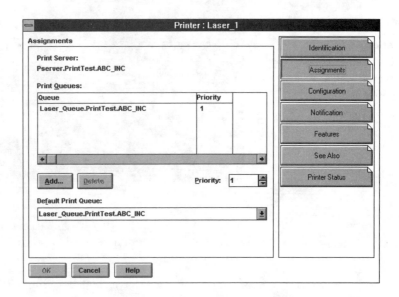

- A plotter may not work as a network printer using a software print server. Plotters need to have a real-time dialog with the application software to accept commands. You may need to attach the plotter directly to the workstation that uses it. Also, hardware print servers, which may work, are available.

- Although a NetWare 5 print server can handle a total of 256 printers, that many printers cause a heavy load on one server. You may see slow network performance with as few as five or six printers, depending on the type of server. Consider loading another print server on a separate server or dedicating a server to print services.

- If you change any configuration in the Print Server or Printer objects, you need to bring the print server down and back up before the changes take effect.

- If the print server's behavior is inconsistent, try running the DSREPAIR utility on a server. This utility finds any problems in the NDS definitions of the Print Server, Printer, and Print Queue objects. DSREPAIR is discussed in more detail in the NetWare 5: CNA/CNE Administrator and Design Study Guide. Figure 17.8 shows the opening screen in DSREPAIR.

**FIGURE 17.8**

The DSREPAIR utility may fix problems with printing NDS objects.

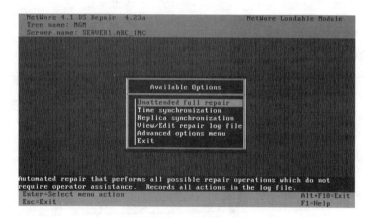

- Check the Novell support areas on CompuServe or the Internet to see if updated versions of PSERVER.NLM, NPRINTER.NLM, or NPRINTER.EXE are available. Although the versions included with NetWare 5 work in most situations, they may have errors when working with certain products or in certain configurations.

- Be sure that the port driver (NPRINTER.NLM or NPRINTER.EXE) is running on the workstation or server that the printer is attached to. (This is not necessarily the same machine that PSERVER.NLM runs on.)

### Troubleshooting PSERVER.EXE

Earlier versions of NetWare included PSERVER.EXE, a print server that could run on a standalone DOS workstation. PSERVER.EXE is not included in NetWare since versions 4.*x*, but you may still be using a NetWare 3.1*x* print server with NetWare 5 or have both versions on your network. Here are some possible problems with PSERVER.EXE:

- Be sure the workstation has at least 512KB of free conventional memory, plus 10KB for each printer. If you need more memory, remove any TSR programs. PSERVER.EXE requires only DOS and the network drivers.

- To take the print server down, use PCONSOLE. Select Print Server options, then Print Server Information and Status. Change the status from Running to Down. Sometimes this will not work; you may have to turn the workstation's power off and on.

- Be sure that the workstation's NET.CFG file contains the following line:

```
SPX CONNECTIONS = 60
```

- If this line is not included, the print server may function normally but will display errors as soon as it gets busy or after a length of time.

# Troubleshooting Remote Printers

NetWare 5 uses NPRINTER.EXE (DOS) or NPRINTER Manager (Windows 95) for remote, or workstation, printers. This utility receives jobs from the print queue and sends them to the printer itself. In a printer attached to a server, this function is handled by NPRINTER.NLM. The workstation version runs as a TSR (terminate and stay resident) utility under DOS. Here are some tips for avoiding potential problems with NPRINTER:

- Be sure that NPRINTER is running with the correct printer specified. You can check this from the AUTOEXEC.BAT file or in the user's login script.

- Other TSR programs may conflict with NPRINTER. Remove them from the AUTOEXEC.BAT or CONFIG.SYS file, and see if the problem is fixed.

- Never allow an application to print to a local printer port directly while NPRINTER is running. At best this prints in the middle of a network-printing job, and at worst, it crashes the workstation. Always use CAPTURE, and print to the network print queue.

- If the workstation crashes, the printer stops; there isn't much that can be done about this.

- If the workstation runs Windows, there may be conflicts. NPRINTER works under Windows in most cases but may disagree with certain Windows applications.

- If you are running Windows 3.1*x*, be sure to start NPRINTER before Windows is started. Do not start it from a DOS session under Windows.

NetWare 3.1*x* included a utility, RPRINTER.EXE, which provided the same functions as NPRINTER.EXE for remote printing. RPRINTER does not work with NetWare 5 queue-based printing. If you are using RPRINTER, consider switching to NPRINTER. It is much more reliable than RPRINTER, especially under Windows.

# Novell Distributed Print Services Concepts

**A**nyone who has set up network printing knows that it is far from simple. There are many steps and details and, if one step is not done correctly, network printing won't work. To that end, Novell got together with Hewlett-Packard and Xerox to develop a next-generation printing technology that would be easy to configure and use and at the same time be very powerful. This technology is called Novell Distributed Print Services (NDPS). The main advantage to NDPS is simplified management and ease of setup. Instead of three objects to configure in NDS, you only need to configure one (called the *Printer Agent*, which is discussed later). Additionally, some printers come with technology where they can be plugged in to the network and the users will be able to print immediately, without any further configuration.

To understand how this new technology works, you need to be familiar with the various components of NDPS.

## NDPS Components

NDPS is made up of several components, each with a specific function. Not all components are required for NDPS to function properly, but they may be required in special situations. The major components of NDPS are:

- The NDPS Manager
- The Printer Agent
- The NDPS Broker
- The NDPS Gateways

### The NDPS Manager

The *NDPS Manager* is just what it sounds like, a software component that manages the printing process. It is used to create and manage the various Printer Agents (discussed next). If you are familiar with the old queue-based printing technology (discussed later in this chapter), the NDPS manager performs some of the same functions as the print server.

A single NDPS Manager can support an unlimited number of Printer Agents. But, typically you will create one NDPS manager for each server that you want to be able to manager printers. Remember that only one NDPS manager can be loaded per server.

The NDPS Manager can be loaded from the server console by typing either **NDPSM** or **LoadNDPSM**. Additionally, when you create a Printer Agent, if there isn't an NDPS Manager already loaded, one will be automatically loaded.

### The Printer Agent

In traditional NetWare queue-based printing, there are three NDS objects that need to be set up. In NDPS, there is really only one, the Printer Agent. The Printer Agent is the entity on the network that controls and manages the printer. It combines the functionality of the three objects into one. There is one agent for each printer on the network. All the printing and management happens through the agent.

The agent can be either software, loaded on a NetWare server, or embedded within the hardware of a network-connected printer. Some printers have a network interface that is NDPS compatible (like Xerox and HP JetDirect printers). These printers have the Printer Agent embedded within the network interface itself. When these printers are connected to the network, they will contact the NDPS Broker and announce themselves as a new printer. The NDPS Manager will then automatically make them available to the workstations and users can print. This capability has been given the name Plug-and-Print.

## The NDPS Broker

The NDPS Broker is the component of NDPS that gives it some of the new features. NDPS needs to have a broker so that workstations can take advantage of the more advanced features of NDPS. When you install NDPS, the installation program checks to see if a broker is needed. A broker is needed if:

- There isn't one on the network.
- The one that is on the network is more than three hops away from the server you are installing NDPS on.

The NDPS Broker provides three distinct services for NDPS:

- Service Registry Services (SRS)
- Resource Management Services (RMS)
- Event Notification Services (EMS)

**Service Registry Services (SRS)**   Under NetWare 4.*x*, printers used to advertise themselves using IPX and SAP. Now that NetWare 5 can use IP, however, a new system had to be developed to keep track of all the printers.

Service Registry Services is the component of the NDPS broker that allows public access printers to register themselves to NDPS. It keeps a list of all the public access printers so that workstations can find them. When a new printer is available on the network, it registers itself with the SRS component of the broker.

**Resource Management Services (RMS)**   One of the nicest new features of NDPS is the ability of NDPS to automatically download the printer driver (as well as banners, fonts, and printer definition files) to the workstation when the printer is installed. When a workstation connects to an NDPS printer, the Printer Agent contacts the Resource Management Services (RMS) component of the broker to find out what components can be downloaded to the workstation.

The Resource Management Services component of the NDPS Broker keeps all the printing resources (like printer drivers, printer fonts, and printer definition files and banners) in a central location on a server.

**Event Notification Services (EMS)**   When there are problems with the printer, NDPS can notify the user and the administrator of the location of the problem as well as its nature. If you'll recall, queue-based printing could only notify via NetWare broadcasts. NDPS, however, can notify users and administrators via several methods including NetWare broadcasts, log files, and e-mail.

## The NDPS Gateways

At the time of the writing of this book, there aren't that many network printers that are NDPS-aware (those that have an NDPS Printer Agent embedded in the network interface). For this reason, Novell provides three NDPS Gateways for the various types of printers (Hewlett-Packard, Xerox, and a generic Novell gateway). The NDPS Gateways allows the NDPS clients to:

- Manage the printer

- Get status information from the printer

- Send jobs to non–NDPS-aware printers

- Access queue-based printing system with NDPS

- Send jobs across platforms (From NetWare to UNIX or Macintosh systems)

# NDPS Printer Types

The NDPS Manager specifies two types of NDPS printers. The two types of NDPS printers are public access and controlled access.

A *public access printer* is a printer available to every user on the network with no restrictions. Unfortunately, because of its public nature, a public access printer has very low security. But, the nicest thing about public access printers is that they provide the true Plug-and-Print capabilities mentioned earlier. Finally, it should be noted that when the administrator configures an NDPS public access printer, it has no corresponding NDS object.

On the other hand, a *controlled access printer* has an NDS object. The NDS object of a controlled access printer allows an administrator to manage all the functions of that printer, which also means that the printer access can be restricted. A controlled access printer has more security and more administrative options than a public access printer.

# Troubleshooting NDPS

Troubleshooting NDPS is much like troubleshooting queue-based printing. The following sections cover some tips that make troubleshooting NDPS much easier.

## Getting Started

When you experience printing problems, the first thing you should note is any error message. Error messages, although cryptic, will give you an indication that something is wrong. Most software (including NetWare) comes with documentation that will tell you what the error message means and how to resolve it. If the documentation doesn't have it, check Novell's website (www.novell.com) because there may be an update since the documentation was printed.

A few common errors and their solutions are:

- A "print job was rejected" error message indicates that the spooling volume may be full or have a space restriction. Removing the restriction or removing unneeded files should correct the situation.

- A "Can't connect to the Printer Agent" error indicates that the NDPS Manager or Broker may not be loaded. Remember that the LOAD NDPSM command in the AUTOEXEC.NCF is not added by default, so it may not reload when you reboot. To prevent the problem, add the LOAD NDPSM to the AUTOEXEC.NCF.

If there are no error messages, or the error messages lead you down a dead end, you can try some quick fixes. If the problem affects all workstations, you could try:

- Turn the printer off and on to purge the job.

- Notice if the printer is getting a hardware error and correct it before continuing.

- Check the Printer Information screen in the Novell Printer Manager for NDPS error messages.

- Check the server console for error messages.

- Check the cabling to the printer.

- Search the Support Connection website for updates or possible causes.

- Make sure you have the most current NDPS software.

If the problem affects only one workstation, try some different options:

- See if any changes have been made on the workstation since the printer last worked.

- Check the local printer configuration (like job configurations or printer form settings).

- Check the job list to see if the print job is getting to the spooler and that the printer hasn't been set to pause printing.

Another thing that will help you get started troubleshooting is to determine your printing environment. That is, understand the issues involved in printing from different platforms, including:

- If you are using NDPS as your printing environment, NSPSM.NLM and BROKER.NLM must be loaded. If you are using queue-based printing, PSERVER.NLM must be loaded.

- Remember that NDPS supports only Windows clients. All other platforms must use queue-based printing.

- If you have Print Queue, Printer, and Print Server objects in your NDS tree, more than likely you are using queue-based printing

- NDPS requires Novell Client 2.2 or higher and the configuration of Printer Agents.

- Queue-based printing requires any Novell client and the configuration of Print Queue, Printer, and Print server objects.

The last basic item to remember is that issues exist when using queue-based printing and NDPS together.

- If you have a printer that can only take its jobs from a print server and print queue, but the clients are set up to print to printer agents, you can configure the printer agent to transfer a job to a print queue.

- If you have older clients that can only send to print queues (like old NETX and VLM clients), but that now need to print to NDPS-only printers, you can configure the Printer Agent to pull jobs from the print queue, emulating a print server.

## Narrowing Down the Problem

If the quick fixes don't work, you may need to narrow the problem down. Otherwise, you may be chasing problems that aren't really there. Here are a few things to remember when trying to narrow the problem down:

- To determine if the problem is related to one workstation or all workstations, send the same job from other workstations to the same printer.

- Ask yourself if this workstation could ever print to this printer. If so, check to see if something has been changed since it last worked. If the answer is yes, then most likely, the thing that was changed is the source of the problem.

- Check the setup. Was it done correctly? Check the documentation that was made when you installed NDPS.

## Determining Platform-Specific Issues When the Problem Affects Only One Workstation

When you have different types of workstation operating systems on your network, there are a few concepts you must keep in mind. Each operating system has its own printing issues. DOS, Macintosh, UNIX, and OS/2 operating systems can only use queue-based printing. Make sure that a print server (PSERVER.NLM) is functioning, or ensure that a Printer Agent has been configured to emulate a printer server and print queue.

- Windows 95, 98, and NT can use NDPS. Make sure that they are running the most current version of the client.

- Check out the "Troubleshooting Print Queues" and "Troubleshooting Print Servers" sections earlier in this chapter.

## Isolating Printing Problems Affecting One Windows Workstation

If the problem is related to only one workstation, there are several things you can check. First of all, check the status of the printer you are trying to print to in the Windows Control Panel. Make sure that the correct driver is installed and that the printer is not paused.

Next, check to see which port the printer is printing to. On Windows 95 and NT workstations, go to Start ➤ Settings ➤ Printers, right-click the printer you are having problems with and choose Properties. Select the Details tab and notice the value in the Print to the following port field. If it has been set up correctly, an NDPS printer object name will appear in the menu bar and the word NDPS will appear somewhere in the Print to which port field (Figure 17.9).

**F I G U R E  17.9**

Printer properties screen  (Note NDPS01 in the Print To: field.)

In addition to the Properties screen of the Windows 95 printer, you can also check the status of the printer using the Novell Printer Manager. The Novell Printer Manager shows all the installed NDPS printers and their status. The executable is located in SYS:PUBLIC\WIN32\ and is called NWPMW32.EXE. Figure 17.10 shows an example of the Novell Printer Manager screen.

**F I G U R E  17.10**

Novell Printer Manager screen

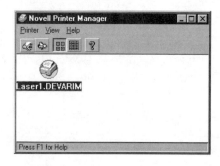

You can tell if an NDPS printer is functioning properly using the Novell Printer Manager. If there is a problem, you can find out by running the printer manager, selecting the printer you want status on, and choosing Printer ➤ Information. This will display a menu similar to the one in Figure 17.11. As you can see, the printer is experiencing a problem. The area under the words State Details shows the possible causes of the problem. In this case, the printer isn't connected. If the errors don't make sense, you can click the Help button in the lower right hand corner to get further information.

**FIGURE 17.11**

The Printer Informa-
tion screen of Novell
Printer Manager

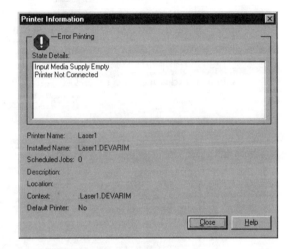

## Tracking Jobs Using Workstation Tools

Everyone has done it. You print to a network printer. The print job doesn't appear in the output tray of the printer. The instinctive reaction is something that has been dubbed "the toothpaste effect." When your toothpaste tube clogs up (as they occasionally do), the natural response is to squeeze as hard as you can in hopes of forcing the plug out. This action usually works; unfortunately, the toothpaste usually gets all over everything. The instinctive reaction when the print jobs get stuck in the network print apparatus is to send the job several more times in hopes of forcing the job out the other side.

Just like the toothpaste example, no good can come of trying to force the print jobs. The reason the jobs won't print isn't because they're stuck, but because there is something wrong with the printing mechanism. It usually means that the printer is offline or out of paper. When the condition is corrected, all the jobs that have been waiting patiently will get printed.

Managing the toothpaste effect is best accomplished with training. Help the users overcome their tendency to automatically print again when their jobs don't appear at the printer. Granted, it doesn't come easy. But, remind the users that patience is a virtue and their jobs will print.

To check how many jobs are waiting to be printed, there are many methods. The easiest method, as an administrator, is to use NetWare Administrator to list the jobs that are waiting to be printed on a specific printer. To do this, start NetWare Administrator, select the Printer Agent you want to see the job list for, right click and choose Details. On the first page that appears (Printer Control), there will be a button called Jobs. Click it and select Job List. The Window in Figure 17.12 will appear. From here you can delete jobs, reorder jobs, and see the status of individual jobs.

**FIGURE 17.12**

The Job List screen for a Printer Agent

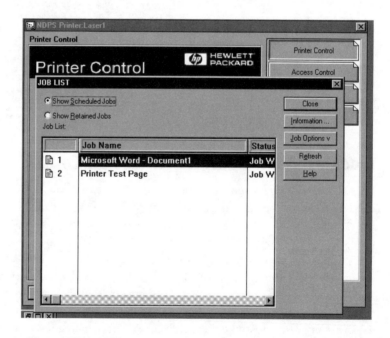

You can view the same information from a Windows 95 workstation using either the printer instance found in the Printers control panel or the printer instance in the Novell Printer Manager. To view the job list from the

Printers control panel, go to Start ➤ Settings ➤ Printers and double-click the printer you want to see the job list for. The screen shown in Figure 17.13 will appear. From this screen you can stop or pause printing, plus you can view which jobs are waiting to be serviced.

**FIGURE 17.13**

The Windows 95 printer job list

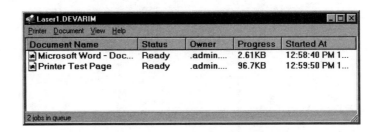

| Laser1.DEVARIM | | | | |
|---|---|---|---|---|
| Printer  Document  View  Help | | | | |
| Document Name | Status | Owner | Progress | Started At |
| Microsoft Word - Doc... | Ready | .admin.... | 2.61KB | 12:58:40 PM 1... |
| Printer Test Page | Ready | .admin.... | 96.7KB | 12:59:50 PM 1... |
| 2 jobs in queue | | | | |

The same procedure will work for Windows NT 4.0.

To view the job list using Novell Printer Manager, open the printer manager, and right click the printer you want to see the job list for. Choose Jobs... from the quick menu that appears to display the list of print jobs that are waiting to print (Figure 17.14). If you double-click a job in this list, you can modify the details of the print job, including priority, capture settings, and other administrative settings. You can also right click a job and pause or cancel a job.

## Checking Printer Output with Test Files

When you think you've got the connection between workstation and printer working, it's best to perform a test print. There are two main ways of doing this.

### From the Properties of the Printer in Windows 95/NT

Every printer instance in Windows 95 or NT has the ability to print a sample test page. When you installed the printer for the first time, you were asked if you want to print a test page. You can print a test page by opening the Printers folder under Start ➤ Settings, then right click the printer you want to print a test page from. When the page in Figure 17.15 appears, click the Print Test Page button.

FIGURE 17.14

Novell Job Manager printer job list

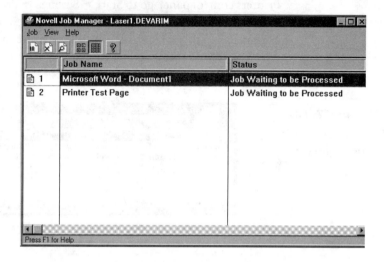

FIGURE 17.15

Using the printer properties to print a test page

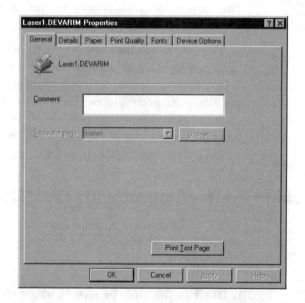

## Printing a Printer-Ready Test File Using Drag-and-Drop Printing

A printer ready test file is one that is formatted and ready to be sent directly to the printer. Printers can accept either ASCII text (.TXT) files, PostScript (.PS or .EPS) files, or Printer Control Language (PCL) files. Make sure you know which type of file formats your printer supports before attempting this test. Most printers can accept ASCII text files.

With this method, you must open both Windows Explorer and the Novell Printer Manager. Position the windows so you can see both on the screen at the same time (see Figure 17.16). Navigate to the location of the test file you want to print in Windows Explorer. Then, drag the file to the printer you want to test. The file will then be printed on the printer you selected.

**F I G U R E   17.16**

Printing a test file using the drag-and-drop method

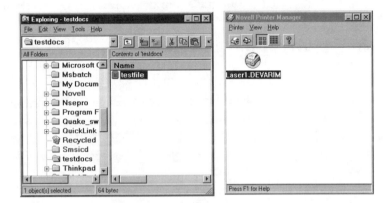

## Printing Problems That Affect All Users

The best way to solve printing problems that affect all users is to work your way backward from the problem printer to the workstation. Some things to check are:

- Check to see if the printer is connected properly, online, and ready to print.

- Using NetWare Administrator, check the Printer Agent object and see if it shows any errors.

- Make sure all the software components (including the Printer Agent, NDPS Manager, and NDPS Broker) are loaded and functioning properly.

- Using the NDPS Remote Printer Management feature in NetWare Administrator, push the newest printer driver out to all the workstations.

# Review

Printing is one of the most complicated network services provided by NetWare 5 and probably the most prone to problems. This chapter has covered tips on troubleshooting problems with the printer itself, the connections, print queues, print servers, and workstation (remote) printers.

## Network Printing Overview

The network printing process includes the following key components:

- In order to print to a printer on the network, you must first send the data to a *print queue*. The print queue stores each set of data, or *print job*, that it receives. The jobs are then sent, one at a time, to the print server. Print queues serve two main purposes:

  - They allow you to continue working while the printer prints. Your workstation quickly sends the job to the print queue, and NetWare performs printing, without using your workstation.

  - They allow multi-user printing. Many users can add jobs to the queue, and they are printed in the order received. A complete job is always printed before another job starts.

- The *print server* accepts print jobs from print queues, and sends them to the appropriate printer. In NetWare 3.1*x*, print servers were limited to 16 printers; in NetWare 4 this limit has been increased to 256, which allows you to use a single print server for the entire network. You create the Print Server object in NDS. The properties of the Print Server object provide identification information and define the list of printers the server can send jobs to.

- You must create a *Printer object* to represent each network printer. The properties of the Printer object identify the printer and list the print queues that the printer accepts jobs from. Other properties define the type of printer, and how it is accessed. Printers can be attached to a server, to a workstation, or directly to the network.

- CAPTURE is a TSR (terminate and stay resident) program that allows you to *redirect* printing to a network printer. You specify a local printer port (usually LPT1, LPT2, or LPT3) in the CAPTURE command line. After the CAPTURE command is executed, any printing that your workstation sends to this port is redirected to the network queue you specified.

- Before data is sent to the printer, it is sent to the *port driver*. The port driver receives data from the print server and transmits it to the printer. The port driver is also called NPRINTER and is run by NPRINTER .EXE, NPRINTER.NLM, or the Windows 95 NPRINTER Manager utility.

The print queue, print server, and printer objects handle a typical print job in this order:

1. The application sends the data to the CAPTURE program.

2. When the application finishes sending the print job, CAPTURE sends it to the print queue.

3. The print server takes jobs from the top of the print queue and sends them to the port driver.

4. The port driver (NPRINTER) receives the job and sends it to the printer.

5. The printer prints the job.

## Printer Problems

There are several types of printers, each with its own set of problems:

- Dot matrix printers use a set of pins that move forward and press a ribbon against the paper, making a dot. These printers are commonly used for invoices, checks, and continuous forms. They are loud and prone to problems, but they do work with multi-part forms.

- Ink jet printers are a more modern version of the dot matrix printer. They use a similar dot pattern, but liquid ink is forced through tiny nozzles to create the dots on the paper. These printers are typically faster than impact dot matrix printers, and much quieter. Because there's no impact in ink jet printing, they won't work with multi-part forms.

- Laser printers use a laser (or a matrix of LEDs, in some cases) to fuse toner particles onto the paper. Laser printers have the highest quality, and high-speed models are available. They do have their share of problems, though, and are usually the most expensive.

- Other printers include daisy-wheel and band printers. Most of these types of printers are now antiques, but they're still used in many companies.

Most of the problems you encounter with printers will be simple ones:

- Is the printer out of paper? With laser printers, you may have specified manual feed when sending the job, and the printer may be waiting for paper to be inserted.

- Is the ribbon, ink cartridge, or toner running low?

- Is the printer unplugged, turned off, or set to offline?

- Is the connection between the printer and the workstation or server in place?

- Have you created the NDS objects needed for printing and configured them correctly?

When you've eliminated the obvious, move on to the less obvious solutions:

- Check the paper path, the path the paper travels as it enters and exits the printer. Look for any obstruction—usually a torn piece of paper.

- Clean the printer, and see if the problem is fixed. Vacuum dust from all areas, and remove any paper fragments. Clean ink-covered surfaces carefully, using a cotton swab dipped in alcohol.

- Check the printer's environment. High humidity, heat, cold, or even a leaky roof could cause problems.

- Most printers have a self-test routine. Check the manual, and run a test. If it works, the problem is probably with the network or connections.

## Connection Problems

There are three possible ways a printer can be connected:

- Server printers are attached directly to a file server.

- Workstation printers, or remote printers, are attached to a network workstation.

- Directly connected network printers are attached to the network directly, using a hardware device or a card within the printer.

There are two common interfaces for printers, serial and parallel. The interface you use depends on the interface supported by the printer and the port available on the workstation or server. Parallel connections are the most common, but serial connections are still used on many printers.

Here are some of the parameters associated with serial printing. In all cases, the same parameters must be set at the printer and at the workstation or server.

- Baud rate is the rate at which data is sent. Speeds range from 1,200 baud to 57,600 baud.

- Parity specifies whether extra bits of data are sent for error checking. Options include even, odd, mark, space, and none.

- Data bits are the number of bits used to represent a character. Usually seven or eight.

- Stop bits are the number of bits sent between characters. Usually ranges from zero to two.

- Flow control is the method used for the printer to tell the host to slow down to allow it to print the data it has received. Values are typically XON/OFF (software), DTR/RTS (hardware), or none.

A parallel printer connection sends eight bits of data at once. Because the speed, flow control, and other parameters are standard, there are no parameters to set for a parallel connection. Although you can purchase parallel printer extension cables, you should avoid increasing the distance beyond the limit (15 feet).

Here are some solutions to connection problems:

- Run the printer's self-test. Refer to the manual to see how to perform the self-test; it usually involves holding down one of the buttons on the printer while turning the power off and on.

- If the self-test doesn't work, turn the power off and on, and then try the self-test again.

- If the self-test still doesn't work, the problem must be with the printer itself.

- If the self-test works, try printing a screen next. If the printer is attached to a workstation, you can press Shift+Print Screen from any DOS application. If the printer is attached to a server, you can either take the server down and try a print screen from DOS or connect the printer to another workstation.

- If printing a screen doesn't work, the problem is between the printer and the workstation or server—most likely with the cable.

- If printouts are split into several pieces, try increasing the timeout setting in CAPTURE.

## Print Queue Problems

If jobs are not listed in the print queue, check the following:

- The CAPTURE command may not be executing. Type **CAPTURE SH** to view settings, and be sure they are correct.

- Be sure your application is sending data to the correct port, as listed in the CAPTURE command.

- Check that the CAPTURE command includes either the timeout (TI) or autoendcap (AE) options. Try typing **CAPTURE /EC** to end the capture manually. If that works, you need to add a timeout or autoendcap to the command.

- Check the available disk storage on the volume where the print queue is stored—usually the SYS volume. If the volume is almost out of space, queue files will not be created.

If none of these solutions is effective, the print queue files may be corrupt. Print queue files are stored in the QUEUES directory, usually under the SYS volume. Delete all the files in this directory, and send another job.

If jobs never leave the print queue, check these items:

- Check the printer itself.

- Make sure PSERVER.NLM is running on a server.

- Make sure that the port driver (either NPRINTER.NLM or NPRINTER.EXE) is running on the server or workstation where the printer is attached.

## Print Server Problems

Follow these steps to diagnose a print server problem:

1. Be sure the print server is running on a server. You can load it by typing this command: **LOAD PSERVER** *name*, where *name* is the name of the Print Server object.

2. In the PCONSOLE utility, select Print Server Information, then Print Server Information and Status. Be sure the print server is running.

3. Take the print server down using PCONSOLE, and then reload it using the LOAD PSERVER command. This action stops any jobs that are currently printing.

4. Make sure that you have created a Print Server object to handle printing and that you have configured it correctly.

5. Be sure that each user has rights to the Print Server object. Placing the Print Server object in the same context as the users who use it is a good way to ensure this.

6. Check whether the server is low on RAM. If there is insufficient memory, PSERVER.NLM may not run properly.

7. Check for a hardware conflict in the server. You may wish to change the IRQ setting or set polled mode instead of an IRQ.

8. Check the Queues Serviced by Printer option in PCONSOLE or in the Printer object's properties. Be sure the correct queue or queues are listed.

## Remote Printer Problems

Remote printing is handled by NPRINTER.EXE. Here are some tips for avoiding potential problems with NPRINTER:

- Be sure that NPRINTER is running with the correct printer specified. You can check this from the AUTOEXEC.BAT file or in the user's login script.

- Other TSR programs may conflict with NPRINTER. Remove them from the AUTOEXEC.BAT or CONFIG.SYS file, and see if the problem is fixed.

- Never allow an application to print to a local printer port directly while NPRINTER is running. At best, this prints in the middle of a network-printing job; at worst, it crashes the workstation. Always use CAPTURE, and print to the network print queue.

- If the workstation crashes, the printer stops; there isn't much that can be done about this.

- If the workstation runs Windows, there may be conflicts. NPRINTER works under Windows in most cases but may disagree with certain Windows applications.

- If you are running Windows, be sure to start NPRINTER before Windows is started. Do not start it from a DOS session under Windows.

# NDPS Overview

Novell Distributed Print Services (NDPS) is Novell's new printing technology. It has the following features:

- All queue-based functionality has been consolidated from three NDS objects to one, the Printer Agent.

- NDPS is backward compatible with queue-based printing.

- NDPS was developed cooperatively with Xerox and Hewlett-Packard.

## NDPS Components

NDPS is made up of the following components:

- NDPS Manager is responsible for managing the Printer Agents.

- NDPS Broker has several responsibilities and functions, including:

  - Event Notification Services (ENS) is responsible for keeping track of errors and notifying users and administrators of problems via e-mail or NetWare broadcasts.

  - Service Registry Services (SRS) keeps track of all the public access printing agents on the network so that they can be found by workstations.

  - Resource Management Services (RMS) keeps track of all printing resources (like printer drivers, printer configurations, and banner pages) in a central location so they can be distributed automatically.

- Printer Agent  (the software component) is responsible for managing the printer and reporting status to the network. It replaces most of the functionality of the Print Queue object, Printer object, and Print Server object in queue-based printing.

- Gateways **provides** support for non–NDPS-aware printers in an NDPS environment. Three gateways come with NDPS: Novell, Xerox, and Hewlett-Packard.

### NDPS Printer Types

There are two types of NDPS printers, public access and controlled access.

- Public access printers have no NDS object. They are created automatically when an NDPS aware printer is plugged into the network. Any user can use them without restriction

- Controlled access printers are NDS objects and have restrictions that control who can print to the printer. Additionally, controlled access printers have more management features.

## NDPS Troubleshooting

There are several categories of tips for troubleshooting NDPS. They fall into seven major categories:

- Getting started:   Try some quick fixes to see if you can eliminate the problem with too much trouble.

- Narrowing down the problem:   Determine whether or not the problem is related to one workstation or several.

- Determining platform specific issues:   Remember that only Windows platforms can use NDPS. All others must use queue-based printing.

- Isolating the problem on one workstation:   Check the various sources listed in this chapter to see if you can fix the workstation.

- Tracking print jobs with workstation tools:   If the toothpaste effect is causing you problems, use the workstation tools to determine how the print jobs are moving through the printing system.

- Checking printer output with test files:   Try printing a test file to the printer to determine where the problem lies.

- Printer problems affecting all users:   If a printing problem affects all users, trace the problem backward from printer to workstation.

# CNE Practice Test Questions

1. What NDS objects are used for printing?

   A. Print Server, Print Queue, Port Driver

   B. Print Server, Print Queue, Printer

   C. Printer, Print Server, Port Driver

   D. CAPTURE, Printer, Print Server

2. The number of printers controlled by a NetWare 5 print server

   A. Is limited only by the server's memory

   B. Is limited to 16 printers

   C. Is limited to 256 printers

   D. Is limited to 3 parallel printers and 2 serial printers

3. What are three basic types of network printer?

   A. Workstation, Server, Queue

   B. Workstation, Server, Directly connected

   C. NDS, Bindery, Workstation

   D. Dot Matrix, Laser, Daisy Wheel

4. What program do you use to configure a workstation printer?

   A. RPRINTER

   B. REMOTE

   C. WPRINTER

   D. NPRINTER

**5.** Which is the correct order of components used when a print job is processed?

    **A.** CAPTURE, print queue, printer

    **B.** CAPTURE, print queue, print server, port driver, printer

    **C.** CAPTURE, port driver, print server, print queue, printer

    **D.** Port driver, CAPTURE, print queue, print server, printer

**6.** Which common printers are used with networks?

    **A.** Laser, dot matrix, ink jet

    **B.** Laser, daisy wheel, band

    **C.** Dot matrix, ink jet, daisy wheel

    **D.** Dot matrix, ink jet, dye sublimation

**7.** Which of the following conditions does NOT cause the printer to stop in the middle of a job?

    **A.** Overheating

    **B.** Out of paper or paper jam

    **C.** Incorrect print server configuration

    **D.** Ribbon or ink supply low

**8.** The parameters for a serial printer do NOT include

    **A.** Baud rate

    **B.** Data bits

    **C.** Stop bits

    **D.** Cable pinout

**9.** What is the official limit for a parallel printer cable?

    **A.** 5 feet

    **B.** 15 feet

    **C.** 300 feet

    **D.** 50 feet

**10.** Which of the following should you try *first* if a printer has a problem?

   **A.** Restart PSERVER.NLM.

   **B.** Run the self-test.

   **C.** Replace the printer cable.

   **D.** Check for a corrupt print queue.

**11.** If a printer works in the self-test but not from the network, where is the problem?

   **A.** The cable

   **B.** The print queue

   **C.** The print server

   **D.** Any of the above—not enough information to tell

**12.** If the printer works in a self-test but does not print a screen from the workstation, where is the problem?

   **A.** The workstation or cable

   **B.** The print queue

   **C.** The print server

   **D.** Any of the above—not enough information to tell

**13.** Which type of printer does NOT generate a lot of heat?

   **A.** Dot matrix (9-pin)

   **B.** Ink jet

   **C.** Laser

   **D.** Dot matrix (24-pin)

**14.** If the printer jams on multi-part forms, what should you try *first* to correct the problem?

   **A.** Using a different paper

   **B.** Adjusting the print head distance

    **C.** Replacing the ribbon

    **D.** Replacing the print head

**15.** If the printer does not print at all, which is NOT likely to be the problem?

    **A.** A print queue or print server configuration error

    **B.** A bad connection or disconnected cable

    **C.** The ribbon is worn and needs replacing

    **D.** Printer is turned off or offline

**16.** A laser printer printing completely black pages is a symptom of

    **A.** Bad cartridge or broken charge corona wires

    **B.** Out of toner

    **C.** Incorrect print server configuration

    **D.** Dirty fuser roller

**17.** What should be used to clean toner spilled on clothing, hands, or furniture?

    **A.** Acetylene or other solvent

    **B.** Cold water

    **C.** Very hot water

    **D.** A dry cloth

**18.** What is the correct command to display CAPTURE settings?

    **A.** CAPTURE /?

    **B.** CAPTURE /S

    **C.** CAPTURE SH

    **D.** CAPTURE /EC

**19.** Where are the print queues stored?

**A.** The SYSTEM directory

**B.** The PUBLIC directory

**C.** The QUEUES directory

**D.** The PRINT directory

**20.** What is the correct syntax to load the print server WEST?

**A.** PSERVER WEST

**B.** LOAD PSERVER /NAME=WEST

**C.** LOAD PSERVER, WEST

**D.** LOAD PSERVER WEST

**21.** If Printer, Print Server, or Print Queue NDS objects are corrupt, what should you try running?

**A.** DSREPAIR

**B.** DSMERGE

**C.** BINDFIX

**D.** PCONSOLE /REPAIR

**22.** The NetWare 3.1*x* PSERVER.EXE requires which command in NET.CFG?

**A.** PREFERRED SERVER

**B.** SPX PROCESSES = 50

**C.** SPX CONNECTIONS = 60

**D.** SPX = 50

**23.** What is the correct method of stopping a print server?

**A.** UNLOAD PSERVER at the file server console.

**B.** From within PCONSOLE at the workstation.

**C.** Turn the server off and back on.

**D.** Use the RESTART SERVER command at the server.

**24.** Which component of NDPS is responsible for managing the printer agents?

**A.** NDPS Manager

**B.** NDPS Broker

**C.** Print Server

**D.** Printer Agent

**25.** You have set up your network to use NDPS. No one can print to the new public access printer. What should you check first?

**A.** That the workstations have the newest driver

**B.** That NetWare Administrator is running

**C.** That the printer is online

**D.** That the broker has configured the NDPS Printer Agent

**26.** A user is complaining that none of their print jobs are printing. What tools should you use to see if the printer has been paused?

**A.** Windows 95 printer instance

**B.** Novell Printer Manager

**C.** NetWare Administrator

**D.** NDPS Broker

**27.** Which component of the NDPS Broker makes automatic driver download possible?

**A.** SRS

**B.** ENS

**C.** RMS

**D.** EMS

**28.** If you are getting "Can't connect to the Printer Agent" errors on all workstations, which component of NDPS may not be loaded/functioning?

 **A.** NDPS Broker

 **B.** NDPS Manager

 **C.** NDPS Gateway

 **D.** Printer Agent

**29.** Which NDPS component is responsible for allowing non–NDPS-aware printers to be used in an NDPS-only printing system?

 **A.** NDPS Broker

 **B.** Printer Agent

 **C.** NDPS Manager

 **D.** NDPS Gateway

**30.** Which NDPS gateways come with NDPS and are installed by default?

 **A.** Novell

 **B.** HP

 **C.** Xerox

 **D.** Canon

# CHAPTER

# 18

## Disaster Recovery and
## Network Optimization

# Roadmap

This chapter covers common techniques used to optimize the network and server as well as the most common techniques used to recover from a data loss or other disaster.

### Topics Covered

- Recovering from a disaster
- Patching the NetWare Operating System
- Server abend and lockup recovery techniques
- Troubleshooting network performance bottlenecks
- Using LANalyzer for Windows

### Skills You'll Learn

- Come up with a disaster recovery plan using Novell and other third-party utilities
- Determine how to find the most current patches for your NetWare server and how to install them
- Troubleshoot server abends and lockups
- Troubleshoot server and network performance problems
- Use LANalyzer for Windows

---

**W**hether it's an earthquake, fire, hardware failure, or simply the janitor unplugging the file server in the middle of the night, disaster will eventually strike your network. This chapter covers what you can do to recover after a disaster. In addition, it discusses the process of optimizing the network to improve its speed and performance.

# Recovering from Disaster

**W**hen a disaster hits and you find that your network data has been corrupted, there is no bigger relief than knowing that you have backed up your data on a reliable backup system. The necessity of having a secure backup system cannot be overemphasized. Along with backup systems, the following sections cover the possible solutions when data is corrupted and discusses applying patches to the operating system.

## Establishing a Dependable Backup System

To determine whether your backup system is reliable, consider the following:

- Can you successfully restore selected parts of your backups to a disk test area on your server (without overwriting current data, of course)?

- Does your backup software allow you to verify-after-write? This feature is crucial because it allows you to make sure that data is actually being written to the backup medium.

- Do your backup logs indicate that all files backed up are actually stored on the backup medium?

- Do you rotate tapes rather than overwrite the most recent copy?

- Do you back up as often as you go home from work (lunch breaks excluded)?

- Does your backup software back up the NDS database as well as the file system?

- Do you keep one or more copies of a backup at a separate site in case of disaster?

These are minimum requirements. Alone, they will not ensure complete safety, but they are certainly capabilities you need in a solid backup system.

## Recovering Data

For those times when disaster does strike and your backup system fails to back you up, you have at least three options:

- Novell's VREPAIR utility, included with NetWare 4.11 and older versions

- Professional data-recovery services

- Third-party utilities

Because these items are so important when you are trying to recover data, the following sections look at each one individually.

### VREPAIR

VREPAIR is a software data-recovery utility included with NetWare. If your problem is not hardware-based, it may help. Although it should not be used for serious disk problems, it can correct minor structure errors on volumes. The VREPAIR menu is shown in Figure 18.1.

**F I G U R E  18.1**

VREPAIR scans the disk and finds errors.

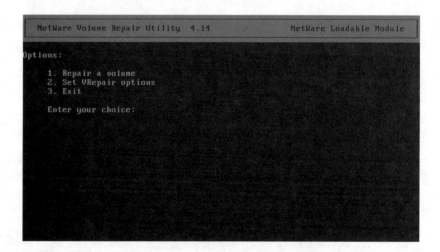

VREPAIR is most useful under the following conditions:

- Data has been corrupted by a power failure.

- A directory mirroring error is indicated when the server is booted.

- A volume won't mount or a data-read error appears, as a result of hardware failure.

In order to run VREPAIR on a volume, the volume must first be dismounted. You may find that you need to run VREPAIR several times to correct all errors. Because one or more volumes may be damaged or unavailable when a disaster occurs, you should keep a copy of VREPAIR.NLM on the DOS partition.

## Professional Data Recovery Services

When you are dealing with serious, critical data loss without reliable backups, professional data-recovery services may prove helpful. If money and time are no obstacle for your organization, professional services are often an excellent way to recover from hardware-related disasters.

Experts who can recover virtually any data that is still intact on a drive provide these services. They usually charge at least a couple of thousand dollars and require that you send your hardware to them (unless you want to pay much more for an on-site job). If you do choose to go this route, you can probably find a few professional data-recovery or disk repair services listed in your local telephone directory, in the Computer Services section.

## Third-Party Utilities

Before you consider a professional data-recovery service, you may want to investigate the variety of third-party utilities available. Here are a few of the options:

- NETUTILS3 is a collection of utilities for NetWare 3.1*x*. It includes NETSCAN3 for volume repair, NETFILE3 to repair and edit corrupt files, and NETDISK3 to edit sectors directly. These utilities can go beyond VREPAIR's capabilities and restore the disk to working order.

- Check-It Pro is a utility that allows you to control and investigate all aspects of disk configuration. Although it is a DOS utility, it can diagnose problems on NetWare server disks.

- OnTrack Data Recovery, a professional data-recovery service, also offers software to recover files yourself. This software is fully NetWare-enabled and has many features.

- STAC, makers of the popular Stacker disk-compression utility, has introduced Replica, a full-scale system for NetWare that manages backups, replicates data, and allows recovery of inaccessible files and servers.

# Patching the NetWare Operating System

Although the NetWare operating system is thoroughly tested, you may encounter problems. If you experience data loss, a server crash, or other problems and are unable to correct them, they may be the result of an actual bug in NetWare. Novell releases *patches* for NetWare that correct the problems that have been discovered. To find a list of patches available for your operating system, check the Novell Support Connection website or CD-ROM. (See Chapter 13 for information about these resources.)

Patch files that you download are in self-expanding compressed format so they don't take as long to download. The file format looks something like this:

*VVVYYZ.EXE*

Where *VVV* is the version of the product that you are patching, *YY* is either PT (passed test) or SP (support pack) and *Z* is the revision of the patch. Some examples of patch files would be

- IWSP5A.EXE (IntraNetWare Support Pack 5a)
- 311PTA.EXE (Patch for NetWare 3.11 )
- CLIBA.EXE (CLIB.NLM patch)

## Types of Patches

There are three types of patches, and each has a different behavior when you install it on a server.

- A *Static* patch makes permanent changes to the SERVER.EXE file. This type of patch CANNOT be removed. Make sure that you back up the SERVER.EXE file before you patch the one on the server. NEVER patch the SERVER.EXE on a distribution disk (the disk that comes from Novell when you buy NetWare).

- A *Semi-static* patch is a NetWare Loadable Module (NLM) that can be loaded while the server is up and running, but can't be unloaded without restarting the server.

- A *Dynamic* patch can be loaded and unloaded while the server is functioning. Unloading the patch will restore the NetWare server to its former, unpatched, state.

## Applying Patches on a NetWare 5 Server

When you have determined which patch(es) you need for your server, you must plan to apply them. Applying patches to a NetWare server is done in the same manner as installing other types of software. The first step is to back up the server and verify the backup. Then, download the patch you need and expand it into a directory on the server (SYS:\PATCHES\NW5SP1\).

You will need to have a drive mapped to that location from your workstation to expand it there because the compression/decompression program runs in DOS for most patches.

The next step varies depending on which version of NetWare you are using. If you are using NetWare 4.11 or earlier, you must type **LOAD INSTALL** at the server prompt to start the installation utility. If you are using NetWare 5, you can simply type **NWCONFIG** at the server prompt to invoke the NetWare Configuration Utility.

When you have started the appropriate utility, use the up and down arrow keys to navigate to product options. Press Enter to select it, and the product options screen shown in Figure 18.2 will appear.

**FIGURE 18.2**

Product options
screen

From this screen, select "Install a product not listed" and press Enter. The installation utility will ask you where the files are for the software you want to install. If you just pressed Enter here, it would look in the default location (A:\). But the software you want to install is located on the server in a directory already. So, to change the location of the installation files, press F3 and type in the path on the server where you expanded the patch files. The path should be in NetWare format (that is, SYS:\PATCHES\NW5SP1\). After you have typed in the path, press Enter to begin the installation.

The installation routine should prompt you for anything else it needs. When the files have finished copying, you may need to restart your server. So, when planning to patch your server, you may want to pick a time when there aren't that many people on the server. Or, at least notify your users ahead of time that the server will be down for a time.

# Server Abend and Lockup Recovery Techniques

Every CNE will have to deal with an abend or a server lockup at one time or another. For this reason, Novell chooses to test you on your knowledge of these problems and what you can do to minimize their effects.

## Abends

An *abend* is an abbreviation for ABnormal END. It is a situation that occurs when a NetWare server has to stop a program because it did something unusual.

### Errors That Cause Abends

Typically, abends are the result of bad programming or misconfigured hardware. There are two types of errors that cause abends:

- Errors that the processor detects
- Errors that the operating system detects (called consistency check errors)

**Processor-Detected Errors**   When a processor detects that there is a problem, it can either issue an exception or an interrupt to stop a program or process. An *interrupt* is a call from an external device saying that it needs attention. An *exception* is the result of a problem that the processor detected while executing an instruction. These exceptions can be classified as traps, aborts, or faults. What type of exception it is depends on whether the instruction can be restarted or how it is reported.

There are two major types of exceptions, non-maskable interrupts (NMIs) and processor-detected exceptions. Non-maskable interrupts are hardware errors and aren't handled by NetWare directly; you must reconfigure the hardware to solve the problem. A processor-detected exception is any other exception that occurs that the processor detects (usually related to software).

**Operating System–Detected (Consistency Check) Errors**   NetWare has internal software diagnostics, called consistency checks, that are constantly running. These checks monitor and validate the critical functions of the operating system including memory, disk, and communications processes. The errors are detected by software, not by the CPU (as in processor-detected errors).

When an abend occurs and displays a failed consistency check error, it indicates that a portion of memory has become corrupt. The abend can be caused by any number of problems including a bad memory chip, invalid data that somehow got passed from the network card to the operating system, a corrupt NLM, or a bad driver for a piece of hardware.

## Recovering from an Abend

Since NetWare 4.11, NetWare has had the capability of recovering from an abend. In earlier versions (before 4.11), an abend meant that all processes were stopped, and no further interaction with the server was possible. Abend recovery usually meant restarting the server, or getting into the debugger, which most people didn't care to do.

Starting with NetWare 4.11 (and including NetWare 5), servers have had the ability to keep functioning after an abend with a few options as to what to do about the abend. Some of the new abend recovery features include

- Placing all abend messages into a special log file called the ABEND.LOG, for later troubleshooting. This file is placed in SYS:\SYSTEM by default.

- Giving detailed information about the abend. In addition to the older abend text (error message and hex memory segment information), NetWare will give a paragraph of information about the conditions surrounding the abend.

- Shutting down the offending process so that the server can keep functioning

These new functions are enabled by default. There are a few SET parameters that can be changed to customize the way the abend recovery works. Table 18.1 details the three options.

**T A B L E   18.1:**   Abend Recovery SET Parameters

| Parameter | Values | Default | Description |
| --- | --- | --- | --- |
| AUTO RESTART AFTER ABEND | 0-3 | 1 | 0=Don't recover from abend. 1=Force delayed restart for NMI & software exceptions, suspend process for Page Faults. 2=Force delayed restart for all abends. 3=Force immediate restart. (This option only applies to NetWare 5.) |
| AUTO RESTART AFTER ABEND DELAY TIME | 2-60 | 2 | How long the server should wait (in minutes) before performing the delayed restarts for options 1 & 2 in AUTO RESTART AFTER ABEND. |
| CPU HOG TIMEOUT | 0-3600 | 60 | How long (in seconds) the server should wait before killing a process that is monopolizing the CPU so that no other application can use it. |

Sometimes an abend recovery will cause the server console to hang. In this case, a controlled restart of the server may not be possible. But, you can still safely shut down the server by pressing <CTRL>+<ALT>+<ESC>. The server will then ask you if you want to down the server. Answer yes by pressing **Y**, and the server will safely dismount all volumes and force a downing of the server, preventing data corruption from occurring (as might happen if you simply shut the server off).

## Analyzing Abends

The ABEND.LOG file is a valuable source for troubleshooting information. It contains all the information you'll need to find out what kind of problem it is. Figure 18.3 shows part of a sample log file from a server abend. The numbers in the brackets (<1>, etc) were added to make discussion easier.

**F I G U R E   18.3**

Sample ABEND.LOG file

<1>Server S1 halted Wednesday, November 25, 1998  12:32:19 pm
<2>Abend 1 on P00: Server-5.00a: Nonmaskable Interrupt Processor Exception (Error code 00000030)

<3>Registers:
   CS = 0008 DS = 0010 ES = 0010 FS = 0010 GS = 0010 SS = 0010
   EAX = 00000003 EBX = D016E238 ECX = 05BF3EF0 EDX = 00000004
   ESI = D0190040 EDI = 00000000 EBP = 05BF3ED0 ESP = 05BF3EC0
   EIP = D016E442 FLAGS = 00000293
   D016E442 C3            RET
   EIP in ABENDEMO.NLM at code start +00000442h

<4>Running process: Abendemo Process
Created by: NetWare Application
Thread Owned by NLM: ABENDEMO.NLM
Stack pointer: 5BF3CE0
OS Stack limit: 5BF0000
Scheduling priority: 67371008
Wait state: 5050170  (Blocked on keyboard)
<5>Stack: D016E299  (ABENDEMO.NLM|MenuAction+61)
   D2027602  (NWSNUT.NLM|NWSShowPortalLine+3602)
   --00000003  ?
   --00000000  ?
   --05BF3F20  ?
   --D0176040  (ABENDEMO.NLM|DoDoubleFault+7BF0)
   --00000001  ?
   D2027949  (NWSNUT.NLM|NWSShowPortalLine+3949)
   --00000010  ?
   --05BF3EF0  ?
   --00000000  ?
   D2027BD9  (NWSNUT.NLM|NWSShowPortalLine+3BD9)
   --0000000B  ?
   --00000000  ?
   --00000000  ?

<6>Additional Information:
   There may be some bad memory either on an adapter card or on the motherboard. If the problem continues, try replacing the main system memory or adapter cards to prevent future parity errors.

1. Line #1 shows the server name and the date and time the error occurred. This line is useful in gathering trend data. If a server abends every day at about the same time, you can track down the problem by finding out what occurs every day at the time (like a certain user logs on, for example).

2. Line #2 shows the number of the abend, the processor that is reporting the abend, and the type of abend that occurred. In Figure 18.3, Abend 1 means this is the first abend that has occurred in the time that the server has been up. P00 means that processor 0 is reporting the abend. (The server used in Figure 18.3 only has one processor.)

3. Line #3 shows the values that are stored in the processor's registers at the time of the abend. It also shows where the Execution Instruction Pointer (EIP) is currently pointing (the "EIP=" line).

4. Line #4 shows which process was running when the abend occurred, not necessarily the process that caused the abend, but which process was active.

5. Line #5 shows the stack trace. The stack is an area of memory that applications use for temporary storage of certain application values.

6. Line #6 is probably the most useful line to those people inexperienced in the day-to-day operating of a NetWare server. This line will give you a clue as to the possible causes of the abend.

## Server Lockups

Server lockups typically happen less often than abends, but they are still common. It is pretty obvious when a lockup occurs, because the server won't respond to any input (either from the console, or through the network). Several things can cause lockups. For example, a process can get locked in an infinite loop and take up all the processor's time. Lockups can also be caused by hardware. If a piece of hardware, like a network card, stops functioning, the server can lock up when it tries to access the hardware. Basically, the same items that can cause abends, can also cause lockups. A lockup will occur if the operating system can't handle the problem with an abend.

There are two different types of lockups that can occur:

- Full server lockup
- Partial server lockup

### Full Server Lockups

When a full server lockup occurs, all activity on the server stops. Additionally, any connections to the server will be dropped, because the server won't be responding to any are-you-still-there type packets. The server will not recover from a full server lockup and will have to be powered off and powered back on to bring the server up again.

### Partial Server Lockups

Partial server lockups can be somewhat difficult to diagnose. They are often the result of a busy or overtaxed server. A partial server lockup will respond to users' requests, but may take much longer than usual. Entering commands at the console is possible, but responses take several minutes. You can usually tell when a partial server lockup has occurred by switching to the MONITOR .NLM. If the processor utilization percentage stays consistently at 100% for 30 seconds or more, a partial lockup has occurred.

Partial lockups sometimes resolve themselves. But, more often than not, after several minutes, they will lock the server up completely in a full server lockup.

## Abends and Lockup Troubleshooting Steps

The steps for troubleshooting lockups and abends are the same. These steps should help you determine if the abends are caused by simple items and, therefore, have quick fixes. Novell recommends using the following steps when troubleshooting abends and lockups:

- Gather information about the problem.

- Understand the problem and identify possible causes.

- Test possible solutions.

- Use debugging tools, if needed.

- Resolve the problem.

- Document the problem.

## Gather Information about the Problem

Just like with most other problems, the first step is to gather information about the problem, which gives you the tools you need to troubleshoot the problem. Some of the types of information you should gather are

- Any error messages that appear
- Hardware configuration
- Versions of operating system, drivers, and other software
- List of NCF files and their contents
- Any known issues from the Support Connection website
- A list of the most recent changes made to the system
- The situation and events surrounding the crash

There are many tools available to help you gather this information, including Novell's ManageWise, Intel's LANDesk manager, and others. Novell Technical Services has an NLM you can download from the Support Connection website called CONFIG.NLM. The CONFIG.NLM will put all the relevant server configuration information into a file called CONFIG.TXT in the SYS:SYSTEM directory.

CONFIG.NLM is part of TABND2.EXE, which you can download from the Files area on the Support Connection website.

## Understand the Problem and Identify Possible Causes

In this step, you try to narrow down the problem using information gathered in the last step. To do this, ask yourself the following questions:

- Does the problem happen at a certain time of day or coincide with a specific event?
- Can the problem be duplicated or is it a random occurrence?
- When did the problem start? Does it coincide with a recent event (like installing new software)?
- Is the problem consistent? Does the exact same error message appear every time?

- Are all drivers and NLMs current and at the most recent patch level? (If you call tech support, you know they will ask.)

- How often does the problem occur?

- Is there any new hardware in the server that might be causing this problem?

- Is there any new software on the server that might be causing the problem?

- Is there any other new hardware or software on the network (like a new server or print server box)?

- Are all components on the server certified to work with NetWare? (Check `http://developer.novell.com` for a current list.)

- Is the hardware configured correctly with the right drivers for the hardware being used?

- If the server is locked up, can you do anything at the server? Can you toggle between screens with ALT and ESC?

- What symptoms occurred prior to the crash?

- Can you gather any conclusions from the symptoms and information?

## Test Possible Solutions

After you have finished asking yourself these questions, you probably have a good idea what the solution is. When you determine a solution, you should try it to see if it solves the problem. A few of the most common solutions are

- This is the most common solution. Download the most current drivers and patches and apply them.

- Replace defective or suspect hardware.

- Remove multiple components and simplify the configuration.

- Consult your coworkers and peers. If you don't know the solution, or have never seen it before, there's a good chance one of your coworkers or peers has. User groups can be a great source of this kind of information.

## Use Troubleshooting Tools, If Needed

Novell has several tools available for troubleshooting NetWare. Some of them come with NetWare 5. Three of these utilities are

- MONITOR.NLM
- Server memory image file
- Network analyzers

**MONITOR.NLM**   MONITOR.NLM comes with NetWare 5 and can be used to gather statistics on just about every aspect of the server's operation. Unfortunately, most of the statistics that it keeps aren't historical. MONITOR shows statistics like processor utilization, errors, LAN statistics, and memory statistics.

**Server Memory Image File**   When abends occur, you have the option of copying the contents of the server's memory at the time of the abend to a file on the DOS partition (a *core dump*). This action is normally considered to be a last resort. You should not perform a core dump unless Novell Technical Services instructs you to do so, because the file it creates is the same size as the amount of memory it occupies in the server (a server with 128MB of RAM, will have a 128MB core dump file).

This file is then sent to Novell Technical Services for an analysis of the problem.

**WARNING**   Your DOS partition must have free disk space on your DOS partition equal to or greater than the memory installed in the server. Otherwise, you won't be able to do a core dump.

**Network Analyzers**   Network analyzers take information directly off the network to determine if the information being sent over the network is valid. They can also be used to determine bottlenecks and traffic statistics. Two examples of network analyzers are Novell's ManageWise and Novell's LANalyzer.

### Resolve the Problem

After you have determined the problem and tried your solution, you can implement the solution and resolve the problem. If you have further difficulties, contact your Novell Authorized Reseller or Novell Technical Services.

### Document the Problem

This step is probably the most overlooked step. When the problem is solved, most people breathe a sigh of relief and move on. Unfortunately, if you don't document the problem and its solution, the same problem might happen again, and you will have to repeat the entire troubleshooting process.

The best way to document the problem is to keep a logbook in the server room and update it every time a problem occurs with the date, the server affected, the problem, and the solution. You could also use a word processing file stored on your workstation or on a server. The advantage to the latter approach is that the file is completely searchable, and you can search for previous instances of a problem.

# Troubleshooting Network Performance Bottlenecks

In addition to abends and lockups, there is one other major area that causes problems. Performance bottlenecks can frustrate users as well as administrators. Bottlenecks aren't problems so much as they are design issues. If a network or server is designed properly, performance bottlenecks should be minimal (if not eliminated entirely).

There are four areas that typically cause performance bottlenecks:

- Network I/O problems
- Processor problems
- Bus I/O problems
- Disk I/O problems

## Network I/O Problems

Network I/O problems can cause bottlenecks in heavily used servers and networks. High use servers like web servers, video servers, and imaging servers typically have network I/O problems.

The best way to check a NetWare 5 server to see if it is experiencing network I/O bottlenecks is to use the MONITOR.NLM and check the following statistics under LAN/WAN Drivers:

- Transmit failed, packet too big

- Transmit failed, miscellaneous error

- Receive failed, adapter overflow condition

- Receive failed, packet too big

- Receive discarded, no available buffers

- Receive failed, miscellaneous error

If these statistics are high or you can watch them grow over a period of only a few seconds, chances are you have a network I/O bottleneck.

Network I/O problems can result from poor network design, too many stations on the same segment, cabling problems, and other physical network problems. Because network I/O problems can be caused by so many diverse causes, many different tools must be used to troubleshoot them.

Network I/O problems can be resolved in any number of ways:

- Upgrade the network topology to a faster topology.

- Segment the network with bridges or routers so there are fewer stations per segment.

- Resolve cabling problems so there are no physical cable problems.

## Processor Problems

At the rate processor speed increases, processor speed is rarely an issue. However, if you are running CPU-intensive server-based applications, make sure you are running a faster processor than the software's recommended minimum. Additionally, if you have server processor performance bottlenecks, consider upgrading to bus mastering LAN and disk controller adapters to take some load off the processor.

## Bus I/O Problems

Most servers are designed with high-speed busses (PCI or EISA), so bus I/O is usually not a limitation. If you happen to be using a server that is using a slower speed bus, consider upgrading to a server that has one of these higher speed busses. Also, upgrading to bus mastering LAN and disk adapters (if your bus supports them) can increase performance.

## Disk I/O Problems

If you have optimized your LAN performance as well as your bus and processor I/O speed, the bottleneck could be your disk subsystem. The number of disks, rotation speed, and speed of the disk interface can all play a part in the efficiency of your disk subsystem.

The best way to tell if the disk subsystem is the bottleneck is to use the MONITOR.NLM utility to check the number of dirty cache buffers. If this number stays high and grows over a few minutes, your disk subsystem can't process disk requests fast enough.

There are several things you can do to increase your disk subsystem's overall performance:

- Upgrade to a faster disk technology.

   - Fast SCSI II transfer data at 10MB/second

   - Fast/Wide SCSI II transfer data at 20MB/second

   - Ultra Wide SCSI transfer data up to 80MB/second

- Use bus mastering disk controllers.

- Use multiple disks to replace a single disk in a RAID configuration.

# Using LANalyzer for Windows

If you've ever spent hours searching for the sources of network cabling problems, you know they aren't easy to find. There is a tool that can help you with this, as well as with optimizing the performance of your network connections. A *protocol analyzer* is a program that monitors network activity, gathers statistics, and provides guidelines for optimizing performance. Novell's protocol analyzer is LANalyzer for Windows.

LANalyzer is available at an extra cost from Novell. It has many more features than listed here; however, this should give you an understanding of the basics, which is all the CNE test requires.

LANalyzer runs on a Windows workstation attached anywhere in the network. In order to properly monitor and diagnose the performance of the network, you may want to run it on workstations at several different points on the network.

The main LANalyzer screen, called the Dashboard, is shown in Figure 18.4.

**FIGURE 18.4**

The LANalyzer Dashboard includes indicators of network performance.

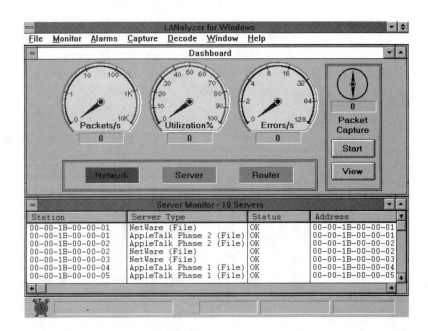

The dashboard includes several useful indicators:

- Packets displays the actual number of packets traveling across the network. If the number is high, you probably have a lot of network bandwidth and lots of traffic.

- Utilization displays the percentage of the network cable's bandwidth that is being used. If the percentage is above 50, you may need to add network segments to increase the available bandwidth.

Bandwidth refers to the amount of data a cable can carry, measured in bits per second. Generally, a high bandwidth increases throughput and performance.

- Errors displays a count of errors that have occurred, packets that have required resending. If this gauge shows any activity at all, something is wrong on the network: a disconnected cable, a bad network card, or a short.

- Packet Capture captures packets. Click the Start button to begin monitoring activity on the network for a period of time, and then display statistics for that time. Packet Capture makes it easy to determine the peak usage times for the network and the times when errors occur.

The Dashboard screen also shows the Server Monitor, which lists servers detected on the network and parameters for them. Another list you can view is called the Station Monitor, shown in Figure 18.5. It displays a list of workstations (logged-in users) on the system. You can watch network traffic for each user and determine if anyone is using a lot of bandwidth and slowing down the system. (This could be caused by a bad network card or cable on the workstation.)

**FIGURE 18.5**

The LANalyzer's Station Monitor displays active workstations on the network.

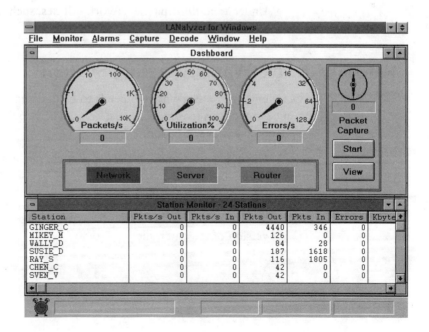

The most important use of LANalyzer is to monitor trends on the network, such as ways in which the network is used and the times that the most usage occurs. You can use the Packet Capture option to monitor the network for an extended period of time, then display a graph showing trends as they develop, which can help you detect problems with the network and find the sources of errors.

# Review

This chapter covered what you can do when disaster strikes your network. In addition, it discussed the process of optimizing the network so that you can improve its performance and help decrease the chance of disasters.

## Disaster Recovery

Several points are important for disaster recovery:

- Establish and test a dependable backup system.
- Understand the VREPAIR utility and its use.
- Use professional data-recovery services when they are worth the cost.
- Understand third-party network utilities, such as NETUTILS3 and Check-It Pro.

## Patching the NetWare Operating System

Occasionally, the NetWare OS needs to be updated with bug fixes as they come out. For this reason, you must know where to find patches and how to update the server with them.

- Patches can be found at the support connection website (`http:// support.novell.com`).
- Patch files are typically in the format *VVVYYZ.EXE. (VVV* is the product being patched, *YY* is the type of the patch file, and the *Z* is the version of the patch file.)

## Server Abend and Lockup Recovery Techniques

Abend stands for ABnormal END. An abend occurs when the server OS detects a hardware or software error. Lockups occur when hardware or software monopolizes the CPU and won't release it to other processes. There are two types of lockups, full server and partial server. When full server lockups occur, the server stops responding to all requests. Partial server lockups stop responding for a short period of time, then return control to the console.

There are a few steps you should follow when troubleshooting abends and lockups.

- Gather information about the problem.
- Test possible solutions.
- Use Troubleshooting tools:
  - MONITOR.NLM
  - Server memory image file
  - Network analyzers
- Resolve the problem.
- Document the problem.

## Troubleshooting Network Performance Bottlenecks

Network bottlenecks are the other category of server and network problems. A bottleneck is an area of the network that can't keep up with the rest of the network. Network performance bottlenecks can be divided into four major areas:

- Network I/O problems
- Processor problems
- Bus I/O problems
- Disk I/O problems

## LANalyzer for Windows

A protocol analyzer monitors network activity, gathers statistics, and provides guidelines for optimizing performance. Novell's protocol analyzer is called LANalyzer for Windows. LANalyzer runs on a Windows workstation on the network. LANalyzer is available at an extra cost from Novell.

With LANalyzer, you can watch for trends on the network, such as how the network is used and when it is used most often. You can use the Packet Capture option to monitor the network for an extended period of time, and then display a graph showing trends as they develop to help you detect problems with the network and find the sources of errors.

# CNE Practice Test Questions

1. Which of the following is NOT an important test for backup software?

   **A.** Can it back up files?

   **B.** Can it restore files?

   **C.** Does it rotate tapes?

   **D.** Can it back up from tape to tape?

2. If a server disk will not mount due to errors, which utility should you try first?

   **A.** LANalyzer

   **B.** VREPAIR

   **C.** DSREPAIR

   **D.** DISKSCAN

3. When can you run VREPAIR?

   **A.** At any time while the server is running

   **B.** Only when no users are logged in

    **C.** Only when the volume is dismounted

    **D.** Only on a new server

**4.** Which utility allows you to install operating system patches on a Net-Ware 5 server?

    **A.** INSTALL.NLM

    **B.** NWCONFIG.NLM

    **C.** CONFIG.NLM

    **D.** PATCHMAN.NLM

**5.** The MONITOR utility does NOT show statistics for

    **A.** Memory utilization

    **B.** Scheduling

    **C.** Bandwidth usage

    **D.** LAN cards

**6.** Which file is the correct file to download for the fourth revision of the NetWare support pack?

    **A.** IWSP4A.EXE

    **B.** NWSP4.EXE

    **C.** SP4.EXE

    **D.** SP4NW4.EXE

**7.** Which of the following can cause abends?

    **A.** Software issues

    **B.** Hardware issues

    **C.** Bad network packets

    **D.** All of the above

**8.** Which of the following best describes a LANalyzer?

    **A.** A packet analyzer

    **B.** A protocol analyzer

    **C.** A workstation analyzer

    **D.** A server monitor

**9.** Which LANalyzer feature lists users?

    **A.** Server Monitor

    **B.** Station Monitor

    **C.** Connection Monitor

    **D.** User Monitor

**10.** Which of the following is the main LANalyzer display?

    **A.** Console

    **B.** MONITOR

    **C.** Dashboard

    **D.** Control Center

**11.** Which feature in LANalyzer allows you to monitor the network and capture details?

    **A.** Packet Capture

    **B.** Network Display Monitor

    **C.** Dashboard

    **D.** Statistical Analyzer

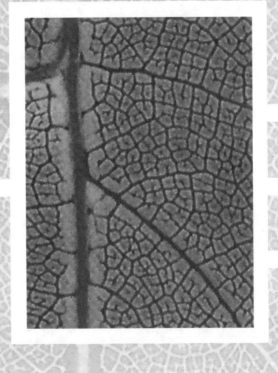

# APPENDICES

# APPENDIX

# A

Answers to Practice Test Questions

# Chapter 1 Answers

1. Centralized computing is best described as

   **A.** Computing taking place on the motherboard, rather than the peripherals

   **B.** When data processing is completed at corporate headquarters

   **C.** Computing that centers around a mainframe computer

   **D.** Server-centric networking

   Answer: C

2. Which of the following is NOT characteristic of the distributed computing model?

   **A.** Clients with internal processing power

   **B.** Exchange of data and services

   **C.** Clients with data storage capacity

   **D.** Clients serving mainly as input/output devices

   Answer: D

3. What is a WAN?

   **A.** A wide-apple network

   **B.** A work-associate nexus

   **C.** A wide area network

   **D.** A work-area network

   Answer: C

4. Which one of the following is currently NOT a common network service?

   **A.** Print services

   **B.** File services

   **C.** Communication services

   **D.** Photocopying services

   Answer: D

5. What is a protocol?

   **A.** A set of rules of communication that allow network devices to communicate

   **B.** A device used by proctologists

   **C.** A hardware device used by TCP/IP

   **D.** The most important part of the CPU

   Answer: A

6. What are the three main types of file storage?

   **A.** Online storage

   **B.** Offline storage

   **C.** Nearline storage

   **D.** Downline storage

   Answer: A, B, C

7. What is the primary function of a print queue?

   **A.** Ensure that fonts maintain precise integrity

   **B.** Store print jobs before they are printed

   **C.** Provide important information about printer specifications

   **D.** Store backup paper for the printer

   Answer: B

8. Which one of the following is NOT a type of message service?

   **A.** E-mail

   **B.** Workgroup applications

   **C.** Directory Services

   **D.** Secretarial databases

   Answer: D

# Chapter 2 Answers

1. Thin Ethernet uses which type of cable?

   **A.** UTP

   **B.** STP

   **C.** Coaxial

   **D.** Fiber-optic

   Answer: C

2. Which type of cable supports the highest bandwidth?

   **A.** UTP

   **B.** STP

   **C.** Coaxial

   **D.** Fiber-optic

   Answer: D

**3.** Which device is used to send data over telephone lines?

**A.** Repeater

**B.** Hub

**C.** Bridge

**D.** Modem

Answer: D

**4.** What is the most common connector used with UTP cable?

**A.** RJ-14

**B.** RJ-45

**C.** DB-15

**D.** BNC

Answer: B

**5.** What is the process of converting a signal to analog form?

**A.** Modulation

**B.** Demodulation

**C.** Transmission

**D.** Attenuation

Answer: A

**6.** Which two categories are used to classify repeaters?

**A.** Amplifiers and transmitters

**B.** Amplifiers and regenerating repeaters

**C.** Modems and codecs

**D.** Bridges and routers

Answer: B

**7.** What is the device that connects multiple nodes to the network?

**A.** A modem

**B.** A repeater

**C.** A hub

**D.** An amplifier

Answer: C

**8.** What are the three main types of hubs?

**A.** Passive, active, and FDDI

**B.** Passive, active, and amplifying

**C.** Passive, active, and intelligent

**D.** Passive, regenerative, and amplifying

Answer: C

**9.** Which is the most complicated type of hub?

**A.** Intelligent

**B.** Passive

**C.** Active

**D.** Regenerative

Answer: A

**10.** What device passes signals selectively between network segments?

**A.** A repeater

**B.** A hub

**C.** A bridge

**D.** A modem

Answer: C

**11.** What is sending two signals over the same cable called?

**A.** Routing

**B.** Multiplexing

**C.** Multicoding

**D.** Combining

Answer: B

**12.** What does attenuation refer to?

**A.** A signal growing weaker as it travels

**B.** A signal growing stronger as it travels

**C.** Sending the same signal again

**D.** Increasing the strength of a signal

Answer: A

## Chapter 3 Answers

1. Which of the following devices functions at the Data Link layer?

   A. Repeater

   B. Router

   C. Bridge

   D. Gateway

   Answer: C

2. Which of the following access methods requires centralized management?

   A. Token-passing

   B. Contention

   C. Collision avoidance

   D. Polling

   Answer: D

3. Which flow control method is the most efficient use of network bandwidth?

   A. Dynamic window flow control

   B. Static window flow control

   C. Guaranteed rate flow control

   D. Static rate flow control

   Answer: A

4. Which of the following access control methods is NOT deterministic?

   A. Token-passing

   B. Contention

   C. Polling

   D. Primaries and secondaries

   Answer: B

5. Which of the following physical topologies is most susceptible to a single point of failure?

   A. Star

   B. Mesh

   C. Ring

   D. Bus

   Answer: D

6. Which transmission synchronization method introduces a single point of failure into the network?

   A. Asynchronous

   B. Isochronous

   C. Synchronous

   D. Oversampling

   Answer: B

7. In which logical topology is the data seen and received by every device on the network?

   A. Bus

   B. Ring

   C. Mesh

   D. Cellular

   Answer: A

8. Which analog encoding method uses the presence or absence of a transition to encode data?

   A. FSK

   B. PSK

   C. ASK

   D. MUX

   Answer: B

9. Which multiplexing technique can be used on baseband channels?

   A. FDM

   B. MUX

   C. ASK

   D. TDM

   Answer: D

10. How would a polar digital signal encoding scheme in which a –3 V represents a 1 and a +3 V represents a 0 be categorized?

    A. Current-state

    B. State-transition

**C.** Unipolar

**D.** Guaranteed state change

**Answer:** A

# Chapter 4 Answers

1. Which Transport layer addressing method identifies conversations?

   **A.** Connection ID

   **B.** Transaction ID

   **C.** Transport ID

   **D.** Conversation ID

   **Answer:** A

2. What is the name of the table that includes information about hops and ticks?

   **A.** Switching

   **B.** Routing

   **C.** Addressing

   **D.** Hop and tick

   **Answer:** B

3. What type of switching does store-and-forward refer to?

   **A.** Packet switching

   **B.** Message switching

   **C.** Circuit switching

   **D.** Bait and switching

   **Answer:** B

4. Which type of route selection allows intermediate devices to select a packet's next hop?

   **A.** Dynamic

   **B.** Static

   **C.** Virtual

   **D.** Hop

   **Answer:** A

5. Which device is used to connect networks that are running distinctly different protocols?

   **A.** Bridge

   **B.** Repeater

   **C.** Router

   **D.** Gateway

   **Answer:** D

6. Which type of route discovery method does Novell's RIP protocol use?

   **A.** Link-state

   **B.** State-link

   **C.** Vector

   **D.** Distance-vector

   **Answer:** D

7. Which type of packet switching is the closest to message switching?

   **A.** Datagram

   **B.** Circuit

   **C.** Virtual circuit

   **D.** Repeater

   **Answer:** A

8. Which type of address/name resolution uses name servers or directory servers?

   **A.** Service-provider-initiated

   **B.** Service-requester-initiated

   **C.** Name/directory initiated

   **D.** Address/name initiated

   **Answer:** A

9. Which connection service is concerned with alleviating network congestion?

   **A.** Transport layer error control

   **B.** Network layer error control

   **C.** Transport layer flow control

   **D.** Network layer flow control

   **Answer:** D

**10.** What does the term *aggregation* refer to?

A. Dividing messages into segments of the proper size

B. Combining segments into messages at the destination device

C. Combining small messages into one segment

D. Combining small segments into one message for transport

**Answer:** C

## Chapter 5 Answers

**1.** Which layer is responsible for encryption?

A. Application

B. Presentation

C. Session

D. Transport

**Answer:** B

**2.** A walkie-talkie would be an example of which kind of dialog?

A. Simplex

B. Half-duplex

C. Full-duplex

D. Broadcast

**Answer:** B

**3.** Which type of communication requires the most cooperation between operating systems?

A. Remote operation

B. OS call interception

C. Full-duplex

D. Collaborative computing

**Answer:** D

**4.** Which encryption method does NetWare 5 use?

A. Public key

B. Private key

C. Algebraic

D. Transposition

**Answer:** A

**5.** Which character code set is the one most commonly used on microcomputers and LANs?

A. ASCII

B. EBCDIC

C. Shift-JIS

D. Unicode

**Answer:** A

**6.** Which translation method does "little endian" have to do with?

A. Bit order

B. Byte order

C. File syntax

D. Character code

**Answer:** B

**7.** Which layer is responsible for establishing and maintaining dialogs?

A. Application

B. Presentation

C. Session

D. Network

**Answer:** C

**8.** Which one of the following does not belong in connection establishment?

A. Verify valid user ID and password

B. Assign the connection ID

C. Release the resources on the service provider

D. Specify the services required

**Answer:** C

**9.** Which one of the following is not an Application layer service?

A. File syntax

B. Database

C. Message

D. Print

**Answer:** A

**10.** What does NetWare use SAP for?

   **A.** Passive service advertising

   **B.** Collaborative computing

   **C.** Active service advertising

   **D.** Character code translation

   **Answer:** C

# Chapter 6 Answers

**1.** Which 802.3 standard is the closest to the original Ethernet?

   **A.** 10BaseF

   **B.** 1Base5

   **C.** 10Base5

   **D.** 10Base2

   **Answer:** C

**2.** Which non-IEEE protocol is very similar to IEEE 802.5 Token Ring?

   **A.** SMDS

   **B.** FDDI

   **C.** SONET

   **D.** PAP

   **Answer:** B

**3.** What access control method does IEEE 802.3 use?

   **A.** CSMA/CA

   **B.** Token-passing

   **C.** CSMA/CD

   **D.** 802.3 Enhanced

   **Answer:** C

**4.** Which IEEE 802 standard defines the LLC sublayer functions?

   **A.** 802.3

   **B.** 802.1

   **C.** 802.4

   **D.** 802.2

   **Answer:** D

**5.** Which WAN protocol can support dynamic IP addressing?

   **A.** X.25

   **B.** PPP

   **C.** SLIP

   **D.** ATM

   **Answer:** B

**6.** Which two layers of the OSI model do the IEEE 802.*x* map to primarily?

   **A.** Transport

   **B.** Network

   **C.** Data Link

   **D.** Physical

   **Answer:** C, D

**7.** Which IEEE 802.*x* standard is often used concurrently with 802.3, 802.4, 802.5, and 802.6?

   **A.** 802.1

   **B.** 802.2

   **C.** 802.7

   **D.** 802.9

   **Answer:** B

**8.** How many Class II Fast Ethernet repeaters can you have in a single collision domain?

   **A.** 2

   **B.** 3

   **C.** 4

   **D.** 5

   **Answer:** A

**9.** In an FDDI network where all the workstations are Class A stations, what is the maximum number of stations that can be connected?

   **A.** 100

   **B.** 250

   **C.** 500

   **D.** 1000

   **Answer:** C

**10.** Which Fast Ethernet standard uses four pairs of Category 3 UTP cabling?

**A.** 10BaseT

**B.** 100Base-T4

**C.** 100Base-TX

**D.** 100Base-FX

Answer: B

**11.** Fast Ethernet uses which media access method?

**A.** CSMA/CD

**B.** CSMA/CA

**C.** Token-passing

**D.** Contention

Answer: A

**12.** What is the maximum number of repeaters that can be used on a 10Base2 network?

**A.** 2

**B.** 3

**C.** 4

**D.** 5

Answer: C

**13.** Which connector is used by 10BaseT Ethernet networks?

**A.** RJ-11

**B.** RJ-45

**C.** RJ-12

**D.** RJ-36

Answer: B

**14.** What is the maximum segment length for a 100Base-FX Fast Ethernet segment?

**A.** 100 Meters

**B.** 185 Meters

**C.** 412 Meters

**D.** 500 Meters

Answer: C

**15.** You can have both 4Mbps and 16Mbps Token Ring devices on the same network operating at different speed.

**A.** True

**B.** False

Answer: B

# Chapter 7 Answers

**1.** A router works at which layer of the OSI model?

**A.** Physical

**B.** Data Link

**C.** Network

**D.** Transport

Answer: C

**2.** A repeater works at which layer of the OSI model?

**A.** Physical

**B.** Data Link

**C.** Network

**D.** Transport

Answer: A

**3.** A bridge works at which layer of the OSI model?

**A.** Physical

**B.** Data Link

**C.** Network

**D.** Transport

Answer: B

**4.** A switch can operate at which layers of the OSI model? (Choose all that apply.)

**A.** Physical

**B.** Data Link

**C.** Network

**D.** Transport

Answer: B, C

**5.** Which bridging technology organizes bridges into a hierarchy, with designated and backup bridges?

 **A.** Transparent

 **B.** Spanning tree

 **C.** Source routing

 **D.** Distance vector

 **Answer:** B

**6.** Which route discovery algorithm is more efficient in larger networks?

 **A.** Link state

 **B.** Distance vector

 **C.** Source routing

 **D.** Transparent

 **Answer:** A

**7.** Which is not a routable protocol?

 **A.** IPX

 **B.** AppleTalk

 **C.** IP

 **D.** NetBIOS

 **Answer:** D

**8.** Every time a packet crosses a router, the router increments which count?

 **A.** Hop

 **B.** Router

 **C.** Destination

 **D.** Hello

 **Answer:** A

**9.** Data Link layer virtual LANs are segmented using which address?

 **A.** Hardware (MAC)

 **B.** IPX

 **C.** TCP/IP

 **D.** Network

 **Answer:** A

**10.** Which network device would be the best choice to divide a network with high traffic into two, lower traffic segments?

 **A.** Repeater

 **B.** Bridge

 **C.** Router

 **D.** Transceiver

 **Answer:** B

**11.** Which network device will connect multiple networks with different topologies and protocols into an internetwork?

 **A.** Repeater

 **B.** Bridge

 **C.** Router

 **D.** Transceiver

 **Answer:** C

# Chapter 8 Answers

**1.** Which IP address is a valid Class C address?

 **A.** 204.153.163.67

 **B.** 189.45.225.23

 **C.** 10.4.2.1

 **D.** 245.142.64.15

 **Answer:** A

**2.** Which IP address is a valid Class B address?

 **A.** 204.153.163.67

 **B.** 189.45.225.23

 **C.** 10.4.2.1

 **D.** 245.142.64.15

 **Answer:** B

**3.** Which IP address is a valid Class A address?

 **A.** 204.153.163.67

 **B.** 189.45.225.23

 **C.** 10.4.2.1

 **D.** 245.142.64.15

 **Answer:** C

4. The process of copying host information from a master DNS server to a replica server is called?

    A. Zone transfer

    B. DNS copy

    C. Replication

    D. Replica updates

    Answer: A

5. Which special IP address refers to the local IP interface?

    A. 255.255.255.255

    B. 197.34.12.255

    C. 197.34.12.0

    D. 127.0.0.1

    E. 172.0.0.1

    Answer: D

6. Which domain is NOT considered a common top level domain?

    A. COM

    B. PRO

    C. EDU

    D. MIL

    E. US

    Answer: B

7. Which top-level domain refers to domains located in Germany?

    A. DE

    B. GE

    C. GY

    D. GER

    Answer: A

8. Where is the HOSTS file located, typically, on a UNIX machine?

    A. SYS:ETC

    B. /etc

    C. C:\ETC

    D. \ETC

    Answer: B

9. What organization is responsible for registering Internet domains?

    A. ARIN

    B. InterNIC

    C. RIPE

    D. APNIC

    Answer: B

10. What organization is currently responsible for keeping track of IP information for Mexico?

    A. ARIN

    B. InterNIC

    C. RIPE

    D. APNIC

    Answer: A

11. What organization is responsible for keeping track of IP information for France?

    A. ARIN

    B. InterNIC

    C. RIPE

    D. APNIC

    Answer: C

12. What organization is responsible for keeping track of IP information for Japan?

    A. ARIN

    B. InterNIC

    C. RIPE

    D. APNIC

    Answer: D

**13.** How many bytes are there in the network portion of a typical Class B IP address?

**A.** 1

**B.** 2

**C.** 3

**D.** 4

Answer: B

**14.** Your workstation is trying to access the website www.ebay.com. When your workstation asks the local DNS server, the local DNS server has no entry for www.ebay.com. Which DNS server does your DNS server query next?

**A.** Root (.)

**B.** Com

**C.** Ebay.com

**D.** www.ebay.com

Answer: A

## Chapter 9 Answers

**1.** Give two reasons for using subnet masks.

Answers: To extend the network

To reduce congestion

To reduce CPU usage

To isolate network problems

To improve security

To use multiple media

**2.** What is a subnet mask?

Answer: A subnet mask is a 4-byte number that is partnered with an IP address to distinguish the network address from the host address.

**3.** If you take a Class B address of 110.132.0.0 and have a subnet mask of 255.255.255.0, what is the range of subnet addresses? Host addresses?

Answer: The subnet address range is 110.132 .0-255.x

**4.** What is the subnet mask of a Class C address of 125.152.38.0?

Answer: 255.255.255.0

**5.** Complete the table.

| Subnet Mask | Subnets | Hosts on Partial Byte |
|---|---|---|
| 10000000 | 2 | 128 |
| 11000000 | 4 | 64 |
| 11100000 | 8 | 32 |
| 11110000 | 16 | 16 |
| 11111000 | 32 | 8 |
| 11111100 | 64 | 4 |
| 11111110 | 128 | 2 |

**6.** What is 11111111.11111111.11100000 .00000000 in decimal? What class address is it?

Answer: 255.255.224.0

**7.** What is 255.240.0.0 in binary? What class address is it?

Answers: 11111111.11110000.00000000 .00000000; Class A with the second byte split.

**8.** The second byte of a Class A address has been split, and the first four bits have been used for subnets (**1111**0000). The IP address is 138.0.0.0, and the subnet mask is 255.240.0.0. What is the total number of hosts available? (TIP: Don't forget the third and fourth bytes.)

Answers: 0.16.255.254 available per byte per subnet; 525 hosts total per subnet; 8400 hosts total.

**9.** The third byte in a Class B address has been split; the first three bits have been used for subnets; the IP address is 152.152.0.0. What is the subnet mask?

Answer: 255.255.224.0

**10.** Using the scenario from question 9, if the first subnet address is 32, then what is the range of host addresses from the third byte? If the subnet address is 140?

**Answers:** 152.152.31-63.x; 152.152.140-171.x

## Chapter 10 Answers

**1.** Which TCP/IP routing protocols allow for variable length subnet masking?

A. RIP I

B. RIP II

C. OSPF

D. NLSP

Answer: B, C

**2.** If an OSPF router is synchronized with a DR or BDR, what is said to exist between the two?

A. Link

B. Imbalance

C. State

D. Adjacency

Answer: D

**3.** Which IP routing protocol would you choose for a large internetwork with hundreds of routers?

A. RIP I

B. RIP II

C. OSPF

D. NLSP

Answer: C

**4.** Which component of the TCP/IP protocol suite provides connection-oriented, reliable transport for upper layer protocols?

A. TCP

B. UDP

C. HTTP

D. IP

Answer: A

**5.** Which protocol translates an IP address into a physical (MAC) address?

A. HTTP

B. TCP

C. ARP

D. UDP

Answer: C

**6.** Which protocol provides World Wide Web document delivery over the Internet using TCP?

A. TCP

B. ARP

C. RARP

D. HTTP

Answer: D

**7.** Which protocol(s) use UDP as a transport protocol?

A. TCP

B. FTP

C. TFTP

D. HTTP

E. BOOTP

F. RIP

Answer: C

**8.** Which protocol is used during an OSPF link state database synchronization?

A. RIP

B. LSA

C. TCP

D. HTTP

Answer: B

**9.** What else must you configure when implementing an OSPF routing environment?

A. Areas

B. Link state synchronization

C. Distance vector table

D. ARP tables

Answer: A

**10.** Which protocol(s) can gather router address information?

A. ICMP

B. TCP

C. SMTP

D. OSPF

**Answer:** A, D

**11.** What kind(s) of information is/are NOT found in the hello packet used in OSPF route discovery?

A. Route information

B. Neighbor information

C. Hello interval

D. Sender's address

**Answer:** A

# Chapter 11 Answers

**1.** Which of the following apply to IPX routers that use RIP?

A. They are not reliable.

B. They suffer from the count-to-infinity problem.

C. They are used most often on a WAN link.

D. They support up to 126 hops.

**Answer:** B

**2.** Which of the following apply to IPX routers that use NLSP? (Choose all that apply.)

A. They are not reliable.

B. They suffer from the count-to-infinity problem.

C. They are used most often on a WAN link.

D. They support up to 126 hops.

**Answer:** C, D

**3.** IPX corresponds closely to which layer of the OSI model?

A. Network

B. Transport

C. Data Link

D. Physical

**Answer:** A

**4.** SPX corresponds closely to which layer of the OSI model?

A. Network

B. Transport

C. Data Link

D. Physical

**Answer:** B

**5.** Which routing protocol is based on link state route discovery?

A. IPX

B. SPX

C. RIP

D. NLSP

**Answer:** D

**6.** Which routing technology uses SAP for service discovery?

A. IPX

B. SPX

C. RIP

D. NLSP

**Answer:** C

**7.** Which is NOT a function of the DR in an NLSP network?

A. Create a pseudonode

B. Remain offline until a router malfunctions, then take over the function of that router

C. Transmit, receive, and convert information to and from RIP/SAP routers to allow NLSP and RIP networks to communicate

D. Manage the synchronization between the DR and individual routers on a particular network

**Answer:** B

**8.** When a RIP router is brought offline, it broadcasts its routing information and the fact that routes it provides are unavailable.

**A.** True

**B.** False

Answer: A

**9.** What protocol should be filtered on a WAN link to decrease broadcast traffic across the link?

**A.** SAP

**B.** RIP

**C.** NLSP

**D.** LSP

Answer: A

**10.** Which protocol provides NetWare clients with access to various services on a NetWare server?

**A.** RIP

**B.** NLSP

**C.** NCP

**D.** CNSP

Answer: C

## Chapter 12 Answers

**1.** What are the services offered by X.500?

**A.** Unified (standard) naming service

**B.** Name and address resolution

**C.** Private key encryption

**D.** Unique object naming scheme

**E.** Object description capabilities

Answer: A, B, D, E

**2.** What are the main features of X.500?

**A.** Scalability

**B.** Simplicity

**C.** Replication

**D.** Connectivity

**E.** Synchronization

Answer: A, C, D

**3.** At what level of the OSI model are X.500 Directory Services processes defined?

**A.** Application

**B.** Session

**C.** Presentation

**D.** Network

Answer: A

**4.** LDAP runs over

**A.** IPX/SPX

**B.** UDP

**C.** TCP/IP

**D.** PBX

Answer: C

**5.** LDAP is used for

**A.** User access to the X.500 Directory

**B.** Server access to the X.500 Directory

Answer: A

## Chapter 13 Answers

**1.** Which is NOT a category of network problems?

**A.** Physical problems

**B.** Electrical problems

**C.** Network design problems

**D.** Viruses

Answer: C

**2.** Which problem is most likely to cause corruption of data?

**A.** Static

**B.** Magnetism

**C.** Crosstalk

**D.** Transients

Answer: B

**3.** What is the most likely cause of a network problem?

A. Viruses

B. User error

C. Static

D. Transients

**Answer:** B

**4.** Which term describes a surge of voltage?

A. Virus

B. Transient

C. Static

D. Noise

**Answer:** B

**5.** Which technique will NOT reduce the possibility of noise?

A. Proper grounding

B. Use of shielding

C. Avoiding interference sources

D. Proper user training

**Answer:** D

**6.** If you handle the internal parts of a computer, what can cause damage?

A. Viruses

B. Noise

C. Static

D. Crosstalk

**Answer:** C

**7.** Which of the following best describes computer viruses?

A. They are a myth.

B. They are usually created accidentally.

C. They cannot affect networks.

D. None of the above

**Answer:** D

**8.** Which source is most likely to have the latest driver for a network card for NetWare?

A. The Microhouse Technical Library (MTL)

B. The Novell Support Connection website

C. The NetWare Support Encyclopedia (NSEPRO)

D. The Encyclopedia of Hard Drives

**Answer:** B

**9.** Which source would you look in for the latest Novell news?

A. The NSEPRO

B. The Novell Support Connection website

C. The MTL

D. None of the above

**Answer:** B

**10.** Which MTL category would show the jumper settings for a hard drive interface card?

A. Hard Drive Controllers

B. Hard Drives

C. Miscellaneous I/O Controller Cards

D. Manufacturers

**Answer:** A

# Chapter 14 Answers

**1.** Which of these technologies is typically the most expensive?

A. Ethernet

B. ATM

C. Token Ring

D. FDDI

**Answer:** B

**2.** What is the most commonly used topology?

A. Ethernet

B. ATM

C. Token Ring

D. FDDI

**Answer:** A

**3.** Which device is used to add connections to ThickNet cabling?

A. A repeater

B. A hub

C. A vampire tap

D. A pigtail

Answer: C

**4.** Which of the following is NOT a disadvantage of ThickNet?

A. High cost

B. Large size

C. Reliability

D. Connection method

Answer: C

**5.** Which device allows you to increase the network's overall length?

A. A repeater

B. A passive hub

C. An active hub

D. A vampire tap

Answer: A

**6.** What is the maximum length allowed for ThickNet cable?

A. 100 meters (330 feet)

B. 100 feet (30.3 meters)

C. 300 feet (90.9 meters)

D. 500 meters (1,650 feet)

Answer: D

**7.** What is the maximum number of segments on a ThinNet network?

A. 5

B. 4

C. 30

D. 100

Answer: A

**8.** What is the maximum length of a ThinNet segment?

A. 925 meters (3,052.5 feet)

B. 200 meters (660 feet)

C. 185 meters (610.5 feet)

D. 100 feet (30 meters)

Answer: C

**9.** What other name is used for ThinNet?

A. 10BaseT

B. 10Base2

C. Ethernet

D. Ethernet_SNAP

Answer: B

**10.** What is the maximum length for an Ethernet UTP (unshielded twisted-pair) connection?

A. 100 meters (330 feet)

B. 200 meters (660 feet)

C. 185 meters (610.5 feet)

D. 151.5 meters (500 feet)

Answer: A

**11.** What is the speed of a Token Ring network?

A. 10 Mbps

B. 4/16 Mbps

C. 100 Mbps

D. 2.5 Mbps

Answer: B

**12.** What is the speed of a 100BaseT network?

A. 10Mbps

B. 4Mbps

C. 100Mbps

D. 2.5Mbps

Answer: C

**13.** Which types of cable can be used with 100BaseT4?

   **A.** Category 3 UTP

   **B.** Category 5 UTP

   **C.** Fiber-optic cable

   **D.** Coax cable

   **Answer:** A, B

**14.** What is the most expensive type of cable?

   **A.** Fiber-optic

   **B.** 10Base2 coaxial

   **C.** UTP

   **D.** ThickNet

   **Answer:** A

# Chapter 15 Answers

**1.** Which is NOT a division of a hard disk?

   **A.** Tracks

   **B.** Cylinders

   **C.** Pages

   **D.** Sectors

   **Answer:** C

**2.** What is the minimum unit of storage on a NetWare 5 volume?

   **A.** A cluster

   **B.** A cylinder

   **C.** A block

   **D.** A track

   **Answer:** C

**3.** What is the time required for the read/write head of a disk drive to reach the data called?

   **A.** Drive latency

   **B.** Seek time

   **C.** Transfer time

   **D.** Access time

   **Answer:** B

**4.** What are the most common hard drive interfaces today?

   **A.** ST-506 and IDE

   **B.** IDE and SCSI

   **C.** IDE and ESDI

   **D.** MFM and RLL

   **Answer:** B

**5.** What is the range of Standard SCSI device numbers?

   **A.** 0 to 7

   **B.** 1 to 7

   **C.** 1 to 16

   **D.** 0 to 6

   **Answer:** A

**6.** What does the stripe on one side of a disk cable typically mean?

   **A.** The cable is faulty.

   **B.** Pin 1 is on that side.

   **C.** Pin 36 is on that side.

   **D.** This is a floppy disk cable.

   **Answer:** B

**7.** Which drive standard uses two cables per drive?

   **A.** ESDI

   **B.** SCSI

   **C.** IDE

   **D.** ST-506

   **Answer:** D

**8.** Which DOS program is used to partition hard disks?

   **A.** FORMAT

   **B.** FDISK

   **C.** SYS

   **D.** PARTMAN

   **Answer:** B

**9.** Which step do you usually NOT have to perform to prepare a disk?

**A.** Partitioning

**B.** Low-level formatting

**C.** High-level formatting

**D.** Setting CMOS drive type

Answer: B

**10.** What do you call two drives using the same controller and containing identical data?

**A.** Duplexed

**B.** Mirrored

**C.** Matched

**D.** RAID 7

Answer: B

**11.** Which is NOT an advantage of disk duplexing?

**A.** Faster disk read access

**B.** Fault tolerance

**C.** Backups are no longer necessary

**D.** One drive still works if the other fails

Answer: C

**12.** What is the NetWare 5 utility used to manage mirrored drives?

**A.** DISKMAN

**B.** PARTMAN

**C.** NWCONFIG

**D.** SERVMAN

Answer: C

**13.** What are the advantages of CD-ROM storage?

**A.** Faster access than hard disks

**B.** Light weight and portability

**C.** Cheaper than floppy disk drives

**D.** All of the above

Answer: B

**14.** Which NLM must you load on a NetWare server to enable a CD-ROM to be used as a NetWare volume?

**A.** NWCONFIG

**B.** MONITOR

**C.** Volumes

**D.** CD-ROM

Answer: D

## Chapter 16 Answers

**1.** Which line, when placed in the SYSTEM.INI file, will enable the Novell Client log file?

**A.** Logging=True

**B.** NWEnablelogging=True

**C.** Startlog=True

**D.** NCStartlogging=True

Answer: B

**2.** What is the minimum amount of RAM required for the Novell Client for Windows 95?

**A.** 8

**B.** 16

**C.** 32

**D.** 64

Answer: B

**3.** What is the minimum amount of RAM required for the Novell Client for Windows NT?

**A.** 8

**B.** 16

**C.** 32

**D.** 64

Answer: C

**4.** Where do you change the size of the log file?

**A.** HKEY_LOCAL_MACHINE/Network/ Client32/LogSize

**B.** Properties of Novell Client for Windows 95 in Network Control Panel

Chapter 17 Answers **619**

**C.** Properties of Novell Client for Windows NT in Network Control Panel

**D.** My computer ➢ logfiles

**Answer:** B

5. Which component of both Novell Clients allows support of Microsoft components and protocols when using the 32-bit ODI modules?

**A.** LSL

**B.** ODI

**C.** TCP/IP

**D.** ODINSUP

**Answer:** D

6. LANalyzer for Windows is an example of which of the following?

**A.** Protocol Analyzer

**B.** Internet Protocol

**C.** Control Panel

**D.** Registry Entry

**Answer:** A

7. Which component of the Novell Client for Windows 95 acts much like the SERVER.EXE component of a NetWare server, providing an interface between the Windows 95 and network services?

**A.** NWFS.SYS

**B.** LAN Driver

**C.** LSL

**D.** NIOS.VXD

**Answer:** D

8. Which component of the Novell Client for Windows NT provides an interface between Windows NT and network services?

**A.** NWFS.SYS

**B.** LAN Driver

**C.** GINA

**D.** NIOS.VXD

**Answer:** A

9. What is the name of the Graphical Identification and Authentication (GINA) file that the Novell Client replaces MSGINA.DLL with?

**A.** NIOX.VXD

**B.** NWGINA.DLL

**C.** NCGINA.DLL

**D.** GINA.DLL

**Answer:** B

10. What is the location in the Windows 95 Registry, of the version of the Novell Client for Windows 95?

**A.** HKEY_LOCAL_MACHINE/Novell/Network/ Version

**B.** HKEY_LOCAL_MACHINE/Network/System Config/Install/Novell/Version

**C.** HKEY_LOCAL_MACHINE/Novell/Install/ System Config/Version

**D.** HKEY_LOCAL_MACHINE/Network/Novell/ System Config/Install/Version

**Answer:** D

# Chapter 17 Answers

1. What NDS objects are used for printing?

**A.** Print Server, Print Queue, Port Driver

**B.** Print Server, Print Queue, Printer

**C.** Printer, Print Server, Port Driver

**D.** CAPTURE, Printer, Print Server

**Answer:** B

2. The number of printers controlled by a NetWare 5 print server

**A.** Is limited only by the server's memory

**B.** Is limited to 16 printers

**C.** Is limited to 256 printers

**D.** Is limited to 3 parallel printers and 2 serial printers

**Answer:** C

**3.** What are three basic types of network printer?

A. Workstation, Server, Queue

B. Workstation, Server, Directly connected

C. NDS, Bindery, Workstation

D. Dot Matrix, Laser, Daisy Wheel

Answer: B

**4.** What program do you use to configure a workstation printer?

A. RPRINTER

B. REMOTE

C. WPRINTER

D. NPRINTER

Answer: D

**5.** Which is the correct order of components used when a print job is processed?

A. CAPTURE, print queue, printer

B. CAPTURE, print queue, print server, port driver, printer

C. CAPTURE, port driver, print server, print queue, printer

D. Port driver, CAPTURE, print queue, print server, printer

Answer: B

**6.** Which common printers are used with networks?

A. Laser, dot matrix, ink jet

B. Laser, daisy wheel, band

C. Dot matrix, ink jet, daisy wheel

D. Dot matrix, ink jet, dye sublimation

Answer: A

**7.** Which of the following conditions does NOT cause the printer to stop in the middle of a job?

A. Overheating

B. Out of paper or paper jam

C. Incorrect print server configuration

D. Ribbon or ink supply low

Answer: C

**8.** The parameters for a serial printer do NOT include

A. Baud rate

B. Data bits

C. Stop bits

D. Cable pinout

Answer: D

**9.** What is the official limit for a parallel printer cable?

A. 5 feet

B. 15 feet

C. 300 feet

D. 50 feet

Answer: B

**10.** Which of the following should you try *first* if a printer has a problem?

A. Restart PSERVER.NLM.

B. Run the self-test.

C. Replace the printer cable.

D. Check for a corrupt print queue.

Answer: B

**11.** If a printer works in the self-test but not from the network, where is the problem?

A. The cable

B. The print queue

C. The print server

D. Any of the above—not enough information to tell

Answer: D

**12.** If the printer works in a self-test but does not print a screen from the workstation, where is the problem?

A. The workstation or cable

B. The print queue

**c.** The print server

**D.** Any of the above—not enough information to tell

**Answer:** A

**13.** Which type of printer does NOT generate a lot of heat?

**A.** Dot matrix (9-pin)

**B.** Ink jet

**c.** Laser

**D.** Dot matrix (24-pin)

**Answer:** B

**14.** If the printer jams on multi-part forms, what should you try *first* to correct the problem?

**A.** Using a different paper

**B.** Adjusting the print head distance

**c.** Replacing the ribbon

**D.** Replacing the print head

**Answer:** B

**15.** If the printer does not print at all, which is NOT likely to be the problem?

**A.** A print queue or print server configuration error

**B.** A bad connection or disconnected cable

**c.** The ribbon is worn and needs replacing

**D.** Printer is turned off or offline

**Answer:** C

**16.** A laser printer printing completely black pages is a symptom of

**A.** Bad cartridge or broken charge corona wires

**B.** Out of toner

**c.** Incorrect print server configuration

**D.** Dirty fuser roller

**Answer:** A

**17.** What should be used to clean toner spilled on clothing, hands, or furniture?

**A.** Acetylene or other solvent

**B.** Cold water

**c.** Very hot water

**D.** A dry cloth

**Answer:** B

**18.** What is the correct command to display CAPTURE settings?

**A.** CAPTURE /?

**B.** CAPTURE /S

**c.** CAPTURE SH

**D.** CAPTURE /EC

**Answer:** C

**19.** Where are the print queues stored?

**A.** The SYSTEM directory

**B.** The PUBLIC directory

**c.** The QUEUES directory

**D.** The PRINT directory

**Answer:** C

**20.** What is the correct syntax to load the print server WEST?

**A.** PSERVER WEST

**B.** LOAD PSERVER /NAME=WEST

**c.** LOAD PSERVER, WEST

**D.** LOAD PSERVER WEST

**Answer:** D

**21.** If Printer, Print Server, or Print Queue NDS objects are corrupt, what should you try running?

**A.** DSREPAIR

**B.** DSMERGE

**c.** BINDFIX

**D.** PCONSOLE /REPAIR

**Answer:** A

**22.** The NetWare 3.1*x* PSERVER.EXE requires which command in NET.CFG?

**A.** PREFERRED SERVER

**B.** SPX PROCESSES = 50

**C.** SPX CONNECTIONS = 60

**D.** SPX = 50

**Answer:** C

**23.** What is the correct method of stopping a print server?

**A.** UNLOAD PSERVER at the file server console.

**B.** From within PCONSOLE at the workstation.

**C.** Turn the server off and back on.

**D.** Use the RESTART SERVER command at the server.

**Answer:** B

**24.** Which component of NDPS is responsible for managing the printer agents?

**A.** NDPS Manager

**B.** NDPS Broker

**C.** Print Server

**D.** Printer Agent

**Answer:** A

**25.** You have set up your network to use NDPS. No one can print to the new public access printer. What should you check first?

**A.** That the workstations have the newest driver

**B.** That NetWare Administrator is running

**C.** That the printer is online

**D.** That the broker has configured the NDPS Printer Agent

**Answer:** C

**26.** A user is complaining that none of their print jobs are printing. What tools should you use to see if the printer has been paused?

**A.** Windows 95 printer instance

**B.** Novell Printer Manager

**C.** NetWare Administrator

**D.** NDPS Broker

**Answer:** A, B, C

**27.** Which component of the NDPS Broker makes automatic driver download possible?

**A.** SRS

**B.** ENS

**C.** RMS

**D.** EMS

**Answer:** C

**28.** If you are getting "Can't connect to the Printer Agent" errors on all workstations, which component of NDPS may not be loaded/functioning?

**A.** NDPS Broker

**B.** NDPS Manager

**C.** NDPS Gateway

**D.** Printer Agent

**Answer:** B

**29.** Which NDPS component is responsible for allowing non–NDPS-aware printers to be used in an NDPS-only printing system?

**A.** NDPS Broker

**B.** Printer Agent

**C.** NDPS Manager

**D.** NDPS Gateway

**Answer:** D

**30.** Which NDPS gateways come with NDPS and are installed by default?

**A.** Novell

**B.** HP

**C.** Xerox

**D.** Canon

**Answer:** A, B, C

# Chapter 18 Answers

**1.** Which of the following is NOT an important test for backup software?

   **A.** Can it back up files?

   **B.** Can it restore files?

   **C.** Does it rotate tapes?

   **D.** Can it back up from tape to tape?

   **Answer:** D

**2.** If a server disk will not mount due to errors, which utility should you try first?

   **A.** LANalyzer

   **B.** VREPAIR

   **C.** DSREPAIR

   **D.** DISKSCAN

   **Answer:** B

**3.** When can you run VREPAIR?

   **A.** At any time while the server is running

   **B.** Only when no users are logged in

   **C.** Only when the volume is dismounted

   **D.** Only on a new server

   **Answer:** C

**4.** Which utility allows you to install operating system patches on a NetWare 5 server?

   **A.** INSTALL.NLM

   **B.** NWCONFIG.NLM

   **C.** CONFIG.NLM

   **D.** PATCHMAN.NLM

   **Answer:** B

**5.** The MONITOR utility does NOT show statistics for

   **A.** Memory utilization

   **B.** Scheduling

   **C.** Bandwidth usage

   **D.** LAN cards

   **Answer:** C

**6.** Which file is the correct file to download for the fourth revision of the NetWare support pack?

   **A.** IWSP4A.EXE

   **B.** NWSP4.EXE

   **C.** SP4.EXE

   **D.** SP4NW4.EXE

   **Answer:** B

**7.** Which of the following can cause abends?

   **A.** Software issues

   **B.** Hardware issues

   **C.** Bad network packets

   **D.** All of the above

   **Answer:** D

**8.** Which of the following best describes a LANalyzer?

   **A.** A packet analyzer

   **B.** A protocol analyzer

   **C.** A workstation analyzer

   **D.** A server monitor

   **Answer:** B

**9.** Which LANalyzer feature lists users?

   **A.** Server Monitor

   **B.** Station Monitor

   **C.** Connection Monitor

   **D.** User Monitor

   **Answer:** B

**10.** Which of the following is the main LANalyzer display?

   **A.** Console

   **B.** MONITOR

   **C.** Dashboard

   **D.** Control Center

   **Answer:** C

**11.** Which feature in LANalyzer allows you to monitor the network and capture details?

**A.** Packet Capture

**B.** Network Display Monitor

**C.** Dashboard

**D.** Statistical Analyzer

**Answer: A**

# APPENDIX

# B

Glossary

**0.0.0.0**   IP address that refers to the default route.

**127.0.0.0**   IP address used to refer to the local TCP/IP interface. It is used by a host to send packets to itself. Also called the loopback address.

**Abend**   Short for abnormal end. This is NetWare's term for a server crash. An abend is frequently caused by an application (NLM) writing to an area of memory that belongs to the operating system.

**Abnormal END**   See *Abend*.

**Active Monitor**   Part of the Token Ring that prevents data frames from roaming the ring unchecked. If the frame passes the active monitor too many times it is removed from the ring.

**Address Recognized Indicator (ARI)**   A special Token Ring source routing frame field that is used to determine if the receiving station is on the local ring. A transmitting station sends a special frame out on the ring with no source routing information. If the frame comes back with the Address Recognized Indicator bit set, the sending station knows the receiving station is on the local ring.

**Adjacency**   Refers to a router's immediate neighbors in an OSPF network routing environment.

**American National Standards Institute (ANSI)**   A non-profit organization responsible for the ASCII code set (American Standard Code for Information Interchange), as well as numerous other voluntary standards.

**American Registry for Internet Numbers (ARIN)**   The organization that distributes registered IP addresses for the Americas.

**Amplitude**   In communications, the distance between the highest and lowest points in a wave. The amplitude controls the strength, or volume, of the signal.

**Amplitude Modulation**   A type of communications that modulates, or makes changes in, the amplitude of the wave in order to transmit bits of data.

**Amplitude Shift Keying**   A multiplexing method that modulates the amplitude of signals to encode multiple signals into a single data stream.

**Analog**   Data that has an infinite number of possible states, rather than the simple 1s and 0s of a digital signal. Audio, video, and voice telephone signals, for example, can all be represented using analog signals.

**ANSI**   See *American National Standards Institute*.

**AppleTalk**   A networking system developed by Apple for use with Macintosh computers. The software for AppleTalk connectivity is built into the Macintosh operating system (MacOS or System 7). NetWare for Macintosh allows connectivity between AppleTalk and NetWare networks by emulating AppleTalk services on the NetWare server.

**Application Services**   Allows client PCs to access and use extra computing power and expensive software applications that reside on a shared computer. Upper layer processes that provide network functionality to clients.

**ARCnet**   Stands for Attached Resource Computing Network. A network topology developed by Datapoint Corporation in 1977. ARCnet uses a token-passing media access method and can use a physical star, bus, or tree topology.

**ARIN**   See *American Registry for Internet Numbers*.

**Asynchronous**   A type of communication that sends data using flow control rather than a clock to synchronize data between the source and destination.

**Asynchronous Transfer Mode (ATM)**   Protocol that covers the functionality of the OSI model's Data Link and Network layers and can operate over Physical layer protocols such as FDDI and SONET/SDH.

**ATM**   See *Asynchronous Transfer Mode.*

**Attenuation**   A communications term referring to a signal decreasing in volume (and amplitude) over a distance. The length of the cable and its resistance can affect the amount of attenuation.

**Authentication**   Part of the login process, during which NDS verifies that the user's password, access rights, and other settings are correct. Authentication is handled by the nearest read/write or master replica.

**Auto Negotiation**   The process of negotiating a connection speed (either 10Mbps or 100Mbps) that 100Mbps Ethernet hubs perform when a NIC connects. This function provides backward compatibility with 10Mbps Ethernet cards in a mixed environment.

**Auto-Reconfiguration**   The automatic corrective action process of a Token Ring network.

**B-ISDN**   See *Broadband ISDN.*

**Backup Bridge**   On the Spanning Tree bridge protocol, the redundant bridge for the designated bridge that will take over as the designated bridge in case the original designated bridge fails.

**Bandwidth**   In network communications, the amount of data that can be sent across a wire in a given time. Each communication that passes along the wire decreases the amount of available bandwidth.

**Baseband**   A transmission technique in which the signal uses the entire bandwidth of a transmission medium.

**Baud Rate**   A way of describing modem communications. One signal transition per second equals one baud.

**Beaconing**   Function of a Token Ring network where the network is able to reconfigure itself in the case of a major failure.

**Beacon**   A special frame on a Token Ring network that is sent out to indicate a problem on the ring.

**Binary**   The numbering system used in computer memory and in digital communication. All characters are represented as a series of 1s and 0s. For example, the letter A might be represented as 01000001.

**Binding**   The process of connecting a communication protocol (such as TCP/IP) to a LAN board driver (such as Ethernet).

**Biphase**   Encoding scheme that requires at least one mid-bit transition per bit interval.

**Bits**   In binary data, each unit of data is a bit. Each bit is represented by either 0 or 1, and is stored in memory as an ON or OFF state.

**Block**   One of the divisions of a hard disk. NetWare stores files on the volume in terms of blocks. In NetWare 3.1*x* and earlier, entire blocks are always used. Block sizes are typically 4K for NetWare 3.1*x*, 4.1*x*, and NetWare 5.

**Blocking**   Bridge port state that will only forward data frames addressed to the bridge's multicast address. It will ignore all frames sent to any other destination address.

**Bridge**  A device that connects two segments of a network and sends data to one or the other based on a set of criteria.

**Bridge IDs**  A unique ID assigned to each bridge on a bridged network using the spanning-tree protocol.

**Bridge Ports**  Connectors on a bridge that allow it to connect to two or more segments.

**Bridging Loops**  Phenomenon that occurs when data frames circle endlessly between two redundant bridges. They are primarily caused by bridges that don't use the spanning tree protocol.

**Broadband**  A network transmission method in which a single transmission medium is divided and shared simultaneously.

**Broadband ISDN (B-ISDN)**  An ISDN technology that has greatly increased data rates of standard ISDN. It is capable of speeds up to 155Mbps and uses fiber-optic technology.

**Broadcast Address**  Packets sent to this address go to all the nodes on the network segment or the sending workstation. For TCP/IP, the broadcast address is 255.255.255.255.

**Brownout**  A condition of lower power where power drops below 120 volts but isn't completely cut off.

**Byte**  The unit of data storage and communication in computers. In PC systems a byte is eight bits, or an eight-digit binary number. A single byte can represent numbers between 0 and 255.

**Cable**  Physical transmission media that has a central conductor (wire or fiber) surrounded by a plastic jacket.

**CAPTURE**  Novell TSR command that allows you to redirect printing to a network printer.

**Carrier**  In communications, a signal that is kept on the line at all times so that the device on the other end knows that it is connected.

**Carrier Sensing**  Method for reducing collisions during data transmissions. In this method, before a device transmits data, it listens to, or senses, the cable to see if it is busy. If it detects a signal, indicating that another station is transmitting, it will wait until the cable is free. If it doesn't detect any traffic, the computer will place its own data onto the medium for transmission.

**CCITT**  See *Consultative Committee on International Telegraphy and Telephony.*

**Cell**  A 53-byte packet that follows a virtual circuit; most commonly used in an ATM network.

**Channel**  A portion of the bandwidth that can be used for transmitting data.

**Channel Addressing**  Type of addressing similar to logical network addressing except that the address is maintained for each connection.

**Checksum**  A number that is calculated based on the values of a block of data. Checksums are used in communication to ensure that the correct data was received.

**Chip Creep**  When integrated circuits gradually lose contact with their sockets because of changes in temperature.

**Choke Packet**  Method of dynamic window flow control that uses a special acknowledgement packet that the receiving device can send when its buffer is nearly full.

**Circuit Switching**   A type of communication system that establishes a connection, or circuit, between the two devices before communicating and does not disconnect until all data is sent.

**Cladding**   A layer of glass that reflects the light back into the core in fiber-optic cable.

**Client**   Any device that attaches to the network server. A workstation is the most common type of client. Clients run *client software* to provide network access. A piece of software that accesses data on a server can also be called a client.

**Client/Server Network**   A server-centric network in which some network resources are stored on a file server, while processing power is distributed among workstations and the file server.

**Coaxial Cable**   One of the types of cable used in network wiring. Typical coaxial cable types include RG-58 and RG-62. The 10Base2 system of Ethernet networking uses coaxial cable. Coaxial cable is usually shielded. The ThickNet system uses a thicker coaxial cable.

**Collaborative Computing**   Computing model that shows computers working together to process the same task.

**Collision**   An error type on an Ethernet network that happens when two stations try to transmit at the exact same time.

**Collision Detection**   Method for reducing collisions during data transmission. During the transmission, the station monitors the cable to ensure that nothing is interfering with the signal being sent. If it detects a collision, it first transmits a jam pattern so that all stations will be made aware of the collision. Then it will stop transmitting and wait for a random amount of time before attempting to retransmit.

**Connection Management (CMT)**   FDDI network management function that assigns connections to workstations that wish to attach to the network and removes them when unattached.

**Consultative Committee on International Telegraphy and Telephony (CCITT)**   A committee sponsored by the United Nations that defines network standards, including X.400 and X.500. This committee has been recently renamed International Telecommunications Union/Telecommunications Standardization Sector (ITU/TSS).

**Contention**   A media access method that basically allows any computer to transmit whenever it has data.

**Controlled Access Printer**   NDPS printer with an NDS object that allows an administrator to manage all the functions of that printer.

**Core Dump**   When a server crashes, you typically have the option of copying the information from memory to a file on the local hard disk. This process (as well as the file) is known as a core dump.

**Count-to-Infinity**   A problem that exists on distance vector routed networks with multiple routers. It occurs when two routers send the same routing information back and forth, incrementing the hop count to the destination network until it reaches infinity. This problem can cause networks to take a long time to converge.

**Crosstalk**   When copper wires that are close together conduct electrical signals, there is a tendency for each wire to produce interference in the other.

**Current-State Encoding**   Category of signal-encoding techniques in which data is encoded by the presence or absence of a signal characteristic or state.

**Custom Device Module (CDM)**   Part of the NetWare Peripheral Architecture (NPA) system of device drivers, the CDM provides an interface between the device and the Host Adapter Module (HAM). The HAM provides communication with the controller.

**Cyclic Redundancy Check (CRC)**   Test where the entire frame is run through a mathematical calculation and the result is appended to the frame in the CRC field and placed on the wire. When the receiving station receives the frame, it reads the CRC field into memory and runs the same mathematical formula against what's left of the frame. If the value of this calculation and the CRC value aren't the same, the receiving data will know that the transmission got changed in some way during the transmission, and the frame is dropped.

**Data Bits**   The number of bits used to represent a character in asynchronous transmissions, usually seven or eight.

**Data Link Layer**   The second to the bottom layer of the OSI model; it provides the first layer of logic on top of the Physical layer.

**Data Packet**   A unit of data being sent over a network. A packet includes a header, addressing information, and the data itself. A packet is treated as a single unit as it is sent from device to device.

**Dedicated Line**   A transmission medium that is used exclusively between two locations. Dedicated lines are also known as leased lines or private lines.

**Dedicated Server**   A server that serves no other purpose except being a server—it cannot be used as a workstation. All NetWare servers since version 3.*x* are dedicated.

**Designated Bridge**   When using the Spanning Tree protocol, the bridge that all frames are forwarded through.

**Designated Router (DR)**   A router elected to speak for all other routers on a network. It performs special functions and has special responsibilities on a network.

**Device Driver**   A piece of software that allows a workstation or server to communicate with a hardware device. For example, disk drivers are used to control disk drives, and network drivers are used to communicate with network boards.

**Digital**   Any signal that has discrete values over time. A digital signal has no transition between values. It is one value one instant (a specific number, like 1) and a different value the next (a second number, like 0).

**Directory**   In NDS, the database that contains information about each of the objects on the network. The Directory is organized into a tree-like structure, the *Directory Tree*, with a [Root] object on top and leaf objects at the bottom. To distinguish it from disk directories, the name of the NDS Directory is always capitalized.

**Directory Services**   The network service that provides users access to the network directory.

**Directory Tree**   An organizational structure applied to a directory that allows directory objects to be more easily found.

**Disabled State**   A possible port state for a bridge. A bridge port in this state is, for all purposes, offline and will not forward frames.

**Disk Mirroring**   A disk fault tolerance method where information is saved to two identical disks simultaneously. One disk is said to be the *mirror* of the other. If one disk fails, the other takes over automatically and handles disk requests.

**Distance Vector**   Route discovery method where each router tells every other router what networks and routes it knows about and how far away they are.

**Distributed Database Model**   Network model in which local servers distribute changes and receive updates in synchronized coordination with other servers, which also distribute changes and receive updates.

**Distributed Print Services**   New type of printing technology that allows the printer and server to talk directly and exchange information. (See *NDPS*.)

**DNS**   See *Domain Name Services*.

**DNS Zones**   Division of the DNS hierarchy where a zone begins at a particular domain and extends downward until it reaches a host or another zone begins. Zones provide logical divisions for the Internet. They may or may not represent physical segments.

**DOD Networking Model**   A four-layer conceptual model describing how communications should take place between computer systems. The four layers are Process/Application, Host-to-Host, Internet, and Network Access. DOD is the acronym for Department of Defense, the government agency that provided the original funding for the development of the TCP/IP protocol suite.

**Domain Names**   Logical names given to IP hosts.

**Domain Name Services (DNS)**   A TCP/IP network service that performs translation of host names into IP addresses. DNS organizes network names into a hierarchy.

**Dot Matrix**   Printer that uses a set of pins that move forward and press a ribbon against the paper making a dot. Patterns of dots create letters and images on the paper.

**Dual-Attached Stations (DASs)**   Another name for Class A FDDI stations. They can be attached to both FDDI rings at the same time.

**Dumb Terminal**   Basically a keyboard and monitor that send keystrokes to a central processing computer (typically a mainframe or minicomputer) and return screen displays to the monitor. The unit has no processing power of its own, hence the name *dumb* terminal.

**Duplex**   A way of classifying communication systems. Full duplex is full two-way communication (both stations transmitting and receiving at the same time); half-duplex means that data can only travel in one direction at a time (one station transmits, the other receives at any one instant).

**Dynamic Window Flow Control**   Type of window flow control that allows the receiving device to adjust its window size; also referred to as floating or sliding window flow control.

**Early Token Release**   Token Ring technology in which the sending workstation releases the token as soon as it's done sending. This technology allows an increase in performance over standard Token Ring technologies.

**Electromagnetic Interference (EMI)**   Noise that affects the signal that is sent through the transmission media. EMI is caused by outside electromagnetic waves affecting the desired signal, making it more difficult for the receiving computer to decode the signal.

**Electronic Mail**   A technology that allows users to send electronic text (and other) messages to people across the world using their computer.

**Electrostatic Discharge (ESD)**   A problem that exists when static electricity buildup discharges into an electronic component, damaging it. It can be prevented by reducing or eliminating conditions that cause static electricity.

**Encoding**   The process by which data or bits are represented in a way that the sender can create a message and the receiver can understand it.

**Error Control**   Connection service that detects corrupted data in received frames and can request retransmission. It ensures reliable data delivery.

**Ethernet**   Network that uses the CSMA/CD media access method. The original Ethernet specifies a CSMA/CD media access method as well as baseband signaling and logic and physical bus topology.

**Event Notification Services (ENS)**   A component of the NDPS broker that notifies users and administrators of events that occur with network printing.

**Fault Domain**   A problem area on the Token Ring.

**Fiber Distributed Data Interface (FDDI)**   An ANSI standard that specifies both the Physical layer and MAC sublayer components of the OSI model for a fiber-based networking topology with dual, counter-rotating rings.

**Fiber-Optics**   One of the media that can be used for network communications. Fiber-optics uses a tiny glass or plastic fiber, and sends a light signal through the fiber.

**File Archiving**   The process of backing up files or offline storage devices such as tapes or optical disks.

**File Services**   The network applications that store, retrieve, or move data on the network.

**File Transfer Protocol (FTP)**   A TCP/IP protocol that permits the transferring of files between computer systems. Because FTP has been implemented on numerous types of computer systems, file transfers can be done between different computer systems (for example, a personal computer and a minicomputer).

**Filtering Database**   A database on a bridge that contains entries for which packet addresses should be forwarded and which should be dropped. The database can be modified either manually by an administrator with the bridge manufacturer's administration software or dynamically by the bridge itself.

**Flow Control**   Connection service that determines the amount of data that can be transmitted in order to prevent a sender from overwhelming a receiver.

**Forwarding**   Bridge port state in which the port can perform both forwarding and learning functions. Also a name for the process by which a bridge or router copies a frame from one segment to another.

**Frame**   A unit of data transmission that corresponds to the Data Link layer of the OSI model.

**Frame Relay**   Packet-switching technology that uses virtual circuits. Frame relay assumes that certain error-checking and monitoring tasks will be performed by higher-level protocols.

**Frequency**   The amount of time it takes for an analog wave to complete one cycle. Frequency is measured in hertz (Hz) or cycles per second.

**Frequency Shift Keying**   A method of encoding data that varies the frequency of a signal to represent various bits.

**Frequency-Division Multiplexing (FDM)**   Method of multiplexing that uses separate frequencies to combine multiple data channels onto a broadband medium. FDM can be used to separate different-direction traffic in a broadband LAN.

**Full-Duplex Ethernet Ports**   Ports on an Ethernet switch that balance incoming and outgoing traffic. In full duplex mode, an Ethernet switch can provide 20Mbps bandwidth from station to hub on regular 10Mbps Ethernet.

**Full-Duplex Transmission**   Transmission in which there is full, two-way communication. See *Duplex*.

**Full Server Lockup**   Error condition characterized by a lack of any activity on the server.

**General Service Responses**   Type of Service Advertising Protocol (SAP) Service Responses that are sent in response to broadcasts.

**Gigabit Ethernet**   Ethernet category for those networks that run at more the 1000Mbps.

**Global Network**   The type of network required to serve multiple organizations and cover multiple continents. The World Wide Web would be an example of this type of network.

**Graphical Identification and Authentication (GINA Module)**   The module of Windows NT that provides a graphical interface for login to a Windows NT computer. This functionality is provided in Windows NT by the file MSGINA.DLL. When the Novell Client for Windows NT is installed, it replaces the MSGINA.DLL file with its own GINA functionality file: NWGINA.DLL. This file allows simultaneous login to Windows NT and Novell NetWare.

**Guaranteed Flow Control**   Flow control method in which the sender and receiver agree on a mutually acceptable transmission rate before transmission begins.

**Guaranteed State Change**   Method of synchronous bit synchronization in which the clocking information is embedded in the data signal. The receiver is guaranteed that transitions will occur in the signal at predefined intervals.

**Half-Duplex Transmission**   Transmission in which data is sent only one way at a time. See also *Duplex*.

**Handshaking**   In network communication, a process used to verify that a connection has been established correctly. Devices send signals back and forth to establish parameters for communication.

**Header**   Headers contain pieces of control information that are read and processed by the corresponding layer on the receiving stack. As the message travels up the stack of the other machine, each layer strips the header added by its peer layer.

**Hello Frame**   In source route determination, in order to determine the route to a station each device sends a special frame called a hello frame to the destination device. As it travels toward the destination device, each bridge that it passes through appends its name and route information to the frame; it responds to the source station, sending it back along the same route. When the original sending station receives the frame, it adds that route information to its database.

**Hello Packet**   In TCP/IP OSPF routing, this packet is sent by a router to identify its neighbors. It is used to acquire and maintain neighbor information as well as ensure two-way communications between them. The hello packet contains the source address of the sending station as well as the priority and hello interval.

**High-Capacity Storage System (HCSS)**   A Novell storage technology that allows seldom-used files to migrate (or move) to a slower speed, larger capacity storage medium. The file will still appear in a directory listing. When the file is accessed, it will be copied from the slower medium back to the hard disk.

**Hold-Down Interval**   The specified time a router waits between calculations of the forwarding database information.

**Holding Time**   How long before a router should expect to wait before receiving another hello packet from a specified router.

**Hop**   The count of every router a packet passes through on its way to its destination.

**Hops Away**   In reference to RIP packet construction, this field contains the number of routes between the router and the network being reported.

**Host**   An addressable computer system on a TCP/IP network. Examples include endpoint systems such as workstations, servers, minicomputers, mainframes, and immediate systems such as routers. A host is typically a system that offers resources to network nodes, similar to a NetWare server's function.

**Host Adapter**   A hardware device that allows communication with a peripheral, such as a disk or tape drive. The host adapter, also called a *controller*, is usually a card that is inserted into a slot on the server's motherboard.

**Host Adapter Module (HAM)**   One of the components of the NetWare Peripheral Architecture (NPA) device driver standard. The HAM provides communication with the *host adapter*.

**Host Table**   Text file set up on the local host with the names of the various hosts on the network that are commonly accessed and their associated IP addresses.

**HTTP**   See *Hypertext Transfer Protocol (HTTP)*.

**Hub**   A device that connects the network to several devices at once. 10BaseT and ARCnet are networking methods that use hubs.

**Hypertext Transfer Protocol (HTTP)**   The protocol used by World Wide Web (WWW) browsers and servers. Uses the connection-oriented transport protocol TCP. It resides at the Process/Application layer of the DOD model.

**IEEE**   See *Institute of Electronic and Electrical Engineers*.

**IEEE 802.*x* Standards**   The generic name for the series of standards developed by the Institute of Electronic and Electrical Engineers 802 subcommittee.

**IEEE 802.1**   Standard that defines standards to the Physical and Data Link layers that allow any two IEEE 802 LAN stations to communicate over a LAN or WAN.

**IEEE 802.2**   This standard defines the Logical Link Control (LLC) sublayer of the entire 802.*x* series of protocols. The standard specifies the adding of special header fields that tell the receiving protocol stack which upper layer sent the information.

**IEEE 802.3**   Standard that specifies many Physical layer attributes such as signaling types, data rates, and topologies.

**IEEE 802.4**   Standard that specifies a physical bus topology, token-passing media access, either 75-ohm copper or fiber-optic media, and either broadband or baseband signaling.

**IEEE 802.5**   Specifies a token-passing media access method. This standard is based on IBM's Token Ring technology.

**IEEE 802.6**   Standard that uses Distributed Queue Dual Bus (DQDB) technology for high-speed data transfer between nodes.

**IEEE 802.7**   Defines several standards for broadband communications including design, installation, and testing.

**IEEE 802.8**   Standard that defines a group (the Fiber-Optic Technical Advisory Group) to work with the other 802 groups to advise them on the various fiber-optic technologies and standards.

**IEEE 802.9**   Defines a standard for Isochronous Ethernet (or IsoEnet). This standard focuses on the integration of voice and data transmissions.

**IEEE 802.10**   Standard that defines a standard way for protocols and services to exchange data securely using encryption mechanisms.

**IEEE 802.11**   Defines standards for implementation of wireless LAN technologies like infrared and spread-spectrum radio.

**IEEE 802.12**   Standard based on 100VG-AnyLAN. When a station has data to transmit, it signals a hub. If another station wants to transmit at the same time, the hub allows the highest priority traffic to get transmitted first.

**Ink Jet**   Type of printer where liquid ink is forced through tiny nozzles to create the dots on the paper. The pattern of the dots form images and text on the page.

**Institute of Electronic and Electrical Engineers (IEEE)**   An international organization that sets standards for various electrical and electronic issues, including the IEEE 802 series, which defines standards for Ethernet and Token Ring networks.

**Integrated Services Digital Network (ISDN)**   A new network standard that allows high-speed communication over ordinary category 3 or 5 copper cabling. It may someday replace conventional phone systems with high-speed, digital lines.

**Intelligent Hubs**   Hubs that have built-in management capabilities that will report errors or problems, as well as allow you to disconnect the devices from the hub remotely.

**Internal IPX Address**   Enables the server to perform internal routing to upper layer protocols.

**International Organization for Standardization (ISO)**   The standards organization that developed the OSI model. ANSI is a member of the ISO.

**International Telecommunications Union (ITU)**   The international standards organization formerly known as the CCITT.

**International Telegraph and Telephone Consultative Committee (CCITT)**   An international standards organization responsible for developing the X.*nn* (for example, X.25, X.500) standards for telecommunications.

**Internet**   A global network made up of a large number of individual networks interconnected through the use of TCP/IP protocols. The individual networks comprising the Internet are from colleges, universities, businesses, research organizations, government agencies, individuals, and other bodies. The governing body of this global network is the Internet Activities Board (IAB). When the term *Internet* is used with an upper-case *I*, it refers to the global network, but when written with a lower-case *i*, it simply means a group of interconnected networks.

**Internetwork Packet Exchange (IPX)**   A connectionless, routable network protocol based on the Xerox protocol XNS. It is the default protocol for versions of NetWare before NetWare 5.

**Internetworking**   The process of connecting multiple local area networks to form a wide area network (WAN). Internetworking between different types of networks is handled by a *router*.

**InterNIC**  Nonprofit organization tasked by the government to assign blocks of IP addresses to people who request them.

**Intranet**  A term for any network that makes Internet-related services, such as e-mail, FTP, and the Web, available to users of a local network.

**Inverse Address (IN-ADDR.ARPA)**  A DNS zone that is used for translating IP addresses into DNS names.

**Impedance**  Cable's resistance to direct or alternating electric currents.

**IP Addresses**  A logical TCP/IP address given to each network entity on a TCP/IP network.

**IP6.INT**  DNS zone used to translate the domain names into Ipv6 addresses.

**IPX External Network Number**  A number that is used to represent an entire network. All servers on the network must use the same external network number.

**IPX Internal Network Number**  A number that uniquely identifies a server to the network. Each server must have a different internal network number.

**IPX Network Address**  An eight-digit hexadecimal number that is used to uniquely identify a particular network segment that is running IPX.

**ISDN**  See *Integrated Services Digital Network*.

**ISO**  See *International Organization for Standardization*.

**Isochronous Transmission**  Method in which communicating devices must depend on another device to provide the timing.

**Jabber Packet**  When a workstation's NIC goes out and begins to talk consistently and incoherently on the network, it creates packets that are larger than 1,518 bytes and contains CRC errors.

**Knowledgebase**  A feature of a vendor's technical support website that allows you to search all the technical support information a vendor has on a particular product or topic.

**LAN**  See *Local Area Network*.

**LAN Driver**  The software component that provides an interface between the Novell Client and the network interface card (NIC).

**LANalyzer for Windows**  Program that allows the viewing of network packets as they pass your workstation. It can display network bandwidth use in a graphical format as well as collisions and errors per second.

**Laser Printer**  Printer that uses a laser to fuse toner particles onto the paper.

**Layers**  The name for divisions in the OSI reference model. The OSI model divides network communication into seven separate processes. Each layer in the protocol stack receives services from the layer below it and provides services to the layer above it.

**Learning**  Bridge port state that tries to determine which nodes are on its associated segment.

**Learning Bridges**  Ability of a transparent bridge to learn which MAC addresses are on which segments by examining the source addresses of every frame that crosses the bridge.

**Link**   The connection between two routers. A link is made when both routers on each side of the connection recognize each other.

**Link State**   Route discovery method that works by transmitting special packets (LSPs) that contain information about which routers that router is connected to.

**Link State Database**   The router's logical map of an internet.

**Link State Packet (LSP)**   A special packet sent by NLSP routers to send routing updates to all routers on the network.

**Link Support Layer (LSL)**   Component of the ODI specification that allows communication between MLID and upper layer protocols. It acts as a switchboard to enable multiple protocols over a single network board.

**Listening**   Bridge port state that is preparing for the learning and forwarding states. A bridge in this state will use its internal timer to wait for the network to settle down between topology change before enabling the learning and forwarding states.

**Load Balancing**   Technology that routers employ to balance the load across multiple routes. If a router discovers that there is more than one way to get somewhere, it can distribute the load.

**Lobe Length**   On a Token Ring network, the distance between a node and a MAU.

**Lobe Ports**   Ports in MAUs where the cables from the workstations connect.

**Local Area Network (LAN)**   A network that is restricted to a local area—a single building, group of buildings, or even a single room. A LAN often has only one server, but can have many, if desired.

**Logical Ports**   Ports used by the CAPTURE command to redirect a workstation printer port to a network print queue. The logical port has no relation to the port to which the printer is actually attached, or the *physical port*.

**Login Script**   A set of commands that are automatically executed when a user logs in. NetWare 5 includes Container, Profile, User, and Default login scripts. Up to three of these can be executed for each user. The login script consists of a special type of command called *login script commands*.

**Logical Bus Topology**   Type of topology in which the signal travels the distance of the cable and is received by all stations on the backbone.

**Logical Link Control (LLC)**   Sublayer of the Data Link layer in charge of establishing and maintaining links between the communicating devices.

**Logical Ring Topology**   A logical network topology where all network signals travel from one station to another, getting read and forwarded each time.

**Logical Topology**   Path the signal takes as it travels around the network.

**Loopback Address**   Usually referring to the TCP/IP address 127.0.0.0

**Mainframe**   A computer that has all the processing power on the network and supports several hundred users' simultaneous connections. It uses terminals and front-end processors to connect the users with the main processing unit and shared disk storage.

**MAN**   See *Metropolitan Area Network*.

**ManageWise**   Comprehensive network management system developed by Novell, Inc. It includes components for server management, protocol analysis, network trend tracking, segment monitoring, and centralized workstation and network management.

**Master Database Model**   Network model in which a single server receives all changes and additions and sends them all to secondary database servers. Changes must be initiated at the master database.

**Media Access Control (MAC)**   Sublayer of the Data Link layer that controls the way multiple devices share the same media channel. It controls which devices can transmit and when they can transmit.

**Media Independent Interface (MII)**   Specification for an interface between the Media Access Control (MAC) layer of Fast Ethernet and the three Physical layer implementations. It allows Fast Ethernet to run over any of the three Physical layer implementations (called Physical layer devices or PLDs) by simply changing an external transceiver on the network card.

**Message Switching**   A type of network communication that sends an entire *message,* or block of data, rather than a simple packet.

**Metropolitan Area Network (MAN)**   A network spanning a single city or metropolitan area. A MAN is larger than a local area network (LAN), which is normally restricted to a single building or neighboring buildings, but smaller than a wide area network (WAN), which can span the entire globe. The term *MAN* is rarely used outside of Novell education courses.

**Microhouse Technical Library (MHTL)**   A collection of electronic encyclopedias that provide network professionals with technical information about hard drives, network interface cards, I/O cards, and other computer hardware.

**Microwaves**   A type of unbounded network transmission media. Microwaves are most often used to transmit data across satellite links and between earth-based equipment, such as telephone relay towers. Microwave transmission is commonly used to transmit signals when bounded media, such as cable, cannot be used.

**Modem**   A device used to convert the digital signals produced by a computer into the analog signals required by analog telephone lines, and vice versa. This process of conversion allows computers to communicate across telephone lines.

**Modulation**   The way data and bits are represented in a way that the sender can create a message and the receiver can understand it.

**MODULES Command**   NetWare console command that helps determine what NLMs are loaded and their associated versions.

**MONITOR.NLM**   NetWare server utility that can be used to gather statistics on just about every aspect of the server's operating. It shows statistics like processor utilization, errors, LAN statistics, and memory statistics.

**Multi-Mode Fibers**   Fiber-optic fibers that can support multiple signals on the same strand of fiber.

**Multi-Station Access Unit (MSAU)**   The central connecting device on a Token Ring that connects all stations together.

**Multiple Link Interface Driver (MLID)**   Piece of software that controls and understands a network card. Also commonly known as the network card (NIC) driver.

**Multiplexer**   A device that combines different signals so that they can be transmitted simultaneously across the same transmission media. The signals are later separated at the receiving end in a process called demultiplexing. Often abbreviated as Mux.

**Multipoint Connection**   A type of network design in which a single transmission medium, frequently called the backbone network, is shared by multiple network devices. An example of multipoint connections would be a network using a bus topology, which could have several computers and printers all connected on a single Ethernet cable. The opposite of a multipoint connection is a point-to-point connection.

**NDPS**   See *Novell Distributed Print Services.*

**NDPS Broker**   The component of Novell's Distributed Print services that is responsible for maintaining NDPS services. It is the component responsible for registering new printers and distributing printer drivers to workstations automatically. If NDPS is to be used on a network, an NDPS broker must exist.

**NDPS Gateways**   A software component of NDPS that allows printing from third-party printing systems.

**NDPS Manager**   Software component that manages the printing process.

**Nearest Service**   Type of SAP Service Responses that is sent in reply to specific queries.

**NetWare Client Requester**   Portion of the Novell Client for Windows 95 that does most of the higher level functions for the Novell Client software, including redirections file and print requests and caching files for network transmission and reception.

**NetWare Core Protocol**   The core protocol for the functionality of NetWare.

**NetWare Link Services Protocol (NLSP)**   The link state routing protocol used by IPX.

**NetWare Loadable Module (NLM)**   An application or program that executes on the NetWare server. NLMs are used for device drivers, LAN drivers, and applications such as backup software. A variety of utilities NLMs are provided with NetWare 5, and others are available from third parties.

**NetWare Peripheral Architecture (NPA)**   A new system introduced with NetWare 4.1 that specifies a new type of *device driver*, used to control disk and tape drives. The driver is divided into two modules: a host adapter module (HAM) and a custom device module (CDM) for each device attached to the host adapter. Older device drivers use a single program with a .DSK extension. These older drivers cannot be used with NetWare 5.

**Network Address**   A unique address that identifies each node, or device, on the network. The network address is generally hard-coded into the network card on both the workstation and server. Some network cards allow you to change this address, but there is usually no need to do so.

**Network Basic Input/Output System (NetBIOS)**   A Session layer protocol that opens communication sessions for applications that want to communicate on a LAN.

**Network Control Panel**   Troubleshooting resource used to configure the various networking components for Windows 9$x$.

**Network Interface Card (NIC)**   Physical device that connects a computer or other network equipment to the transmission medium used. When installed in a computer's expansion bus slot, a NIC allows the computer to become a workstation on the network.

**Network Operating System (NOS)**   The software that runs on a file server and offers file, print, and other servers to client workstations. NetWare 5 is a NOS. Other examples include NetWare 3.1*x*, Banyan VINES, and IBM LAN Server.

**Network Services**   Services are simply what computers have to offer on a network. Examples would include print services, file services, e-mail, and database services.

**Network Support Encyclopedia (NSEPro)**   Novell's database of technical information documents, files, patches, fixes, NetWare Application Notes, Novell lab bulletins, Novell professional developer bulletins, answers to frequently asked questions, and more. The database is available from Novell and is updated approximately ten times per year.

**Network Terminator**   A device attached to the end of a cable segment. It contains an electrical device called a resistor. Its function is to connect the two conductors together partially to stop the reflection of network segments.

**NIC**   See *Network Interface Card.*

**Node**   In TCP/IP, an IP addressable computer system, such as workstations, servers, minicomputers, mainframes, and routers. In IPX networks, the term is usually applied to non-server devices, workstations, and printers.

**Novell Directory Services (NDS)**   The system NetWare 5 uses to catalog objects on the network—users, printers, volumes, and others. NDS uses a *Directory tree* to store this information. All of a NetWare 5 network's resources can be managed through NDS.

**Novell Distributed Print Services (NDPS)**   A new printing technology co-developed by Novell, Hewlett-Packard, and Xerox that simplifies printing administration and setup. Printers are now represented by *printer agents* and managed by the *NDPS Manager.* In some cases, a printer can be plugged into the network and be available to network clients without administrator intervention.

**NSEPro**   See *Network Support Encyclopedia.*

**Object**   In NDS, any resource on the network. Users, printers, and groups are examples of *leaf objects.* Another type, container objects, is used to organize other objects.

**Object-Oriented Applications**   Programs that can accomplish complex tasks by combining smaller applications. By using a combination of objects, object-oriented applications gain the ability to handle large tasks.

**Object Trustee**   See *Trustee.*

**Ontrack Data Recovery for NetWare (ODRN)**   Software that when loaded on a server can aid in the recovery of data from a damaged disk.

**Open System Interconnection (OSI)**   A model defined by the ISO to conceptually organize the process of communication between computers in terms of seven layers, called protocol stacks. The seven layers of the OSI model provide a way for you to understand how communication across various protocols takes place.

**OSI**   See *Open System Interconnection.*

**Oversampling**   Method of synchronous bit synchronization in which the receiver samples the signal at a much faster rate than the data rate, which permits the use of an encoding method that does not add clocking transitions.

**Packet**   The basic division of data sent over a network. Each packet contains a set amount of data along with a header, containing information about the type of packet and the network address to which it is being sent. The size and format of packets depend on the *protocol* and frame types used.

**Packet Switching**   A type of data transmission in which data is divided into packets, each of which has a destination address. Each packet is then routed across a network in an optimal fashion. An addressed packet may travel a different route than packets related to it. Packet sequence numbers are used at the destination node to reassemble related packets.

**Packet Type**   In reference to RIP packet construction, this field indicates which type of packet is being sent, a request or response.

**Paper Path**   The path the paper travels as it enters and exits the printer.

**Parity**   Error checking mechanism used with asynchronous transmission. The parity bit is tacked onto the end of each byte.

**Partial Server Lockup**   When a server will respond to users' requests, but may take longer than usual.

**Partition**   NetWare uses disk partitions to divide a hard disk. A disk can contain a single NetWare partition, which is used to hold one or more NetWare volumes. In addition, it can have a DOS partition, used to boot the server and hold the SERVER.EXE program.

**Patch**   A piece of software that fixes a problem with an existing program or operating system. Patches are like Band-Aids for software. Most often they can be downloaded from the original software vendor's support website.

**Peer-to-Peer Network**   A local area network in which network resources are shared among workstations, without the use of a file server.

**Phase**   The relative state of one wave relative to another wave measured in degrees.

**Phase Shift Keying**   A way of encoding data by changing the phase of an analog signal to represent digits of a digital number.

**Physical Bus Topology**   A backbone configuration in which all the computers tie into one long cable segment. It is a multipoint connection. Both ends of the network segment must be terminated to avoid harmful signal reflections and the machines are attached to the common media via some type of connector.

**Physical Cellular Topology**   Network configuration that is wireless. The network is made up of circular areas called cells. Each cell is serviced by a central station or hub. Communication takes place through radio signals that carry data from nodes within the cell to the central station. The central station can then route data to devices in other cells by way of their central stations.

**Physical Layer**   The bottom layer of the OSI model. The Physical layer consists of the physical media, such as cable, and the electrical specifications that determine its functionality. It also controls the physical layout or structure of the network and defines the rules for bit-transmission encoding and timing.

**Physical Mesh Topology**   Network configuration that has a link between each and every device in the network.

**Physical Port**   In NetWareprinting, the port to which a printer is actually attached, which differs from the *logical ports* used in the CAPTURE command for printer redirection.

**Physical Star Topology**   Network that requires a central hub (usually a concentrator or repeater) Each computer has a dedicated cable to the hub.

**Physical Topologies**   The physical layouts of networks, such as bus, star, or ring.

**Ping**   A TCP/IP utility used to test whether another machine is online. A ping program sends a request to the other machine, waits for a reply, and displays the time the reply took to arrive. An implementation of this utility, WinPing, is included with the IPX/IP Gateway software.

**Platen Knob**   The knob that advances the paper on a dot matrix printer.

**Point-to-Point**   Network communication in which two devices have exclusive access to a network medium. For example, a printer connected to only one workstation would be using a point-to-point connection.

**Point-to-Point Protocol (PPP)**   Protocol used with dial-up connections to the Internet. Its functions include error control, security, dynamic IP addressing, and support for multiple protocols. PPP provides physical device addressing at the MAC sublayer and LLC-level error control.

**Poison Reverse**   Option for distance vector routing software that determines the hop count of any path from which it receives updates to be infinity.

**Polar Encoding Scheme**   An encoding scheme that can use both positive and negative voltages for encoding data.

**Polling**   Media access control method that uses a central device (master or controller) to regulate access to the network. This central device queries secondary devices in a certain order to see if they have information to transmit. If the device being queried has information to transmit, it will do so. Then another device will be polled.

**Port Driver**   A component of NetWare queue-based printing. The port driver accepts data from the print server and sends it to the printer. The port driver can be a hardware device, NPRINTER.EXE on a workstation, or NPRINTER.NLM on a server.

**PPP**   Stands for Point-to-Point Protocol. This protocol allows the sending of IP packets on a dial-up (serial) connection. Supports compression and IP address negotiation.

**Print Head**   Part of either a dot matrix printer or ink jet printer that forms the image on the paper.

**Print Job**   A file that has been sent by a client for printing. Print jobs are stored in a *print queue* until they can be serviced by the print server.

**Print Job Configuration**   A set of parameters for network printing. These are similar to the parameters in the CAPTURE command. Print Job configurations can be set for user and container objects.

**Print Queue**   The area used to hold the list of print jobs that are waiting to print. The print queue is managed through the Print Queue object in NDS. Print jobs are sent from the print queue to the print server one at a time.

**Print Server**   A device that is used to manage printing. The Print Server NDS object is used to manage printing. The print server itself can run on a NetWare 5 server (PSERVER.NLM) or in a hardware device. Net-Ware 3.1*x* included PSERVER.EXE, which ran on a DOS workstation; it is not supported in NetWare 5.

**Print Services**   The network services that manage and control printing on a network allowing multiple and simultaneous access to printers.

**Printer Agent**   The NDPS entity on the network that controls and manages the printer.

**Printer Object**   Properties of the Printer object identify the printer and list the print queues that the printer accepts jobs from.

**Printer Redirection**   The process of mapping a logical printer port in the workstation to a network printer. The user can then print to the port as if it were an actual printer, and the print job will be sent to the print queue. The CAPTURE utility is used to start redirection.

**Priority**   Value used by routers to determine which router is the DR. The highest value in this field indicates the DR.

**Processor-Detected Exception**   An exception that occurs that the processor detects (usually related to software).

**Protocol**   A method of communicating between NetWare servers and clients. The protocol is the language used for sending data. Data is divided into packets specified by the protocol. IPX is the typical protocol for NetWare networks.

**Protocol Analyzers**   A category of network analysis tools that examine packets at the lower layers of the OSI model. They aid in determining problems that may not be easily determined by other means.

**Protocol Stacks**   A group of protocols that are stacked on top of each other as part of a communication process.

**Protocol Suite**   A collection of protocols that are associated with and that implement a particular communication model (such as the DOD Networking Model, or the OSI Reference Model).

**Pseudonode**   An imaginary node all routers on the network connect to in IPX when using NLSP.

**Public Access Printer**   NDPS printer available to every user on the network with no restrictions.

**Public Switched Telephone Network (PSTN)**   Includes the network used for ordinary telephone calls and modem communications, as well as dedicated lines that are leased by customers for private, exclusive use. Numerous services that facilitate computer communication across PSTN are offered by commercial service providers.

**Pure IP**   The only protocols running on the network are those related to the TCP/IP specification.

**Registry Editor (REGEDIT)**   Program that comes with Windows 95 that allows you to view and change all the settings in the Windows 95 Registry.

**Relay Entities**   Entity inside a router that performs the forwarding and filtering services inside a bridge. The information found in the filtering database is used to determine whether a packet should be forwarded or dropped.

**Remote Printer**   See *Workstation Printer*.

**Replica Name Servers**   DNS servers that contain a copy of the DNS database.

**Resistor**   An electrical device found inside of a network terminator.

**Resource Management Services (RMS)**   Component of the NDPS broker that keeps all the printing resources, like printer drivers, printer fonts, and printer definition files and banners in a central location on a server.

**Return-to-Zero**  Encoding scheme in which the signal transitions to zero in the middle of each bit interval. A positive voltage level transitioning to zero could represent a 0, and a negative voltage transitioning to zero could represent a 1.

**Ring Length**  Distance between Multistation Access Units (MAUs).

**Ring In Ports**  MAU ports that receive signals from other MAUs.

**Ring Management (RMT)**  Built in FDDI network management function that finds and resolves problems in the ring.

**Ring Out Ports**  MAU ports that send signals on to other MAUs.

**Ring Topology**  Network that is set up in a circular fashion. Data travels around the ring in one direction, and each device on the ring acts as a repeater to keep the signal strong as it travels. Each device incorporates a receiver for the incoming signal and a transmitter to send the data on to the next device in the ring. The network is dependent upon the ability of the signal to travel around the ring. If the signal is halted from making its rounds, communication comes to a standstill.

**RIP**  Stands for Routing Information Protocol. A distance vector routing protocol used on many TCP/IP internetworks and IPX networks. The distance vector algorithm uses a fewest-hops routing calculation method.

**Root Bridge**  On a spanning tree network, the bridge responsible for initiating configuration messages, which are then sent to all bridges and forwarded by the designated bridges. The root bridge can notify all bridges that a change has occurred on the network and the bridges need to reconfigure to adapt to the change.

**Route Determination**  When each node on a source routing network builds its own table of routes.

**Route Discovery**  The process where the routing tables are built and maintained with information about the various segments of an internetwork.

**Router**  A device that connects two dissimilar networks and allows packets to be transmitted and received between them.

**Router Information Protocol (RIP)**  Vector route discovery protocol that IPX uses. It uses hops and ticks to determine the cost for a particular route.

**Routing Information Table**  Database within a router that tells the router the location of the network on the internetwork from the router's point of view.

**RS-232**  The most common serial communication system in use. One or more RS-232 serial ports are included on most PCs sold today. This standard supports modems, printers, and other serial devices.

**SAP Service Queries**  Type of SAP packet that is sent by a client to determine the names and services located on a specific server.

**SAP Service Responses**  Type of SAP packet that is sent in response to SAP Service Queries.

**Semi-Static Patch**  An NLM that can be loaded while the server is up and running but can't be unloaded without restarting the server.

**Sequence Control**  Connection service that allows a receiver to reassemble the pieces of a message into their original order.

**Sequenced Packet Exchange (SPX)**  Provides the connection-oriented packet delivery for IPX. It provides packet fragmentation, sequencing, and reassembly for packets that are too big for the Data Link layer.

**Serial Connection**   Data communications method that sends data one bit at a time, one after another.

**Serial Line Internet Protocol (SLIP)**   Protocol used with dial-up connections to the Internet. It functions at the Physical layer only, and does not provide error control or security.

**Server Printer**   One of the methods of attaching a printer to the network, probably the most common. The printer is attached to a printer port on the NetWare server. The port driver, NPRINTER.NLM, is used to drive the printer.

**Service Advertising Protocol (SAP)**   The protocol used for various NetWare 5, as well as 2.*x*, 3.*x*, and 4.*x*, services. Single reference timeservers use this protocol to broadcast time information to the entire network at once.

**Service Data Units**   Data packages found at each layer comprised of data and headers from the layers above.

**Service Provider**   Novell's term for a computer that is offering a service on the network. Any example of this would be a server.

**Service Registry Services (SRS)**   Component of the NDPS broker that allows public access printers to register themselves to NDPS. It keeps a list of all the public access printers so that workstations can find them.

**Service Requester**   A term for a computer that asks for services on the network.

**Shielded Twisted-Pair**   A type of wiring that includes a pair of conductors inside a metal or foil shield. This type of media can support faster speeds than non-shielded wiring.

**Signaling**   The way that data is transmitted across the medium. It involves using electrical energy to communicate.

**Simple Network Management Protocol (SNMP)**   A management protocol used on many networks, particularly TCP/IP. It defines the type, format, and retrieval of management information about nodes.

**Simplex Transmission**   A type of transmission that can go one way only. Duplex is the alternative.

**Single-Mode Fibers**   Optical fibers that allow a single light path and are typically used with laser signaling.

**SLIP**   Stands for Serial Line Internet Protocol. A protocol that permits the sending of IP packets on a dial-up (serial) connection. Does not by itself support compression or IP address negotiation.

**SNA**   See *Systems Network Architecture.*

**SNMP**   See *Simple Network Management Protocol.*

**Socket Identifiers**   Addresses that uniquely identify each process running on a server. Used within IPX packets to identify which service sent the packet and which process should receive it.

**Source-Routing Bridge**   Bridge that does not contain a filtering database but relies on the sending devices to include bridging information in the MAC header in the data frame.

**Spanning Tree Protocol**   Bridge protocol that uses a special packet called the bridge protocol data unit (BPDU) that bridges can use to communicate with one anther.

**Spikes**   A power problem that occurs when transients rise and decay randomly and lasts less than a second.

**Split Horizon**   Option for distance vector routing that prevents a router from advertising any routes on the network it received them from.

**Standby Monitors**   A monitor on a Token Ring that waits for its turn to be the active monitor.

**Start Bit**   A bit that is sent as part of a serial communication stream to signal the beginning of a byte or packet.

**State-Transition Encoding**   Category of signal-encoding techniques that uses transitions in the signal to represent data as opposed to encoding data by means of particular voltage level or state.

**Static Patch**   Patch that makes permanent changes to the SERVER.EXE file.

**Static Window Flow Control**   Type of window flow control that uses fixed sized windows. The number of frames that fit in the receiving device's buffers usually determines the size of the window.

**Station (Node) IPX Address**   Twelve-digit hexadecimal number based on the MAC address of the network that is used to uniquely identify a station on an IPX network.

**Station Management (SMT)**   Built in FDDI network management function that provides the auto-reconfiguration feature and allows the monitoring of the ring's status using specialized software.

**Stop Bit**   A bit that is sent as part of a serial communication stream to signal the end of a byte or packet.

**Store-and-Forward Mode**   Mechanism used by transparent bridges in the forwarding state. It receives a packet on one port, reads the value of the CRC field and addresses fields, and stores the frame in memory while the CRC and address restrictions from the filtering database are checked for validity.

**SupportSource**   Novell CD-ROM based program that accesses many technical databases. It provides a single screen interface for these databases that allow them to be searched for specific technical information.

**Synchronous Transmission**   A type of transmission that uses a clock to control the timing of bits being sent.

**System Identification (System ID)**   Indicates the internal IPX address of the designated router.

**System Network Architecture (SNA)**   An IBM network architecture used with minicomputers.

**Switching Hub**   Also known as a switch, a switching hub is basically a multiport bridge. A switch-based network eliminates contention problems associated with regular Ethernet hubs.

**T-Connector**   A connector used in Ethernet and ARCnet, as well as other thin coax systems, that connects the coaxial cable to the workstation while keeping the two ends connected.

**TCP/IP**   Stands for Transmission Control Protocol/Internet Protocol. Generally used as shorthand for the phrase *TCP/IP protocol suite*. It is the protocol developed by the DOD for use in the Internet. By most counts, the leading network protocol suite in use on networks today. This is due, in no small part, to the popularity of the Internet.

**Telnet**   A TCP/IP terminal emulation protocol that permits a node, called the Telnet client, to login to a remote node, called the Telnet server. The client simply acts as a dumb terminal, displaying output from the server. The processing is done at the server.

**Terminal Emulation**   The process of emulating a terminal, or allowing a PC to act as a terminal for a mainframe or UNIX system.

**Terminator**   A device (basically a resistor) placed at the end of a coaxial cable segment to indicate that the last node has been reached.

**Thermistor**   Device in a dot matrix printer that detects high temperatures and shuts down printing.

**Throughput**   The amount of data that has been sent over a given time. For example, 10BaseT Ethernet has a theoretical maximum throughput of 10Mbps. In practice, the throughput depends on the quality and length of wiring, and is usually slightly less.

**Time-Division Multiplexing (TDM)**   Multiplexing technique in which a channel is divided into time slots. Each of the devices communicating over this multiplexed line is allocated a time slot in a round-robin fashion. TDM can be used with a baseband media or an individual channel of a broadband FDM system.

**Time Domain Reflectometers (TDRs)**   IPX protocol analysis tools that send out signals to a responder device and record the details of the return signal.

**Token Passing**   Media access method in which a small token is passed around in an orderly fashion from one device to the next. The station that is in possession of the token has control of the media, which gives it permission to transmit. If a station has data to send, it must wait for control of the token before it can transmit the information. After a station has transmitted its data, it will retransmit the token. The next device can then use it to gain control of the media and transmit its data.

**Token Ring Network**   Common example of a logical ring topology. It is wired by connecting stations to a central hub, called a multi-station access unit (MSAU). The signal travels in a ring from workstation to workstation and is only routed through the MSAU.

**Topology**   A type of network connection or cabling system.

**Transient**   A high voltage burst of current.

**Transmission Media**   Physical cables and wireless technology across which computers are able to communicate. These media provide a network with physical connections.

**Transparent Bridge**   Type of bridge where the sending device is unaware that the destination device may be on a segment on the other side of a bridge.

**Trojan Horse**   In reference to computers, a program that is designed to hide in the disguise of something harmless, waiting for the right moment to do its deed.

**Trustee**   Any object that has been given rights to an NDS object or file. Trustee rights can include explicit, inherited, and effective rights.

**Twisted-Pair Cable**   Two color-coded, insulated copper wires that are twisted around each other. A twisted-pair cable consists of one or more twisted-pairs in a common jacket.

**Twisted-Pair**   A type of wiring used for network communications, which uses copper wires twisted into pairs.

**UDP**   Stands for User Datagram Protocol. UDP uses a connectionless, non-guaranteed packet delivery method. It resides at the Host-to-Host layer of the DOD Networking Model.

**Unipolar Encoding Scheme**   Encoding scheme that uses two levels for encoding data. One of the levels is zero, which could represent a binary 1, and the other level can be either positive or negative.

**UNIX**   A multitasking operating system, created by AT&T's Bell Labs, that is used on a wide variety of computers, including Internet servers.

**Unshielded Twisted-Pair Cable**   Twisted-pair cable consisting of a number of twisted-pairs with a simple plastic casing.

**Virus**   In reference to computers, a pernicious computer program that alters stored files or system configuration and copies itself onto external disks or other computers.

**VREPAIR**   Software data-recovery utility included with NetWare.

**Wide Area Network (WAN)**   A network that extends across multiple locations. Each location typically has a local area network (LAN), and the LANs are connected together in a WAN. Typically used for *enterprise networking*.

**Window Flow Control**   Method used at the Data Link layer that uses buffering to allow the sending device to get a few frames ahead of the receiving device.

**Wireless Media**   Transmission media that employ higher electromagnetic frequencies (radio waves, microwaves, and infrared waves). Wireless media are necessary for networks with mobile computers or those that transmit over large distances, such as enterprise and global networks.

**Workstation Printer**   A printer that is attached to a workstation on the network. In NetWare 3.1*x* these were referred to as *remote printers* and handled by the RPRINTER.EXE program. In NetWare 5 they are handled by the NPRINTER.EXE program.

**World Wide Web (WWW)**   A term used for the collection of computers on the Internet running HTTP (hypertext transfer protocol) servers. The Web allows for text and graphics to have hyperlinks connecting users to other servers. Using a *web browser*, such as Netscape Navigator or Microsoft Internet Explorer, a user can link from one server to another at the click of a button.

**Worm**   In reference to computers, a destructive or dangerous program that fulfills a specific function at a specific location.

**Wrapping**   System fault-tolerance feature that takes effect when a break occurs in a cable on a Token Ring network. Token Ring and FDDI use this technology to reconfigure around a fault.

**Zone Transfer**   Process where a replica name server copies the master DNS database from the master name server to itself.

# Index

**Note to the Reader:** Throughout this index **boldfaced** page numbers indicate primary discussions of a topic. *Italicized* page numbers indicate illustrations.

# NETWARE® 5 CNE®
## STUDY GUIDES FROM
# NETWORK PRESS®

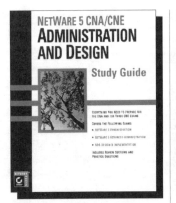

**NetWare® 5 CNA℠/CNE®:
Administration and
Design Study Guide**

ISBN: 0-7821-2387-2
864 pp.; 7½" X 9"
$44.99, Hardcover

**Covers:**

NetWare® 5 Administration
(the CNA test)

NetWare® 5 Advanced
Administration

NDS Design & Implementation

**NetWare® 5 CNE®:
Core Technologies
Study Guide**

ISBN: 0-7821-2389-9
512 pp.; 7½" X 9"
$44.99, Hardcover

**Covers:**

Networking Technologies

Service & Support

**NetWare® 5 CNE®:
Integrating Windows®
NT® Study Guide**

ISBN: 0-7821-2388-0
448 pp.; 7½" X 9"
$39.99, Hardcover

**Covers:**

Integrating Windows® NT®

**NetWare® 5 CNE®:
Update to NetWare® 5
Study Guide**

ISBN: 0-7821-2390-2
432 pp.; 7½" X 9"
$39.99, Hardcover

**Covers:**

NetWare® 4.11 to
NetWare® 5 Update

NETWORK PRESS®
SYBEX

www.sybex.com

# Boost Your Career
# with Certification

Detailed information on more than 70 computer and network certification programs, including:

- Computer hardware
- Operating systems
- Software
- Networking hardware
- Network operating systems
- Internet
- Instructor and trainer certifications

**COMPUTER & NETWORK PROFESSIONAL'S CERTIFICATION GUIDE**

J. SCOTT CHRISTIANSON
AVA FAJEN

**Available May 1998**
ISBN: 0-7821-2260-4
512 pp; 5 7/8 x 8 1/4; Softcover
$19.99

# Learn why to get certified, when to get certified, and how to get certified.

NETWORK PRESS® SYBEX

# From the Experts...

## Who bring you Mark Minasi's #1 best-selling *Complete PC Upgrade & Maintenance Guide*, Sybex now presents...

**Nearly a million copies sold!**

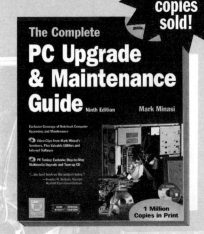

### The Complete Network Upgrade & Maintenance Guide

**BY MARK MINASI, JIM BLANEY, CHRIS BRENTON**

The Ultimate Networking Reference—this book is a practical and comprehensive guide to implementing, upgrading, and maintaining networks, from small office LANs to enterprise-scale WANs and beyond.

ISBN: 0-7821-2259-0
1536 pp., $69.99

### The Complete Website Upgrade & Maintenance Guide

**BY LISA SCHMEISER**

Destined to be the industry's ultimate Website reference, this book is the most comprehensive and broad-reaching tome, created to help you turn an existing site into a long-lasting sophisticated, dynamic, effective tool.

ISBN: 0-7821-2315-5
912 pp., $49.99

### The Complete PC Upgrade & Maintenance Guide, 9th edition

**BY MARK MINASI**

After selling nearly <u>one million copies</u> of its previous editions, the 9th edition carries on the tradition with detailed troubleshooting for the latest motherboards, sound cards, video boards, CD-ROM drives, and all other multimedia devices.

ISBN: 0-7821-2357-0
1600 pp., $59.99

www.sybex.com

©1998, Sybex Inc.

SYBEX